DAVID FULTON

A

Practical Treatise

ON

PATENTS, TRADE MARKS

AND

DESIGNS

WITH A

Digest of Colonial and Foreign Patent Laws

THE TEXT OF THE

PATENTS, DESIGNS, AND TRADE MARKS ACTS, 1883 TO 1888

(CONSOLIDATED)

Elibron Classics
www.elibron.com

Elibron Classics series.

ISBN 0-543-97735-8 (paperback)
ISBN 0-543-97734-X (hardcover)

This Elibron Classics Replica Edition is an unabridged facsimile of the edition published in 1894 by Jordan & Sons, London.

A

Practical Treatise

ON

PATENTS, TRADE MARKS

AND

DESIGNS.

A

Practical Treatise

ON

PATENTS, TRADE MARKS

AND

DESIGNS,

WITH A

Digest of Colonial and Foreign Patent Laws;

THE TEXT OF THE

PATENTS, DESIGNS, AND TRADE MARKS ACTS, 1883 TO 1888

(CONSOLIDATED);

THE RULES, FEES, AND FORMS RELATING TO PATENTS, DESIGNS, AND TRADE MARKS CONSOLIDATED; THE INTERNATIONAL CONVENTION FOR THE PROTECTION OF INDUSTRIAL PROPERTY; PRECEDENTS OF AGREEMENTS, ASSIGNMENTS, LICENCES, MORTGAGES, &c.; AND A FULL ANALYTICAL INDEX.

BY

DAVID FULTON, A.M.I.C.E.,

Fellow of the Chartered Institute of Patent Agents, and of the Middle Temple,

BARRISTER-AT-LAW.

JORDAN & SONS,

Companies' Registration Agents, Printers, and Publishers,

120 CHANCERY LANE, LONDON, W.C.

1894

PREFACE.

THIS work is intended to constitute a complete and concise guide to the Patents, Designs, and Trade Marks Acts of 1883 to 1888. While it is hoped that the work will be found of sufficient fulness to serve as a handy text-book for the use of the Legal Profession and of Patent Agents. the chief object of the writer has been to convey to Inventors, Patentees, Manufacturers, Traders, and the public generally a clear and definite explanation of the nature and scope of the privileges conferred by those Acts, and of the procedure by which such privileges are obtained. The author has, therefore, tried to select and enlarge more particularly upon those questions which a long and varied personal experience has shown him to be the chief points of practical interest to those to whom the book is mainly addressed.

While acknowledging the learned labours of Dr. EDMUNDS upon Patents, and of Mr. SEBASTIAN upon Trade Marks, it may be noted that, so far as the writer is aware, the present is the first and only existing treatise in which all three subjects of the

Patents, Designs, and Trade Marks Acts have been discussed with reasonable fulness by the same author.

It may, therefore, be claimed that there is room for such a work, as, irrespective of the statutory *vinculum* which exists between Patents, Designs, and Trade Marks, it not unfrequently happens that those who are interested in one of these subjects are also to some extent interested in the others.

The contents of the book have been arranged in their relative order of importance. Part I. relates to Patents; Part II. to Trade Marks; Part III. to Designs. In addition to these, Part IV. presents, in alphabetical order, Concise Digests of all Patent Laws in Foreign Countries and in the Colonies. These have been prepared from the latest available information, and the chief characteristics of each law have been grouped under certain specific headings with which it is essential that British patentees should make themselves acquainted.

Following these will be found the Acts of 1883 to 1888 in a consolidated form, and the Rules framed by the Board of Trade from 1890 to 1893 have also been consolidated and added. The essential portions of the International Convention have been incorporated, and the work concludes with some simple precedents of Agreements, Assignments, Licences, and Mortgages of Inventions and Patents, together with extracts from certain Statutes bearing upon the interpretation and construction of such documents.

With a view to abolishing foot-notes, and to obviate needless multiplication of references, the author has been sparing in his allusions to decisions, and has selected as illustrations only those cases which bear directly and unmistakeably upon the points under consideration. All important rulings which have been reported up to the time of going to press have also been noted, as well as all recent changes in the rules, fees, and procedure, so that the work will be found well up to date.

In the tabulated list of cases cited, a short note is appended to each, stating the essential point or points affected by the ruling.

To prevent the work from exceeding the prescribed limits, purely litigious proceedings in Patent matters have not been specifically dealt with, and have been but briefly referred to in the Trade Marks and Designs portions. To have enlarged upon these matters would not only have unduly swelled the bulk of the book, but would also have been to some extent out of place in view of its specific and practical nature and objects. Besides, the essentials in such actions, so far as mere procedure is concerned, are now so well known to both branches of the profession that the necessity for their separate treatment has largely disappeared. The important factor is that those having the conduct of such actions should thoroughly understand the principles which govern the patentability and limits of an invention, or the registrable nature and the extent of possible claims in or under a Trade Mark or Design, and these principles it is hoped will be clearly apparent from a study of the matter constituting the body of the book.

As the volume deals with what are practically three distinct heads of subject-matter, a separate Index has been prepared for each part, so as to avoid confusion, and the Tables of Cases have been arranged upon the same principle.

DAVID FULTON.

3 Essex Court, Temple,
July, 1894.

CONTENTS.

PART I.—PATENTS.

PART II.—TRADE MARKS.

PART III.—COPYRIGHT IN DESIGNS.

PART IV. FOREIGN AND COLONIAL PATENTS.

THE PATENTS, DESIGNS, AND TRADE MARKS ACTS, 1883 TO 1888 (CONSOLIDATED).

PATENTS RULES, 1890 TO 1892 (CONSOLIDATED).

DESIGNS RULES, 1890 TO 1893 (CONSOLIDATED).

TRADE MARKS RULES, 1890.

TWELVE SHORT PRECEDENTS OF AGREEMENTS, ASSIGNMENTS, LICENCES, MORTGAGES, &c.

KEY TO ABBREVIATED REFERENCES TO REPORTS.

Beav. - - -	Beavan's Reports.
B. & S. - - -	Best & Smith's Reports.
C. B. N. S - -	Common Bench Reports, New Series.
C. & P. - - -	Carrington & Payne's Reports
Dav. P. C. - -	Davies' Patent Cases.
De G. J. & S - -	De Gex, Jones & Smith's Reports.
De G. & J. - -	De Gex & Jones's Reports.
De G. M. & G. - -	De Gex, Macnaughten & Gordon's Reports.
Dig. - - -	Sebastian's Digest of Trade Mark Cases.
E & B. - - -	Ellis & Blackburn's Reports.
Griff. P. C. - -	Griffin's Patent Cases (pub 1887).
Griff. A. P C - -	Griffin's Patent Cases before Comptroller-General and Law Officers (pub. 1888).
Good. P C. - -	Goodeve's Patent Cases.
H. Bl. - - -	H. Blackstone's Reports.
H & N. - - -	Hurlstone & Norman's Exchequer Reports.
Johns. - - -	Johnson's Reports.
L. J. Ch. - - -	Law Journal Reports, Chancery.
L. R. Ch. App. - -	Law Reports, Chancery Appeals.
L. R. Q B. D. - -	Law Reports, Queen's Bench Division.
L. R. Ch. D. - -	Law Reports, Chancery Division.
L. T. N. S. - -	Law Times Reports, New Series.
N. Lon. Jour. - -	Newton's London Journal of Arts and Sciences.
Popham - - -	Popham's Reports.
P. O. R. - - -	Reports of Patent, Design, and Trade Mark Cases.
Q. B. - - -	Queen's Bench Reports
Stark. R - - -	Starkie's Reports.
Web P.C. - -	Webster's Patent Cases.
W. R. - - -	The Weekly Reporter.

TABLE OF CASES.

PART I.—PATENTS.

Title of Case.	Where reported.	Pages in this book.	Chief point or points affected by decision.
Dollond's Patent (*re*)	2 H. Bl. 43	32	Prior secret use by one person no bar to subsequent grant of patent to another person.
Dunnicliffe *v.* Mallett	7 C. B. N. S. 209.	72	Assignee of specific part of patent may bring action alone for infringement of that part.
Edmunds's Patent (*re*)	Griff. P. C 281.	59	Comptroller or law officer takes no cognisance of what transpires abroad.
Ehrlich *v.* Ihlee - -	5 P. O. R. 437.	29	The application of an old thing to a new use is sometimes patentable.
Fawcett's Patent (*re*)	Good. P. C. 10.	55	Comptroller has power to correct informalities in opposition papers at hearing.
Felton *v.* Greaves -	3 Car. & P. 611.	37	Bad title invalidates patent.
Foxwell *v.* Bostock -	4 De G. J. & S. 298.	46	In combination patents, old parts should be differentiated from new.
Gandy *v.* Reddaway -	2 P. O. R. 49.	50	True reading of claim sometimes settled by extraneous evidence.
Garthwaite's Patent (*re*).	Griff. P. C. 284.	59	Grant disputed before Comptroller or law officer might be issued jointly to opponent and applicant.
Gibson *v.* Brand- -	1 Web. P. C. 627.	46	In combination patents old parts should be differentiated from new.
Green's Patent (*re*) -	Griff. P. C 286.	61	First applicant might formerly have incorporated subject-matter of second application by other inventor. Remedied now by third ground of opposition. (*See re* Hetherington)
Guest *v.* Barrow -	5 P. O. R. 312.	61	In opposition cases, references to prior patents must not be forced on applicant.
Hampton's Patent (*re*)	Griff. A. P. C. 13.	57, 68	Caution should be exercised in accepting Comptroller's decision *in toto* before time for appeal expires.
Hancock *v.* Somervell	39 N. Lon. Jour. 158.	32	Publication of product not disclosing mode of manufacture will not bar grant of patent for mode of manufacture.
Harris *v* Rothwell -	4 P. O. R. 225.	34	British patent anticipated by German prints in Patent Office Library.

Title of Case.	Where reported.	Pages in this book.	Chief point or points affected by decision.
Harwood *v.* Gt. N. R. Co.	2 B & S. 22, 194.	29	Generally, old thing applied to new use not patentable. (But *see* Ehrlich *v* Ihlee.)
Heald's Patent (*re*) -	8 P. O. R. 429.	59	Invention of servant is not necessarily property of master.
Herrburger *v.* Squires	6 P. O. R. 194.	34	Prior publication of drawing alone may anticipate subsequent patent.
Hetherington's Patent (*re*).	7 P. O. R. 419.	62	Prior applicant not allowed to incorporate interim subject-matter belonging to after-applicant even when the same only appears in the drawings.
Jones's Patent (*re*) -	Griff. A.P.C. 33.	56	In oppositions, applicant may define limits of opponent's specification by references to evidence of public knowledge.
Jupe *v.* Pratt - -	1 Web. P. C. 145.	28	Where new principle is described, if one practical mode of carrying into effect is shown, any other mode for same object treated as piracy.
Kay's Patent (*re*) -	1 Web. P. C. 568.	5	Instances to show cost of patent under ancient practice.
Kurtz *v.* Spence -	5 P. O. R. 161.	88	In action for threats, damages, to be reasonable, must have been actually sustained.
Lake's Patent (*re*) -	Griff. A. P. C. 35.	55	Informalities in opposition papers may be corrected by Comptroller at hearing.
Lake's Patent (*re*) -	Griff. P. C. 294.	59	Patent may be issued jointly to applicant and opponent.
Lake's Patent (*re*) -	5 P. O. R. 415.	59	Comptroller or law officer not bound to notice transactions abroad.
Lancaster's Application (*re*).	Griff. P. C. 293.	56	Samples as illustrations may be used at hearing, though not included as exhibits
Lane Fox *v.* Kensington Electric Co.	9 P. O. R. 221.	40	Disconformity between provisional and complete specifications.
Lawrence *v.* Perry -	2 P. O. R. 179.	44	Drawings not absolutely necessary even in mechanical specification.
Lister *v.* Leather -	8 E. & B. 1018.	52	Essential part of combination cannot be taken and used for similar purpose with other combination. (*See* Proctor *v.* Bennis, *infra*.)
Lister *v.* Norton -	3 P. O. R. 199.	33	Effect of publication under subsequently dropped provisional. (*See* Oxley *v.* Holden, *infra.*)

Title of Case.	Where reported.	Pages in this book.	Chief point or points affected by decision.
Lucas *v.* Miller - -	2 P. O. R. 155.	41	Legitimate developments of invention during provisional protection.
Macfarlane *v.* Price -	1 Web. P. C. 74.	46	In combination patents, old to be differentiated from new.
Mathers *v.* Green -	L. R. 1 Ch. App. 29.	64, 72	Co-owners may work patent independently, but not license. (*See* Steer *v.* Rogers, *infra.*)
Mills *v.* Carson - -	10 P. O. R. 9	75	In exclusive licence, provisions for payment of renewal fees.
Minter *v.* Mower -	1 Web. P. C. 142	49	A claim which is too wide vitiates patent.
Morgan's Patent (*re*)	5 P. O. R. 186.	82	Grounds of application for revocation of patent.
Morgan *v.* Seaward -	1 Web. P C. 171.	31	Confidential and experimental manufacture not publication.
Moser *v.* Marsden -	10 P. O. R. 350.	18	Commercial and practical success of slight improvement weighs in favour of patent.
Murchland *v.* Nicholson.	10 P. O. R. 417.	31	One unsound claim invalidates whole patent.
Neilson *v.* Harford -	1 Web. P. C. 295.	26, 28, 52	Claim for bare principle bad, unless coupled with means for carrying into effect. (Jupe *v.* Pratt.)
Nobel *v.* Anderson -	11 P. O. R. 113.	25	Chemical specifications construed narrowly.
Nuttall *v.* Hargreaves	8 P. O. R. 450.	40	Disconformity between provisional and complete.
Otto *v.* Linford - -	146 L.T.N.S. 35.	28, 52	Principle must be coupled with practical means.
Otto *v.* Steel - -	3 P. O. R. 109.	34	Book not catalogued and inaccessible to public not anticipatory publication.
Oxley *v.* Holden -	8 C. B. N. S. 666.	33, 37	Effect of publication under subsequently dropped provisional. (*See* Lister *v.* Norton, *supra.*)
Parnell's Patent (*re*) -	5 P. O. R. 126.	65	Agreement made before application not registrable unless invention identified
Patent Type Co. *v.* Richards.	1 Johns. 381	44	Slight variations from claimed proportions permissible to patentee.
Pether *v.* Shaw - -	10 P. O. R 293.	50	Failure of claimed alternative vitiates patent.
Pharmaceutical Society *v.* Piper.	L. R. 1893, 1 Q. B. 686.	89	"Patent Medicines" held to mean medicines protected by letters patent.

Title of Case.	Where reported.	Pages in this book.	Chief point or points affected by decision.
Proctor *v.* Bennis -	4 P. O. R. 333.	21, 52	"Pith and marrow" of combination cannot be pirated, even although such essential element has not been separately claimed.
Redges *v.* Mulliner -	10 P. O. R. 21.	74	Discontinuance of licence.
Reg. *v.* Cutler - -	14 Q. B. 372	50	Failure of claimed alternative vitiates patent.
Rex *v.* Metcalf - -	1 Web. P. C. 141.	37	Incorrect title vitiates patent.
Russell's Patent (*re*) -	2 De G. & J. 130.	59	Opposed patent may be issued jointly to applicant and opponent.
Saxby *v.* Gloucester Waggon Co.	L. R. 72 Q. B. D. 305	19	Obvious combination not patentable. (*See* Williams *v.* Nye, *infra.*)
Simpson *v* Holliday -	12 L. T. N. S. 29.	44, 47, 50	Evident error need not vitiate patent. Failure of claimed alternative. (Reg. *v.* Cutler.)
Smith's Patent (*re*) -	Griff. P. C. 268.	48	Definition of *quantum* of claim.
Steers *v.* Rogers -	10 P. O. R. 245.	64	Co-owners of patent may work independently. (Mathers *v.* Green, *supra.*)
Stevens *v.* Keating -	2 Web. P. C. 182.	25, 49	Claims for processes. One bad claim vitiates whole patent.
Stewart *v.* Casey -	9 P. O. R. 9	70	Assignments of patents should be by deed. Trusts excluded from register.
Stewart's Patent (*re*)	3 P. O. R. 7	85	Evidence of opponent in objections to extension of patent.
United Horse Nail Co. *v.* Stewart.	2 P. O. R. 122.	34	Not necessary to prove actual perusal of anticipatory publication in public library.
United Horse Nail Co. *v.* Swedish Horse Nail Co.	6 P. O. R. 8	36	Claim for impracticable modification vitiates whole patent.
Vickers *v.* Siddell -	7 P. O. R. 292.	40	Disconformity between provisional and complete.
Vorwerk *v.* Evans -	7 P. O. R. 265.	24	Claim for new product sustainable.
Wenham *v.* May -	4 P. O. R. 303.	21	Essential of patented combination considered as protected *per se.* (Proctor *v.* Bennis, *supra.*)
Williams *v.* Nye -	7 P. O. R. 62	19	Mere stringing together of known parts not patentable combination.
Young *v.* Rosenthal -	1 P. O. R. 33	51	Effects of word "substantially" as used in claims.

PART II.—TRADE MARKS.

Title of Case.	Where reported.	Pages in this book.	Chief point or points affected by decision.
Adams's Mark (*re*) -	9 P. O. R. 174.	120	Held that word "patent" in *old* mark was an essential that could not be removed by amendment.
Allsopp & Sons' Mark (*re*)	5 P. O. R. 316.	120	Old marks may to a limited extent be amended.
American Tobacco Co. *v*. Guest.	9 P. O. R. 218.	125	Innocent infringer of registered mark not always cast in costs.
Apollinaris Co.'s Marks (*re*).	8 P. O. R. 137	119	"Aggrieved persons" defined.
Baker *v*. Rawson -	45 Ch. D. 519.	119	Mark represented on registration as old, when really not so.
Burgess *v*. Burgess -	3 De G. M. & G. 896.	96	Defendant restrained from using sign similar to plaintiff's, though of same name
Californian Fig Syrup Co.'s Mark (*re*).	6 P. O. R. 126.	105	Foreign mark registered abroad is not *on that account alone* registrable here.
Carter Medicine Co.'s Mark (*re*)	9 P. O. R. 401.	104	Foreign mark registered abroad is not *on that account alone* registrable here.
Cartier *v*. May - -	Dig. 200	125	Breach of injunction, direct and indirect
Cheavin *v*. Walker -	5 Ch. D. 863	109	Article described in trade mark (or otherwise) as "patent" when no patent exists or patent expired considered in equity as deceptively described.
Churton *v*. Douglas -	Johns. 174	140	A person must not use his own name so as to deceive.
Condy *v*. Mitchell -	37 L.T. N. S. 268.	122	On dissolution of partnership, unless otherwise provided, each partner may use partnership marks.
Edwards *v*. Dennis -	30 Ch. D. 454	103, 110, 119, 121	If registration of mark is wrongful from the first, mark may be expunged at any time.
Grossmith's Mark (*re*)	60 L. T. N. S. 612.	117	Period of non-user of mark, amounting to abandonment.
Guinness, Son & Co.'s Marks (*re*).	5 P. O. R. 316.	120	Old marks may to a limited extent be amended.
Hanson *v*. Harrison -	9 P. O. R. 186.	122	Rights of partners, when separated, to marks of partnership business.
Hendriks *v*. Montague	17 Ch. D. 643.	140	A company registering under the Companies Acts cannot appropriate the name of an existing unregistered company.
Holloway *v*. Holloway	13 Beav. 209	95	A man's own name must not be so used as to be an instrument of fraud

Title of Case.	Where reported.	Pages in this book.	Chief point or points affected by decision.
Shipwright *v.* Clements	19 W. R. 599	121	Trade mark inseparable from business.
Singer Co *v.* Loog -	8 App. C. 15	137	A name never actually impressed on the goods as a mark may, nevertheless, constitute a trade mark, and as such may be infringed.
Singer Co. *v.* Spence -	10 P. O. R. 297.	128, 137	Patentee of expired patent cannot restrain use of his name to describe the principle or article made according to former patent, but he may do so when such use of name might lead the public to believe him to be the manufacturer.
Singer *v.* Wilson -	2 Ch. D. 434	124	In action for infringement all that is necessary is to show that mark has been taken.
Slazenger *v.* Feltham	6 P. O. R. 531.	129	Use of trade mark identified with patent which has been declared invalid.
Southern *v.* How -	Popham, 144	91	First recorded trade mark case. (*Temp.* Elizabeth.)
Spratt *v.* Ward - -	11 Ch. D. 240	125	Trade mark cases usually heard by judge without jury.
Turton *v.* Turton	42 Ch. D. 128	140	Where no *mala fides* is shown, mere liability to confusion between two businesses of the same name will not justify an injunction.
Upmann *v.* Forester -	24 Ch. D. 231	124, 125	Innocent infringer of trade mark.
Van Duzer (*re*) -	34 Ch. D. 623	98	Registrable invented or fancy words must convey no meaning to average Englishmen, or must be non-descriptive and non-deceptive.
Wood's Mark (*re*) -	32 Ch. D. 247	119	A registered mark allowed by owner to be applied to different makers' goods becomes vitiated and may be cancelled.
Worthington's Mark (*re*)	14 Ch. D. 8	126	A mark not the same in detail but having the general appearance of a registered mark is considered an infringement.
Wotherspoon *v.* Currie	L. R. 5 H. L. 508.	139	A geographical name, long in use, may be sustained by first long user. (Montgomery *v.* Thompson.)
Wragg's Mark (*re*) -	29 Ch. D. 551	118, 119	Marks common to trade or previously used by others, not registrable, and if registered may be expunged. (*Re* Thewlis & Blakey *v.* Hughes & Young, 10 P. O. R. 369.)

PART III.—DESIGNS.

Title of Case.	Where reported.	Pages in this book.	Chief point or points affected by decision.
Adams *v.* Clementson	L. R. 12 Ch. 714.	148	Portrait of eminent person applied to manufactured articles held not to be registrable design. (But see judgment dissenting from this in Saunders *v.* Weil, *infra.*)
Bach's Design (*re*) -	6 P. O. R. 376.	150	Mere change of material, shape of article remaining the same, does not constitute new design.
Blank *v.* Footmann -	5 P. O. R. 653.	149, 151	Exhibiting unregistered design to customer, taking order, and leaving sample, held to be publication. Method of marking goods in bulk. (See also *re* Sherwood; Heinrichs *v.* Bastendorff, Winfield *v.* Snow.)
Cooper *v.* Symington	10 P. O. R. 264.	145	Design of old appearance obtained by new device held to be invention, not design *e.g.* corset busks marked to imitate lacing, but actually secured by studs and eyes.
Harrison *v.* Taylor -	4 H & N. 815.	145	New combination of old patterns may form new design: *e.g.*, placing large-space honeycomb fabric (old) over small-space honeycomb fabric (also old).
Hecla Foundry *v.* Walker.	6 P. O. R. 554.	142, 143	Designs to be judged by the eye. Utility to be ignored.
Heindrichs *v.* Bastendorff.	10 P. O. R. 160	149, 151	Merely showing unregistered design to one or two persons, not publication. Slight error in marking goods not material.
Hothersall *v.* Moore -	9 P. O. R. 27	146, 151	Obvious combination of old patterns held invalid (old centrepiece and old border in a duster). Insufficient marking in bulk. Publication in one class is publication in all.
Johnson *v.* Bailey -	11 P. O. R. 21.	152	Failure of manufacturer to keep die in good order, resulting in imperfect marking of goods, held to destroy copyright.
Le May *v.* Welch -	L. R. 28 Ch. D. 24.	146	Limits of what will constitute design. (Collar containing combination of three characteristics, all separately old in collars, held not a new design.)

PART I.—PATENTS.

CHAPTER I.

INTRODUCTION.

Existing law of Patents, Designs, and Trade Marks.

AT the present day Patents, Designs, and Trade Marks are granted and registered under the provisions of "The Patents, Designs, and Trade Marks Acts, 1883 to 1888." The union of the three species of property in the titles of these Acts seems to imply a closeness of similarity which does not really exist. A few words will serve to differentiate them.

Patents, Trade Marks, and Designs differentiated.

Patent.

Where a Patent has been granted, say for a new description of lamp, the manufacture and sale of the lamp become a monopoly, and every lamp of the same or substantially the same construction which is made and sold by others, without leave or licence, is a distinct damage and loss to the Patentee.

Trade Mark.

But where a trader has registered a Trade Mark for a lamp which is not the subject-matter of a Patent, all the world may make and sell precisely the same lamp, with this restriction only, that they must not sell it under the registered trade mark, for this would be to represent the article as having been made by the owner of the trade mark.

Design.

A Design, on the other hand, like a Patent, has reference to the specific substance or *corpus* of an article, but rather from an artistic or configurative than from a functional point of view. Thus the patented portion of the lamp might relate to a new automatic safety extinguisher, which might be made and applied and be operative in several forms and still be within the scope of the Patent, while the Design Copyright might refer to the decorative stand supporting the lamp, which could not be varied from the registered design without going outside the limit of protection.

To follow the subjects of this work in their relative order of importance, it is proposed to treat First, of PATENTS; Secondly, of TRADE MARKS; and, Thirdly, of DESIGNS.

CHAPTER II.

THE ORIGIN AND HISTORY OF PATENT LAW.—THE PATENT LAW AMENDMENT ACT, 1852.—THE PATENTS, DESIGNS, AND TRADE MARKS ACTS, 1883 TO 1888.

TO ASSIST the reader to a proper understanding of Patent Law as now existing, it may not be unprofitable to give a short sketch of its earlier history.

Origin of Letters Patent for Inventions.

Letters Patent for Inventions are the offspring, or rather the survival, of the ancient Royal Grants of Monopoly. From the earliest times it has been recognised that the Sovereign was at liberty to exercise the prerogative of making special grants to subjects. These grants were made known by "Open Letters," or *Litteræ Patentes*, addressed to all subjects of the realm, so that the privileges granted should not be questioned from want of knowledge. It is evident that from the first, new inventions, new manufactures, and advances in arts and sciences, were considered favourable subjects for protection by these Royal Grants. It may be said that the first Patent for an Invention of which we have record was issued by King Edward III. in favour of an alleged discovery of the philosopher's stone.

Crown Grants.

First recorded Patent for Invention.

With lapse of time, however, the perverted custom of granting monopolies in the exercise of trades and in the sale of goods grew to such an outrageous extent, that in the reign of Elizabeth a vast number of commodities, representing in some cases the merest necessaries of life, were in the hands of patentees or monopolists, who used their powers in the harshest and most arbitrary manner to enforce their rights. The supplies of coal, salt, vinegar, iron. steel, bottles, glass, lead, oil, tin, sulphur, pots, brushes, currants, and numbers of other products, natural and artificial, home and foreign, were governed by monopolists, who stood so little on conscience that, in certain places, that prime necessity of life, salt, rose from sixteen pence a bushel to fifteen shillings. According to the historian Hume, a list of these things, read in the House of Commons, brought to his feet an indignant member, who vowed to his astounded hearers that if things were allowed to go on at this rate "bread itself would be reduced to a monopoly."

Early trade monopolies and their abuse.

But this represents the high-water mark of monopolies, and in the succeeding reign of James I. the whole vicious system was done away with by the famous *Statute of Monopolies*. At one stroke of the pen the bulk of these unjust and restrictive privileges was declared "utterly void and of none effect, and in no wise to be put in use or execution." One of the exceptions to the general extinction of monopolies was made by Sections 5 and 6 of the Statute, in favour of Patents for Inventions, then in force and thereafter to be granted, and this is still the basis upon which patent rights stand at the present day. For example, by the 6th Section the term of a patent is limited to fourteen years, and the subject-matter is shortly defined as "any manner of new manufactures, which others at the time of making such letters patents and grants shall not use." The patent must be granted to the true and first inventor; the invention must be novel; the privilege must not be contrary to law, nor mischievous to the State, nor hurtful to trade, nor generally inconvenient. The term

Statute of Monopolies 21 Jac. I. c. 3), 1624.

Monopolies abolished.

Sections 5 and 6 reserve patents for inventions and become the basis of patent right.

Subject-matter and conditions of Patents defined.

of fourteen years seems to have been fixed by doubling the usual period of apprenticeship—*i.e.*, seven years.

Reasons for fixing the duration of patent right.

Probably the draftsman of the section reasoned that if the inventor of a new manufacture trained an apprentice in the art for seven years, it was but just that he should have the services of the skilled workman, at skilled workman's wages, for another seven years, before the pupil should be at liberty to exercise the art for his own personal advantage. Indeed, under the earliest practice it was customary to insert a proviso in the grant, requiring the inventor to take apprentices during the last seven years of the term, if he had not done so before.

After-history of patent law.

The privilege of Letters Patent for Inventions, having been thus saved from the general wreck of Monopolies brought about by the Statute of James I., thereafter passed through a long period of comparative obscurity, to endeavour to trace which would only weary without instructing the reader. As to the procedure in obtaining a patent, this became a model of circumlocution.

Circumlocutive procedure in early times.

Petitions, declarations, reports, references, warrants, stamps, bills, and seals were bandied about from office to office, existing only for the extraction of fees from the patentee. The Home Office, the Law Officers' Chambers, the Patent Bill Office, the Signet Office, the Privy Seal Office, the Letters Patent Office, and finally the Lord Chancellor's Office, each appeared in turn with mystic powers and itching palm. Nor must the Enrolment Office, the Petty Bag Office, and the Office of the Rolls Chapel be forgotten, although these were chiefly repositories of the enrolments and beyond the purview of the patentee.

Lord Coke instances this multiplication of fee-exacting offices as an example of "the wisdom of prudent antiquity, that whatsoever should pass the great seal should come through so many hands, to the end that nothing should pass the great seal . . . . that was against law or inconvenient." But we moderns may be pardoned for surmising that institutions for which so clever an apologist could only find so meagre an excuse were ripe for removal.

Separate patents for England, Scotland, and Ireland.

England, Scotland, and Ireland had each its separate patent, the fees for protection in all three amounting to about £300. With the addition of attorneys' and other charges, the entire cost to the patentee of a patent covering the United Kingdom cannot, in those days, have been less than from £500 to £700. *In re Kay's Patent* (1 Web. P. C. 568) the accounts showed the patent to have cost £500. Up to the reign of Queen Anne no Specification seems to have been required, but after 1711 the enrolment of a Specification became compulsory.

As time went on, and as the volume of patent business increased, the attention of legislators was directed more and more to projected improvements in the patent law. Slight changes in the procedure were made, and the power of entering a disclaimer of any part of his Specification was granted to the patentee by 5 & 6 Will. IV. c. 38. The right of application for extension of the term of fourteen years was provided for under 7 & 8 Vict. c. 69. Following these Acts, there came—

5 & 6 Will. IV. c. 38. (Disclaimer.)
7 & 8 Vict c. 69. (Extension.)

The Patent Law Amendment Act, 1852.

Patent Act of 1852.

The changes effected by this Act were important.

One patent for the United Kingdom.

One patent now covered Great Britain and Ireland, the Channel Islands, and the Isle of Man. The whole business of the Commissioners of Patents was conducted in one office under a responsible head. The stages of procedure were reduced to—(1) The Application, with Provisional or Complete Specification; (2) Giving notice of intention to proceed with the application; (3) Applying for the Warrant and Seal; and (4) Filing the Complete Specification (if this had not been done at the time of application). This option of filing a provisional description of the invention at the time of application, and following it up within six months afterwards with a Complete Specification, was a new element in patent procedure which has proved extremely satisfactory in practice.

Introduction of Provisional Specification.

Under the Act of 1852 the mere stamp duties payable on obtaining a patent amounted to £25, and the sums payable at the end of the third and seventh years respectively were £50 and £100, so that the total amount

Fees under Act of 1852.

payable in stamps alone, on a patent obtained and kept in force for the full term of fourteen years, was £175.

Agitation for changes in procedure.

In course of time an agitation sprang up calling chiefly for a reduction of the stamp duties, and for the adoption of the American system of examination into novelty and patentability. This agitation gathered force as years went on, and finally resulted in the passing of the present Act of 1883. A careful consideration of much conflicting testimony led the framers of the Bill to exclude the examination system. There is no reasonable doubt that, in spite of the popular clamour for its adoption, the system of examination, as now in force in America and Germany, has many evils which will always militate against its adoption here. That any examiner, whether principal or secondary, should have the power to pare down claims or absolutely to refuse the grant of a patent, is going too far. In many cases, no doubt, the examiners are able to refer to a prior invention, the same or nearly the same as that of the applicant, and in such a case no sensible man could feel aggrieved at the refusal of his application. But where, as is sometimes the case in America, and very frequently the case in Germany, the examiner exercises a perverse ingenuity in discovering anticipations and analogies that are apparent to no one but himself, and exhibits a crass determination not to be convinced of his error, the drawbacks of the examination system become too apparent to be ignored. Besides, apart from rejections on the score of anticipation, it is not unusual for a manufacturer who has invented some apparently slight but really important and valuable advance in his art to have his application for a patent in those countries met by the objection that it is not patentable subject-matter, advanced possibly by an official who knows absolutely nothing of the industry in question, and who is quite incapable of appreciating the advantages and importance of the invention submitted to him. Thus it has frequently happened that inventions which have realised large sums of money in royalties in England have been refused protection in America and in Germany on the plea of lack of novelty or of patentability. It may seem, and no doubt it is, a pity that

Examination system considered.

patents should be granted over and over again for the same thing; but the writer is persuaded that more injustice would be done than good effected by the adoption of the system of examination, if accompanied with the power of arbitrary refusal or arbitrary dictation as to the form the Claims shall assume. As to the supposed security of patents which have been granted under the examination system, it is sufficient to state that as large, if not indeed a larger, proportion of patents granted in the United States are declared invalid in courts of law than is the case with patents granted in this country.

PATENTS, DESIGNS, AND TRADE MARKS ACTS, 1883 TO 1888.

Act of 1852 not an originating Act.

If the reader has followed the foregoing historical *résumé*, it will have been noted that the Act of 1852 made no real change in the principles of patent law. It was merely an amending Act, by which the procedure was simplified, the cost decreased, the United Kingdom placed under the scope of one patent, the principle of the Provisional Specification adopted, and sundry regulations promulgated relating to the conduct of litigation.

Patents, Designs, and Trade Marks Acts, 1883 to 1888.

Procedure simplified and fees reduced.

No change was effected in fundamental principles, and no attempt made to define afresh the subject-matter of patents. For a definition of the expression "Invention" the reader of the Act was referred to the old Statute of Monopolies. As in the case of the Act of 1852, so it is with the Act of 1883. By this Act the procedure has been still further simplified. The fees and stamps on the obtaining of a complete patent are reduced from £25 to £4, while the fees for maintaining the patent in force during the full term of fourteen years have, under recent Rules, been reduced from £150 to £95.

These and sundry provisions having reference to the regulations of legal proceedings, the amendment of Specifications, oppositions, &c., represent the bulk of the changes made by the present Acts.

Having thus glanced broadly at the origin and development of patents for inventions up to the present day, we can now with greater profit proceed to discuss the present patent law It will be found that almost every phase of the subject which need be touched upon can be grouped under one of the following headings:—

1. Procedure in Obtaining Patents.
2. Who may be a Patentee.
3. Subject-Matter of Patents.
4. The Specifications (Provisional and Complete).
5. Oppositions to Applications.
6. Sealing of the Patent.
7. Amendment of Specifications.
8. Assignments, Licences, &c.
9. Extension of Patents.

CHAPTER III.

PROCEDURE IN OBTAINING PATENTS.

Application for patent.

AS FAR as the merely formal steps are concerned, an application for a patent is a very simple matter. The respective forms and stamps are on sale at all postal money order offices in the United Kingdom, and when filled in can be delivered or posted direct to the Patent Office in London. The application papers consist of a declaration (Form A), stamped with £1, in which the applicant must insert his full name, address, and occupation, and give the title of the invention. He must declare that he is the true and first inventor; that the same is not in use by any other person or persons to the best of his knowledge and belief; and must sign his name at the foot of the form. If the inventor wishes to apply for provisional protection only, he will receive with Form A two unstamped copies of Form B, upon which he should write and sign his Provisional Specification. The declaration and two copies may then be posted to the Comptroller-General at the Patent Office, and the business is complete.

How to fill in forms.

Signature of applicant.

By return of post the applicant will receive his certificate of filing, and in the next week's issue of the *Illustrated Official Journal (Patents)* the application is advertised. In about three weeks or a month afterwards (granted that his Specification is sufficiently intelligible, and that his papers have been filled up according to the instructions given) he will receive the certificate of acceptance, and this also is advertised. The Specification itself is kept secret during the term of provisional protection. At any time within nine months from the date of his application the applicant may file his Complete Specification. The form for this (Form C) can also be purchased at a postal money order office. These forms are supplied in duplicate, and one copy bears a stamp of £3. The Complete Specification must be prepared in accordance with this form and upon the lines and limits laid down by the Provisional. It should conclude with a clear statement of what the inventor claims as new, and should, when necessary or desirable, be accompanied by line drawings executed in indian ink, and without the use of colour or brush shading, so as to be suitable for reproduction by photo-lithography. Such drawings are to be made on cardboard sheets, in duplicate, size 13 inches in height by 8 inches in width, or, if this is too small, 13 inches in height by 16 inches in width. A marginal line should be placed round the sheets half an inch from the outer edge. On one of the copies of the drawing (marked "Original") the reference lettering should be in indian ink; the other copy should be marked "true copy," and the lettering should be in blue pencil. Both copies should be signed. When the Complete Specification has been dispatched to the Patent Office, a certificate of filing will in due course be received by the applicant. The examiners in the Patent Office now compare the Provisional with the Complete Specification, and if they accord with one another, and are properly prepared in compliance with the Rules, a certificate of acceptance is issued and advertised in the aforesaid Official Journal. About three weeks afterwards the Complete, together with the Provisional Specification, is generally printed and

Certificate of filing.

Advertisement of application.

Acceptance.

Complete Specification.

Drawings.

Differences in duplicate copies of drawings.

Comparison by examiners of Provisional with Complete.

Acceptance of Complete.

Publication of Specifications.

Period for opposition.

published. Within two months from the date of the Journal in which such advertisement appears, any person interested in so doing may give notice of opposition to the application. But if these two months should pass without opposition being offered, a patent is sealed and issued to the applicant.

Sealing of Patent.

Provisional Specification may be dispensed with.

The foregoing is an exact account of the procedure when a Provisional Specification only is filed with the application, and afterwards followed up by a Complete Specification. But it should be said here that the applicant has the option of filing a Complete Specification in the first instance instead of a provisional description. Each course has its advantages, and the simplest plan will be to lay these in order before the reader.

Advantages of filing Provisional Specification with application.

First.—If application is made for provisional protection only in the first instance, the advantages are that the preliminary cost is less, while the applicant has nine months during which he may, without fear, test the value of his invention either publicly or privately, improve upon the details, make searches as to its novelty, sell or agree to sell his discovery or its products, and, in short, deal with his invention just as if he had a patent, except in this respect, that he has no right of action against infringers until he has obtained his patent, and then only in respect of infringements committed after publication of his Complete Specification (Patent Act, Section 13). To these should be added the consideration that, as the Provisional Specification may be a document much less exact in its terms than a Complete Specification, an application for provisional protection may be filed at a stage in the conception of the invention when it might be impossible or injudicious to give full details.

Time is also given to consider the subject of foreign patents. Lastly, if the invention should prove disappointing, the application may be abandoned without incurring further expense, and without rendering the invention public property, seeing that the Specifications of all abandoned applications are never published, but remain secret. Therefore, if the applicant should afterwards be able to remedy the defects in his invention, there is nothing to prevent him from renewing and completing his application, granted that he has not in the meantime published his idea, or that some other inventor has not crept in after the date of his first, but before the date of his second application. In practice the vast majority of applications are accompanied in the first instance by a Provisional Specification only.

Secondly.—If application is made accompanied by a Complete Specification, the advantages which exist are much less obvious. Where an agent is employed, there is, no doubt, some slight saving in agency fees. The total stamp amounts are the same in either case—viz., £4. The acceptance and publication of the Complete places the applicant at once in a position to deal with infringers as soon as he gets his patent into his hands. On the whole, it may be said that a Complete Specification should accompany the application only where the details of the invention are fully worked out, and where the applicant has no reasonable doubt of the novelty, utility, and assured practical success of his invention.

Filing Complete in first instance.

In the foregoing description of the mode of procedure it has been assumed that the Provisional and Complete Specifications are prepared by the inventor himself. But, if the writer may be allowed to express an opinion, grounded upon long experience, the preparation of the Specification by the inventor himself is not a course to be recommended. No prudent man attempts to draw a conveyance, mortgage, will, or other legal instrument without the assistance of a properly qualified adviser, and this care is no less essential in the case of Patent Specifications. The fatal facility with which any person, fired by some crude idea, can rush into a post-office, buy a form, scribble a few incoherent lines, and breathlessly post the whole to the Comptroller, is by no means an unmixed benefit, and has its result in a flood of rubbish poured into the Patent Office every year. Probably a very large proportion of the applications thus made would never have been filed at all had they been submitted in the first instance to the calmer judgment of an experienced and properly trained patent agent.

Some reasons for the employment of Patent Agents.

But, apart from this, should the invention really contain some valuable subject-matter, the assistance of a professional adviser would in many instances have enabled the inventor to reap results of which his own precipitancy and self-confidence have deprived him. Undoubtedly there are many inventions so simple that a plain man using plain language can express the gist of his invention sufficiently well to satisfy requirements. But in all cases the burden is laid upon the applicant, that the Specification and Claims shall be prepared with "reasonable skill and knowledge," and if these essentials are wanting, nothing can save the patent from being upset should it come to be tested in a court of law.

To return from this digression, it has been said that, where a Provisional Specification has been first filed, the Complete should be lodged before the expiry of the succeeding nine months. If, from any excusable cause, this term should elapse without the Complete being filed, an additional month within which to lodge the Complete may be had upon payment of a fine of £2. If no Complete is filed within the extreme allotted time—that is, within ten months from the date of application—the application is considered to be abandoned.

Time for filing Complete may be extended for one month.

Duties of the examiners with regard to Complete Specification.

The examination of the Complete Specification has already been referred to. If the examiner should report that the Complete Specification does not properly describe the invention, or goes beyond the Provisional, or that the claims are absent or imperfect, or that more than one invention is claimed, the Comptroller may refuse to accept the Specification until these faults have been corrected. If the applicant disputes the justice of these objections, he may appeal to the Law Officer, who will either sustain or rebut the Comptroller's decision.

Comptroller's objections to Specifications may be appealed against.

Oppositions will be treated under the heading specially devoted to that subject (see Chapter VIII.).

Patent dated as of date of application.

If no opposition is entered, or if the opposition is unsuccessful, the patent is issued and dated as of the day of application.

Duration of patent.

The patent is granted for fourteen years, and covers the United Kingdom of Great Britain and Ireland and the Isle of Man.

At the end of the fourth year, annual payments are required to keep the patent in force. According to the most recent scale the annual fees are as follows:— Renewal fees on patent.

	£	s.	d.
Before the end of the fourth year, and in respect of the fifth year	5	0	0
Before the end of the fifth year, and in respect of the sixth year	6	0	0
Before the end of the sixth year, and in respect of the seventh year	7	0	0
Before the end of the seventh year, and in respect of the eighth year	8	0	0
Before the end of the eighth year, and in respect of the ninth year	9	0	0
Before the end of the ninth year, and in respect of the tenth year	10	0	0
Before the end of the tenth year, and in respect of the eleventh year	11	0	0
Before the end of the eleventh year, and in respect of the twelfth year ...	12	0	0
Before the end of the twelfth year, and in respect of the thirteenth year ...	13	0	0
Before the end of the thirteenth year, and in respect of the fourteenth year ...	14	0	0

If by accident the payment of an annual tax should be overlooked, an extension of time of from one to three months can be had to pay the annuity, on payment of the following fines:— Time to pay renewal fees on patent may be extended from one to three months.

	£	s.	d.
On extension of time for one month ...	1	0	0
,, ,, ,, two months ..	3	0	0
,, ,, ,, three months ...	5	0	0

In the event of the Letters Patent being lost or destroyed, the Comptroller may, on a satisfactory explanation of the disappearance of the original, cause a duplicate to be sealed and issued on payment of a fee of £2. Duplicate of lost Letters Patent may be obtained.

The question of Amendments of Specifications will be treated under its proper heading (see Chapter X.).

CHAPTER IV.

WHO MAY BE A PATENTEE.

Persons entitled to become patentees.

ANY person, of either sex, whether a British subject or an alien, may be a patentee. Even those who are generally considered under legal disabilities, such as infants and lunatics, may become patentees, so long as the necessary documents are prepared in the prescribed manner. No inquiry is made by the Patent Office as to the age, sanity, or coverture of the applicant.

It is submitted that exceptions to this general rule exist in the case of the Sovereign, on the principle that the Crown cannot make a grant to itself. Again, although many such patents exist, it may be doubted whether a beneficed clergyman can legally become a patentee, in view of the prohibition from trading under 1 & 2 Vict., Cap. 106, Sections 28 to 30. The question whether an alien enemy is incapacitated as a patentee was raised, but not decided, in *Bloxam v. Elsee* (1 Web. P. C. 132). The probability is that he would not be ousted on that account alone.

Joint patentees.

Two or more persons may make a joint application for a patent, and it is provided that an application may legally be made by the inventor or inventors in conjunction with another or with others who are not joint inventors. Thus an invention may be patented in the joint names of the inventor and a capitalist with whom he has agreed to associate himself. The name or names of the actual inventor or inventors should, however, be specified in the declaration.

Inventor and non-inventor.

Importers.

The term "Inventor" is not under the Act confined to a person who evolves an invention from his own mind. The term is also used to designate one who first introduces or imports an invention from abroad. A patent granted to such an applicant would be perfectly valid if it could be shown to be unknown and unpublished in this country at the date of the application. However, if the invention has been previously patented or protected abroad, the foreign inventor has the privilege, in those countries which have become parties to the International Convention, of making an application here within six months and obtaining the same date as that of the original patent abroad. In countries "beyond the sea"—such, for example, as America—an additional month is allowed.

Rights of foreign inventors under International Convention.

If an inventor should die before applying for a patent, his legal representatives may make the application, and if his death should occur after the application, but before completing, his legal representatives may proceed and obtain the grant of the patent.

Rights of legal representatives of deceased inventor or applicant.

A person resident in this country may patent in his own name an invention communicated to him by the actual inventor abroad. In such cases it is usual, though not essential, to indicate the source from which the knowledge has been derived.

Communicated inventions.

CHAPTER V.

SUBJECT-MATTER OF PATENTS.

IT HAS been said that neither in the Patent Law Amendment Act of 1852, nor in the more recent Acts of 1883 to 1888, has any attempt been made to define the meaning of the term "Invention." In both instances the reader is referred back to the ancient Statute of Monopolies. Referring, then, to Section 6 of this Statute, we find that letters patent and grants of privilege are limited in favour of **"the sole working or making of any manner of new manufactures**

Definition of "Invention."

Statute of Monopolies, Section 6.

within this realm to the true and first inventor and inventors of such manufactures, which others, at the time of making such letters patent and grant, shall not use, so as also they be not contrary to the law nor mischievous to the State by raising prices of commodities at home, or hurt of trade, or generally inconvenient."

"Invention" means new manufacture.

Therefore the subject-matter of letters patent must be some "*manner of new manufactures.*" It is very unlikely that the old draftsman in setting down this definition of subject-matter had any glimpse of the magnitude of the interests that would be created by this Section 6 of his Bill. The clause was the earliest legislative recognition of the public policy of allowing temporary privileges to the inventors of new manufactures. It is the basis of our present law, and the cradle of the still more gigantic patent system in force across the Atlantic.

The discussions that have taken place upon the true meaning of the "working or making of any manner of new manufactures" only prove how unintentionally well chosen and comprehensive the expression really is. "Manufacture" has been held to be synonymous with "invention," and to mean not only the process of making, but also the thing produced. For example, "manufacture" as applied to hatting might mean (*a*) the machinery by which the hat is made, or (*b*) the successive steps or processes to which the hat body is subject, or (*c*) the hat itself. It was admitted, says Chief Justice Eyre in *Boulton v. Bull* (1795, 2 H. Bl. 482), that "manufacture" is applicable not only to things made, but to the practice of making; to principles carried into practice in a new manner; to new results of principles carried into practice. Thus the term excludes a mere barren principle, no matter how great the discovery may be, so long as no immediate practical result useful to individuals or to trade is brought about. In other words, the mere laying bare of a physical law or force which has been in existence since the world began, no matter how tremendously it may increase the scope of our knowledge and the sum of our wealth, cannot be patented. Thus, to instance extreme

"Manufacture" means both manner of making and product.

But does not include bare principle.

cases, Newton could not have patented his discovery of the laws of gravity; nor Harvey his, of the circulation of the blood; nor Franklin his, of electricity. But lesser minds coming after these great intellects may, by cunning devices, put these newly awakened Titans into harness, so that they shall grind corn, pump water, or carry messages, and for these devices patents will be granted

Manufacture includes processes. *Crane v. Price.*

At one time it was doubted whether the language of the statute extended to processes, but the decision in *Crane v. Price* (1842, 4 M. & G. 580) affirmed emphatically that it did. Therefore a process, whether it be chemical or mechanical, is good subject-matter for a patent.

For the purpose of splitting up subject-matter into a few heads which may repay separate examination, it will serve to consider patentable inventions as divisible into the following six classes, viz.:—

Classes of subject-matter.

(1) New and useful machines or things, for new or old purposes, and improvements in existing machinery or things.

(2) New and useful combinations of mechanical parts or of materials.

(3) Improvements in existing manufactures, processes, or parts of processes.

(4) Novel and useful results of chemical and mechanical processes.

(5) New or improved processes, for which special machinery may or may not be necessary.

(6) New principles, when coupled with a mode of carrying the same into practical effect.

A short examination of each of these heads, with an example attached, will assist the reader to understand them more fully.

(1) *New and Useful Machines for New or Old Purposes, and Improvements in Existing Machinery.*

New or improved machinery.

A new machine or contrivance may also be for an entirely new purpose, or it may be for use in connection with an old purpose. The first is an extremely rare class of invention. The second is most common. As an example of the first, take the subject of the transmission of speech over a long distance by electricity. Here was a new purpose, and the telephone, with its vibrating plates, transmitter and receiver, formed a new apparatus for this new purpose. Therefore the telephone was a patentable invention of the highest order—namely, a new apparatus for a new purpose. As an example of a new machine for an old purpose, one of many will suffice. Sewing is among the oldest of arts. But the first sewing machine was an absolutely new contrivance for this old purpose: therefore it formed patentable subject-matter.

Improvements in existing machinery may be said to form the bulk of patented inventions. For example, there are hundreds of patented improvements on the original sewing machine. Indeed, in all classes of machinery of which large quantities are used, an improvement which to an outsider may seem but a very slight advance is often the source of fortune to its inventor, and is patentable subject-matter. In *Moser v. Marsden* (10 P. O. R. 350) Lopes, L.J., says that a new mode of using an old machine by altering it, involving the exercise of invention and ingenuity in its application, is good subject-matter for a patent. In the above case, in which the Court of Appeal affirmed the validity of the patent for the well-known Moser "raising" machine, the evidence showed that the advance effected by the patentee upon prior inventions for the same object, although apparently slight, had *practically* been exceedingly successful, and this had great weight with the Court in supporting the patent. Additions to or improvements on existing patented machinery or things may also be made, and in their turn patented. If the improvement is separable from, and is no essential part of the existing patented machine or thing, it may be made and sold separately. But if it forms an integral part of the machine or thing, and is useless apart from it, it would evidently be of little advantage to the inventor, as he could not make use of the original invention without the sanction of the original patentee. On the other

Consideration given to great practical success of slight improvement.

Improvements on existing patented inventions.

hand, the original patentee could not make use of the improvement without the permission of the second patentee, and, as a consequence, the second patentee might find his reward in selling or licensing to the original patentee.

(2) *New and Useful Combinations of Mechanical Parts, and of Materials.*

Although patents are granted for combinations, it must be said at the outset that a combination to warrant a patent should show invention. Obvious combinations are not good subject-matter. Therefore, in every case it is necessary to take the merits into consideration, to decide whether or not the effecting of the combination shows the exercise of invention. And, first, take the simplest form of combination—viz., the mere coupling together of two well-known things which have heretofore acted separately, but which on being connected give a continuous operation. A good example of this is to be found in *Williams v. Nye* (7 P. O. R. 62). The plaintiff in this case had merely taken a well-known mincing-machine and an equally well-known machine for filling skins, and connected them together, so that the mincing and filling operations were continuous, instead of being interrupted as before. The result was a sausage-making machine which was proved to be most useful, meritorious, and economical. Nevertheless, the Judges of the Court of Appeal expressed themselves as satisfied that there had been no such exercise of the *inventive* faculty as to make the plaintiff's machine subject-matter for a patent. Even where the combination was apparently not quite so easy to effect, the patent could not be upheld. In *Saxby v. Gloucester Waggon Co.* (L. R. 72, Q. B. D. 305) a decision adverse to the patent was grounded on the same objection, although this was less obvious than in *Williams v. Nye.*

Combinations.

Combination must show "invention."

Still, even this simplest type of combination—viz., the connecting of two well-known machines—might be patentable if the method and means used to connect them required invention. For example, merely to place a folding machine in line with a printing machine so as to print and fold continuously instead of separately as before, would not be invention if nothing more were done. But if the continuous printing and folding involved some necessary transmitting mechanism, requiring design and the exercise of invention, to pass each printed sheet to the folders, then the combination would be patentable subject-matter.

Combination of a concretion and an abstraction not patentable.

It is unsound to claim the combination of a concrete thing with an abstract property or qualification. Chief Baron Pollock in trying, although not very happily, to express this, once said, "You cannot have a valid claim for the combination of 2½*d.* with a pound of butter." An example will help the point to be better understood. We will suppose that rollers covered with porcelain were well known as being the best rollers that could be used for crushing grain. Suppose it were afterwards discovered that to make one roller run a little faster than the other produced a grinding as well as a crushing effect, which vastly improved the result, by separating the germ from the starch part of the grain. Here is a real invention. It cannot be said that the idea is unpatentable. But, at all events, the claim that was really made—viz., "The combination of porcelain rollers with *differential velocity*"—proved to be untenable.

Almost the largest class of patented inventions is that of combinations of mechanism. These may consist of combinations of mechanical parts or groups of parts. The combination may consist of mere rearrangement, addition, or subtraction. The parts or the groups must not be independent of each other, nor must the connection of the groups be known or obvious. The combination may consist entirely of old parts or groups, and in such a case the patentee is usually tied somewhat closely to the arrangement shown and described. Therefore, an infringer might, by changing the combination to a greater or less extent, place himself outside of the scope of the patentee's claims.

Combinations which include new element.

On the other hand, a combination may include an entirely new element, which is, however, dependent for its utility upon its connection with the combination. Here the patentee is in a better position, and any attempt to evade or use an equivalent for the described combination, so long as the new element is pirated, will be severely scrutinised by the Court. A good example of this was instanced in the case of *Proctor v. Bennis* (4 P. O. R. 333). The subject of the patent was a mechanical stoker for feeding coal into boiler furnaces. Before the date of Proctor's patent, mechanical stokers had been in use in which there was a reciprocating fuel-pusher working horizontally, and drawn slowly back and shot quickly forward by an arrangement of springs, shafts, and tappets. Proctor had an arrangement of springs, shafts, and tappets almost identical with what had been used before, but instead of a sliding pusher he had a flap, hung vertically upon a hinge pivot. It was shown at the trial that the circular sweep of the pivoted flap had great advantages over the horizontal pusher, as being a more close approximation to the swinging and spreading action of hand stoking. The pivoted flap was not claimed separately for the specific purpose, as, strictly speaking, it ought to have been, but was claimed in combination with the specified arrangement of shafts, springs, and tappets, the latter having almost no feature of novelty. The defendant had altered this arrangement so as to differ from that of Proctor, but had appropriated the pivoted flap, evidently relying upon this not having been separately claimed. This, however, did not save him. In spite of the fact that no specific separate claim had been made for the hinged flap, this was described in the judgment as the "pith and marrow" of the invention, and the decision was, that the defendant, having taken the gist of the invention, although he avoided the actual combination shown and claimed, must be held to have infringed.

Proctor v. Bennis.

In *Wenham v. May* (4 P. O. R 303) the patentee had invented a gas lamp in which wire gauze screens were used in certain specified positions, the said gauze screens being claimed "as described and shown." The defendants also used gauze screens, but not in the same positions as in the plaintiff's lamp, their defence being, practically, that they had not infringed the specific combination claimed. It was held that both upon the evidence and the Specifica-

Wenham v. May.

tion, the object of the plaintiff's invention was to equalise and regulate the regenerative air-currents by means of wire gauze screens, irrespective of the specific arrangement, and that the defendants by adopting such gauze screens had infringed the essence of the plaintiff's patent. A lesson on the essential of an apparatus or combination may also be had from a consideration of the *Automatic Weighing Machine Company's* case (9 P. O. R. 41).

In passing from mechanical combinations to those of materials we enter another field. A number of possible examples could be easily suggested. Thus, different materials may be mechanically mixed so as to produce new and useful results, such as linoleum floorcloth for example. New compositions of colours, varnishes, and cements might be so produced. In the same manner, the combination of two materials, viz., caoutchouc with a woven fabric, results in a new product, *i.e.* a waterproof cloth; or the combination of two or more metals results in a new alloy. All of these are patentable.

(3) *Improvements in Existing Manufactures, Processes, or Parts of Processes.*

In order to differentiate the selected heads that have been set down as representing the main divisions of subject-matter, and so to avoid repetition, it will be necessary to consider the word "manufacture," not always in the broad and general terms extracted from the Statute of Monopolies, but sometimes in its narrower and more generally understood sense.

Restricted meaning of "manufacture."

"Manufacture" under the present heading must therefore be taken to represent the "making of anything by hand or by art," such, for instance, as the weaving of cut pile fabrics, the making of lead piping, or the production of gas.

For example, in the manufacture of pile fabrics, instead of the usual plan of weaving the pile in loops and cutting these loops by an after operation, an inventor might produce a new method of weaving pile fabrics face to face in a double web, and cut the pile by the after operation of separating one fabric from the other, thus saving time both in the weaving and in the pile-cutting. Another inventor might propose to cut the pile in the very act of weaving, each pick as it is beaten up being severed by a series of knives worked from the healds. Both of these inventions would be patentable improvements in that special manufacture.

Again, take the production of lead piping For many purposes, lead, although it makes so convenient and cheap a tubing, is unsuitable. Metals of a higher cost have therefore to be used. But suppose a cheap and easy method were invented of thinly lining the interior of the lead pipe in the course of manufacture with this superior metal, so that all the advantages of the more expensive metal were obtained at the cost of only a slight increase in the price of the lead tubing. Here would be a patentable improvement in the manufacture of such tubing, based both upon the mechanism, if new mechanism had been devised, and also in respect of the new product—viz., the lined lead tubing.

Then to glance at a supposititious improvement in the manufacture of gas. The improvement might relate to the retorts, or to the purifiers, or to the materials distilled in the retorts; or the inventor might make an entire change in the process, and, as has been lately done, manufacture gas from a mixture of decomposed steam or water gas and vaporised oil.

Just as an inventor may effect a radical change in the whole of a mechanical or chemical manufacture or process, so the invention may relate to a part only of the process.

(4) *Novel and Useful Results of Chemical and Mechanical Processes.*

It was at one time doubtful whether a new product, apart altogether from its mode of manufacture, could be maintained as good subject-matter for a patent. It may, however, be safely taken that when, by mechanically mixing or chemically compounding selected substances in a new manner, products are obtained having novel and useful qualities, such products are patentable.

A new product is patentable.

Examples of patentable products.

In examples of mechanical admixtures of materials, resulting, for instance, in a new artificial stone, or a new cement, where there is no invention in the process of mixing or making, but only in the selection of the materials, clearly the materials separately and apart from each other cannot be claimed as destined for that purpose. It is only when amalgamated and formed into the new and useful thing, whether artificial stone or cement, that they become appreciable subject-matter. Therefore the proper object to which to direct the claim is the product. In the same manner, the novel result of a chemical process, such as a new dye, is a product capable of being patented. But the results of mere changes or variations in operations capable of indefinite change are doubtful subject-matter, even when the product is something appreciably different from what has been produced before. For example, although a number of patents are taken out for so-called new cloths, produced merely by a rearrangement of the ordinary operations of a weaver's loom, it is more than doubtful whether any such patent could be sustained, unless the result exhibited an advance of such importance as to justify the maintaining of the patent. But, to go a step further than this, if an undoubtedly new article—that is, a new product—is produced by the operation of specially designed mechanism, the opinions expressed on the bench are all in favour of a claim being made for the product itself as well as for the mechanism by which it is produced. For example, in *Vorwerk v. Evans* (7 P. O. R. 265) the claim for the product was sought to be declared bad by the defendants. It may be explained that the object of the invention was to produce a waistband for ladies' skirts and petticoats. Before the date of the patent, waistbands had been cut from woven material to the required circular shape, of course with considerable waste of material. The patentees invented a mode of weaving such waistbands to the required curved shape, and a specially designed loom, with sectional warps and conical drawing rollers, was designed and described in the specification. Now, no such waistband had ever been so made or woven before. It was an entirely new article of manufacture. A specific claim was made for it The defendants attacked this claim, but Cotton, L.J.. in giving judgment, defended such a claim and said, "If there is a new thing produced, and that is useful and complies with other requirements, then in my opinion there could be a thoroughly good patent taken out for that."

(5) *New or Improved Processes for which Special Machinery May or May Not be Necessary.*

If the result or product of a process is good subject-matter for a patent, it is clear that a new or improved process itself, whether applied to the making of a new product or to the manufacture of an old product, is equally good subject-matter. Where both process and product are new, both may be claimed: where the product is old and the process new, the process can be claimed. Thus in *Stevens v. Keating* (2 Web. P. C. 182) Pollock, C.B., said, "The real invention may not be so much for the thing when produced, as for the mode in which it is produced, and its novelty may consist not so much in its existence as a new substance, as in its being an old substance produced by a different process." Processes.

As far as processes generally are concerned, the old case of *Crane v. Price* (1 Web. P. C. 393) settled the point that a new process is a patentable invention. Chemical processes also may be said to stand upon a more favourable footing than mechanical processes, in respect of anticipation by analogous processes.

In the case of *Badische Anilin v. Levenstein* (4 P. O. R. 449) it was held that the prior use of an analogous chemical invention will not go far as an anticipation of an after invention. The cause of this is, probably, that analogy and deduction in chemistry are not so obvious as in mechanical operations. This same rule holds good in cases of alleged infringement. Thus, in *Nobel's Explosives Co. v. Anderson* (11 P. O. R. 113) the plaintiffs, who had claimed the use of a *soluble* nitro-cellulose in the manufacture of a certain explosive, were unable to succeed against the defendant, who used *insoluble* nitro-collulose. Analogy does not go far in chemistry.

A process may be new and the product may be new, yet the process may be worked by apparatus which has been in common use before, and cannot be claimed merely because of its application to a new purpose. But in some cases the apparatus for carrying out the process may require to be specially devised, and then it may constitute a separate invention.

Patent might contain claims for new apparatus, new process, and new product.

Thus there might be an invention in which apparatus, process, and product may all be new, and in such a case each may constitute subject-matter for a separate claim.

(6) *A New Principle Coupled with a Mode of Carrying the Same into Practical Effect.*

Bare principles not patentable.

It has again and again been laid down by the highest authorities that a principle *per se* cannot be patented. In practice, one of the difficulties attending the general application of the rule is, whether the particular invention under consideration is or is not within the vague lines which define a principle.

It is undoubtedly true that the discovery of an abstract and fundamental law of nature or of a natural or scientific truth—such, for example, as the law of gravity, the circulation of the blood, the principles of electricity—cannot be validly patented. But, although our knowledge of these things is the result of logical reasoning, thoughtful observation, and well-weighed deduction, nevertheless they are in no sense inventions. Columbus, although he discovered America, did not invent it. But, passing from these landmarks in human progress to the consideration of smaller issues, it is questionable whether it is not too much the custom to seek to narrow down the field of invention, by describing as principles, and therefore as unpatentable, matters which are really improvements legitimately due to invention, and relating rather to practice than to principle. Take, for example, the well-known "hot-blast" case of *Neilson v. Harford* (1 Web. P. C. 295), which is quoted so often as a test case on this very matter of principle. The action was tried in 1841, at a time when patent actions were remarkably rare,

Neilson v. Harford.

and when judges had but little opportunity of making acquaintance with technical matters. The invention was simple. Prior to the date of Neilson's patent, iron-smelters had used a blast of *cold air* to blow up the smelting furnaces. Neilson's improvement was that he *heated* the blast. The advantages which have been derived by the iron industry of this country from this simple advance have been held to be incalculable. Fortunately for the patentee, the Court held that his claim was not for the hot blast *per se*, but for the hot blast in conjunction with the means by which the blast was heated. Otherwise it is perfectly plain, from the observations of the judges, that had it been construed that Neilson claimed "heating the air-blast of smelting furnaces" irrespective of any air-heating means, his patent would have been considered bad, as laying claim to a principle.

Principle must be claimed in conjunction with means for carrying into effect, but such means need not show invention.

It was not and cannot be pretended that the air-heating means involved any invention at all. Neilson briefly alluded to a heating box as a suitable means. But the invention lay altogether in the use of a hot blast. The least intelligent of ironmasters, when once told in three words what the object of the invention was—viz., to "heat his blast"—would have had no difficulty in constructing at once a more or less efficient heating means, such as a heating box, or a cylinder, or a heating coil, or a jacketed flue. He would have been astounded if he had been told that the patentable part of the invention lay, not in the grand secret of heating the air-blast, but in the self-evident heating means at his feet, although this had scarcely given him any trouble to devise, and had called for the exercise of no invention at all. During the hearing of the above case of *Neilson v. Harford*, Alderson, B., said, "I take it that the difference between a patent for a principle and a patent that can be supported is, that you must have an embodiment of the principle in some practical mode, described in the Specification, of carrying the invention into practical effect, and then you take out your patent, not for the principle, but for the mode of carrying the principle into effect." It is useless to speculate whether the Court, constituted as it is to-day, might not, in the case of *Neilson v. Harford*, have given a different ruling upon the question as to whether the mere heating of the blast fell within the domain of principle. The precedent has been established, and all that can be said is, that wherever it is a question of claiming anything which seems to be of the nature of a principle, the rule is to claim it in conjunction with, and as effected by, the means for carrying the principle into effect, however simple and self-evident such means may be.

Rule for drawing claims in patents for principles.

Practically the same conclusions were arrived at in the case of *Boulton & Watt v. Bull* (2 H. Bl. 493), the plaintiffs being the patentees of the separate condenser in steam engines. This difference, however, might be noted, that the means for carrying into effect the principle or plan of separate condensation were not self-evident, like the air-heater, but might have called for the exercise of the inventive faculties. Still more so was this the case in *Otto v. Linford* (146 L. T., N. S. 35). One of the chief features of this invention was what Jessel, M.R., called the "idea," or principle, of putting a cushion of air between the explosive mixture and the piston of a gas engine, so as to regulate or make gradual what would otherwise be a sudden shock. "Of course," said his Lordship, "that could not be patented. I do not read the patent so; I read the patent as being to the effect that the patentee tells us that there is the idea which he wishes to carry out; but he also describes other kinds of machines which will carry it out, and he claims to carry it out substantially by one or other of these machines. That is the subject of a patent." It will, however, be evident to the reader that the mere "idea" of interposing this elastic fluid cushion in the cylinder would be but a half-told tale if the ingenious mechanism for carrying it into effect were not also described and shown.

Boulton & Watt v. Bull.

Otto v. Linford.

Jessel, M.R., on the patenting of a principle.

Alderson, B., whose remarks in *Neilson v. Harford* have already been quoted, said in the later case of *Jupe v. Pratt* (1 Web. P. C. 145), "You cannot take out a patent for a principle. You may take out a patent for a principle coupled with a mode of carrying the principle into effect. . . . . . . If you have done that, then you are

Alderson, B., on the same.

entitled to protect yourself from all other modes of carrying the same principle into effect, that being treated by the jury as a piracy of your original invention." The *Automatic Weighing Machine Company*—who were patentees of a weighing machine having three essential parts, a weighing apparatus, an indicating apparatus, and a *break between the two* which was closed up by the insertion of a coin so as to make the machine act automatically—have had more than a dozen actions against various infringers, who, while adopting the principle of their machine, used in some cases strikingly different apparatus. But the *Company* have nearly always been successful, and have practically established that any mechanism carrying out their principle is an infringement (see 9 P. O. R. 41, and 10 P. O. R. 442).

Old things applied to new uses sometimes patentable.

The application of an old article to a new use is sometimes patentable, but it will depend upon the amount of invention involved in effecting the new application. Thus in *Ehrlich v. Ihlee* (5 P. O. R. 437), although circular cards had long been used in looms, their application to mechanically played musical instruments was held to be patentable.

The mere substitution of one material for another to effect a like purpose is not patentable. For example, the manufacture of stair-rods from mahogany instead of brass would not be patentable, and an application for such has been refused.

In *Harwood v. Great Northern Railway Company* (2 B. & S. 194, 22) a patent for fishplates, to connect the rails of permanent way, was held to be bad because a similar mode had been in vogue for connecting timber baulks. Inventions having immoral or illegal objects are also unpatentable.

CHAPTER VI.

FURTHER ELEMENTS IN SUBJECT-MATTER: INVENTION, NOVELTY, AND UTILITY.

THE remaining necessary elements in subject-matter are INVENTION, NOVELTY, and UTILITY.

INVENTION.

The amount of invention necessary to make an improvement fit subject-matter for a patent has to some extent been already treated in the last chapter, under the foregoing heads of Subject-Matter. But upon this point it is absolutely impossible to give any general rule. Each case must be judged upon its own merits, and the reported decisions are always governed by the special circumstances of each case, so that an attempt to generalise from them would only mislead. For example, an argument that the improvement was obvious and the advance but little has been met successfully by showing the great demand for and large sale of the article, or that, although similar articles had been made in large quantities by various manufacturers before, the so-called *obvious* improvement had never suggested itself to them.

Instances in which alleged "obvious" nature of invention may be rebutted.

NOVELTY.

The whole of the subject-matter of claims must be new.

Every invention for which a patent is obtained must also possess the element of novelty. The grant of a patent being upon the assumption that it is "*a new manufacture*" which the inventor is giving to the public, anything which disproves this view militates against the validity of the grant.

It is therefore of the utmost importance that the novelty of the invention should be established before the expense of obtaining a patent is incurred. And it must be remembered that if it should transpire that the subject of even one only of the claims is old, the whole patent is invalid, at least until amendment of the Specification has been effected. For example, in a recent case tried in the Court of Session, Scotland (*Murchland v. Nicholson*, 10 P. O. R. 417), the patentee of an apparatus for milking cows brought an action for infringement. Unluckily, however, for the plaintiff, it turned out that the fifth claim in his Specification, for a quite unimportant detail, was not novel. The whole patent was therefore held to be invalid. The Lord Chief Justice Clerk, in delivering judgment, said, "I cannot but regret that the complainer, who, I think, had a good and patentable invention, should have made a claim which is bad in an unimportant detail of his apparatus. Unfortunately, the law is, as stated by the Lord Ordinary, that this claim being bad, the whole patent must fall." One bad claim vitiates the whole patent.

The broad rule is that if the invention has by any means whatever become known to the public, either by prior use or by prior publication, no patent can be afterwards granted for it. The reason is that in such circumstances the patentee has nothing to give to the public in return for the grant from the Crown, nor can the public be deprived of the right freely to use what they already possess. Nature of patentee's contract with the Crown.

Prior Use.

Prior use by the public, or even by the inventor himself, if effected in a public manner, will destroy the validity of a patent granted after the date of such prior use. As to prior use by the inventor himself, such use to prevail against his right to a patent must be open and undisguised. Mere experiments in his own closet or workshop, or mere confidential disclosure to or experimental user by another, will not destroy the inventor's right to a patent. For example, in *Morgan v. Seaward* (1 Web. P. C. 171) the patentee had invented a paddle-wheel, and had two pairs of such wheels made for him by an engineer, whom he had cautioned to keep silence. The wheels were made, packed, and exported before the date of the patent; but, Experimental prior use not publication.

in spite of these facts, the patent was sustained. The bulk of cases go to show that the inventor is allowed a reasonable latitude in experimenting with his invention, even although such experiments should be known to one or two besides himself. But this doctrine must not be pushed too far.

Secret prior use by another will not vitiate patent granted to independent inventor.

Prior use by some one who has practised the invention secretly, and in a mode known only to himself, will not invalidate a patent granted to a subsequent independent inventor. In *Dollond's Patent* (2 H. B. 43) the fact of a similar object-glass for telescopes having been made in 1720, in a manner which was an undisclosed secret, did not upset the patent. It may be said also that it is possible to obtain a valid patent for a process which one's next-door neighbour may have used for years, but used only as a personal and jealously guarded secret.

Prior use might sometimes constitute merely prior existence. But where the new article, although seen and handled by several persons before the date of the patent, did not on the face of it disclose the secret of production, the patent has been upheld. Thus in *Hancock v. Somervell* (39 New. Lon. Jour. 158) the alleged anticipation amounted to this, that samples of the invention (which was a shoe of vulcanised rubber) were sent up and down for the purpose of attracting customers, although not actually sold. It could not be shown that the secret of the manufacture was discovered or made known by or to any of those who saw the sample shoes, and as a result the patent was upheld.

Publication under provisional protection afterwards abandoned.

Another incident of prior user, or it might be of prior publication, falls to be considered under the following not unusual circumstances. It sometimes happens that an applicant, after having obtained provisional protection for an invention, and after having under such provisional protection advertised and sold articles made in accordance with the invention, determines for some reason to drop the first provisional during the currency of the protection, and obtains a fresh provisional protection for substantially the same invention.

Under such circumstances it has been asked if such

publication, under the first provisional, does not destroy the novelty of the invention as protected under the second application.

There are two cases under the former Act of 1852, in which it was held that, assuming the invention in the two provisional specifications to be the same, the abandonment of the first provisional specification did not void a patent, granted, *within the original period of provisional protection*, upon the second application, even if actual user and publication could be shown to have taken place during the currency of the first provisional protection, and before the second application was made.

The cases referred to are those of *Oxley v. Holden* (8 C. B. R., New Series, 666) and *Lister v. Norton* (3 P. O. R. 199). Mr. Justice Chitty in the latter case held himself bound by the decision in *Oxley v. Holden*, and pointed out that such a conclusion might very fairly be drawn from the wording of the 8th Section of the Act of 1852.

Oxley v. Holden. Lister v. Norton

This section said that during provisional protection the invention might be "used and published without prejudice to *any* letters patent to be granted for the same." On the other hand, Section 14 of the present Act (corresponding to Section 8 of the Act of 1852) says, after referring to the acceptance of the application, that the invention may be publicly used "without prejudice to *the* patent to be granted for the same." Some authorities are inclined to hold that the use of the definite article identifies the patent with the original application, and that if this is abandoned in favour of a re-application, public user in the interval will vitiate novelty. Others see no material difference between the effect of Section 14 of the present Act and Section 8 of the former Act, and therefore maintain that the rulings referred to above would remain unchanged in the case of applications made under the present Act.

The old and the present Sections compared.

No decision has yet been given on the point, but it is submitted that if the matter were again considered under the present Statute, there is a strong probability that the former rulings would not be sustained.

Probable effect of present Act.

Prior Publication.

Publication in book, periodical, or drawing.

An invention may be published in this country, by being described in some newspaper or book, or in the specification of some prior patent. It is not necessary that such newspaper or book should have been issued in this country. It might be a foreign book or newspaper, and be printed in a foreign language. The publication might even be effected by an engraving, if the invention should be unmistakeably set forth therein. But it will not suffice to prove the mere existence of such book or publication in this country. It should be proved that it has been actually seen and consulted by members of the public, or has been in such a situation that it was at the disposal of anyone who cared to see or consult it. Thus, if a book in a public library stood in its proper place on the shelves, and figured in the catalogue, it would not be necessary to prove specifically that it had ever been read or consulted by a member of the public. Its presence would be considered as publication. In *Harris v. Rothwell* (4 P. O. R. 225) a knitting machine patent was declared invalid because of the presence, in the Patent Office Library, of two German specifications which described a similar knitting machine. It was not considered essential to prove that they had ever been really consulted (see also *United Horse Nail Company v. Stewart and Company*, 2 P. O. R. 122). But if, instead of being shelved and catalogued, the book had been lying in some back room, and its presence unknown until disinterred by some chance finder, that would not be considered to be an anticipatory publication (*Otto v. Steel*, 3 P. O. R. 109).

Book must be accessible to the public.

Publication may be made in a foreign language.

Publication by drawing.

A drawing in a prior specification, illustrating, without any description, the subject-matter of a subsequent invention, will be held to be publication (*Herrburger v. Squires*, 6 P. O. R. 194); but the meaning of the drawing must be unmistakeable, and no favourable construction will be put upon anything uncertain. When the anticipation consists of descriptive matter only, the description must be such as to enable a competent person to carry the invention into effect. Consequently there can be but few unmistakeable letterpress descriptive anticipations of mechanism, unless it is of the most simple construction.

The field which should be most carefully scanned in searches to establish or to break down a claim to novelty is that afforded by the published specifications of home and foreign patents. The classified indexes and class abridgments of subject-matter which are now published, and which, together with the specifications, can be consulted at the Patent Office Library or in the public libraries of most large towns, render this task of searching comparatively easy.

Utility.

The remaining element in subject-matter is, Utility. The invention may be novel and most ingenious, but unless it fulfils a useful purpose, and is useful and beneficial to the public, a valid patent cannot be obtained. And by "Utility" is not meant the mere capacity to be put to a useful purpose. Mr. Justice Grove, in charging a jury, said that in his opinion "Utility means an invention better than the preceding knowledge." In other words, a machine, however ingenious, which performed a given operation in an inferior and faulty manner as compared with an existing machine, would not be good subject-matter.

Invention must be useful.

"Utility" means increased serviceableness.

The utility of an invention is always a question of fact and a matter of proof. The commercial success of a patent will have great weight in attesting its utility, and Chief Justice Tindal has remarked that better evidence of the utility of an invention could not possibly be had than the fact that attempts were being made to infringe it.

Utility is matter of proof.

In drawing the claims of an invention, care should be taken to confine the invention within its limits of usefulness. The natural desire to cover as much ground as possible has often led to the making of claims which break down when put to the test.

For example, an inventor, having practically proved the utility of his invention as applied to three things, might, by analogy, be led to conclude that it would be equally useful as applied to a fourth. If practice should prove that he has overlooked several objections, and that it is not useful for this fourth purpose, his fourth claim would constitute a fatal flaw in his patent.

In the *United Horse Nail Co. v. Swedish Horse Nail Co.* (6 P. O. R. 8) a patent was declared void, because the sixth claim referred to a mode of punching nail-blanks, which the evidence showed could not be carried out in an economical and useful manner.

If a patent is granted for an improvement upon an existing patent which has been shown to be lacking in utility, the improvement will remain good if it is in itself a useful invention.

CHAPTER VII.

PROVISIONAL AND COMPLETE SPECIFICATIONS AND CLAIMS.

Having thus reviewed the essentials of subject-matter of patentable inventions, it will now be competent to proceed to a consideration of the Specifications. In the foregoing pages the origin of the Specification has been indicated, and an attempt made to contrast the advantages and disadvantages of filing a Provisional or Complete Specification with the application. In the following references to the Specification, it will be assumed that the ordinary course of filing a Provisional with the application would be followed.

The Title.

Title must describe nature of invention.

In drawing or filling in the declaration, the first thing that requires to be settled is *the title* of the application. This is an important point, and care should be exercised in choosing a title which will accurately describe the nature of the invention. The Patent Office examiners will decline to accept a title which is not, in their opinion, properly descriptive, and the Comptroller has power to decline to date and number such imperfect application, so that the applicant may find himself greatly delayed and hampered by defects in his title.

Function of examiners with regard to title.

In choosing a title, directness and simplicity of expression are to be preferred to the vague generalities that are sometimes used. The title should be wide enough to cover all that the applicant has really invented, without stretching aimless tentacles towards improbable uses which the Specification fails to make out. For example, in *Cochrane v. Smethurst* (Dav. P. C. 354) the invention really consisted in an improved street-lamp, but the patentee had entitled it "A method or methods of more completely lighting cities, towns, and villages." It was held that the title was too wide. Again, in *Felton v. Greaves* (3 Car. and P. 611) the patent was held to be bad, because the title contained a reference to certain articles to which the invention turned out not to be applicable.

Title should not be too vague.

But, in avoiding this danger, care must be taken not to run to the opposite extreme of making the title so narrow as not to fully cover the field of the invention. In *Oxley v. Holden* (8 C. B., N. S., 666, 705) the title was "Improvements in the Doors and Sashes of Carriages." In his Specification the patentee said that, although he had shown and described his invention as applicable to carriage doors and windows, the improvements were applicable to any descriptions of doors and windows subject to vibration. It was sought to dispute the patent on the score of disconformity between the title and body of the Specification, and the Court so far sustained the contention as to hold the patent to be good only within the limits of the title, that is to say, only as applied to *carriage* doors and windows.

Nor should title be too restricted.

In *Rex v. Metcalf* (2 Stark. R. 249) the patent was upset because of what was alleged to be a misdescription of the nature of the invention in the title. A brush made to diminish towards the point by the arrangement

Misdescription in title.

of hairs of unequal length, was called in the title a "tapered brush," which it really was if looked at broadly. Lord Ellenborough directed the jury that it was not a "tapered," but an unequal brush, and upon these grounds the verdict went against the patentee.

It must be said, however, that this case happened in the days when, as has been said, the Courts exercised ingenuity not to save, but to upset patents. It may safely be submitted that such a decision would be impossible at the present time.

A form of title, which at any rate possesses the demerit of being unnecessarily cumbrous and awkward, is where the applicant seeks to explain at length, technical terms or names of machines in his title. Thus, instead of saying "Improvements in Carding Engines," to say "Improvements in that class of machinery, for preparing, drawing out and cleaning textile fibres, known as Carding Engines," is a pedantic excess of quite unnecessary caution. Patent Specifications are addressed to people having knowledge of the arts and manufactures, and if one were to stop to explain to the uninitiated the meaning of every technical term used, the drafting of such documents would be laborious indeed.

"Fancy" titles.

Another mistaken fashion of drawing a title, much in vogue with inventors who prepare and file their own Specifications, is to use a fancy name in describing the invention. Thus in examining the Official Journal one frequently comes upon such titles as "The 'Simplex' Bottle-Stopper," or "Smith's 'Triumphal' Cue-Tip." All such titles are disallowed by the Comptroller-General, and the applicant requested to amend his papers in this respect.

The Provisional Specification.

Since the time of its introduction under the Amendment Act of 1852, the Provisional Specification accompanying the application has been made use of in the bulk of cases, in so far at least as the applications of British inventors are concerned. Under the present Act the conditions governing the Provisional Specification are practically the

Function of Provisional Specification.

same as before. Now, as then, the Provisional Specification must accurately *ascertain* the nature of the invention. This does not mean that a mere intimation of the inventor's object will suffice. It must be a clear and sufficient record of the proposed mode in which the invention is to be carried out. The rule to be followed is this, that "the Provisional Specification must state distinctly and intelligibly the whole nature of the invention, so that the Comptroller may be apprised of the improvement and of the means by which it is carried into effect."

Not that all details are to be minutely described or indicated too carefully; on the contrary, the chief value of the period of Provisional Protection is to enable these details to be elaborated or created in the light of practical experiment. It is a sketch which must contain the gist, the grouping, and the main arrangement of the finished picture—that is to say, the Complete Specification—which will be afterwards amplified from it. And just as the making of an effective sketch is sometimes a truer test of the artist's power than the painting of a finished picture, it must not be considered that anything will suffice for a Provisional Specification, and that all faults can be remedied in preparing the Complete Specification. The Provisional should rather correspond to a well-prepared and broadly laid foundation, upon which the superstructure of the Complete may afterwards be reared with some promise of stability.

Provisional to be looked upon as a foundation for the Complete Specification.

The Provisional remains a secret document until it is published with the Complete Specification. If no Complete Specification is filed, the Provisional Specification is destroyed, and its contents remain secret.

Provisional never published unless followed by Complete.

THE COMPLETE SPECIFICATION.

The Provisional Specification having broadly described the improvement, it remains for the Complete Specification to "*particularly* describe and ascertain the nature of the invention, and in what manner the same is to be performed."

In considering a Provisional Specification, in furtherance of which it is intended to construct a Complete Specification, the first duty of the draftsman is to ascertain and digest the contents of the Provisional, and then to see that the matter of the Complete, upon which it is proposed to found claims, does not extend beyond the scope of the Provisional. Certain writers have doubted whether, under the Act of 1883, the mere fact of disconformity between the Provisional and Complete Specifications would now invalidate a patent. But recent cases have entirely disposed of any such doubts. In *Vickers v. Siddell* (7 P. O. R. 292), Lord Halsbury, L.C., is responsible for the following dictum:—

There must be conformity between Provisional and Complete.

"It is suggested that the new machinery of the Comptroller and the examiners has superseded the power of raising any objection to the conformity of the Provisional and the Complete Specifications. I am unable to take that view. I think it is an essential condition of a good patent that the invention described in the Provisional should be the same as that in the Complete Specification, and I think the third Sub-section of Section 26 preserves this as a ground upon which a patent may be revoked."

This deliverance was followed in the case of *Nuttall v. Hargreaves* (8 P. O. R. 450), in which the plaintiff's patent was declared invalid upon the ground of disconformity. The patent was for a beer-tap, and one of the claimed features of novelty was a wire-gauze strainer in the tap to prevent the passage of impurities. This strainer was not referred to in the Provisional Specification at all, and this was held to establish fatal disconformity. In the still more recent case of *Lane Fox v. Kensington and Knightsbridge Electric Lighting Co.* (9 P. O. R. 221), a decision adverse to the patentee was founded chiefly on similar grounds.

These recent cases being under the present Act, and pointing so unmistakeably to the fatal effect of disconformity between the Provisional and Complete, it will be unnecessary to disinter any of the prior cases under the old Act, in which precisely the same deductions were drawn. It will therefore be essential to guard carefully against claiming any important part of the invention as a novel feature which is not foreshadowed in the Provisional Specification. If it should be decided to include such excess features in the description for the purpose of making the whole more complete, it would be a point of prudence expressly to disclaim them, lest the usual terminating phrase of a Claim, such as "substantially as hereinbefore described," &c., or as "herein described," might, in the case of one or certain of the Claims, be held to include the new matter.

Specifications must be drawn in the most strict good faith.

It cannot be impressed too strongly upon inventors that in Patent Specifications honesty of purpose and directness of expression are best. The patentee or patent agent who seeks to import into a Patent Specification those ambiguously cunning phrases which are so common in many other legal documents gets but little consideration at the hands of the Court. Obviously, unless the actual words employed were presented for consideration, it is impossible to say how far expressions used in the Provisional Specification would warrant amplification and separate claims in the Complete. It can only be said that all that is necessary is to show that an improvement was suggested, or could reasonably be said to be within the limits of the language used in the Provisional Specification, and, if this is so, such an improvement is good subject-matter for the Claims. Apart from this, it may be said that where a general descriptive sketch of a newly invented machine or article has been given in the Provisional, and details which have been afterwards designed in perfecting the invention should present in themselves features of novelty, rendering them specially useful for that particular machine or article, such details may be separately claimed for that specific purpose, although it would not do to claim them generally for that and for other purposes.

Some latitude allowed in claiming improvements suggested during provisional protection.

As an illustration of this it will suffice to refer to the case of *Lucas v. Miller* (2 P. O. R. 155). The subject-matter of the plaintiff's patent was an improved bicycle lamp. After his Provisional was filed, a further improvement suggested itself in the form of clip washers, for more easily suspending the lamp to the hub of the driving wheel. These washers, although not mentioned in the Provisional, were fully described in the Complete Specification, and were claimed as part of the combination. The defendant pointed out the discrepancy between the Provisional and Complete, and disputed the validity of the patent on that ground. But Kay, J., held that these suspending washers, by virtue of their close functional connection with the lamp, constituted an improvement which the inventor was right in making and was perfectly entitled to claim.

Specification must contain sufficient and full instructions for working the invention.

Another point to be observed in preparing the Complete Specification is, that it must be sufficient and full.

When an applicant files his Complete he is fulfilling his part of a contract with the public. On the one hand, he gains the exclusive monopoly of his invention for a fixed period of fourteen years. For that privilege he undertakes, by means of his Specification, so to instruct the public that at the end of his monopoly they will be able to use his invention as fully and advantageously as himself. Therefore, any ambiguity, suppression, or misdirection is a breach of faith, which only requires to be laid bare to destroy the privilege.

Specification must be prepared with reasonable skill and knowledge.

Accordingly, all Specifications should be prepared in as transparently honest a manner as possible, and with all the marks of anxiety on the part of the patentee thoroughly to instruct his readers in the best methods, known to him at the time, of carrying his invention into effect. Reasonable skill and knowledge must be apparent in the preparation of the Specification, and a patentee will not be excused for shortcomings on account of ignorance. Specifications and drawings must be prepared so as to be intelligible and complete, and the Court will not study to piece together what it was the duty of the inventor to make plain. In *Allen v. Duckett* (10 P O. R. 397), the Specification turned out to be so badly prepared that the Court was satisfied that the nature of the invention had not been properly ascertained. "Can anybody," said Hawkins, J., "reading this Specification, form any judgment as to what the object of the invention is? . . The more I look at it, the more satisfied I am that both the Provisional and the Complete Specifications are absolutely wanting in the essential features which ought to present themselves upon both Provisional and Complete Specifications, and I therefore hold that it is bad for that reason."

The Specification is addressed to persons who are competent to understand and carry out processes or manufactures akin to the subject-matter of the patent. Therefore, it is not necessary that technical terms and trade expressions should be explained, unless they are more than ordinarily obscure or uncommon. Thus, if the invention deals with electricity, the inventor may use the scientific and accepted terms common among electricians; if with chemistry, those terms which are common knowledge with chemists. So in an invention connected with a loom, for example, the patentee may safely presuppose an acquaintance on the part of his readers with the ordinary mechanism and operations of weaving. For it would be insufferable that a chance mention of a shuttle, reed, picking-stick, or weft fork, should be a signal for the writer to stop and carefully explain to the reader what these were.

Intelligibility of Specification subject to "the ordinary workman test."

As a development of this implied knowledge on the part of the reader, the Courts have in turn come to assess the sufficiency of a description by what is known as "the ordinary workman test."

This means that a Complete Specification will be held to be sufficient in law, if the directions are plainly enough given to enable a person of average intelligence, and conversant with that particular industry, to carry the invention into effect.

The reader is not to be called upon to exercise extraordinary intelligence or invention, or to fill in evident gaps left by the patentee. But he must duly exercise his trade knowledge and trained intelligence as a workman in interpreting the instructions of the patentee. In *Crossley v. Beverley* (3 C. & P. 513), the defendants asserted that the description of a gas-making apparatus was incomplete because no mention was made of the condenser. Lord Tenterden, C.J., brushed this objection aside, saying that "a workman who was capable of making a gas apparatus would know that he must put in a condenser."

To go a little further than this, it may be said that where a patentee in his description makes an error which is on the face of it an error, and which could not possibly mislead anyone acquainted with the subject-matter, such error will not vitiate his patent.

Errors in Specification, how far excuseable.

This was the opinion of Lord Westbury, L.C., in *Simpson v. Holliday* (12 L. T., N. S. 99). But his Lordship nevertheless went on to say that this was not a correct statement of the law when applied to errors which were only discoverable by experiment and further inquiry. In a Complete Specification, a patentee is not tied down to exact and definite proportion or detail, if the nature of the invention reasonably admits of variation. Thus, in the description of a new alloy, the proportions of metal to form the alloy should be stated specifically; but where variations might be made in these proportions without essentially affecting the nature or utility of the alloy, it is quite permissible for the patentee to say so and to indicate the limits within which such variations might be made (*Patent Type Founding Company v. Richards*, 1 Johns. 381). On the same grounds, a combination claim, consisting of several parts, would not be defeated by mere variation or substitutes, where the characteristics of the combination were preserved. In short, whether in mechanical or chemical combinations or processes, a reasonable latitude will always be allowed in construing the Specification. Wherever a Complete Specification can be made more easily understood by the addition of drawings, these should be incorporated.

Reasonable latitude allowed in construing Specification.

Drawings.

It was said by North, J., in *Lawrence v. Perry* (2 P. O. R. 179), that drawings are not an absolute necessity even for the explanation of mechanical patents. But that was under the Act of 1852, and Sub-section 4 of Section 5 of the present Act says that a Complete Specification *must* be accompanied by drawings if required. There is little doubt, therefore, that it is an essential that drawings should be used wherever possible. Language is at the best a very poor and misleading substitute for a representation of the thing itself, and, besides, a faithful and careful drawing is of use in explaining what might otherwise be an ambiguity in the description. Thus, if the descriptive part were to tell the reader something which is absurd, perhaps something so misleading that if it stood alone the very validity of the patent might be imperilled, if that misleading statement is coupled with a reference to the drawing, the error in the description can be explained and neutralised, so long as the drawing is so unmistakeably clear and correct that a competent person can at once see for himself that a mistake has been committed.

Drawings sometimes of value to correct and limit faulty description.

In making a drawing, the great object should be to clearly illustrate the subject-matter of the invention. This is sometimes so far lost sight of, that an inventor, in illustrating an improvement in locomotive furnace bars for example, is content with nothing less than giving several complete views of an entire locomotive engine and tender. The result is, that the illustrations of the improved bars are dwarfed, and the Specification encumbered by the presence of matter that has nothing to do with the invention.

Drawing should be confined to subject-matter of invention.

Perspective drawings or isometrical projections should be used where possible, as these appeal to the understanding of a much wider class than is the case with purely mechanical drawings.

As the drawings attached to the Specification are now reproduced by photo-lithography, and generally to a reduced scale, it is incumbent upon the patentee to see that his drawings are neat, black, clear, and distinct, and to as large a scale as the prescribed sizes of sheet will conveniently hold.

Mode of reproducing drawings for publication.

It should be mentioned that, under Sub-section 4 of Section 5 of the present Act, it is provided that when drawings have been filed with the Provisional Specifications, these drawings can be referred to in the Complete Specification without the necessity for filing fresh copies of the drawings.

Drawings filed with Provisional may be referred to as illustrations of the Complete.

Old matter should be differentiated from new.

In pursuance of the advice already given, as to the exercise of absolute good faith in preparing the Complete Specification, it might be useful also to point out the advantage of differentiating the old from the new in a Specification, especially where a combination is concerned. As Cresswell, J., says in *Gibson v. Brand* (1 Web. P. C. 627), "Every party is bound to tell the public clearly by his Specification what he claims, and what they may do or may not do without risk of an action for infringing his patent."

Macfarlane v. Price. No distinction between old and new.

In *Macfarlane v. Price* (1 Web. P. C. 74) certain improvements in umbrellas and parasols were described, no distinction being made as to which of the details were new and which were old. The patent was infringed by the use of a certain part shown in the drawings, and admittedly of the essence of the invention. But Lord Ellenborough, C.J., nonsuited the plaintiff on the ground that no one could be fairly expected to gather from the Specification what the novel parts really were.

So in *Foxwell v. Bostock* (4 De G. J. & S. 298) certain improvements in a sewing machine were so described that Lord Westbury held that no one could properly distinguish between what was new and what was old, and on that account declared the Specification insufficient. This differentiating of the new from the old need not of course be carried out where common knowledge or the knowledge of the ordinary skilled workman is sufficient to point out the old parts.

But differentiation between old and new not always necessary.

For example, if the invention refers to a new equilibrium valve for governing the passage of steam to the valve chest of a steam engine, and the Specification describes the valve in connection with an ordinary ball governor, it would not be necessary to disclaim the governor, for every one knows how old that is. But if the valve itself were partly old, it might be necessary to point out what parts of the valve were new and constituted the improvement. As regards an improvement upon a foregoing invention or existing patent, it will be sufficient, for the purposes of differentiation between old and new, to indicate the Specification of the first invention.

When two or three methods of carrying an invention into effect are described in the Specification, and one of them turns out to be useless, the patent is invalid (*Simpson v. Holliday*, 12 L. T., N. S. 99). All claimed modes of carrying the invention into effect should have utility.

In construing Specifications of Letters Patent for Inventions, the practice of the Courts seems to have gone through a pendulum-like swing before settling down to the present rule of reasonable and fair construction. In former times, letters patent for inventions suffered from the vestiges of that odium which attached to the bad old monopolies. As a result, when a patent came into Court it was subjected to the most keen and searching scrutiny. The leaning of the Court was always dead against the patentee and in favour of the public. This might be termed the period of *malevolent* construction of Specifications. But early in the present century more liberal conceptions concerning the inventor and his mission began to prevail, and the practice of the Courts swung into what has been called the *benevolent* construction. Construction of Specifications. Former modes of construing Specifications.

That, in its turn, has been succeeded by a very evident determination on the part of the Court to allow itself to be influenced neither by the benevolent nor the malevolent theory of construction, but to give fair consideration to the meaning of the language employed and to decide accordingly. Present practice in construing Specifications.

When confronted by counsel with examples of former practice, several eminent judges have expressed themselves upon the principles of construction.

In *Clopper v. Smith* (1 P. O. R. 89, 90) Bowen, L.J., gives an excellent exposition of the rules governing the Courts at this day. Chitty, J., in *Lister v. Norton* (3 P. O. R. 203), speaking of the construction of a Specification, says, "It ought to be construed, like any other legal document, as a whole. It certainly ought not to be construed malevolently; I will not say it ought to be construed benevolently; I do say it ought to be construed fairly. It must be read by a mind willing to understand, not by a mind desirous of misunderstanding." Chitty, J., on construction.

Claims.

Next to a clear and comprehensive setting forth of the invention in the body of the Complete Specification, the most important task of the patentee is the framing of the Claims, by which he points out and fences off the real fruits of his brain. Prior to the present Act of 1883 it was not necessary to conclude the Specification with Claims, although, for their own sakes, patentees usually did so. Now, however, every Complete Specification must end with "a distinct statement of the invention claimed."

Claims became essential to Specifications in 1883

Simple as the requirement may seem, it is sometimes a matter of considerable difficulty to select and limit in clear and comprehensive language, not only the pith and gist of the invention, but also the subsidiary and collateral claims that may spring from the main trunk.

Power of Comptroller to require Claims in Complete.

The Comptroller-General of the Patent Office has power to require that something in the shape of a Claim shall be appended to the Complete; but as to the form and substance of the Claim, or its agreement with the invention described in the Specification, he has no power to interfere, and does not attempt to guide the applicant. It appears that there must be some attempt to indicate the scope of the invention in the Claim. Herschell, S.G., in *re Smith's Patent* (Griff. P. C. 268), expressed an opinion that to say "I claim the invention described in the Specification" would not be a Claim that should be accepted by the Comptroller. But he also said that if the Claim read, "I claim the improved bicycle substantially as described," such a phrase might be accepted, as it clearly pointed to a particular machine.

Claim must have specific reference to invention as described and shown.

The primary rule in drawing a Claim is to take care that the Claim shall not cover anything more than the actual invention. In the act of working out an invention, and preparing the Complete Specification, it is often the case that extensions of the uses of, and changes in, the apparatus, begin to suggest themselves more or less vaguely to the inventor, some of which he thinks might possibly lead to evasion if hit upon by other inventors. In this state of mind, Claims are prepared, in which, not content with claiming the substance of the invention, the patentee endeavours also to secure some foothold in case of possible developments of his idea by others. With this object the Claim is drawn in vague terms, which the patentee flatters himself not only cover the design originated by himself, but would trip up anyone who might come within measurable distance of his domain. **Danger of "fishing" Claims.**

This ambition has often proved fatal to his own patent, and in thus snatching at the shadow the patentee runs great risk of losing the substance.

In *Steven v. Keating* (2 W. P. C. 181) the patentee had described a mode of making a new cement by the use of sulphuric acid with limestone or chalk. The gist of the invention was the employment of the acid for the purpose. Not content with having proved the usefulness of sulphuric acid for his purpose, the patentee said, in the body of his Specification, that other acids might be used, and claimed the process in combination with the use of acids "as hereinbefore described." This was held to be a Claim for every acid, and, as it was proved that certain acids would not do, the Claim was upset as being too wide. **Claim must not be too wide.**

Again, in *Minter v. Mower* (1 W. P. C. 142), the patentee of an automatically self-balancing chair, instead of claiming his own construction of the chair, which was both novel and useful, claimed "the application of a self-adjusting leverage to the back and seat of a chair, whereby the weight on the seat acts as a counter-balance to the pressure against the back of the chair, as above described." It was shown at the trial that a form of chair acting upon this claimed principle, but infinitely less cleverly constructed than the plaintiff's, had been made and sold before the date of his patent. It was held that Minter's Claim, instead of being confined to his own invention, was wide enough to cover the anticipatory chair also, and was therefore bad.

If an essential part of a combination, operation, or process, or an alternative arrangement or process, described and claimed, should turn out to be useless, the patent is bad. The first would put an entire stop to the useful function of

Modifications of invention claimed must possess utility, or the whole will be vitiated.

the machine or would nullify the process and is clearly a fatal defect (see Lord Denman's remarks in *Reg. v. Cutler*, 14 Q. B. 372). The second—viz., the failure of an *alternative* arrangement or process—is not so clearly a reason for upsetting a patent. The principle seems to be that the Court says, "Here you have two methods presented to you as equally useful. You are told that one is as good as the other. Having nothing to serve as a guide, you may choose the useless method. It fails. Practically, therefore, you are put to experiment to prove what is useful and what is useless, and that is distinct failure of a patent." In *Simpson v. Holliday* (12 L. T., N. S. 99) two methods of preparing dyes were described. The method first described was perfectly successful; the second (an alternative method) was a failure. The patent was held invalid on that account. Similarly, in *Pether v. Shaw* (10 P. O. R. 293), Kekewich, J., held the plaintiff's patent bad because, of two alternatives suggested in the Claim, one was of no use, although the other had proved highly successful. It must be remembered that the Claim is always read together with the Specification: therefore where a Claim is made, and direct qualifying reference is had to the Specification, the Claim is limited thereby, and the reader must go to the Specification to learn the extent of the limits. But, as this course is very apt to lead to doubt and uncertainty, it is unquestionably better to formulate in the Claim itself the feature which it is desired to secure.

The body of the Specification may limit and explain the Claim.

True meaning of Claims sometimes settled by evidence outside of the Specification.

Sometimes the interpretation of the true meaning of a Claim is a matter for settlement by evidence. That is to say, that, though a Claim may seem too wide to an outsider, it may have a more restricted meaning to a person well acquainted with the industry in question. Thus in *Gandy v. Reddaway* (2 P. O. R. 49) the Claim was for "constructing belts or bands for driving machinery, of cotton, canvas, or duck *woven hard*," &c. It was shown that at least ten classes of "hard woven" canvas were known in the market. Of these, numbers two, three, and four only were suitable for the purposes of the invention. The other classes were useless. The plaintiff endeavoured to show that a workman acquainted with this class of manufacture would, without further instructions, have used number two, three. or four, and would never have thought of using any of the other numbers. It is to be gathered from the judgment that if this had been established on evidence, the Court might have upheld the patent. But no such evidence was forthcoming, and, consequently, the patent was held invalid.

"Substantially as hereinbefore described" is a phrase often appearing as the termination of a Claim. The words are used sometimes with the intention of giving increased breadth to a Claim, sometimes for the purpose of narrowing it. In *Young v. Rosenthal* (1 P. O. R. 33) Mr. Justice Grove gave it as his opinion that it was unnecessary to use any such word as "substantially" to qualify a Claim. The elasticity sought to be obtained in a Claim by such a qualification, either by increasing or limiting its ambit, was already given by the law. "The law says, if a man, although not literally infringing the letter of the patent, yet substantially infringes it, it is an infringement." It is certainly reasonable to consider that all expressions which mean that anything practically or substantially the same will be deemed an infringement of the described invention are unnecessary and might as well be left out. They do no good, for of course it is always for the Court to decide what is and what is not an infringement, and no amount of fencing with such expressions as "mere mechanical equivalents," or "substantially the same arrangement of parts," &c., so commonly found in Specifications, will influence the Court in any way.

Grove, J., on the use of the word "substantially" in Claims.

The subject of how far it is safe to claim anything savouring of a principle has already been referred to in the foregoing pages (see Chapter V., on "Subject-Matter"). It seems proper, however, at this point to repeat the rule already laid down, that although a bare principle *per se* cannot be patented, yet, if the principle is new, and a method of carrying it into effect exists or has also been devised, the principle, coupled with the mode of carrying it into effect, may be patented. If this is done, any other mode of carrying the principle into effect which another

Principles.

person might seek to use will be very narrowly scrutinised, and, if possible, held to be within the limits of the first patent.

The chief expressions of judicial opinion upon this point are to be found in *Neilson v. Harford* (1 Web. P. C. 370) and *Otto v. Linford* (46 L. T. 39).

Combination Claims.

Combinations, whether chemical or mechanical combinations of material, or combinations of parts or motions in machinery, or combinations of methods in industrial processes, are all fit subject-matter for Claims.

Products.

When the invention refers to a combination of materials mechanically mixed or combined so as to produce a new concrete or a new alloy or a waterproof fabric, or where the combination is chemically effected so as to produce a new dye or agent, the proper Claim to frame is for the special product made, from the materials and in the manner described.

In novel combinations the novel elements should be separately claimed.

When the invention refers to combinations of machinery, not only should the combination as a whole be claimed, but those parts of the combination which are new should also be separately claimed. It has, however, been held that where a part of a combination which is undoubtedly new has not been so separately claimed, but figures only as an integer in the combination, such part cannot be taken and used for a similar purpose, even though wrapped up in a different combination.

This was a dictum of Lord Campbell in *Lister v. Leather* (8 E. & B. 1018), and a similar view was taken in *Procter v. Bennis* (4 P. O. R. 333). It is, however, much safer not to depend upon such rulings, but to make a positive Claim for the novel element, apart from the particular combination in which it figures.

The following rules may be useful as guides in the preparation of Claims:—

Rules for the preparation of Claims.

(1) Everything which is not claimed is understood to be disclaimed.

(2) The Claim should not embrace more than the actual invention.

(3) A Claim should be expressed in the clearest and most concise language; should refer unmistakeably

to the invention described in the Specification; and should not contain any vague and speculative phrases.

(4) If the invention discloses a new principle, the Claim should be for the principle, coupled with the means for carrying it into effect.

(5) If the invention relates to a new thing or product, the Claim should be for the product, and the method of producing it should also be claimed, if that also involves invention.

(6) In Combination Claims, if the invention consists purely of the combination, the combination only should be claimed. If the combination contains new parts, or parts new as applied to the purposes of the invention, these parts also should be separately claimed.

Extension of time for filing Complete.

When by inadvertence, or because of the incomplete nature of his experiments, or from any excusable cause, the applicant has failed or finds himself unable to file his Complete Specification before the expiry of nine months from the date of application, an extension of time for one month may be obtained, on payment of a fine of £2. No further enlargement of time can be had.

CHAPTER VIII.

OPPOSITION TO GRANT OF PATENT.

Provisional Specification a secret document.

It has already been said that the Provisional Specification, during the period of provisional protection, is a secret document. Its tenor is unknown to the public, and opposition thereto is not contemplated by the Act. It has also been said that when the Complete Specification has been filed, examined, and accepted, the fact of acceptance is advertised

Advertisement of acceptance of Complete invites opposition.

in the Official Journal. This advertisement is accompanied by a notification that all persons interested in opposing the grant of a patent on the indicated application may, at any time within two months from the date of the Journal, give notice of opposition. At the same time, the Specification and drawings are thrown open to public inspection at the Patent Office, and the printing of the Specification is usually effected within about three weeks after acceptance.

In all cases the Specification is published and placed on sale in ample time to give an intending opponent, not resident near the Patent Office, every opportunity of examining it at his leisure, before filing his notice of opposition.

Persons entitled to oppose (before Comptroller).

The words of the Act (Section 11) are that "any person" may oppose, but the grounds of opposition are set forth as follows:—

Grounds of opposition.

(1) That the applicant has obtained the invention from the opponent, or from a person of whom he is the legal representative.

(2) That the invention has been patented in this country on an application of prior date.

(3) That the Complete Specification describes or claims an invention other than that described in the Provisional Specification, and that such other invention forms the subject-matter of an application made by the opponent in the interval between the leaving of the applicant's Provisional Specification and the filing of the Complete Specification.

Notice of opposition.

The notice of opposition (which bears a ten shilling stamp) must set forth the grounds upon which the opponent intends to rely. The Patent Rules provide that the notice must be signed by the opponent, be accompanied by an unstamped copy, and must give an address for service in the United Kingdom. If one of the grounds of opposition should be that the invention has been already patented in this country, the number, title, and date of the patent should be given. It may be noted that a person whose Complete Specification has been accepted, but not yet sealed, is on the footing of a patentee in thus opposing. So long as the notice of opposition undeniably places the applicant in possession of the real grounds of opposition, quibbling objections to mere informalities in the notice will not affect its validity, and the Comptroller has power to amend either before or at the hearing (see *re Airey*, 5 P. O. R. 348; *re Lake*, Griff. A. P. C. 35; *re Faucett*, Goodeve, P. P. 10).

Declarations by opponent in support of opposition.

On receiving the notice of opposition the Comptroller transmits the unstamped copy to the applicant. If the opponent intends to follow up his notice of opposition by declarations in support, which might or might not be necessary, he must do so within fourteen days after the expiration of two months from the date of the advertisement of the acceptance of the applicant's Complete Specification. On leaving these declarations at the Patent Office he must send a list of them to the applicant.

Declarations by applicant in reply.

Counter declarations by opponent.

Within fourteen days from the date of receiving this list, the applicant may leave declarations in answer, delivering also a list to the opponent; and within a further period of fourteen days, the opponent may leave declarations in reply. These last declarations must be confined strictly to reply. In some cases, further declarations or rejoinders might be filed by the parties, but only by special leave of the Comptroller, and in most instances the declaratory evidence is closed by the opponent's reply.

Declarations not essential in some cases.

But always necessary when fraud or bad faith is alleged.

As to the advisability or non-advisability of filing declarations, it may be said that this depends greatly on the grounds of opposition. Where the grounds are simply a reference to a prior patent, declarations seem scarcely necessary, as the question will, after all, be decided from a comparison of the two Specifications. But where the grounds are that the applicant obtained the invention from the opponent, or wherever fraud is alleged, declarations are absolutely necessary as evidence in support, since no examination on oath can take place before the Comptroller, and mere oral *ex parte* statements would be of little avail.

State of public knowledge may be

To meet a reference to a prior Specification by an opponent, the applicant may produce any evidence of public shown in declarations to limit scope of Claims in Specification.

knowledge which will tend to limit the ambit of the opponent's Specification or reference.

Thus, in *re Jones* (Griff. A. P. C. 34) the applicant sought to minify the scope of the opponent's patent by citing several Specifications prior to the opponent's. The opponent objected, but the Law Officer intimated that it was material that he should be informed of the state of public knowledge.

Exhibits.

For this purpose exhibits may be filed with the declarations. Specimens of the inventions under consideration, or of matters imputed by the declarations, may be exhibited to the Comptroller or Law Officer, to assist him in understanding the drawings or explanations. Thus, in *re Lancaster* (Griff. P. C. 293) the applicant sought to demonstrate the action of his spring piston packing to the Law Officer by means of a specimen. The opponent asked that this should be barred, but the Solicitor-General (Gorst) said it assisted him very much to see the specimen, and he would look at it to better his understanding of the drawings.

Hearing before Comptroller.

When the evidence is complete, one of the parties may apply for a hearing, and the Comptroller appoints a time, at least ten days' notice of the hearing being given to the parties. A hearing fee of £1 is payable by each side. At the hearing, the parties themselves may appear, or their agents or solicitors, or they may be represented by counsel. As a rule the applicant begins, the opponent follows, and the applicant replies; but where the *onus probandi* lies on the opponent—as, for example, where the applicant is charged with fraud—the opponent begins. At the hearing the opponent must confine himself strictly to the grounds of opposition stated in his notice, and generally the hearing is little more than an oral urging of the chief points made in the declarations.

Decision.

The Comptroller, who is generally assisted by one or two of the chief examiners, seldom gives his decision at the hearing, but notifies the parties in writing. If either or both of the parties should be dissatisfied with the Comptroller's decision, appeal can be made to the Law Officer, notice of such appeal to be filed at the Patent

Appeal to Law Officer.

Office within fourteen days from the date of the decision. In the event of an appeal being contemplated, or being probable, it is not advisable for the successful party in the meantime to bind himself to unqualified acceptance of the decision, as it is conceivable that such acceptance may trammel him in using his old evidence or producing new evidence to resist the appeal before the Law Officer.

Possible danger of unqualified acceptance of Comptroller's decision.

The proceedings before the Law Officer amount to a rehearing of the case, and if the successful party before the Comptroller has, by his premature unqualified acceptance of the decision, practically acceded to the exclusion or to a certain reading of parts of his evidence, he may be precluded from reproducing or giving effect to these before the Law Officer. At all events, he will have deprived himself of the power to file new evidence which may have come to his knowledge since the hearing before the Comptroller.

In *re Hampton and Facer* (Griff. P. C. 13) the successful applicants accepted the Comptroller's decision in their favour without qualification. The unsuccessful opponent appealed to the Law Officer. The applicants then applied under L. O., Rule 8, for leave to file evidence to show that the opponent's invention had been in use by others before the date of his patent; but, as they had accepted the Comptroller's decision *in toto*, Clarke, S.G., refused leave.

When notice of appeal has been given, the Comptroller transmits all the papers in the case to the Law Officer's clerk. When the date of the hearing has been appointed, seven days' notice is given to the parties and to the Comptroller.

Proceedings before Law Officer.

The hearing before the Law Officer is limited to the points raised in the notice of appeal. The whole or a part only of the Comptroller's decision may be questioned, and if the party upon whom the appeal is served wishes to do so, he may question other parts of the Comptroller's decision by counter-appeal. The evidence before the Law Officer must be the same as that used before the Comptroller, and no further evidence will be admitted, save as to matters which have occurred or come to the knowledge of either party since the date of the decision

Evidence.

appealed against, except with the leave of the Law Officer upon application for that purpose. In *re Bailey's Patent* (Griff. P. C. 269) Davey, S.G., decided that this rule related to evidence pure and simple, and refused to allow the Specification of a prior patent to be put in as proof of public knowledge. He said that such was not evidence, but an additional ground of opposition. But the practice seems unsettled, for in *re Jones* (Griff. A. P. C. 33) the same Law Officer admitted certain Specifications of prior date to the opponent's for the purpose of showing public knowledge.

Persons entitled to oppose before Law Officer.

It has been said that any person may oppose the grant of a patent before the Comptroller. But in appeals to the Law Officer, only such persons as are in his opinion entitled to be heard will be granted a hearing. Practice has established that those persons who are so entitled to be heard are as follows:—(1) The patentee of an existing prior patent; (2) the grantee of a prior expired patent; (3) a person from whom or from whose legal representative the invention has been wrongfully obtained; (4) a later applicant who alleges that the Complete Specification of the prior applicant contains matter not referred to in his Provisional Specification, but comprised in the after application of the opponent; (5) a licensee under a prior patent; (6) an assignee and manufacturer under a lapsed patent.

Applicant or opponent whose Complete has been accepted, considered as "patentee."

As has already been said, an applicant whose Complete Specification has been accepted is, for opposition purposes, in the position of a patentee, and the invention disclosed in his Complete Specification is for this purpose a patented invention.

Costs (before Law Officer).

Opposition cannot be founded upon mere description in a prior Specification. The invention must be claimed. The Comptroller-General has no power to award costs, but the Law Officer usually allows a sum for costs to the successful party. The average allowance is from five to ten guineas, but considerably larger sums have been awarded where costs have been heavy. An appellant who withdraws before the hearing is liable to pay costs.

The ground of opposition that the applicant obtained

the invention from the opponent or his legal representative only holds good in the case of communications passing in this country. If the information has been acquired abroad, the applicant, being the first importer, is in the shoes of the true and first inventor (*re Edmunds*, Griff. P. C. 281; *re Lake*, 5 P. O. R. 415).

In supporting an allegation that the applicant has obtained the invention from the opponent, the evidence requires to be very strong, especially if fraud is alleged.

Rule in evidence where fraud is alleged.

Neither the Comptroller nor the Law Officer will stop a patent except upon evidence so conclusive that, in their estimation, no jury could fail to find for the opponent. There have been cases following the precedent laid down by Lord Cranworth in *re Russell* (2 De G. & J. 130), where the facts were such as to lead the Law Officer and Comptroller to issue the patent jointly to the applicant and opponent, as, for instance, in *re Lake* (Griff. P. C. 294) and *re Garthwaite* (Griff. P. C. 284).

Case of patent being divided between applicant and opponent.

Witnesses or declarants may be cross-examined before Law Officer.

As there is no provision for cross-examination of the declarants or other witnesses before the Comptroller, the latter will often, when the evidence is conflicting, take such a course as will cause the parties to go to the Law Officer, before whom cross-examination is permissible.

Master's rights in servant's invention.

The relationship of master and servant does not give the master any rights in the servant's invention, even if the servant works out the invention in his master's time and with his master's tools. Thus in *re Heald* (8 P. O. R. 429) Clarke, Solicitor-General, said, "I am not aware of any authority which lays down that the invention of a servant, even made in the employer's time, and with the use of the employer's materials, and at the expense of the employer, thereby becomes the property of the employer, so as to prevent the person employed from taking out a patent for it." But where an inventor employs a workman to work out an invention, improvements in detail, invented or suggested by the workman, become the property of his employer, and the workman cannot afterwards take out a patent for these improvements. This was very plainly stated by Davey, Solicitor-General, in *re David & Woodley* (Griff. P. C. 26). Said the Solicitor-

Solicitor-General Clarke in *re Heald*.

David & Woodley.

General, "I am of opinion that if a workman is employed by an inventor to make a model for the purpose of carrying out his invention, and the workman suggests improvements in detail of the machine, which are adopted in the machine or model as completed, these suggestions are the property of his employer, and the workman cannot afterwards take out a patent for them."

Opponent's patent must be very similar to applicant's to prevent sealing.

When the opposition is based upon the ground of a prior patent, the similarity between the inventions must be very close to stop the patent. All the reported cases show that in most instances of refusal to seal a patent the inventions have been practically identical, so that it would serve no useful purpose to instance causes of refusal.

When the differences between the interfering inventions are at all appreciable, or if sufficient cause is shown to make it a matter of reasonable doubt, the patent is usually granted. The Comptroller and the Law Officer are guided in this lenity by the consideration that if the applicant's patent turns out to be really an infringement of the opponent's, the opponent has his remedy in a court of law, or by petition for revocation.

Apart from the refusal of a patent *in toto*, the Specification and Claims may be modified as the result of opposition. For example, it is frequently the practice to enforce the insertion of explanatory or disclaiming clauses referring to the existing state of knowledge, and sometimes to prior patents, so as clearly to show the limits of the applicant's Claim.

Reference to opponent's patent.

For example, an opponent, although he may be unsuccessful in stopping the patent, may compel a reference in the applicant's Specification to the opponent's prior patent, coupled with a disclaiming clause. This is a condition which is seldom pleasing to applicants; but its weight as an acknowledgment may be modified, if the applicant pleases, by adding references to other patents prior to the opponent's, which in their turn may seem to limit or affect the opponent's patent.

There is no doubt that references of this kind are obnoxious, and tend to affect the value of the patent in the eye of a possible purchaser.

Guest v. Barrow.

In *re Guest v. Barrow* (5 P. O. R. 312) Webster, A.G., clearly showed his distaste for too indiscriminate references of this nature:—"I have never considered that a prior patentee has any right to be specially named, unless the applicants are willing to name him, and unless it is clear that there is no other publication except the one that is mentioned."

Opposition on ground of applicant having incorporated opponent's later improvement in his (applicant's) Complete.

The last of the three grounds of opposition—viz., that the Complete Specification describes or claims an invention other than that described in the Provisional Specification, and that such other invention forms the subject-matter of an application made by the opponent in the interval between the leaving of the applicant's Provisional Specification and the leaving of his Complete Specification—was introduced by the Amending Act of 1888. The additional ground was intended to remedy a possible abuse, such as was disclosed in *re Green* (Griff. P. C. 286), where the applicant's patent was refused although the Specifications made it clear that the opponents had not originally in their Provisional Specification contemplated certain improvements for which the applicant had thereafter made provisional application. These improvements came to the knowledge of the opponents, and were included in their Complete Specification after the filing of the applicant's Provisional Specification. When the applicant filed his Complete Specification, the opponents stopped the patent by showing that his improvements were included in their Complete Specification. The Law Officer admitted the hardship, but was obliged to refuse the applicant's patent. However, by the Amending Act of 1888 such a miscarriage is now rendered impossible. It will be evident that but for this provision occasional injustice might have been done.

Re Green.

For example, let us suppose that A on the 1st of January files a Provisional Specification of an automatic prepayment gas meter, in which no means are described for adjusting the delivery to the local or current price of gas. Suppose that B on the 1st of March files a Provisional, also describing a meter of that class, and containing a description of means for so adjusting the delivery. If B were to publish a description of his invention, or put his meter into the market, so that A gained full knowledge of B's invention, A might formerly have included part of B's meter—say, for example, the adjustable delivery part—in his Specification, and B would have been powerless to stop A's patent, while A could have stopped B's.

Now, however, all this is remedied, and even if A were to describe part of B's invention without laying claim to it, B might oppose the patent and get such part of the description expunged. In *re Hetherington* (7 P. O. R. 419) the Complete Specification of the applicant described, but did not claim, a modified arrangement of flexible bend for carding engines not appearing in his Provisional Specification. The opponents had filed a subsequent application which contained a description of this arrangement of flexible bend. The applicant's patent was allowed to go forward only upon condition that the description of the opponents' flexible bend should be struck out.

CHAPTER IX.

SEALING OF THE PATENT.

Patent sealed as of date of application.

EVERY Patent is dated and sealed as of the day of application.

Letters Patent are sealed with the Seal of the Patent Office, having the same effect as if sealed with the Great Seal of the United Kingdom. The use of the Great Seal for this purpose was discontinued in 1878.

Period within which sealing must be effected.

The sealing must be effected within fifteen months from the date of application, unless under special circumstances, over which the patentee has no control—such, for example, as delay caused by opposition, in which case the Law Officer may direct the sealing at any time. When an applicant dies before the expiry of the fifteen months, the patent may be granted to his legal representative and sealed within twelve months of death. If an extension of time of one month has been obtained for filing the Complete Specification, a patent may be sealed within nineteen months from the date of application.

Patent granted to legal representative of deceased applicant.

Under the terms of the grant the patent privilege lasts for fourteen years, and is maintained in force by payment of the following annual renewal fees, which come into existence at the end of the fourth year:—

Duration of patent.

Annual taxes.

	£	s.	d.
Before the expiry of the fourth year, and in respect of the fifth year	5	0	0
Before the expiry of the fifth year, and in respect of the sixth year	6	0	0
Before the expiry of the sixth year, and in respect of the seventh year ...	7	0	0
Before the expiry of the seventh year, and in respect of the eighth year ...	8	0	0
Before the expiry of the eighth year, and in respect of the ninth year ...	9	0	0
Before the expiry of the ninth year, and in respect of the tenth year	10	0	0
Before the expiry of the tenth year, and in respect of the eleventh year ...	11	0	0
Before the expiry of the eleventh year, and in respect of the twelfth year ...	12	0	0
Before the expiry of the twelfth year, and in respect of the thirteenth year	13	0	0
Before the expiry of the thirteenth year, and in respect of the fourteenth year	14	0	0

When by accident the payment of the annual tax has been overlooked, an extension of time can be obtained on payment of the following fines:—

Extension of time to pay annuities.

	£	s.	d.
On extension of time for one month ...	1	0	0
,, ,, ,, two months ...	3	0	0
,, ,, ,, three months ...	5	0	0

Nature of patent property.

A patent falls under the head of personal estate. As such it is transmissible by assignment, devolution, or by operation of law, as, for example, to a trustee in bankruptcy.

Co-patentees.

When a patent has been granted to more than one person, the mutual rights and obligations of the co-patentees are worthy of a short consideration. Their position is in no degree that of an ordinary commercial partnership. As a matter of fact it is hardly possible at the present time to define exactly their respective positions. It has been said that their position must be deduced from the wording of the grant, but no decision is in existence based upon the actual wording of the present form of grant. The leading case on the subject is that of *Mathers v. Green* (L. R. 1 Ch. App. 29), which was decided in 1865 under the wording of the old grant, which differs to some extent from the present. The decision arrived at in that case was that each co-owner of a patent can assign his share and sue for an infringement independently of the other or others. He can work the patent himself and for his own benefit without accounting to his co-patentees, and can also grant licences under his own hand. This was the substance of Lord Cranworth's deliverance in the Court of Appeal. Lord Romilly, M.R., in the Court below, ruled that a co-patentee who granted a licence independently of his fellow-patentees was liable to account to them for their proper share of the royalties accruing under such a licence.

Mathers v. Green.

The decision in *Mathers v. Green* was approved and followed in the House of Lords in the more recent case (1893) of *Steers v. Rogers* (10 P. O. R. 245). The defendant was part owner of a moiety of a patent by assignment, and was mortgagee of the other moiety. It was sought to make the defendant liable to account to the mortgagor for a share of the profits made by working the patent, but without success, the House of Lords approving and confirming the judgment of Romer, J., in the lower Court, that a part owner of a patent, even when only so by assignment, can work the patent, without accounting to his co-owner.

Steers v. Rogers.

Rights of assignee of part of patent.

Of course a mortgagee alone of a patent or share in a

patent would not be in the same position, but must account for profits as mortgagee in possession in the usual way.

It is therefore incumbent upon co-patentees clearly to define their relative positions and rights by means of a properly prepared agreement, which would prevent any co-owner from taking an unfair advantage of his fellows. For example, it might be provided that no one of the co-owners should use the invention without the consent of the others, or without accounting to them for the profits. Again, it might be mutually agreed that none of the owners should sell his share without the consent of the others, or that the patent should be sold only in its entirety. Provisions should be made also regarding the granting of licences, the payment of renewal fees, the prosecution of infringers, and other points likely to breed differences if unprovided for.

Desirable to define mutual rights of co-patentees by agreement.

A Register of Patents is kept at the Patent Office in accordance with Section 23 of the Patents Act. Every patent upon being sealed is entered upon this Register, and all dealings with the patent, whether by assignment, licence, amendment, or extension, and in short everything affecting the validity or proprietorship of the patent, should be entered on the Register by those concerned.

Register of Patents.

The patent is registered immediately upon being sealed, and, as the Comptroller recognises no property in the invention until after the grant, no documents affecting to deal with the patent will be registered until the patent has been sealed.

Documents affecting to deal with patent not registrable until after sealing.

No notice of any trust can be entered on the Register. An agreement made *before* the filing of an application, and referring to proposed dealings with the patent to be afterwards obtained, was refused entry on the Register even after the sealing of the patent.

Notices of trust not entered on Register.

Agreements made before filing of application should unmistakeably refer to invention afterwards protected.

This was decided in *Parnell's Patent* (5 P. O. R. 126), but North, J., in refusing the motion to compel entry on the Register, declined to lay down as an absolute rule that no document executed before the date of application could be entered on the Register after sealing. Probably an agreement made before the date of application, but having attached to it, as an exhibit, a model or description and drawing of the invention, would be capable of registration, if the model or description or drawing corresponded clearly with the invention for which application was afterwards made.

Assignments and licences registrable by assignees and licensees.

An assignment, licence, or other deed affecting the ownership or use of the patent should be immediately registered by the person claiming to be entitled under the assignment, licence, &c. The fee for each entry in the Register is ten shillings.

Procedure in registering.

A request for entry should be left at or posted to the Patent Office, together with the original assignment, licence, or other document, and also a copy of the same. The Comptroller, having made the entry in the Register, returns the original, bearing his certificate of entry, but retains the copy. If the assignment, licence, or other document should refer to other documents of title, not being matters of record, an official or certified copy of these should accompany the request. A body corporate may be registered as proprietors, in its corporate name.

Register of Patents open to public inspection.

The Register of Patents is open to inspection by the public, and a certified copy of any entry may be had on payment of a small fee. The Register is *primâ facie* evidence of any matters directed or authorised to be inserted therein.

Certified extracts from Register taken in evidence.

Written or printed copies or extracts, certified by the Comptroller, and bearing the seal of the Patent Office, of patents, specifications, or of registers, books, and other documents kept there, are admitted in evidence, without proof or production of the originals, in all courts of law.

Rectifications of Register.

The Register may be rectified by an order of Court made on the application of any person aggrieved.

CHAPTER X.

AMENDMENT OF SPECIFICATION.

IT OFTEN happens that after the Complete Specification has been filed, or it might be after the patent has been obtained, the applicant or patentee finds that he has claimed too much, or that in some other respect his Specification requires amendment. Provision for this has been made in Section 18, Sub-section 1, of the Patents Act. The sub-section is as follows: *Reasons for seeking amendment.* *Section 18.*

"An applicant or patentee may, from time to time, by request in writing left at the Patent Office, seek leave to amend his Specification, including drawings forming part thereof, by way of *disclaimer*, *correction*, or *explanation*, stating the nature of such amendment and his reasons for the same." *Limits of amendment.*

The words in italics show the limits within which amendments must be confined. The amendment may consist in striking out, correcting, or making more clear, but it must not in the smallest degree increase the scope of the patent. Even where terms, which are purely those of correction or explanation, are used in an amendment in such a manner as to give the faintest suspicion that their tendency might be to increase the ambit of the Specification, they are rigorously excluded.

The most usual cases of amendment are those in which the patentee has found that his claim is too wide; but there are also instances where the amendment may be only of the nature of correction or explanation.

In some cases a mistake in the drawing has been allowed to be amended without altering a word in the Specification. *Drawings.*

There is practically no more difficulty in amending the Specification of a patent which has been sealed than there is in amending a Specification not yet sealed. In the former case the official fee is £3, and in the latter case £1 10s.

Application to amend must be signed by applicant or patentee.

The request for leave to amend a Specification must be signed by the applicant or patentee. The amendment or amendments should be shown in red ink on an officially certified copy of the printed Specification. If accepted by the Comptroller, the request to amend is advertised in the Official Patent Journal, and generally in one or two newspapers. For example, if the patent relates to knitting machines, the Comptroller might require the proposed amendment to be advertised in a district devoted to such an industry, for instance in Leicester. If to cotton machinery, it might be required to be advertised in Manchester. The heading of the advertisement invites opposition from anyone interested.

Advertisement of application to amend.

Specification may be amended more than once.

The words "from time to time" in Section 18 would seem to show that a Specification may be amended and re-amended any number of times. Persons entitled to amend include assignees and mortgagees.

Persons entitled to amend.

Although it is permissible for an applicant, on filing his Specification in the first instance, to refer to the defects or shortcomings of patented inventions of prior date, he will not be allowed to do so in an amendment (*re Hampton & Facer*, Griff. P. C. 13). The time within which opposition to an amendment will be entertained is one month from the date of the advertisement in the Official Journal. The notice of opposition bears a stamp of ten shillings. It must contain the full name and address of the opponent, and state the reasons of opposition. The applicant is advised of the opposition by the Comptroller, and thereafter declarations are filed by the opponent in support of his opposition within fourteen days of the expiry of one month from the date of the advertisement. The proceedings and rules as to declarations are identical with those already described with reference to the opposition to the grant of a patent.

Oppositions to amendments.

Procedure on opposition.

Comptroller's decision subject to appeal.

The decision of the Comptroller is subject to an appeal to the Law Officer, whose decision is final.

Amendment on terms.

Section 20 of the Patents Act provides that, where an amendment by way of disclaimer, correction, or explanation has been allowed under this Act, no damages shall be given in any action in respect of the use of the invention before the disclaimer, correction, or explanation, unless the patentee establishes to the satisfaction of the Court that his original claim was framed in good faith and with reasonable skill and knowledge.

Specification or Claims must in first place be framed in good faith and with reasonable skill and knowledge.

The concluding words of this section plainly show that the patentee will not be protected from the consequences of his own ignorance or want of skill, or of perfect honesty and straightforwardness in preparing his Specification. Good faith alone will not serve him if he has blundered in other ways, nor will the greatest skill and knowledge avail if he has not used these to make everything in his Specification as plain as he possibly could. These are axioms not only as regards the conditions of amendment, but in every case where the patent requires to be subjected to legal tests.

Comptroller may impose conditions in granting amendment.

As Section 20 does not absolutely prohibit the bringing of an action for infringements committed before the amendment, it is within the province of the Comptroller or Law Officer to impose conditions, if good cause is shown by the opponent.

Patent *sub judice* may be amended on terms as to costs &c.

Where action for infringement has been taken on a patent, and the plaintiff discovers, from the defence or from some other cause, that his patent has been partly anticipated or is otherwise defective, he may apply to the Court for leave to amend his Specification *by way of disclaimer;* and the Court may direct that in the meantime the trial of the action shall be postponed. Permission to amend a Specification in such a case is usually coupled with the condition that the costs of the action up to the time of leave being given, and, generally speaking, all costs occasioned by the application for leave to amend, are to be paid by the applicant, whether the action succeeds or fails.

CHAPTER XI.

ASSIGNMENTS OF PATENTS.

A patent or a share in a patent is an assignable property.

THE form of grant being to the patentee, his executors, administrators, and "assigns," it follows, from the terms, that a patent is assignable. And not only is it assignable as a whole, but any part or share of the patent may be dealt with, or the right to use a distinct and separate part of the invention may be bought and sold. Further, a patent may be assigned for any place in or part of the United Kingdom, and such district or divisional assignments are by no means uncommon.

Assignment should be by deed.

An assignment should be by deed (*per* Lindley and Bowen, L.JJ., in *Stewart v. Casey*, 9 P. O. R. 9); for the grant itself being under seal, it follows, as a rule of law, that things which are created by deed can only be assigned by deed.

If, however, an instrument not under seal purports to be an assignment of a patent, it is submitted that it would act as an agreement to assign, and specific performance could be enforced on this ground.

Contingent assignment.

An agreement to assign a patent upon the happening of a certain event would operate as an assignment without further assurance, upon the happening of the event.

Patent of bankrupt patentee passes to trustee.

If a patentee, or the proprietor of a patent, or of a share in a patent, should become bankrupt, his interest or share passes to the trustee in bankruptcy.

In drawing an assignment, any form of words which clearly transfers the proprietorship of the patent from the assignor to the assignee will serve.

Heads of assignment.

The usual course is first to indicate the patent grant, distinguishing it by number, date, and title. If the assignor is himself an assignee, the devolution of title should be set forth.

Next come the words purporting to assign the patent,

together with the rights and powers of the patentee, the consideration being here set forth.

Covenants.

The covenant for title is implied, in accordance with the Conveyancing Act, 1881, if the assignor describes himself as the "beneficial owner" or "trustee." Next should follow a covenant for the validity of the patent, as far as the acts of the assignor are concerned. In addition, it is sometimes considered prudent to insert an express covenant as to any improvements upon the patent that may thereafter be made by the assignor. If this were not done, a patentee or assignor might immediately afterwards produce an invention which might entirely supersede the invention he had sold.

Future improvements.

Provision for payment of annuities.

When the assignment deals with a share of a patent only, or is an assignment for a specified district, it is advisable to make provision for the payment of the annuities: otherwise an assignee might find himself compelled, for his own sake, to pay the annuities which would keep the patent in force, not for his benefit alone, but for the benefit of others upon whom he would have no claim for repayment.

Payment of annuities by co-proprietors.

In all cases where there are several co-owners of a patent, it is advisable to make specific arrangements as to the payment of their proportions of the annual renewal fees by the respective owners. The mutual rights and duties of the co-owners should also be laid down and limited.

Mutual rights of co-proprietors.

It has already been said that a co-patentee or part owner might himself, and without the concurrence of the others, manufacture the invention or make profits without accounting to the others. This might fall hardly on the others, as a manufacturer capable of turning out large quantities of the patented goods might, so long as he was owner of a small share in the patent, do so with impunity, and without paying a farthing to his co-patentees. They, on the other hand, might be unable to get the manufacture taken up by others, so that the owner of, say, one-sixth of a patent might be making large profits, while the holders of the remaining five-sixths were making nothing.

To prevent this, an agreement should be made binding

the present or future co-owners to account to each other for the profits made by them respectively, and to act in concert when granting licences. With regard to the latter, however, it should be said that in *Mathers v. Green* (L. R. 1 Ch. 29) an unreversed portion of the judgment of the lower Court held that where one of several joint patentees grants a licence, he is bound to account for the profits to his co-patentees.

Co-proprietorship might be resolved into trust.

In the event of the co-owners objecting to the quasi-partnership brought about by such an agreement as has been indicated, the patent could be assigned to trustees for the owners, the trustees being authorised to grant licences for the benefit of the owners, keep accounts of all profits, and distribute them in the proportions of ownership. The trustees would also be empowered to pay the renewal fees as they fall due, to provide for all current costs and expenses, and to institute or defend any proceedings at law in respect of the patent or trusteeship.

Corporations as proprietors.

A patent may be assigned to a body corporate in its corporate name, and such body corporate is entitled to be registered as the proprietors of the patent.

Persons other than patentee entitled to sue for infringement.

An action for infringement of a patent may be brought by the assignee, and the assignees of a bankrupt patentee may bring it. Where a distinct portion of a patent has been assigned, the assignee of that portion can act alone in bringing an action for infringement of this part of the invention. This was laid down by Erle, C.J., in *Dunnicliff v. Mallett* (7 C. B., N. S. 209, 227).

All assignments should be entered in the Register of Patents.

CHAPTER XII.

LICENCES.

By a Licence, the patentee relaxes the prohibition contained in the grant of Letters Patent against the public, in favour of a certain person—viz., the licensee—whereby the licensee is allowed to exercise the privilege originally granted exclusively to the patentee. Nature of licence by patentee.

Licences may be classed as *Exclusive*, *General*, and *Restricted*. Classes of licences.

An *Exclusive* Licence is a licence which is granted to one person or firm only. The patentee may reserve the continued use of the invention to himself personally, or he may exclude himself and his assigns. The exclusive licence may be for a fixed period, or it may be terminable by notice, or upon the happening of a contingency, or it may be for the full term of the patent and without power of revocation, in which case it amounts to, and for some purposes is treated as, an absolute assignment. Exclusive.

A *General* Licence is a licence which is granted to several different licensees. General.

A *Restricted* Licence may be described as a licence to use only a part of the invention, or to use it only for a certain purpose or within a certain district. Restricted.

A licence to a manufacturer to make a patented article implies a licence to those who purchase the goods from him to re-sell to the public without direct authority from the licensor.

A licence is a personal right granted to the licensee, and cannot, therefore, be assigned or transferred by him, unless a power of assignment or transfer is specifically granted in the instrument. Neither can sub-licences be granted by a licensee, unless the power to do so is expressly conferred. Licence a personal right not transferable.

Licences should be under hand and seal, but a licence of a less formal nature, even when granted by word of mouth, would be perfectly good as betwixt licensor and Licences should be under hand and seal.

But less formal licences can be enforced as between the parties.

licensee, especially so if royalties have been paid and accepted. Such a licence could not, however, be registered in the Patent Office, nor could the licensee sue in the name of the licensor or otherwise for infringement by outsiders, as he might do if he were an exclusive licensee under deed.

Caution to be exercised in accepting licence.

The terms of a proposed licence should be very carefully scanned by the intending licensee: otherwise he may find himself for ever estopped from questioning the validity of the patent, although all the world besides may use it.

Estoppel.

Generally speaking, the mere relationship of licensor and licensee implies that the taker of the licence admits the validity of the patent, and is therefore estopped or hindered from denying a matter already stated or admitted by him. Consequently estoppel might take effect even where the licence was not under seal, or merely in the form of a letter, or even where the licence is verbal. As a rule such estoppel would exist only while the licence remained in force, or until the patent had been declared void in legal proceedings between the licensor and third parties (*Cheetham v. Nuthall*, 10 P. O. R. 321).

But where more than the ordinary covenants have been imported into the instrument, or where the licence is for the full term of the patent, or where the taker of the licence agrees not to question the validity of the patent, the fettering of the licensee might be correspondingly severe, and complete estoppel set up.

In the absence of such restrictive terms in the licence, a licensee who wishes to discontinue should give immediate notice in writing to the licensor, and at the same time cease to use the invention (*Redges v. Mulliner*, 10 P. O. R. 21).

When the relationship of licensor and licensee has been thus properly determined, the licensee may afterwards dispute the validity of the patent—that is to say, if he again commences to manufacture under the patent, he will require to be dealt with as an ordinary infringer, and not as being estopped under his former licence.

Terms of licence should give

A rehearsal of the indicated possible difficulties points to the conclusion that, as it is to the interest of the licensor to bind the licensee as much as possible by the terms of the instrument, on the other hand it is to the interest of the licensee to decline to accept anything that may too greatly hamper him in the future. Therefore the question of estoppel consequent upon recitals and statements in a licence, and actual or implied admissions on the part of the licensee, should be carefully considered before acceptance of the licence. If the licensor will make the concession, the most prudent course is to provide for discontinuance of the licence at once, on the patent being declared invalid, and expressly to bar admissions of the validity of the patent. reasonable freedom to both parties.

Again, from the point of view of the licensor it may be said that equal caution is required, lest, in seeming to guarantee more than can be substantiated, the question of failure of consideration should leave the licensee at liberty to dispute the licence. For example, the expressions "as beneficial owner" or "as trustee" would, under the Conveyancing Act of 1881, imply certain covenants for title which, as far as licensors are concerned, are best omitted from licences. Risks of the licensor.

Further, if the licence is exclusive, and no rent reserved, the licensor might well object to be too stringently bound by covenants for title and for validity, seeing that his only advantage from the licence will depend upon the enterprise of the licensee. At the same time he should have power of revocation for breaches of covenants, or in case the royalties do not reach a reasonable figure per annum within a given period. Otherwise an interested manufacturer might take an exclusive licence, for the express purpose of locking the patent up.

In the case of an exclusive licence, the payment of the renewal fees by one or other of the parties should be expressly provided for. In the absence of such provision, neither would be bound to pay these, and the responsibilities of the licensee might continue, although the patent had lapsed. Exclusive licence should provide for payment of annuities by one of the parties.

An instance of this occurred in the case of *Mills v. Carson* (10 P. O. R. 9). Here an exclusive licence was granted to the defendants by the patentee for the then unexpired term of patent right for the con- *Mills v. Carson.*

sideration of £100 per annum. Nothing was said in the licence as to who should pay the renewal fees. Neither of the parties paid the next renewal fee, so that the patent lapsed. The licensee then declined to pay the next instalment of annuity to the plaintiff. On action being taken by the patentee's assignee, it was held by the Recorder, by the Divisional Court, and by the Court of Appeal, that nothing having been said in the deed about the payment of those fees, the licensee had no right to throw the onus of payment upon the patentee, and that he must pay and continue to pay the annuity prescribed in the deed for the term of years for which the patent would have lasted had it not been allowed to lapse. An ordinary licensee cannot sue alone in respect of infringements, but must join with the patentee. Even in the case of an *exclusive* licensee, his right to sue alone has never been expressly admitted by the Court, and the usual practice is to make the patentee co-plaintiff.

Right of licensee to sue when licence exclusive and irrecoverable.

When the licence, in addition to being exclusive, is irrevocable, and no payments are being made under it, the licence is virtually an assignment, and it seems reasonable to submit that the licensee may sue for infringements without making the licensor a party, although even this has never been directly decided.

Further covenants in licence.

The licensee usually covenants to pay the royalties and other sums agreed upon; to keep proper books of account; to allow inspection and the taking of extracts; and to make periodical returns, verified by statutory declaration, if required. He should also agree to stamp, number, or otherwise distinguish the goods where this is possible.

All questions as to mutual assistance in litigation, detection of infringements, the patenting of improvements, terms of revocation of licence, settlement of disputes by arbitration, &c., may be set forth in the instrument according to the arrangements of the parties.

Fraudulent licensor may be sued for recovery of moneys paid.

Where it is apparent that the licensor has acted fraudulently, all royalties and sums paid to him under the licence are recoverable.

Registration of licences.

Licences should be entered on the Register of Patents, and a registration fee of ten shillings is payable thereon.

When the licence is by deed, and no premium or fixed sum is payable on the making, the consideration being therefore uncertain, it must bear a stamp of ten shillings, under the Stamp Act of 1870. Where a fixed sum is paid, an *ad valorem* stamp is required, whether the licence is by deed or otherwise. Where the licence contains a provision for the payment of a minimum royalty, the revenue authorities require the payment of duty upon the gross minimum royalty reserved, although the licence may contain power for either of the parties to terminate the licence at any time. Stamping.

Compulsory Licences.

Section 22 of the Patents Act provides for the grant of compulsory licences. The petitioner for such a licence must establish— Compulsory licences.

1. Default of the patentee to grant licences on reasonable terms; also Grounds for enforcing compulsory licences.

2. One of the three events mentioned in the section, viz.—

(*a*) That the patent is not being worked in the United Kingdom; or

(*b*) That the reasonable requirements of the public cannot be supplied; or

(*c*) That any person is prevented from working or using to the best advantage an invention of which he is possessed.

It may be added that this section has proved almost inoperative since the beginning of the Act. Up to the time of writing, only three applications for compulsory licences have been made, and none of the three ever came to a hearing. It is, therefore, impossible to say upon what terms a compulsory licence would be granted.

An application for the compulsory grant of a licence is heard before the Board of Trade. An unsuccessful applicant has no appeal from the decision of the Board; but a patentee who may have been ordered to grant a licence might dispute the mandamus by which the order of the Board is enforced, so that practically he has a right of appeal. Board of Trade decides on compulsory licences.

CHAPTER XIII.

AGREEMENTS.

AGREEMENTS also play an important part among documents affecting the working and proprietorship of patents and inventions.

Agreements before or after application.

Agreements may be made either before or after an application for the grant of a patent, and may be for divers objects. For example, if a poor inventor should make an application in conjunction with a person who has had no share in evolving the invention, but whose functions will be those of paying the expenses of obtaining the patent and of introducing the invention commercially, such an arrangement should form the subject-matter of agreement prior to the application being made; for if this is not done, the mere presence of the co-applicant's name would vest him with legal rights in one half share, which it might be difficult to disprove if he should afterwards refuse to enter into the intended agreement. Other reasons for agreement might arise in the case of a money loan from some one to pay the cost of the patent and afterwards to introduce it, the lender to acquire a share in the patent. Such pre-application agreement should distinctly identify the invention: otherwise the Comptroller might refuse to register it (if this should afterwards become necessary), on the ground that he had no means of verifying the representation that the invention mentioned in the agreement was the same as that afterwards protected.

Agreement before application should ascertain invention.

Agreements to ascertain mutual rights of co-patentees.

In the case of joint applicants or patentees, an agreement might be made either before or after the grant of the patent, limiting and defining the mutual rights of the parties, so that no one should have an undue advantage over his co-patentees.

Agreement to purchase.

A share in an invention and in the patent to be afterwards obtained may be purchased even before application is made for a patent, and an agreement may be based upon this sale, in which the inventor binds himself to asssign a share in the patent as soon as it shall have been issued.

Legally, until the Letters Patent are actually sealed and issued there is no vendible property existing: therefore an absolute assignment by deed of a patent for which application only has been made is not effectual. All that can be done is to make an agreement to assign when the patent is issued, and specific performance of such a contract will always be enforced. Absolute assignment made only after grant of patent.

CHAPTER XIV.

THE REGISTER OF PATENTS.

WHEN A Patent is sealed, the Comptroller causes it to be entered by its date, number, and title, together with the name of the patentee, in the Register of Patents, which is a book kept at the Patent Office and containing particulars of everything affecting the existence and proprietorship of each patent so entered. Thus, the Register will contain entries of assignments, licences, amendments, extensions, payment of renewal fees, and other incidents in the life of a patent. The Register is *primâ facie* evidence of any matters inscribed therein. No notice of any trust will be entered on the Register, but registration of an assignment containing trusts would not be refused. For example, it was held in *Stewart v. Casey* (9 P. O. R. 9) that the true construction of Sections 23, 85, and 87 of the Patents Act of 1883, and the Patents Rules, Section 85, only excludes from the Register simple notices of trust, and not documents affecting the proprietorship

Register.

Trusts not registrable.

of a patent, whether by creating trusts or otherwise; and that equitable assignments of a patent, or of a share in a patent, may be entered on the Register as documents affecting the proprietorship.

Documents dated before the actual sealing of Letters Patent, but after the date of application, will be accepted for entry on the Register, but only after the sealing of the patent.

Documents relating to dealings with invention before application, as a rule, not registrable.

In the majority of cases, documents referring to dealings with an invention before application has been made for a patent, are not capable of being entered on the Register at any time. The reason is, that the Comptroller would have great difficulty in satisfying himself that the invention referred to in the document sought to be registered was the same as that afterwards protected and patented. For example, suppose that the invention referred to in the document was "Improvements in Prime Motors," and that the application afterwards made had precisely the same title, it is conceivable that this title might serve for fifty different inventions, and that the invention contemplated in the document was for an improvement on the cut-off valve of a steam engine, while the application, although bearing the same title, might refer to an entirely different part of, and be applicable to, an entirely different class of motor.

Still it is evident, from the words of North, J., in *Parnell's Patent* (5 P. O. R. 126), that where the invention referred to in the document and the invention afterwards patented are *unquestionably* the same, registration will not be refused. Therefore, in such an agreement, a sketch and description of the invention should be attached, so as to identify it with the subject-matter of the application to be afterwards made.

Each volume of the Register is preserved for twenty-one years from the date of the latest patent recorded in it.

Persons entitled to register.

When a person becomes entitled to a patent, or to an interest therein, by agreement, or by transmission, or by operation of law, he should forward a request to the Comptroller for the entry of his name on the Register as complete or partial owner of the patent.

The request should be made according to Form "L,"

and should be signed by the person requesting to be registered as proprietor.

A body corporate may be registered as proprietors in its corporate name, and in such a case the request should be signed by an authorised agent. Bodies corporate

The request on Form "L" in the case of an assignment, and on Form "M" in the case of a licence should be accompanied by the original assignment, licence, or other document, and by an attested copy of the same, which is retained by the Comptroller.

If the assignment or other instrument should refer to a document or documents affecting the title and not in the possession of the Comptroller, the original or an official or attested copy must be left with the Comptroller. References to collateral documents.

Certified extracts from the Register are furnished by the Comptroller on payment of a small fee, and the Register is open to the inspection of the public every week-day. Thus a proposing purchaser or licensee can satisfy himself concerning all registered dealings with the patent. Certified extracts from Register obtainable.

Where rectification of the Register has been ordered by the Court, the order directs due notice of the rectification to be given to the Comptroller, who will thereupon amend the Register. Rectification by order of Court.

CHAPTER XV.

MISCELLANEOUS.

Revocation of Patents.

The old action of *Scire facias* having been abolished by the Act of 1883, revocation of a patent is now obtained by petition to the Court. Abolition of *Scire facias.*

This petition is not presentable in the Court of the County Palatine of Lancaster, but it may be sent for trial at assizes before a judge without a jury. Petition for revocation.

The "Court."

The "Court" means the High Court of Justice in England, the High Court of Justice in Ireland, and the Court of Session in Scotland.

A petition for revocation may be presented by—

Persons entitled to apply for revocation.

(1) The Attorney-General for England or Ireland, or the Lord Advocate in Scotland, or any person authorised by them.

(2) Any person alleging that the patent is obtained in fraud of his rights, or of the rights of any person under or through whom he claims.

(3) Any person alleging that he, or a person through whom he claims, was the true inventor of the subject-matter of the patent.

(4) Any person alleging that he, or any person under or through whom he claims an interest in any trade, business, or manufacture, had publicly manufactured, used, or sold, within this realm, before the date of the patent, anything claimed by the patentee as his invention.

Advisable always to obtain fiat of Law Officer.

Under paragraphs 2, 3, and 4, a person may present his petition as of right; but upon other grounds he must obtain from the Attorney-General in England or Ireland, or the Lord Advocate in Scotland, his fiat or leave to present the petition. This fiat is not issued as a matter of course; but even where the applicant can present his petition under paragraphs 2, 3, and 4, it is sometimes better to fortify the petition with the fiat of the Attorney-General or Lord Advocate, so as to decrease the possibility of the petition failing, upon the ground of insufficient *locus standi*.

It must, however, be said that in *Morgan's Patent* (5 P. O. R. 186), Chitty, J., held that, granted the petitioner is qualified to present the petition himself, under paragraphs 2, 3, and 4, the patent may be attacked on any other ground.

Procedure to obtain fiat.

To obtain the fiat of the Attorney-General, the following papers should be sent to the patent clerk:—

(*a*) A memorial to the Attorney-General asking his authority, and stating all the circumstances.

(*b*) A statutory declaration verifying the statements in the memorial.

(*c*) Two copies of the proposed petition and of the particulars proposed to be delivered with it.

(*d*) The certificate of a barrister that the petition is proper to be authorised by the Attorney-General.

(*e*) A certificate by a solicitor that the proposed petitioner is a proper person to be a petitioner, and that he is in a position to pay the costs of the petition if unsuccessful.

If the Attorney-General think fit, he may direct that the patentee shall have notice, and be allowed to appear before him and show cause why the fiat should not be issued.

Particulars of objections. The petitioner must deliver with his petition particulars of the objections upon which he means to rely. These may be amended from time to time with leave of the Court, but when complete, no evidence will be admitted in proof of any objection not included in the particulars, except by leave of the Court or a judge. If such leave is given, it will in most cases be on the usual terms—*i.e.* payment of costs by the petitioner up to the time of his making application to amend particulars.

A petition for revocation is properly an action, and the issues are the same as in an action to try the validity of a patent.

Patent revoked may in cases of fraud be transferred to petitioner. When a patent is revoked on the ground of fraud, the successful petitioner, if he is the true inventor, can have a patent granted to him for the invention, as of the date of revocation, but expiring at the same time as the original revoked patent would have expired.

Prolongation of Patents.

Period within which petition for prolongation must be presented. Section 25 of the Act of 1883 refers to the extension of the term of a patent, and provides that a patentee may present a petition to Her Majesty in Council, praying that his patent may be extended for a further term; but such petition must now be presented at least *six months* before the time limited for the expiration of the patent.

Grounds for granting petition.

Sub-section 5 is to the effect that if the Judicial Committee report that the patentee has been inadequately remunerated by his patent, it shall be lawful for Her Majesty in Council to extend the term of the patent for a further term, not exceeding seven, or in exceptional cases fourteen years; or to order the grant of a new patent for the term therein mentioned, and containing any restrictions, conditions, and provisions that the Judicial Committee may think fit.

Periods of extension.

Persons entitled to apply for prolongation.

As the term "patentee" includes, under Section 46, any person who is for the time being entitled to the benefit of the patent, it follows that not only can the original patentee present a petition for extension, but also the executor or administrator of a deceased patentee, or an assignee of a patentee who has sold his interest.

Petitioner must present full accounts.

In presenting a petition for extension, the applicant must state fully and fairly everything relating to the patent, and be prepared with complete sets of profit and loss accounts, so that approximately exact results of the working under the patent may be laid before the Committee. Anything savouring of suppression or designed confusion will most certainly result in the throwing out of the application.

It is much better plainly to state an even apparently damaging fact than to try to suppress it, for there is no tribunal more impatient of want of good faith than the Judicial Committee.

A petition for the extension of a patent dated after the 31st of December, 1883, will require to be presented within six months before its expiry.

But a petition for prolongation of a patent dated before that time may be presented any time before the expiry of the patent.

It must, however, be "prosecuted with effect"—*i.e.* some definite step must have been taken by the Judicial Committee before the patent expires. It is therefore better, even in the latter case, to present the petition within the six months.

Advertisement of notice of intention to petition.

Notice of the intention to petition for extension requires to be advertised in the *London Gazette*, and also in newspapers circulating in districts where the inhabitants are likely to be interested in the subject-matter of the patent. The petition must actually be presented within one week from the last insertion of the advertisement in the *London Gazette*.

On or before the day fixed for the hearing of the petition, any person may enter at the Council Office a caveat, addressed to the Registrar, objecting to the extension. The opponent is not required to show such personal interest as in the case of opposition to the grant of a patent or amendment of a Specification before the Law Officer. Opposition to petition. Any person may oppose.

It is advisable to state fully all the particulars of objection to the extension in the caveat; but in *Stewart's Patent* (3 P. O. R. 7) evidence of prior user, not included in the particulars, was admitted, although this resulted in the loss of the costs by the opponents, who were successful. Particulars of objection.

The Attorney-General may give evidence of objections on behalf of the Crown, irrespective of the particulars. Objections by the Crown.

When an extension is opposed, four weeks' notice of the hearing must be given by the applicant to the opponent, and the applicant must also advertise the date of hearing in the *London Gazette* and such other newspapers as the order may name. Procedure in opposition.

At least a week before the hearing, the petitioner must lodge at the Council Office six printed copies of the Specification and four copies of the balance sheet, showing the expenditure and receipts relating to the patent.

At the hearing, the petitioner and opponent may appear either personally or by counsel. The Attorney-General is always present to watch the case in the interests of the Crown, and may interpose, even although no caveat has been entered. The rules of evidence are the same as in courts of law. Hearing of petition.

In examining the request for extension, the Judicial Committee will take into consideration the merits of the invention as regards the public, and the remuneration obtained from it by the patentee or his representative or assignee.

The three chief points to be proved by the petitioner are— Points to be enlarged upon by petitioner.

(1) The merit of the invention.

(2) That every possible effort has been used to make the invention commercially successful.

(3) That, without any fault of his own, the petitioner has been unable to reap a sufficient reward.

As far as merit is concerned, the chief thing to make plain is the great utility of the invention to the public.

Profits on foreign patents to be shown.

Where foreign patents have been obtained for the invention, this should be stated and the accounts should show the expenditure and receipts in connection with these.

Deductions from profits.

Where a certain profit has been made, deductions from this will be allowed for personal expenses of the petitioner, during the periods when he devoted himself exclusively to the pushing of the patent.

Law costs not allowed to be deducted.

It seems that law expenses incurred by the patentee in maintaining his patent rights are not allowed to be deducted from the profits.

Although it is scarcely the function of the Judicial Committee to try the validity of the patent for which extension is sought, still they will not grant extension where the patent is evidently bad. Therefore evidence of anticipation, by the opponent, will be received and given effect to.

Usual period of extension seven years.

As a rule no extension is granted for a longer period than seven years, but in rare instances ten and even fourteen years' extensions have been granted.

The new Letters Patent are sealed and dated as of the date of expiration of the original patent. No new Specification requires to be filed.

Restraint of Threats.

Under former Acts threats not restrainable.

Before the Act of 1883, a patentee might almost with impunity send out circulars threatening legal proceedings on account of alleged infringements of his patent. He was then under no compulsion to bring any action in furtherance of his threats, and unless the party aggrieved could prove that these threats were injurious, untrue, and made maliciously and in bad faith, he had no remedy. So long as the patentee could make out any case that he had, or believed he had, reasonable ground for uttering such threats, he was safe.

Now, however, Section 32 of the Act of 1883 provides that "Where any person claiming to be the patentee of an invention, by circulars, advertisements, or otherwise, threatens any other person with any legal proceedings or liability in respect of any alleged manufacture, use, sale, or purchase of the invention, any person or persons aggrieved thereby may bring an action against him, and may obtain an injunction against the continuance of such threats, and may recover such damages, if any, as may have been sustained thereby, if the alleged manufacture, use, sale, or purchase to which the threats related was not, in fact, an infringement of any legal rights of the person making such threats: Provided that this section shall not apply if the person making such threats with due diligence commences and prosecutes an action for infringement of his patent."

Now Section 32 provides for restraint of threats for infringement.

Section does not apply if action is taken with due diligence.

The manner of conveying such threats is not very material, so long as it reaches the interested parties or their customers, and is calculated to have a restraining or injurious effect. For example, threats conveyed by circular or advertisement are not the only grounds of action: it has been held that threats made in a private letter, or in the course of correspondence (even when without prejudice), or at an interview, or when conveyed by a solicitor's letter, come within the meaning of the section.

What constitutes an actionable threat.

The threat must be in respect of something which has been done or is being carried on. As Bowen, L.J., expressed it in *Challender v. Royle* (4 P. O. R. 374), a merely general warning "to pirates not to pirate, and to infringers not to infringe," and that the patentee has a patent which he intends to enforce, is not in itself an actionable threat. But, even in the case of such a general statement the circumstances will be narrowly inquired into, and in the event of proof of damage an action would be maintainable.

Threat must relate to particular infringement.

General warning not a threat.

The remedies of an aggrieved person are, an action to recover such damages as may have been sustained, and an injunction against the continuance of the threats. These remedies are concurrent. Damages will be awarded only where actual injury has been sustained. Thus, in *Kurtz v.*

Remedies of threatened person.

Spence (5 P. O. R. 161), where the threats had been conveyed in a correspondence conducted "without prejudice," and where the plaintiffs had not gone to any expense for plant or machinery for the manufacture of the alleged infringing invention, a reference as to damages was refused.

Procedure where plaintiff questions validity of defendant's patent.

The plaintiff in such an action may question the validity of the defendant's patent, but in this case the action is conducted as if the defendant had brought an action against the plaintiff for infringement of his patent, the defendant having the first and last word.

"Reasonable time" within which party using threats should bring his action for infringement.

Three months after the utterance of the threats complained of has been considered a reasonable time within which to bring an action for infringement of the patent. The bringing of this action extinguishes the right of the person threatened to his remedy for the threats under Section 32.

Offences and Penalties.

Section 105.

Section 105 of the Act of 1883 provides that "Any person who represents that any article sold by him is a patented article, when no patent has been granted for the same, shall be liable for every offence, on summary conviction, to a fine not exceeding five pounds."

Penalty for falsely marking articles as "patented."

A person shall be deemed to represent that an article is patented if he sell the article with the word "Patent," "Patented," or any word or words expressing or implying that a patent has been obtained for the article, stamped, engraved, impressed, or otherwise applied to the article.

Expired patent.

It is not an offence under this section to continue to mark an article as "Patent" after the patent has expired.

How articles under provisional protection should be marked.

Where an invention has been provisionally protected only, it is an offence to mark or sell it as "Patented." In such a case the best course is to mark on the article, "Patent applied for, No. ."

Penalty for use of Royal Arms.

The succeeding section (106) forbids the use, except under authority, of the Royal Arms, or of arms deceptively similar thereto, in the carrying on of any business or calling, and so as to lead to the belief that the said business or calling is being carried on under royal or official authority. The maximum fine on summary conviction is twenty pounds.

PATENT MEDICINES.

What are popularly known as "Patent Medicines" are distinct from patented inventions, and the term is a misnomer, which it will be no longer legal to use in the way of business. Under the Stamp Medicines Act of 1812, stamps, for application to any particular proprietary medicine, may be had from the Secretary of Stamps and Taxes, Inland Revenue, Somerset House, London. The applicant is required to pay for the preparation of the plate from which his stamps are to be printed, and this plate is kept in the custody of the Secretary, and used only for the purpose of printing the stamps which the owner may require. As has been said, such stamped proprietary medicines have hitherto been known and sold as "Patent Medicines," although not the subject of Letters Patent. Now, however, it is clear that anyone describing and selling medicines of this description as "Patent Medicines" will be liable to a penalty. In the *Pharmaceutical Society v. Piper* (L. R. 1893, 1 Q. B. 686) Collins, J., distinctly held that patent medicines meant "Medicines the subject of Letters Patent."

Patent medicines.

Patent medicines, so termed, must now be the subject of letters patent.

PATENT AGENTS.

Under the Supplementary Act of 1888 it was provided that after the 1st of July, 1889, no person shall be entitled to describe himself as a Patent Agent, whether by advertisement, by description on his place of business, by any document issued by him, or otherwise, unless he is registered as a Patent Agent. Any person contravening the section is liable on summary conviction to a fine not exceeding twenty pounds. The term "Patent Agent" means exclusively an agent for obtaining patents in the United Kingdom. The passing of this Act was a most necessary recognition of the importance to the public of the Patent Agent's profession. Up to the date of the Act there had been no means whatever of excluding incompetent persons from practising, much to the detriment of the public. In

Penalty for false description as "Patent Agent."

Roll of Patent Agents

forming the roll, it was of course impossible to shut out many of these incompetent practitioners, or to prevent the entry of others with very slender claims to admission. But, in spite of this drawback, it may fairly be said that the great body of the profession as it now exists approaches a respectable level, and will at the present rate of progress eventually attain a very high standard of efficiency. Admission to the roll is now only to be obtained after proof of proper professional training for at least seven years, as a pupil under a Registered Patent Agent, and after passing very searching qualifying examinations, which are held from time to time under the Register of Patent Agents Rules, 1889 to 1891.

Training and requirements now necessary to qualify for admission to Roll of Patent Agents.

Chartered Institute of Patent Agents.

The Institute of Patent Agents, which was intended to constitute a representative body of the chief Patent Agents of the United Kingdom, was formed in 1882, and was incorporated by Royal Charter in 1891. The Fellows of this Institute have alone the privilege of styling themselves Chartered Patent Agents. The transactions of the Institute are published annually in a volume edited by the Secretary.

PART II.—TRADE MARKS.

CHAPTER I.

INTRODUCTION.

The custom of a maker of goods adopting a distinctive mark to affix to his merchandise is very ancient.

Origin of trade marks.

Antiquarians point to such distinctive makers' marks upon objects identified with various periods in the world's history, and there is no doubt that in the most remote times a workman whose goods had acquired fame by reason of his skill marked his products so as to show their origin.

First recognition at common law.

Within our own historical purview, the Common Law soon began to take note of and punish fraudulent imitations, and to recognise and protect the right of the producer to have his distinctive mark reserved exclusively to himself. The first case which has been recorded, although in all probability not the first dealt with by the Courts, is that of *Southern v. How*, which occurred in the reign of Elizabeth, and in which damages were given to a clothmaker on proof of piracy of his distinctive mark. It is true that in after cases, the Courts, suspicious of creating anything that seemed to savour of monopoly, for some time hesitated to declare that there was any actual right of property in a trade mark; but early in the present century this ceased to be a matter of doubt. It became apparent that the exclusive possession of a distinctive trade mark was in no sense a monopoly likely to be injurious to the public, but was in reality a protection to them.

Trade mark no monopoly.

It was of advantage to the trader, because he was thereby enabled to reap with more certainty the custom to which his skill and enterprise entitled him. It was also a protection to the public, because in buying an article bearing a well-known mark they were more certain of getting something which possessed acknowledged and approved qualities.

Bacon, V.C., upon trade marks, and their ownership.

The accepted principles upon which the Courts now proceed in trade mark cases are best expressed in the following deliverance of Bacon, V.C , in *Ransome v. Graham* (51 L. J. Ch. 897) : "A manufacturer who produces an article of merchandise which he announces as of public utility, and who places upon it a mark by which it is distinguished from all other articles of a similar kind, with the intention that it may be known to be of his manufacture, becomes the exclusive owner of that which is henceforth called his trade mark. By the law of this country (and the like law prevails in most other civilised countries) he obtains a property in the mark which he so affixes to his goods. The property thus acquired by the manufacturer, like all other property, is under the protection of the law, and for the invasion of the right of the owner of such property the law affords a remedy similar in all respects to that by which the possession and enjoyment of all property is secured to the owners."

Persons entitled to acquire and use trade marks.

It will be noted that the learned Vice-Chancellor, in the foregoing quotation, speaks only of a "manufacturer" adopting a trade mark for the goods he has made. It must, however, be said that, although this is perhaps the most common ownership of a trade mark, there are many instances where the mark is adopted and applied by those who are not actual makers of the goods to which the mark is attached. Thus one person may weave calico, and another may print or bleach or pack it, and a trade mark might be applied by the printer or bleacher or packer, and be registered by him and recognised as his alone. Or the mark might be applied by a mere middleman, who has no share whatever in the manufacture or treatment of the goods, such as an exporter or importer, who merely buys and sells; or by a person who has selected the goods. In all of these cases the mark belongs to the middleman, and the actual manufacturer, who supplies him with the goods to which the mark is affixed, has no claim to any share in it.

But, apart from manufactured goods, trade marks might be used to distinguish substances which are natural products, such as moulders' sand, coal, mineral waters or mineral oils, fruit and the like. Trade marks applicable to natural products.

Previous to 1875 no means existed for acquiring and protecting trade marks by registration. It was occasionally the practice to enter a trade mark at Stationers' Hall, but this conferred no protection whatever. Therefore in bringing an action against an infringer it was necessary to depend entirely upon the Common Law right, and to prove user before the plaintiff's right to take action was admitted. Trade marks not registrable before 1875.

The Merchandise Marks Act, 1862, had for its main object to subject infringers of trade marks to the operation of the Criminal Law, and the same is the case under The Merchandise Marks Act, 1887. But before the latter date, registration had been provided for by The Trade Marks Registration Acts, 1875 to 1877, and at the present time registration is governed by The Patents, Designs, and Trade Marks Acts, 1883 to 1888. Merchandise Marks Act, 1862. Merchandise Marks Act, 1887. Trade Marks Registration Acts, 1875 to 1877. Patents, Designs, and Trade Marks Acts, 1883 to 1888.

Registration of trade marks is granted to aliens, and the rights of aliens in their marks are protected in the English Courts as rigorously as if they belonged to British subjects.

CHAPTER II.

ON THE NATURE AND DEFINITION OF A TRADE MARK.

PASSING over in the meantime the definitions of trade marks as set out in the Merchandise Marks Acts of 1862 and 1887, and as declared in the Trade Marks Act, 1875, the present statutory definition of a trade mark is to be found in Section 64 of the Patents Act, 1888. The definition as it now stands is as follows:— Definitions of trade marks.

"(1) For the purposes of this Act, a trade mark must

consist of, or contain at least one of, the following essential particulars:

Distinctive reproduction of name.

"(*a*) A name of an individual or firm printed, impressed, or woven in some particular and distinctive manner; or

Signature.

"(*b*) A written signature or copy of a written signature of the individual or firm applying for registration thereof as a trade mark; or

Device &c.

"(*c*) A distinctive device, mark, brand, heading, label, or ticket; or

Invented word.

"(*d*) An invented word or invented words; or

Selected word.

"(*e*) A word or words having no reference to the character or quality of the goods, and not being a geographical name.

Additions.

"(2) There may be added to any one or more of the essential particulars mentioned in this section, any letters, words, or figures, or combination of letters, words, or figures or of any of them, but the applicant for registration of any such additional matter must state in his application the essential particulars of the trade mark, and must disclaim in his application any right to the exclusive use of the added matter, and a copy of the statement and disclaimer shall be entered on the register.

"(3) Provided as follows:

"(i.) A person need not under this section disclaim his own name or the foreign equivalent thereof, or his place of business, but no entry of any such name shall affect the right of any owner of the same name to use that name or the foreign equivalent thereof:

Old word, letter, and figure marks.

"(ii.) Any special and distinctive word or words, letter, figure, or combination of letters or figures, or of letters and figures, used as a trade mark *before the thirteenth day of August, One thousand eight hundred and seventy-five*, may be registered as a trade mark under this part of this Act."

Definitions amplified.

The foregoing definitions are sufficiently clear to speak for themselves, but a short reference to each head may prove of advantage.

First.—A name of an individual or firm printed, impressed, or woven in some particular and distinctive manner; or

Secondly.—A written signature or copy of a written signature of the individual or firm applying for registration thereof as a trade mark.

The first and second heads are practically one and the same, and may be treated together.

Name *per se* not a registrable trade mark.

By itself, and apart from any distinctive manner of printing or impressing, a name may constitute a trade mark—not a registrable trade mark, but still a species of property which can under the common law be made good against all the world, with the exception of *persons of the same name.* For it is clear that although a manufacturer of the name of Smith may have carried on business as a sewing machine maker for many years, and may have made his name famous in connection with sewing machines, he cannot on that account prevent another person of the same name from establishing a similar business, and selling machines under his own name. Smith would have his remedy if Jones were to manufacture sewing machines and sell them under the name of Smith, because it would be reasonable to imply that such a course showed fraudulent intent on the part of Jones to take improper advantage of the fame acquired by Smith. The rule, therefore, is that while as against persons bearing a different name a manufacturer's right in his "name trade mark" is absolute and exclusive, nevertheless as against persons bearing the same name no such exclusive right can be set up.

Common-law remedy for fraudulent use of name.

It must, however, be said that in some cases, even as against persons of the same name, a manufacturer would have his remedy, and a rival may be restrained from the free use of his own name if any fraudulent or unfair conduct in connection with such use can be brought home to him. Apart from the civil remedy, the criminal law will punish fraudulent use of a man's own name. In *Holloway v. Holloway* (13 Beav. 209) a brother of the plaintiff had to submit to an injunction, because it was held that he used his own name in such a manner as to imply a fraudulent intent to pass off his pills and ointment as of the plaintiff's manufacture.

Holloway v. Holloway.

Burgess v. Burgess.

Burgess v. Burgess (3 De G. M. & G. 896) was decided upon similar lines, although within more restricted limits, the defendant being restrained from using any sign or intimation capable of confusing the two establishments in the public mind. These and other cases may be submitted as showing that the mere name of an individual or firm, although not now registrable, is a perfectly valid trade mark, but subject to this disadvantage, that the owners cannot prevent others of the same name from using it also for the same class of business, so long as such others use it honestly.

Name only registrable when reproduced in distinctive manner.

As has, however, been said, a mere trade name never was, and is not now, registrable in itself as a trade mark. It must, as the present Act says, be printed, impressed, woven, or otherwise produced in *some particular and distinctive manner*—that is to say, in some ornamental, fanciful, or peculiar fashion; and it is clear that a copy of a written signature comes under this description, since any one written signature is distinctive from another written signature. A trade name registered in this distinctive manner is then good against all the world—that is to say, *in its distinctive dress.* Except as regards the copy of a signature, the name registered in its distinctive dress need not be the actual name of the individual or firm applying for registration.

Signature.

Thirdly.—A distinctive device, mark, brand, heading, label, or ticket.

Distinctiveness an essential in trade marks.

It will be noticed that each variety of mark set forth is subject to the qualification of distinctiveness. Applications for registration of marks under this heading are closely tested in respect of the essential feature of distinctiveness, and refusals are frequent on account of its absence. The mark must not only be distinctive, *i.e.* noteworthy in itself, but it must also be distinctive as compared with other existing marks.

Device.

The word "device" relates to a picture, such for example as a representation of some real or imaginary animal, or a geometrical or other figure, or crest, or in some cases a portrait.

It has been held that "marks" or lines on an article—

such, for example, as marking tobacco or edibles into squares or figures for the purpose of easy and exact subdivision—cannot be claimed as exclusive trade marks.

It was at one time possible to register pictorial representations of the goods as trade marks to be applied thereto; but the Comptroller will not now accept such pictorial representations as registrable trade marks. (See Official Order in *Trade Marks Journal*, No. 570, February 27th, 1889.) **Representations of goods not registrable.**

It may be taken that initials printed in the ordinary non-distinctive manner are not registrable as trade marks, but initials arranged as a monogram of a sufficiently distinctive character, and especially when combined with some device, are usually accepted by the Comptroller. **Initials.**

A "brand" is a mark for branding on corks, casks, butter-tubs, and the like. **Brand.**

"Heading" is a technical name best known in the Manchester trade, and used to designate coloured or other stripes, or combinations of stripes, woven or printed, as headings or narrow borders upon the selvages or ends of piece goods. Registration of such "headings" is now possible only in the case of combination old marks, and even with old marks registration is extremely unlikely. It is certain that no new mark would now be registered which consists only of coloured stripes or arrangements of stripes as a "heading" to piece goods. An application for such a mark would be refused for lack of distinctiveness. "Heading" has also been interpreted as an additional and auxiliary label applied above the ordinary label upon which the chief mark is printed, but its recognised and usual meaning is that known in the Manchester trade. **Heading.**

"Label" clearly refers to adhesive papers bearing the trade mark and capable of being stuck upon bottles, jars, cases, packets, and the like. **Label.**

"Ticket" describes the case of a mark impressed upon a piece of material, such as pasteboard or metal, and loosely attached to the goods. The examples which most readily suggest themselves are the tickets pinned to the wares of a fancy goods dealer or a clothier. **Ticket.**

Invented words.

Fourthly.—An invented word or invented words.

The Trade Marks Acts, 1875 to 1877, excluded fancy words from registration. The Patents Act, 1883, permitted the registration of fancy words not in common use. A fancy word has always been a favourite form of trade mark, since it is available not only to sight, but to speech and hearing. As a result of the Act of 1883 so many applications were received for the registration of fancy words, most of them both descriptive and laudatory of the goods, that the Courts were obliged to restrict and narrow the construction of the term "fancy word." In the leading case on the subject (*in re Van Duzer*, 34 Ch. D. 623) it was finally decided that a fancy word, to be capable of registration, must be a word having no meaning at all to the average Englishman, such for example as the word "Aeilyton," or, if it has any meaning at all, it must be obviously non-descriptive and non-deceptive.

Definition of "fancy word."

The amending Act of 1888 substituted "invented" words for "fancy" words. In devising an invented word as a trade mark, it should be the aim of the inventor to evolve a word not bearing upon the nature of the goods, and in no degree descriptive of the goods or of the effect produced. For example, "Glazo," as a mark for starch, would probably be refused as being somewhat indicative of the results of using such starch. "Satinine" as a mark for starch, blue, &c., was refused as being descriptive. "Emollio" for face cream, and "Granolithic" for artificial stone, have also been refused on the same grounds.

Examples of descriptive invented words.

Fifthly.—A word or words having no reference to the character or quality of the goods, and not being a geographical name.

Selected words.

Words or expressions registered under this clause need not be "invented" words or expressions.

But, on the other hand, the choice of such existing words or expressions is to some extent limited. Any word or expression savouring of advertisement, recommendation, or description is barred, and these are the very sort of words to which a manufacturer naturally turns. Therefore, an application for "Premier Ebony" as a trade mark for ink would be certain of refusal as being descriptive, and as indicating quality. The term "United Service" has been accepted for soap; "Pharaoh's Serpents" for toys; "Charter Oak" for stoves. But applications of this nature are occasionally refused upon grounds which might sometimes be considered a little far-fetched. Thus, the word "Lady's" to be used in conjunction with the word "Blue" has been refused, because it was thought that to call a blue "Lady's Blue" was by inference a suggestion that this particular blue was of a higher quality than usual.

Examples of meaningless selected words.

Geographical words also are expressly excluded from the category of registrable trade marks, and this rule is very strictly adhered to. Geographical Dictionaries and General Gazetteers are ransacked by the trade mark authorities, with the result that many words which no one ever dreamt of as possessing a geographical signification have turned out to appear in such a list. For example, the word "Camel," which had been already registered before 1888 in connection with driving belts, was refused extension to another class by the Comptroller, after the Amending Act of 1888, because it was discovered that a very small and unimportant parish in Somersetshire bore that name. On appeal this refusal was upheld by the Board of Trade. This excluding clause is intended to prevent in the future the registration of such marks as "Glenfield Starch," "Eton Cigarettes," "Melrose Hair Restorer," "Strathmore Whisky," "Reading Biscuits," "Rugby Portland Cement," and the like.

Geographical words.

Examples of terms not now registrable.

The reason is, that another manufacturer starting business in the same locality might be embarrassed in describing the place of origin of his goods, if the name of the place of origin had been registered as a trade mark by a rival manufacturer. Hence a possible discouragement to trade, which it is no part of the public policy to countenance.

As far as new marks are concerned, the foregoing rules furnish tests by which the registrable or non-registrable nature of a mark can be readily ascertained.

But at the date of the coming into force of the Act, many proprietors of existing and old marks saw themselves in danger of being shut out from registration altogether. As far as "word," "letter," and "figure" trade marks are concerned, it is evident that the new statutory definitions

Old marks.

of a trade mark narrowed the view which traders had been accustomed to take of the limits within which this class of trade marks might be adopted and maintained. Many words, letters, and figures, and combinations of these, not agreeing with the definitions for new marks, were in use before the passing of the Act, and had become so valuable to their owners that to shut them out from registration would have meant the infliction of considerable hardship.

Section 64 allows registration of certain old marks not acceptable as new marks.

A side door was, therefore, opened by Section 64, Sub-section 3 (ii.), under which it is provided that "any *special* and *distinctive* word or words, letter, figure, or combination of letters or figures, or of letters and figures, used as a trade mark *before the Thirteenth day of August, One thousand eight hundred and seventy-five*, may be registered as a trade mark under this part of this Act."

By means of this saving clause an old mark consisting of the particulars set forth, and which would probably be refused as a new mark, may be accepted for registration, provided it fulfils the conditions set forth.

Special and distinctive.

These are, that the word or words, or combination, forming the mark, must be "*special and distinctive*," and that the mark was in use before the 13th August, 1875. As to the interpretation of the term "special and distinctive," the practice of the Patent Office and the effect of a number of decisions tend to show that old marks are not by any means so severely criticised in respect of their special and distinctive nature as are new marks. Many labels and marks which have been in use since before the 13th of August, 1875, and which carry on their faces scarcely any features which can be called special and distinctive, are nevertheless accepted now by the Comptroller.

Conditions of registration as old mark.

Old mark must always have been used in same form.

To be effectual, the requisite prior user must undoubtedly have been as a *bonâ fide* trade mark applied directly to goods within the United Kingdom. The mark claimed must always have been used precisely in the form for which registration is sought. No material addition to or subtraction from the mark as used will be permitted. If the old mark has been altered in any way since the 13th of August, 1875, even although the alteration is but slight, the application to register is almost certain of refusal.

The amount of such prior user is not of much importance. granted that the use has actually taken place and in accordance with the required conditions.

No privileged extension of old mark to new goods.

Registration of an old mark, where such registration implies the enjoyment of privilege in respect of prior use as an old mark, is confined absolutely to the goods upon which the mark has been placed, and does not extend to registration as an old mark in respect of other goods, to which its use has been extended after the 13th of August, 1875. Foreign user is not taken into account, and where goods, whether of British or foreign origin, bearing a certain trade mark, have merely passed through this country on their way to another market, without being exposed here for sale, no privileges are acquired in respect of such prior user.

An incident to the registration of old marks was that, in many trades, different applicants sought to register the same or practically the same mark for the same class of goods. Sometimes the applicants were wholly unaware of the existence of the other marks, and cases arose in which several applicants applied in perfectly good faith to register, as their own, a mark which it turned out had been used by others for an equal or greater length of time in other parts of the country. This was especially the case in devices of a common type, such as anchors, crowns, tridents, &c. Clearly, where ten different manufacturers made ten different applications for the registration of the same mark for the same class of goods, and to which all seemed to have an equal right, it would have been ridiculous, even had it been possible in the face of Section 72, to recognise all of the claims, while to have registered one or two only would have been unjust to the others.

Three Mark Rule.

The Commissioners of Patents therefore formulated what is now known as **The Three Mark Rule.** This was to the effect that an old mark—that is to say, a mark used before the 13th August, 1875—might be registered by different persons in the same trade up to the number of three, and no more. This indulgence was, however, subject to the qualification that if the mark should prove to have been used before the 13th August, 1875, by more than three persons, then it should be treated as a mark *common to the trade*, and not capable of registration by anyone, and if anyone had obtained registration before the Comptroller became aware of the facts, his registration might be cancelled (*re Shewlis & Blakey's Mark* and *Hughes & Young's Mark*, 10 P. O. R. 369). This Three Mark Rule was given effect to in Section 74 of the Patents Act, 1883, which expressly provides that any device which was, before the 13th August, 1875, publicly used by more than three persons, for the same or a similar description of goods, shall, for the purposes of this section, be deemed common to the trade in such goods.

Common marks.

Examples of common marks.

This does not mean that such a common mark is altogether incapable of registration. A common mark consisting, for example, of a word, such as the word "Selected" in the steel pen trade, or "Parchment" in the paper trade; or a combination of words, such as "Bank of England" in the sealing wax trade; or a device, such as a "syphon and glass" in the mineral water trade, or an "anchor" in the umbrella trade; or a combination of words and a device, such as a "crown" with the words "Best Best" in the iron trade, is still registrable, and many such marks have been registered, but only when accompanied by certain additions, whether of words, letters, figures, or devices, which latter are claimed as the distinctive characteristics, all proprietorship in the common mark *per se* being *expressly disclaimed.*

Rule 18 of the "Instructions" issued by the Comptroller runs as follows:—

"In the case of a trade mark used before the 13th August, 1875, common or open marks of any kind may be registered in connection with it; but in the case of a trade mark not so used (*i.e.* a new mark), common or open marks consisting of a word or combination of words only can be registered as a part of the mark.

"In each case the applicant for entry of such common particular or particulars must disclaim the right to the exclusive use of the same in a note at the foot of the application form, such note to be signed by the applicant or his agent."

An owner of such a combination mark is bound to use the combination as registered, and in no other form.

By Section 1 of the Act of 1875, if the owner of a trade mark, whether old or new, failed to obtain registration, he was left powerless to restrain infringement or claim damages. But quickly recognising that there might be cases in which the owner of an old mark had an equitable claim to protection, although his mark might have been held incapable of registration, the Legislature cured this defect in the Amending Act of 1876. The effect of the alteration was, that if the proprietor of a trade mark, in use before the passing of the Principal Act, had applied for and had been refused registration, he might, nevertheless, institute proceedings either for the prevention of wrongful use, or damages for the infringement of such trade mark. Therefore, when an owner of an old mark had applied for registration and had been refused, his possession of the Comptroller's certificate of refusal placed him in a position to exercise whatever rights he might have had in the mark before and independently of the Acts.

Common-law rights of unsuccessful applicants for old marks under Act of 1876.

Certificate of refusal.

Section 77 of the Patents Act, 1883, preserves this arrangement, and is as follows:—

"A person shall not be entitled to institute proceedings to prevent or to recover damages for the infringement of a trade mark unless, in the case of a trade mark capable of being registered under this Act, it has been registered in pursuance of this Act, or of an enactment repealed by this Act, or, in the case of any other trade mark in use before the 13th of August, 1875, registration thereof under this part of this Act, or of an enactment repealed by this Act, has been refused. The Comptroller may, on request, and on payment of the prescribed fee, grant a certificate that such registration has been refused."

Similar provisions under present Act.

The registration of a person as proprietor of a trade mark is *primâ facie* evidence of his right to the exclusive use of the trade mark, and shall, after the expiry of five years from the date of registration, be conclusive evidence of his right to the exclusive use of the trade mark,

Registration *primâ facie* evidence of right to mark.

After five years,

conclusive evidence.

subject to the provisions of the Act (Section 76, Patents Act, 1883). The lapse of five years from registration is, however, no bar to proceedings brought for the purpose of rectifying the Register.

But mark may be expunged even after five years.

Therefore, if the registration of a mark is and has been wrongful from the first, from any cause, it is liable to be expunged from the Register, even after the lapse of five years (*Edwards v. Dennis*, 30 Ch. D. 454).

The registration of trade marks for cutlery and goods within the terms of the Cutlers' Company's Acts is governed by special rules.

Particulars not registrable as marks or parts of marks.

In addition to pictorial representations of the goods, it may be noted that the following particulars are also restricted from registration either as trade marks or as parts of trade marks, viz.:—

(*a*) Names of persons in the possessive case in combination with the names of goods.

(*b*) The Royal Arms or Arms so nearly resembling them as to be calculated to deceive.

(*c*) Representations of the reigning Sovereign or any member of the Royal family.

(*d*) Representations of the Crown or the National Arms or Flags of Great Britain.

(*e*) Such words as "Imperial," "Royal," and the like, either alone or as essential parts of a trade mark.

It has been said that the subjects and citizens of foreign States are upon equal terms with British subjects in obtaining the registration of their trade marks in this country. Sections 103 and 104 of the Act of 1883 further enact that where a subject of a foreign State, which has become a party to the International Convention for the protection of Industrial Property (see Appendix), has made an application for the registration of a trade mark in his own country, he shall be entitled to the registration of his trade mark in this country in priority to other applicants (that is to say, applicants coming after the date of his foreign registration), provided he files his application in this country *within four months* of registration abroad.

Foreigners' rights under International Convention.

These sections, if read literally, would point to the

possibility of the Comptroller being required by a foreign applicant to register a mark under those provisions, which could not be accepted by him if proffered as a new mark by a British subject. Many foreign countries will register almost any description of mark which is presented, and which would, as an original English mark, be certain of refusal here. It may, however, be assumed that the Comptroller would not accept and register as a new mark anything coming to him from a foreign source which did not satisfy the requirements of Section 64.

In *re The Carter Medicine Co.'s Trade Mark* (9 P. O. R. 401), North, J., makes it clear that, in his opinion at least, foreign trade marks, even when registered abroad, should, to insure registration here, conform to the requirements of the British Acts of 1883 to 1888.

It must, however, be confessed that the question is still in an unsettled state, because neither in the above case nor in the analogous instance of *The Californian Fig Syrup Co.'s Mark* (6 P. O. R. 126) were all of the essentials present to compel the Court boldly to confront the consequences of the unhappy wording of Sections 103 and 104.

In such States as have given their adhesion to the Convention, British subjects have, of course, corresponding advantages. Therefore it is to be feared that, if the actual wording of the sections of the British Acts were not given effect to here, British applicants might be differentiated against abroad, greatly to the injury of English commerce.

The probability is, that if the Comptroller were fairly confronted by a foreign applicant, with a mark properly registered in accordance with the rules of the country of origin, however at variance with British requirements, he would grant registration, rather than risk possible reprisals in respect of the registration of greatly more important British marks abroad.

Having thus passed in review the various definitions of trade marks and the qualifications and circumstances which govern registration, this chapter may be fitly closed by a few words of practical advice upon the choice of a trade mark.

Glancing at the list of essentials, as set forth in Section 64 of the Act of 1883, which must be carefully kept in view when deciding upon a trade mark, it is evident that the two most important divisions are—

(1) A distinctive device.

(2) An invented word, or a word arbitrarily chosen, not referring to the goods and not having a geographical significance.

An inspection of the applications advertised in the official *Trade Marks Journal* makes it apparent that, in nine cases out of ten, manufacturers prefer to adopt a distinctive device or picture as their trade mark.

Next in order of popularity appear to be invented and arbitrarily chosen words.

Trade mark should be registered before being put to use.

It is a common indiscretion among manufacturers to design or choose a trade mark, apply it at once to the goods, and seek no protection from registration until the mark has, from its popularity, become a valuable trade property. It then occurs to the user, possibly only after attempts at infringement by others, that it would be advisable to register the mark, and application is made for that purpose. In many cases the response of the Comptroller is to the effect that the mark is not of a registrable nature, or is so similar to another registered mark that acceptance is impossible. Thus the applicant finds himself in this unsatisfactory position, that he must either choose a new mark and regard the time and money spent in advertising and popularising his first mark as thrown away; or he may elect to continue trading under the refused mark with the consciousness that if it should be infringed or fraudulently imitated by a rival, he has only the common-law remedy to depend upon, and can claim none of the advantages which the possession of a certificate of registration would have conferred upon him.

Therefore in designing and deciding upon a device or word as a trade mark, it is advisable that an intending user should first of all make himself certain as to its novelty and acceptability.

The Register of Marks is very jealously guarded against the inclusion of fresh marks which may seem in the smallest degree to interfere with marks already registered. Even where the Comptroller is himself of opinion that the mark applied for is admissible, he will frequently ask the applicant to obtain consent to registration from the registered owner of an existing mark, which may in his estimation present some resemblance, however faint, to the proposed mark, and such permission is not easily obtained. Consent of owner of prior mark.

The proper plan is, therefore, to make an application at once and without loss of time for the registration of the intended mark. Two or three weeks will enable the Comptroller to decide whether or not it is a mark which he can accept. If refused, another mark could then be substituted, and if this is accepted, the trader may then proceed to apply it to his goods with some assurance that he is safe in doing so.

In preparing a "device" trade mark, the design should be broad and simple, so as to be easily remembered when once seen. It should be striking, characteristic, and "distinctive" both in itself and as compared with other marks. Distinctive design must be apparent, and it may safely be said that simple geometric figures and the like, either alone or in combination, stand but little chance of acceptance. Carefully worked little pictures are not easily recognisable at a distance, or at a glance, and a device which is successful as a specimen of the fine arts is not usually the best type of trade mark. As a rule a device which sticks in the memory has something of the grotesque in it. No attempt should be made to introduce representations of the article to which the mark is to be applied. This would infallibly lead to refusal. Existing trade marks in which such representations occur have either been registered as old marks in existence before the 13th August, 1875, or they have been applied for and registered before the present rule against such representations took effect.

It has, however, been held, in the Court of Appeal, that where the shape in which the product is sold is not a necessary, but an arbitrarily given shape, as, for example, blacklead in the form of a dome, a representation of such arbitrarily given shape may be registered as a trade mark (see *in re James*, 33 Ch. D. 392). Doubtful exception to rule that representation of goods not registrable.

When inventing or coining a word as a trade mark, no attempt should be made to refer, either directly or inferentially, to the goods themselves, or to their character, qualities, or effect. "Thermos," for example, has been refused as a trade mark for woollen underclothing, as being suggestive of warmth. In selected words, "Aquarius" has been refused as a trade mark for waterproofs; and many similar examples to the same effect might be given. All words having a geographical significance should also be avoided, and also all words having too close a similarity to known surnames.

Further examples of invented words refused as descriptive.

The remaining forms a trade mark may assume are—

(3) The name of an individual or firm, printed or reproduced in some particular and distinctive manner; and

(4) The copy of a signature.

It is clear that neither of these types is so useful, nor so exclusive, as a "device" or "word" trade mark would be. As to the name, it is only the distinctive manner of printing or reproducing it, or, in other words, the device formed from the name, that constitutes the protected mark. The name itself cannot be confined to one individual. Another of the same name might commence manufacturing the same goods, and would have an equal right to register his distinctively printed name, or his signature, so long as neither imitated the distinctive features of that already registered.

The chief points to be avoided in designing or choosing a trade mark are as follows:—

Features to be avoided in designing trade mark.

(1) *A "device" trade mark* should not include any pictorial representation of the goods, nor of the Royal Arms, nor representations of the reigning Sovereign, nor of any member of the Royal Family, nor of the Royal Crown, nor of the National Arms or Flags of Great Britain.

Word trade marks.

(2) *In a "word" trade mark*, the word or words, whether invented or selected, should not refer to, nor be capable of being construed as referring to, the character, quality, or effect of the goods.

Neither must the word or words constitute a geographical name nor a surname.

(3) *In a "name" trade mark*, the name must not be used in the possessive case in conjunction with the names of goods. Thus, "Bunter's Bath Bricks" is unregistrable even when printed, stamped, or written in some particular and distinctive manner (see official order in *Trade Marks Journal* No. 570, February 27th, 1889). **Name in possessive case.**

(4) *Generally.* Even where the goods are patented specialities, it is advisable not to include the words "Patent" or "By Royal Letters Patent" in the registered mark unless accompanied by the number and date of the patent. **"Patent."**

The reason is this: Should the patent from any cause cease to exist, the trade mark then contains a statement which is not true and is deceptive, and in any proceedings by the owner this would be a most effectual weapon in the hand of a defendant (*Cheavin v. Walker*, 5 Ch. D. 863). On the other hand, should the owner on the expiry of the patent cease to use the word "Patent" in his mark, he might be challenged for using his mark in a form different from that registered.

Such words or phrases as "Registered," "Entered at Stationers' Hall," "To counterfeit this is forgery," &c., must be struck out of all representations of trade marks sent up with applications to register.

CHAPTER III.

PROCEDURE IN REGISTERING A TRADE MARK.

THE mere procedure in registering a trade mark is so simple that a short account will suffice to make it plain.

Persons who may register trade marks.

Any individual, firm, company, or corporation, capable of acquiring and holding property, may register a trade mark.

Foreigners have equal rights with British subjects, provided the mark is actually used on goods sold in this country.

Application forms.

The requisite forms for making application to register trade marks are on sale at all the chief post-offices in the United Kingdom. Form "F," which bears a stamp of five shillings, is the form of application for registration.

Representation of mark.

One of the representations of the mark should be mounted on this form, and the particulars inserted in accordance with the marginal notes which are printed on the sheet.

Classification of goods.

All goods, in respect of which trade marks may be registered, are divided into fifty classes, and the applicant must state the class under which he desires to claim the mark, and also particularise the goods to which the mark is to be applied. This classification will be found in the Trade Mark Rules in the Appendix.

Marks should be registered only for goods actually dealt with.

It is important to note here that an applicant should not claim the mark for goods in which he does not deal or intend to deal. By a recent regulation the Comptroller draws attention to the practice of applying for marks in Class 50 for miscellaneous goods, which he says "it is difficult to suppose would be generally dealt with by the same firm." He goes on to say that care should be taken not to include goods for which the mark is not intended, and that evidence may be asked to show that the goods specified are actually made or dealt in by the applicant. This restraint, which is really applicable to all classes, is directly in the interests of applicants, seeing that registration in respect of goods not traded in may afterwards be made the subject of a motion by some aggrieved person to rectify the Register by expunging or limiting the mark, and this notwithstanding that the mark has been five years on the Register. A case bearing directly upon this point is that of *Edwards v. Dennis* (30 Ch. D. 454). But there is practically no difficulty in getting the Court to expunge a trade mark registered in this improper manner. In a recent motion, heard on the 3rd April, 1894, by Mr. Justice Stirling, *Reddaway & Co.* applied to rectify the Register by expunging certain marks registered by *Peek & Co.* in respect of goods in which *Peek* did not deal. The motion was unopposed, and the order for rectification made accordingly.

The application form, "F," is signed by the applicant, or by his agent duly authorised. If the application is made by a firm, the form may be signed in the firm's name by a partner. If made by a company, the secretary or other officer or a director may sign his own name, adding his proper designation, and also the words "For the Company."

Two additional representations of the mark must accompany the application form "F," mounted on sheets of equal size with the form "F," and bearing the name and address of the applicant or his agent. In Classes 23 to 35 inclusive (textile goods and materials), four additional representations of the mark must be supplied. Additional representations.

Where the representations of the mark are too large to mount on forms "F" and "G," they may be mounted on linen, and folded and fixed to the forms. The papers, when completed, may be delivered or posted to "The Comptroller, Patent Office (Trade Marks Branch), 25 Southampton Buildings, London."

In the course of two or three weeks the applicant will be advised either of the acceptance of his mark, or that it has been objected to or refused by the Comptroller. When refusal takes place it is based either on resemblance of the mark to existing marks on the register, to which the applicant will be referred, or on the ground of non-conformance with the requirements set forth in the last chapter. Dealings of Comptroller with application.

Sometimes the objection of the Comptroller to register a mark on account of its resemblance to an existing mark may be got over by obtaining the consent of the owner of the prior mark. When so objected to, and the resemblance seems remote, it is advisable to sound the owner of the prior mark with the view of obtaining his consent to registration, even where this is not suggested by the Comptroller. If the prior owner gives his consent, the Comptroller will in many cases withdraw his objection.

When the mark is accepted by the Comptroller, the notice of acceptance calls upon the applicant to furnish a wood block or electrotype for the purpose of illustrating the advertisement of the mark in the official *Trade Marks Journal*. Such a block or electrotype should correspond exactly with the representations accompanying the application, Notice of acceptance. Advertisement.

and should not be more than two inches square. If larger, an additional charge of two shillings for each additional inch or part of an inch will be made. The largest space available is eight inches by six inches.

Nothing but the actual mark as applied for should appear on the face of the block or electrotype. The number of the application should be written or printed on the side of the block or foundation of the electrotype.

Trade Marks Journal.

The *Trade Marks Journal* (price sixpence) is published weekly, and contains a print of each mark advertised, with particulars of the class and applicant's name and address. When the mark is not illustrated, as for example in the Cotton Classes, the advertisement refers to a place or places where a representation of the mark can be seen.

Certificate of registration.

If no opposition to registration is offered within one month from the date of advertisement in the Journal, the applicant is called upon to pay the final fee (£1), and the certificate of registration is at once issued. This is the short history of a trade mark application where nothing is done either by the Comptroller or by outsiders to trouble or arrest its progress. But any applicant should be prepared for such a possibility.

Comptroller's objection or refusal.

The Comptroller's objection to register a mark submitted to him, whether based on the ground of nonconformity to the rules, or because of resemblance to an existing mark, is frequently accompanied by an invitation to the applicant to appear before him personally or by representative, and state his case in support of the application. If the applicant does not accept this invitation, or if he fails at the hearing to convince the Comptroller that his mark should be accepted, the mark is absolutely refused. If dissatisfied with the decision of the Comptroller, the applicant may appeal to the Board of Trade, and the Board may either decide the matter, or may if they think fit refer the appeal to the Court.

Hearing in support of application.

Appeal to Board of Trade.

Opposition.

If, on the other hand, the mark should be opposed by a rival trader or by any other aggrieved person who thinks his interests would be imperilled by the registration of the mark, the notice of opposition should be given within one month from the date of the Journal containing the advertisement. The time for opposition might, however, be extended by the Comptroller, on good cause being shown, for a period of not more than three months.

Notice of opposition.

The notice of opposition must state the ground or grounds on which the opponent intends to oppose the registration, and be signed by himself or by his solicitor or agent, and must contain an address for service in the United Kingdom. The form "J" given in the Rules is to be adopted, with such variations as are called for by the circumstances. This form bears a one pound stamp.

When the opponent bases his opposition upon the existence on the Register of a trade mark similar to the mark opposed, the notice must state the date of registration and the number on the Register of such alleged anticipatory trade mark.

Counter-statement by applicant.

Within one month after receipt of this notice of opposition, or within such further time as the Comptroller may allow, the applicant may send to the Comptroller a counter-statement, in duplicate, of the grounds on which he relies to support his application. If he fails to send this counter-statement, he is considered to have abandoned his application.

Declaration by opponent.

The next step is taken by the opponent, who must leave a declaration or declarations containing the evidence upon which he relies to support his opposition. Such declaration must be filed within two months after the expiry of one month (or such further time, not exceeding three months, as the Comptroller may allow) from the date of the advertisement of the mark. The opponent must at the same time deliver a copy of the declaration to the applicant.

Counter-declaration by applicant.

Within one month from the delivery of the said copy, the applicant should leave his declaration or declarations in support of his application, and in reply to the opponent's declarations, and should supply the opponent with a copy thereof.

Reply by opponent.

Within seven days from the receipt of such copy, the opponent may leave further declarations, which should be confined strictly to matters in reply to the statements in the opponent's declarations.

This completes the evidence, and no further declarations can be filed by either party, except with the consent of the other or by special leave of the Comptroller. On completion of the evidence, the Comptroller, upon the application of either party, and on the payment of the prescribed fee (£1), appoints a time for hearing the case, and gives at least seven days' notice of the appointment to the applicant and opponent.

Hearing.

At the hearing, the parties or their representatives attend and state their case fully; the declarations form the groundwork of all that is said, and no opposition is allowed which has not been set forth in, or does not directly spring from, the declarations filed. The decision of the Comptroller is usually signified to the parties in writing, within from one to two weeks from the hearing. Should either of the parties be dissatisfied with the decision, he may appeal to the Board of Trade. Notice of the intention to appeal should be left at the Patent Office within one month from the date of the Comptroller's decision. The notice of appeal must be accompanied by a written statement of the grounds of appeal and of the appellant's case in support. In addition to serving the Patent Office with these papers, a copy of the notice of appeal and of the appellant's case in support must be sent to the Secretary of the Board of Trade, Whitehall Gardens, London, and also to the other party in the matter.

Decision.

Appeal to Board of Trade.

Board of Trade may hear appeal or may refer to Court.

The Board of Trade then decide whether they will hear the appeal or refer the matter to the Court. If they decide to hear the appeal, seven days' notice of the hearing is given to the appellant, and to the Comptroller, and to the respondent. The evidence used at the hearing before the Board of Trade is the same as that used before the Comptroller.

A reference to the Court is always more satisfactory where there are equitable reasons why registration should be granted, although a rigid reading of the Act and the Rules seems to bar registration. The Comptroller and the Board of Trade, however they may wish to help the applicant, always find themselves bound to adhere to the strict letter of the Act and Rules, whereas the Court may exercise such discretion as will prevent hardship.

Although not specified, the Chancery Division of the High Court of Justice is meant by "the Court," and in the case of applications at the Manchester Office "the Court" means also the Lancaster Palatine Chancery (Section 26 of the Act of 1888).

Opposition is usually encountered from the owner of another similar registered mark, but this is not always the case. The opponent might enter opposition upon other grounds.

If an applicant abandons his application immediately upon being notified of opposition, he may be called upon to pay to the opponent such costs of the opposition as the Comptroller may think reasonable. But this is the only stage in the proceedings at which the Comptroller has power to award costs. If the matter proceeds to a hearing, no costs are allowed to either party. Costs.

Even if the case is ultimately heard by the Court, and the opponent is successful, no costs are allowed to him in respect of the proceedings below—*i.e.* before the Comptroller and the Board of Trade.

Sheffield Marks.

The registration of trade marks in respect of goods within the Cutlers' Company's Acts is regulated by special rules. The privileges of the Cutlers' Company are recognised and the regulations mainly expressed in Section 81 of the Act of 1883. Sheffield Register.

The Cutlers' Company was authorised to establish at Sheffield a new Register of Trade Marks, to be called the Sheffield Register, and to this Register were transferred all trade marks for cutlery and kindred goods which had been registered or entered before the 1st of January, 1889, by persons carrying on business in Hallamshire, or within six miles thereof. The Company is also empowered to enter in the Sheffield Register all trade marks which have been assigned by the Cutlers' Company, and actually used before the 1st January, 1884, but which have not been entered in either of the other Registers.

Applications for registration of trade marks for metal goods, if made by persons carrying on business in Hallam-

Procedure in registering Sheffield marks.

shire or within six miles thereof, are to be sent direct to the Cutlers' Company; if made by a person outside this area, the application is to be sent to the Comptroller, who communicates with the Cutlers' Company. When an application is made direct to the Company, they notify the Comptroller of the fact, and if the Comptroller has no objection to make, the application is proceeded with by the Company. As a matter of fact, the Comptroller acts in unison with the Company, and if both are of opinion that the mark may proceed, registration can be effected, and not otherwise.

Any person considering himself aggrieved by refusal of his application by the Company may appeal to the Court.

"Metal goods."

The expression "metal goods" used in the Act is not confined to cutlery, but is explained to mean "all metals, whether wrought, unwrought, or partly wrought, and all goods composed wholly or partly of any metal."

Duration of registration.

Renewal.

When a trade mark has been registered, the period of protection lasts for fourteen years. At the end of that time the registration may be kept in force for another fourteen years upon payment of a renewal fee of one pound, and so on from time to time at the expiry of each successive period of fourteen years, so that the registration of a trade mark may be kept in force for an indefinite time. If this renewal fee is not paid, the Comptroller may remove the mark from the Register within three months from the termination of the fourteen years. If the renewal fee is paid before the termination of the three months, an additional fine of ten shillings is imposed. But even if the three months should pass without payment, and the mark has actually been expunged from the Register, the Comptroller will readily restore the mark if a sufficient explanation is forthcoming, and upon payment of an additional fine of one pound.

Lapse by non-payment of renewal fee.

Rights lost by abandonment, disuse, or acquiescence.

The right to a registered trade mark might also be lost to the proprietor by abandonment, which might mean either total abandonment by prolonged disuse on his own part, or abandonment of his exclusive right by acquiescence in the use of the mark by others, to such an extent as to create common and concurrent right in others. To constitute abandonment, the intention to abandon must, however, be shown. Mere non-user of a trade mark for a length of time does not *per se* show abandonment. The period of time during which a trade mark has been disused would, of course, be an element of importance. It has been said (*in re Grossmith*, 60 L. T., N. S. 612) that non-user for eleven years, during which the sale of the goods had ceased, and all labels had been destroyed, amounted to abandonment. It cannot, however, be said with certainty that the Court would look upon mere disuse of a trade mark, for four or five years for example, as abandonment, unless intention to abandon was clearly present.

Penalty for falsely representing trade mark as registered.

Under Section 105 of the Act, any person who represents a trade mark applied to any article sold by him as "registered" which is not so, shall be liable for every offence, on summary conviction, to a fine not exceeding five pounds.

CHAPTER IV.

RECTIFICATION OF REGISTER BY THE REMOVAL OR LIMITATION OF REGISTERED MARKS.

Application to register equivalent to public use.

By Section 75 of the 1888 portion of the Act, it is provided that application for registration of a trade mark shall be equivalent to public use of the mark, and the date of the application shall be deemed to be the date of the registration. Thus, in instituting proceedings for infringement, the registered proprietor of a trade mark is no longer called upon, as he formerly was, to prove "lawful user" before he can obtain relief in a Court of law or equity for the infringement of his mark. Registration of the mark is now notice to the world, and is equivalent to "lawful user" at common law. It must not, however, be inferred that the owner of a mark which has merely been registered, but not put to use at all, could obtain an injunction against someone afterwards using the mark. The essence of trade mark law is entirely against the assumption that anyone should be permitted to harass his neighbours by registering and shelving a mark, only asserting his proprietorship when another, wittingly or unwittingly, uses the mark for trade purposes.

Mark to be of avail must be actually put to use.

Mark must be new and original.

Again, a mark to be good, even after registration, should in the first place have been original, or either the property or design of the applicant. A person cannot register as a new mark something which has already been used by another person in the same trade (see *Wragg's Trade Mark*, 29 Ch. D. 551). So much may be gathered from the remarks of Cotton, L.J., in *Hudson's Case* (32 Ch. D. 311), and from what was said by the President of the Court of Appeal in the same matter.

Registration *primâ facie*, and after five years conclusive, evidence of owner's right.

When a person has been placed upon the Register as proprietor of a trade mark, this is *primâ facie* evidence of his right to the exclusive use of the mark, and after the expiry of five years from the date of registration it is *conclusive* evidence of his right (Section 76). This, however, is upon the assumption that the registration was in the first place good: if not, it is clear that the title can be challenged, even after the expiry of five years. As Jessel, M.R., remarked in *re Palmer* (21 Ch. D. 53), "The Act only says that after five years the person who has registered a trade mark shall be entitled to the trade mark, but does not say that the mark, as registered, shall be deemed to be a trade mark." As a matter of fact, many trade marks have been expunged from the Register after having been registered for a much longer period than five years.

But title may be challenged even after five years.

Reasons for expunging trade mark.

The reasons for removing a trade mark from the Register are various. In many cases the reasons given by the Court have been practically a revision of the Comptroller's judgment in registering the marks at all, and have to do with inherent defects in the marks themselves, which should have prevented their registration in the first instance. Examples of these are to be found in "name marks," because of the name not being printed or reproduced in a distinctive manner; in "word" marks, because of the word not being distinctive, or being descriptive or deceptive, or common to the trade (*re Wragg's Trade Mark*, 29 Ch. D. 551; also *Hyde & Co.'s Mark*, 7 Ch. D. 724); or where a mark has been registered as an old mark in use before 1875 without being really so (*Baker v. Rawson*, 45 Ch. D. 519). To these may be added marks improperly registered for goods for which they were not used or intended to be used (*Edwards v. Dennis*, 30 Ch. D. 454; *Reddaway v. Peek*, page 110); marks, the registered proprietors of which carry on no business; marks, too similar to already registered marks; marks, improperly registered by a servant of the real owner; and marks, the registered owners of which have allowed others to use them so that they have lost their significance as being distinctive of one maker's goods (*re Wood's Trade Mark*, 32 Ch. D. 247). Examples.

These are the principal grounds upon which a registered trade mark may be successfully challenged and removed from the Register, or restricted as to scope.

Any person who is aggrieved may take proceedings to rectify the Register, and, according to Fry, L.J., any person aggrieved means every person who will in reasonable probability suffer any injury or loss (using the words in a legal and not in a sentimental sense) from the other persons claiming to use the mark" (*in re Rivière*, 53 L. J., Ch. 455). Definition of "aggrieved person."

In *re The Apollinaris Company's Marks* the same Judge, in reviewing the question whether the appellants, the *Vichy Water Company*, were or were not "persons aggrieved" within the Act, said, "We are of opinion that whenever one trader, by means of his wrongly registered trade mark, narrows the area of business open to his rivals, and thereby either immediately excludes or with reasonable probability will in the future exclude a rival firm from a portion of that trade into which he desires to enter, then that rival is an aggrieved person." Trade rival.

Of course a person against whom proceedings have been

Defendant in action.

brought by the owner of an improperly registered trade mark is an aggrieved person, and where the validity of the registration is capable of being attacked, the defendant should not only defend himself from the proceedings, but should also move to rectify the Register.

This is specially advisable if the mark has been on the Register for five years, as the defendant would then be fettered in meeting the charge of infringement by reason of the privileged position thereby acquired by the plaintiff.

Register might be amended.

Without going to the extent of removing the mark entirely from the Register, the entry might, on the application of an interested party, or of the proprietor, be purged of redundance or mis-statement, or the entry might be varied so as to cure the mark of informalities or errors, or to vary the entry in accordance with a change of proprietorship. These variations in the entry may be made with the object of (*a*) restricting the goods to which the mark is stated to be applicable (*re Edwards's Trade Mark*, 30 Ch. D. 454); (*b*) striking out some part of the mark; (*c*) entering a partial disclaimer on the Register; or (*d*) altering the name of the registered proprietor.

As to the extent to which such alterations may be carried, the 92nd Section of the Act simply says that application may be made to the Court for leave to add to or alter a mark in any particular "not being an essential particular" within the meaning of the Act.

Alteration of old marks permissible only in non-essential details.

This permission to alter has been held, but within extremely narrow limits, to apply to old as well as to new marks (see *Guinness, Son & Co.*, 5 P. O. R. 316; *Allsopp & Sons, Limited*, &c., where leave was given to amend old marks by adding the word "Limited" to the names). As to what is an essential particular of a mark, Mr. Justice Kekewich, in *re Adams's Trade Mark* (9 P. O. R. 174), held that the word "Patent" in an old trade mark was so essential that he would not allow the alteration to be made. A new mark would not, however, be so stringently treated, and alterations are more readily allowed than in the case of old marks.

CHAPTER V.

TRANSFER OF TRADE MARKS.

Trade marks transferable only when joined to goodwill of business.

TRADE MARKS can be assigned and transferred only in connection with the goodwill of the business in which the mark has been used. Therefore, the owner of a mark cannot legally dispose of it to another, without at the same time transferring to him at least so much of the business as relates to the goods for which the mark has been registered. Fry, L.J., in *Edwards v. Dennis* (30 Ch. D. 454), has said, "An assignee has no exclusive right to a trade mark, unless the assignment is of a business co-extensive with the trade mark as registered." Again, trade marks which have been registered as a series cannot be broken up and disposed of piecemeal. They must be assigned and transmitted as they were registered—viz., as a series (Section 66).

Registration in series must be followed by transfer in series.

The reasons for this indissoluble union between a trade mark and the goods or business which have made the mark a readily accepted sign of certain qualities, are plain. The reputation of the mark has been made by the goods, and the mark must follow the business in those particular goods. Otherwise it might be made an instrument of fraud. This is so far the case that, in *Shipwright v. Clements* (19 W. R. 599), Vice-Chancellor Malins held that, if a business were sold without any word being said about the trade mark, the mark would be understood and held to pass to the purchaser. This is a rule which holds good in American practice as well as here.

New owner placed on Register.

When a trade mark has thus been assigned or transferred, the new proprietor should at once get his name put upon the Register in place of that of the former owner. This is done by sending to the Comptroller a formal request to alter the Register, showing the particulars of the transfer and that the mark has been accompanied by the goodwill of the business, the whole of the several statements being verified by statutory declaration.

Trade mark an asset in bankruptcy.

On the bankruptcy of the owner of a trade mark, the mark, together with his other effects, passes to his representative in bankruptcy, who has the power to deal with it as with any other asset. When one of the members of a partnership, otherwise solvent, becomes bankrupt, his individual share or interest in the mark cannot be sold, but will pass to the solvent partner or partners. The reason of this is, that the undivided interest in the trade mark is valueless apart from the goodwill. If the owner of a trade mark, carrying on a business, assumes a partner or partners, the trade mark becomes part of the partnership assets, unless specially reserved by the original owner. The new partner or partners is or are entitled to registration as joint owner or owners with the original proprietor.

An asset in partnership.

Disposal of trade mark on dissolution of partnership.

On dissolution of partnership, the mark goes with the goodwill. If one of the partners carries on the old business, the trade mark passes to him with the goodwill, the value of the interest in the mark being accounted for to the retiring partner as one of the partnership assets. But if the partners agree to divide the partnership assets and carry on the same business separately, each is at liberty to use the mark (*Condy v. Mitchell*, 37 L. T., N. S. 268; C. A. 37 L. T., N. S. 766). But a former partner in a dissolved partnership was, in *Hanson v. Game Harrison* (9 P. O. R. 186), prevented from allowing a company carrying on business, with which he afterwards became associated, to use one of the marks of the former partnership. When a trade mark is designed and used in a joint adventure, neither of the parties has a right to the mark after the adventure is closed (*re Jones's Trade Mark*, 53 L. T. 1).

Joint adventure.

Trade mark personal property.

On the death of the proprietor of a trade mark the mark passes to his personal representative with the rest of his personal property. The owner may bequeath his trade mark to whomsoever he pleases, but always in connection with the goodwill of the business.

CHAPTER VI.

LEGAL PROCEEDINGS IN CONNECTION WITH TRADE MARKS.

THE foregoing chapters have dealt mainly with the definition, acquisition, and transfer of trade marks. But even so slight a sketch of the subject as this work professes to embody would be wholly incomplete if an indication were not given of the means by which trade mark property is defended and maintained.

When the registered owner of a trade mark finds that his rights are being infringed, there are three remedies which he may adopt:— Three remedies for infringement of mark.

(1) He may bring an action in the Chancery Division of the High Court for an injunction to restrain the infringer from using the mark, with a claim for damages or an account of profits. Chancery.

(2) He may bring an action in the Queen's Bench Division of the High Court, claiming damages on the ground of false representation. Common law.

(3) He may institute a criminal prosecution under the Merchandise Marks Act, 1887, by summons before a magistrate or justice of the peace, or by indictment. Criminal.

The first is the most usual proceeding; the second is scarcely ever employed, and will not be particularly referred to here; the third is made use of in aggravated cases, and possesses the virtue of being a swift, effective, and comparatively cheap remedy.

ACTION IN THE CHANCERY DIVISION.

The growth of the Chancery jurisdiction in trade marks has been of a gradual nature, but the beneficial description of the remedy by injunction and account, as compared with Chancery Division.

the common-law remedy of damages, has resulted in making it at the present day almost the sole arena for the trial of the civil suit in trade mark cases.

The principles upon which the Courts of Equity act in the case of trade marks are, that the motives of the infringer are immaterial. He may have acted innocently and without the intention of defrauding anyone (see the remarks of Chitty, J., in *Upmann v. Forester*, 24 Ch. D. 231). He may even himself have designed the offending mark, and may have intended to use it as his own mark. He may have been absolutely ignorant of the existence of the mark which he has infringed. All of this matters nothing. The Court's duty is to protect the public, and it is undeniable that as soon as the goods leave the defendant, and pass from hand to hand, they may be made the instruments of fraud, and ultimate purchasers may believe that they were originally manufactured by the person entitled to the genuine mark.

Innocence of infringer not material to issue.

The Court protects the public as well as the owner.

Even when the maker, knowing that they are not the goods of the person entitled to use the trade mark, tells this to the immediate purchaser, thinking thereby to clear himself from the charge of fraud, still he is not absolved, because, as the goods pass on from hand to hand, this representation does not pass on with them, and thus the next purchaser or the public at large may be deceived Consequently, all that has to be done is to show that the trade mark has been taken.

What was originally not fraudulent misrepresentation may afterwards become so.

This is the gist of a deliverance by Sir G. Jessel, M.R., in *The Singer Manufacturing Co. v. Wilson* (2 Ch. D. 434), and summarises the principles of the Court of Chancery in such cases. So that it is not now necessary to show intentional fraud, as would be the case in common law. All that is necessary in equity is to show that the plaintiff has an exclusive right to use the mark, and that the mark has been taken by the defendant (Lord Westbury, C., in *The Leather Cloth Company's Case*, 4 De G. J. & S. 137).

Discovery and inspection.

Where full disclosure of facts is desirable, the Court will grant discovery and inspection, and upon establishment of the plaintiff's allegations will issue an injunction, and will also, if thought necessary, order the delivery up and destruction of the labels or attachments bearing the infringing mark. Or the goods themselves may be ordered to be produced for the erasure of the marks which they bear; or, if this cannot be done without destroying the goods, their destruction might in some instances be ordered.

An innocent infringer will not, however, be so stringently dealt with as a wilful wrongdoer, especially if prompt submission is made. But it is unlikely that he will escape payment of the costs (see Justice Chitty in *Upmann v. Forester*); but note Stirling, J., in *American Tobacco Co. v. Guest* (9 P. O. R. 218), which was the case of an innocent infringer who had made a very small purchase of cigarettes bearing the false mark.

Trial of trade mark cases. As a rule, trade mark cases are heard by a judge without a jury, and even where a defendant in such a case gave notice of trial before a judge and special jury, it was held that the case must be heard without a jury (*Spratt's Patent v. Ward & Co.*, 11 Ch. D. 240).

Application for injunction. In applying for an interlocutory injunction, promptness in taking action is above all things to be recommended to the plaintiff. Delay is looked upon unfavourably by the Court, unless it can be conclusively shown that such delay was necessary to secure the requisite evidence to establish the plaintiff's case.

Terms of injunction. The injunction granted may assume various forms. It might be an absolute order to cease using the offending mark in any way, or the injunction might extend only to a certain feature or to certain features of the mark; or it might be limited by an undertaking on the defendant's part to add something which will make the mark more distinctive as compared with the plaintiff's mark.

Breach of injunction. If the defendant after issue of an injunction should continue to use the disputed mark or something so like it as to be practically the same thing, he is liable to committal for contempt. If, however, it is a question whether the defendant's action constitutes a *direct* breach of the injunction, so as to render him liable to committal, the terms of the injunction may be enlarged so as to include the new breach, and the defendant ordered to pay all costs (*Cartier v. May*, Dig. 200).

A trade mark being personal property, on the death of a plaintiff his representatives are entitled to continue the action.

Grounds of action.

As to the grounds upon which action may be taken, these are so multitudinous that it is impossible to give more than a few instances of cases brought upon diverse issues.

Imitation of a registered mark or of its essential features.

In the rare instances where a trade mark is boldly annexed *in toto*, and where the infringement is palpable, there is of course no difficulty in getting relief. But this is seldom the case, and as a rule the Court has rather to deal with colourable imitations or instances where important or essential features of a mark are taken, without an absolute infringement of the whole. It might even be that, without taking a single individual feature of a mark, a label or ticket or device might be produced by an infringer, which would, under a cursory inspection, deceive a purchaser into the belief that it really was the mark which it was intended to imitate (see James, L.J., in *Worthington's Trade Mark*, 14 Ch. D. 8). Sometimes, again, a representation of some animal or thing forming a trade mark, or an essential part of a trade mark, may become so well known by name alone that any other mark containing a representation of the same animal or thing, no matter how different in appearace or arrangement, would infallibly work injustice to the original owner.

Or of general appearance.

Device mark may be infringed by name mark.

Orr-Ewing v. Johnstone.

For example, in *Orr-Ewing v. Johnstone* (7 App. Cas. 219) the plaintiff had a mark which he applied to red yarn, an essential feature of the mark being the representation of two elephants. From this the goods had come to be known as the "Two Elephant" yarn. The defendants had also begun to use a ticket upon which two elephants figured. It was not contended that there was any deceptive resemblance between the tickets: nevertheless an injunction issued against the defendants, in terms which practically forbade them from representing or alluding to elephants at all in trade marks for this class of goods.

Lord Cranworth in *Seixo v. Provezende.*

Lord Cranworth, in his judgment in *Seixo v. Provezende* (L. R. 1 Ch. 192), says, "I do not consider the actual physical resemblance of the two marks to be the sole question for consideration. If the goods of a manufacturer have, from the mark or device he has used, become known in the market by a particular name, I think that the adoption by a rival trader of any mark which will cause his goods to bear the same name, may be as much a violation of the rights of that manufacturer as the actual copying of his device." The same principle was followed in *Read v. Richardson* (45 L. T., N. S. 54), where the beer of the plaintiffs having become well known in the market as "Dog's Head Beer," the defendants were restrained from using any representation of a dog's head on their bottle labels, no matter how unlike the plaintiffs'.

Dog's Head Beer case.

A colourable imitation of a trade mark, whether consisting of a device or of a word, can generally be restrained, but it depends upon the extent of the resemblance. As far as words are concerned, "Tovril" has been restrained as an obvious imitation of "Bovril," and the use of the word "Steinberg" on pianos has been put down as being too similar to "Steinway." As regards a device, a beehive has been held to be a colourable imitation of a bell of a similar shape, similarly printed on a label. A church within a triangle on a beer label has been suppressed as being too like the triangular mark of Bass. A sprig of grape-vine has been held to infringe a sprig of hop-vine; and a unicorn's head has been considered too similar to a horse's head. But even with these examples it is impossible to do more than generalise. The Court will endeavour to look at the marks from the point of view of the general public, and where there is sufficient resemblance between the marks, relief will be granted.

Imitative words restrained.

Similar devices restrained.

The case of a mark, which is of any value to its owner, becoming public property (or *publici juris*, to use the accepted term) owing to the negligence of its originator, is not likely to occur under present conditions.

Trade mark becoming *publici juris*.

All of the instances that can be quoted occurred before the Registration Act of 1875. "Harvey's Sauce" is a case in point of a designation which was at one time proper to one manufacturer only, but which by neglect or licence had

By neglect or licence.

in time become the designation of an article capable of being made and sold by anyone, under the name of "Harvey's Sauce." The same thing occurred in the case of "Worcestershire Sauce." These, and other marks in a similar category, would have been now of enormous value, had their original owners sustained their rights in them; but, as has been said, similar cases are not now likely to occur.

Other instances where trade marks have become *publici juris* are to be found in the case of trade names given to patented articles. The sewing machine industry furnishes one or two examples, from which it may be drawn that it is permissible to use the name of the original patentees and manufacturers in describing an article the patent for which has expired, so long as the name is sufficiently qualified as to make it plain who are really the manufacturers. *The Wheeler and Wilson Sewing Machine Company*, after the expiry of their patent, tried to prevent other manufacturers from selling machines of their own make as "Wheeler and Wilson Machines," but failed. The same ill success attended suits on similar issues brought by *The Singer Manufacturing Company*, and in the end it was established that a manufacturer, affixing his own name to his machine, could not be restrained from using the name of the original patentees and makers as descriptive of the principle upon which the machines were made, granted that the said patentees are not also represented as the actual makers. In *The Singer Manufacturing Company v. Spence & Co.* (10 P. O. R. 297) the company succeeded in restraining the use of their name by the defendants in such a manner as to induce the belief that the machines sold by the defendants were the manufacture of the plaintiffs.

By operation of natural right.

Similar instances of a name becoming *publici juris* are to be found in the cases of "Galloway Tubes" for boilers, "Worthington Pumps," &c.

A very curious, and to inventors especially a very interesting question, bearing in some degree upon the same subject, was raised during the consideration of the case of the *Linoleum Manufacturing Company v. Nairn* (7 Ch. D. 834). The question was this: Granted that a manufacturer invents and patents an entirely new article, to describe which he invents an entirely new name, and then registers that name as a trade mark, can he preserve the right to be the sole user of the invented name which he has constituted his trade mark, after the expiry of his patent? Mr. Justice Fry, in the course of his judgment, distinctly puts it that he cannot. In the case mentioned linoleum floorcloth was a newly invented article of manufacture. The very name "Linoleum" was new, and had been invented to designate it.

***Semble*, an invented name applied to a newly invented and patented product, and registered as a trade mark, becomes *publici juris* on the expiry of the patent.**

The plaintiff did not, however, register the word "Linoleum" alone as a trade mark. The mark consisted of the words "Linoleum Floor Cloth" printed on the border of a lozenge. In the centre of the lozenge were a *fleur-de-lys* and the words "F. Walton's Patent." Mr. Justice Fry considered the mark to consist of the combination as registered, and refused to allow the plaintiffs to pick out the word "Linoleum," and uphold that to be the really essential part of their trade mark. It must be confessed that, in coming to this decision, he was considerably supported by the acts of the plaintiffs themselves.

Although the Judge did not directly say so, it is not difficult to see, from the drift of his remarks, that, even had the plaintiffs registered the word "Linoleum" alone as their trade mark, he would have refused an injunction. Cotton, L.J., in *Slazenger v. Feltham* (6 P. O. R. 531), evidently adopted this reading of the judgment in the linoleum case.

Slazenger v. Feltham.

Had the word "Linoleum" alone been registered, and had the mark been upheld, the result would practically have been to extend the monopoly of the patent indefinitely, since no one but the patentee could have sold the floorcloth as "Linoleum," even after the expiry of the patent. This extension of the monopoly beyond the period of patent right would clearly be against public policy, and it is plain that in the case of a newly invented article for which a new name has to be found, such as "Dynamite," "Cordite," and "Roburite," and which obtains a worldwide fame under that name, and that name only, it would never do to vest the original makers and patentees with a perpetual right to the only name by which the article is, or possibly can be, known to the public.

Claims when seeking injunction.

Account of profits.

Persons seeking an injunction should as a rule claim an account of profits in preference to damages, owing to the difficulty in proving the amount of damage flowing from the infringement. In the event of the plaintiff proving successful, the account of profits is made out under the direction of the chief clerk, in the chambers of the judge who has granted the injunction.

Owing to the number of questions that arise in making out such an account, it is advisable to place the inspection and examination of the defendant's books in the hands of a reliable accountant. Generally, however, the defendant compromises by the offer of a lump sum, which, in most cases, it is best to accept.

Costs.

As a rule costs follow the result of the action, unless the plaintiff, by delay in bringing his action, or unreasonable treatment of the defendant's offers of compromise, has placed himself in such a position that the Court, while granting the injunction, refuses the plaintiff his costs.

Advertisement of injunction.

The fact of an injunction having been obtained may be published by advertisement in a newspaper or by circular. The terms of such an advertisement should, however, be the subject of careful consideration and trustworthy advice before it is published.

CHAPTER VII.

THE CRIMINAL PROSECUTION.

Merchandise Marks Act, 1887.

"Forging" a trade mark.

FOLLOWING the Merchandise Marks Act of 1862, the new *Merchandise Marks Act of* 1887 makes the forgery of trade marks a misdemeanour. To "forge" a trade mark means the making of a spurious trade mark so like an existing mark for the same goods as to be calculated to deceive. The term also means falsifying a genuine trade mark by alteration, addition, erasure, or other change. If these acts are done without the assent of the proprietor of the genuine trade mark, they constitute offences under the Act, and the person charged must prove that he acted without intent to defraud. In this, the present Act differs from the former Act of 1862, which threw the onus of proving "intent to defraud" upon the prosecutor. It is also an offence to make any die, block, machine, or other instrument, for the purpose of forging or being used to forge a trade mark. "Forging" a block.

The following are the offences and punishments as set forth in the Act, so far as trade marks are concerned:—

OFFENCES.

Section 2 (1). Every person who— Offences.

(*a*) Forges any trade mark; or Forging a trade mark.

(*b*) Falsely applies to goods any trade mark or any mark so nearly resembling a trade mark as to be calculated to deceive; or Falsely applying.

(*c*) Makes any die, block, machine, or other instrument for the purpose of forging or of being used for forging a trade mark; or Making printing block.

(*d*) Applies any false trade description to goods; or False description.

(*e*) Disposes of or has in his possession any die, block, machine, or other instrument for the purpose of forging a trade mark; or Selling or possessing printing block.

(*f*) Causes any of the things above in this section mentioned to be done, General.

shall, subject to the provisions of this Act, and unless he proves that he acted without intent to defraud, be guilty of an offence against this Act.

(2) Every person who sells, or exposes for, or has in his possession for, sale, or any purpose of trade or manufacture, any goods or things to which any forged trade mark or false trade description is applied, or to which any trade mark, or mark so nearly resembling a trade mark as to be Persons committing offences should prove absence of guilty knowledge, and must assist

prosecutor to discover real offenders.

calculated to deceive, is falsely applied, as the case may be, shall, unless he proves—

(*a*) That, having taken all reasonable precautions against committing an offence against this Act, he had at the time of the commission of the alleged offence no reason to suspect the genuineness of the trade mark, mark, or trade description; and

(*b*) That, on demand made by or on behalf of the prosecutor, he gave all the information in his power with respect to the persons from whom he obtained such goods or things; or

(*c*) That otherwise he had acted innocently;

be guilty of an offence against this Act.

PUNISHMENTS AND PENALTIES.

Punishments and penalties.

Section 2 (3). Every person guilty of an offence against this Act shall be liable—

(i.) On conviction on indictment, to imprisonment, with or without hard labour, for a term not exceeding two years, or to fine, or to both imprisonment and fine; and

(ii.) On summary conviction, to imprisonment, with or without hard labour, for a term not exceeding four months, or to a fine not exceeding twenty pounds, and in the case of a second, or subsequent, conviction, to imprisonment, with or without hard labour, for a term not exceeding six months, or to a fine not exceeding fifty pounds; and

(iii.) In any case to forfeit to Her Majesty every chattel, article, instrument, or thing by means of or in relation to which the offence has been committed.

"Trade mark" means registered trade mark.

In Section 3 of the Act it is set forth that the expression "trade mark" used in the Act means a trade mark "registered in the Register of Trade Marks kept under the Patents, Designs, and Trade Marks Act, 1883," and includes any mark protected by law (whether with or without registration) under international arrangements, such for example as the existing International Convention. The term also includes marks registered under the Trade Marks Act of 1875, and of course extends now to the Amending Act of 1888, following the Patents Act of 1883.

It will be seen that, unlike what has been said with reference to the civil remedy, a distinction is drawn between the case of a person who issues or causes to be issued the infringing trade mark, and of him who merely sells articles bearing the false mark. In the former case the circumstances all point to intentional fraud. In the latter case the seller or dealer might have acted quite innocently. In such a case the Act tells him how he must proceed to prove absence on his part of "intent to defraud." He must show where he got the goods, and from whom he obtained them. He must also show that he had no reason to doubt the genuine nature of the mark, and, in short, not only produce every possible proof of his own innocence, but also assist the prosecutor to discover the real offenders.

Innocent retailer.

If a person should be convicted under this Act, he is not thereby relieved from further civil proceedings.

Where a tradesman shifts a genuine label from goods of superior quality to goods of an inferior quality, although by the same maker, such wrongful user of a trade mark would constitute an offence under the Act. Any person untruly representing that a trade mark is registered is liable on conviction to a penalty.

To misapply a genuine label is an offence.

Engravers or lithographers who execute instructions for a block, stamp, or die, well knowing it to be meant for fraudulent purposes, commit an offence under the Act. But an engraver who makes a die or block according to instructions without any such guilty knowledge, and who derives no advantage from the sale of the goods to which the forged mark is applied, can clear himself on proof of innocence in the same manner as the innocent seller. Such persons should give immediate notice that they intend to rely on this defence: otherwise they may have to pay the prosecutor's costs, although discharged from the prosecution

Offences by engravers and lithographers.

Innocent engraver.

Appeal.

A defendant may appeal to the quarter sessions, and if charged before a court of summary jurisdiction he may select to be tried on indictment.

Evidence.

In cases under the Merchandise Marks Act the defendant is allowed to give evidence upon oath, and his wife may in like manner be sworn and subjected to examination like any other witness.

Among the reported cases under the Act there are very few indeed in which the head and front of the offending has been direct imitation of the prosecutor's trade mark. This is owing to the custom that has obtained of taking many cases which would be fitly the subject of criminal prosecution into the Court of Chancery. It may, however, be said that the rules which regulate comparison of the marks and the evidence which would point to intentional imitation and fraudulent intent are much the same as those obtaining in the higher Court.

Rules of evidence in criminal proceedings based upon those in the civil suit.

Therefore, the magistrate, or the justices on a summary proceeding, or the Court and a jury on indictment, would practically, in a question of fraudulent imitation, have to decide the same issues that would arise in the Court of Chancery. Such being the case, the evidence adduced by the prosecutor should be as full and based upon the same principles that would guide the plaintiff seeking an injunction in the High Court, as already explained in foregoing chapters.

An excellent example of a case of criminal prosecution under the Act, and founded upon the alleged fraudulent imitation and forgery of registered trade marks, was decided recently at the London Central Criminal Court before the Common Serjeant (Sir Forrest Fulton), both the traders who labelled and disposed of the goods and the printer of the labels being found guilty and sentenced.

Reg. v. Hughes et al.

The prosecution was instituted by James Epps & Co., Limited, and the defendants (Hughes, Morris, and Fairweather) were indicted for conspiracy to defraud. The prisoners pleaded guilty. The evidence showed that Hughes and Morris had applied the forged labels (which were almost exact imitations of Messrs. Epps's registered labels) to packets of cocoa of an inferior quality; while Fairweather had printed the labels, knowing the fraudulent purpose for which they were intended. Morris and Hughes were sentenced to twelve and five months' hard labour respectively, and Fairweather the printer to four months' (*London Daily Chronicle*, 24th October, 1893).

Another important case, of special interest to the Manchester trade, was decided in the City Police Court, Manchester, in July 1893. The prosecution originated with Messrs. G. & R. Dewhurst, merchants in Manchester, and the defendants, Messrs. Ellinger & Co., were shippers in the same city. Messrs. Dewhurst were the proprietors of a combination trade mark for piece goods, known to the trade as their "Rupee Combination." This combination consisted of—

Reg. v. Ellinger.

(1) A green ticket with a border enclosing a lion, and bearing the name of the firm;
(2) The firm's signature in blue stamped upon the cloth;
(3) A ticket in black and silver, the chief features being a rupee in obverse and reverse;
(4) Figures in blue, stamped on the cloth, and showing the length; and
(5) A coloured stripe "heading."

Example of fraudulent imitation of combination trade mark.

The goods were for export to India. The defendants, shipping to the same markets, had imitated the "Rupee Combination" by arrangements of green and black-and-silver tickets, signature and figures in blue, together with coloured "headings," which, although not identical with, were deceptively similar to the Dewhurst combination. It was pointed out that the items of the infringing combinations, when compared severally with the items of the Dewhurst combination, showed readily recognisable differences, nor was the actual relative arrangement of the items in all cases slavishly copied, while the name of the actual shipper or consignee was plainly printed on the tickets and on the cloth. Nevertheless, the unmistakeable *general* resemblance, coupled with certain damaging evidence as to fraudulent intent, resulted in the conviction of the defendants. An interesting point in this case is that it is one of those which show that in adjudicating upon an alleged imitation or infringement of a trade mark, the nature of the market and the degree of

Susceptibility of ultimate purchaser to deception.

intelligence or civilisation of the ultimate purchasers—in other words, their susceptibility of being deceived—must be taken into consideration. The fact that in this instance the ultimate purchasers were natives of India. who were, according to the evidence, mostly ignorant of English, and incapable of easily distinguishing minor differences where a general resemblance to the genuine mark existed, had a powerful effect in influencing the judgment adversely to the defendants.

Query. Can defendant in criminal proceedings question validity of registration?

It has been a matter of discussion whether a defendant, prosecuted under the Merchandise Marks Act, can avail himself of the privilege, enjoyed by a defendant in the higher Courts, of questioning the validity of the registration of the mark which he has been charged with fraudulently imitating. *Primâ facie* one would think that the criminal charge should not deprive him of that advantage, but the writer is unable to point to any judicial solution of the question.

CHAPTER VIII.

COMMON-LAW TRADE MARKS AND TRADING OR FIRM NAMES.

The foregoing chapters have dealt almost exclusively with trade marks which are in the privileged position of being registered, and which have thereby acquired a status and weight not inherent to unregistered marks.

But it must not be supposed that it is only the owners of registered marks who can obtain relief against infringers or imitators. The user or owner of a mark or of a trade name which is perhaps incapable of registration may nevertheless restrain piracy by the exercise of his commonlaw rights. This is a remedy which is alike open to the trader who never has registered his mark, to him whose mark has been refused, and to the proprietor whose mark has been expunged from the Register. The principle upon which the Court goes is, that, whether the imitated mark or trade name is registered or unregistered, it will restrain the practice of fraud by one person at the expense of another. In an action pure and simple for the infringement of a registered trade mark, as touched upon in Chapter VI., there is usually a valid, tangible mark, and the issue is simply how and in what respect the infringer has invaded the property constituted by the mark. But, as Lord Blackburn said in *Singer Manufacturing Company v. Loog* (8 App. Cas. 15), after referring to frauds committed by the infringement of trade marks, "There is another way in which goods not the plaintiff's may be sold as and for the plaintiff's. A name may be so appropriated by user as to cause it to mean the goods of the plaintiff, although it is not and never was impressed on the goods so as to be a trade mark properly so called or within the recent statutes. Where it is established that such a trade mark bears that meaning, I think the use of the name, or one so nearly resembling it as to be likely to deceive, as applicable to goods not the plaintiff's, may be the means of passing off those goods as and for the plaintiff's." (See also the instructive remarks of Romer, J., in *Singer v. Spence*, 10 P. O. R. 297.)

Lord Blackburn in *Singer v. Loog.*

An unregistered or unregistrable trade mark or trade name, such as is referred to by Lord Blackburn, was first termed a "Common-Law Trade Mark" by Lindley, L.J., in *Reddaway and Co. v. Bentham Hemp Spinning Co.* (9 P. O. R. 503), and the latest writers have adopted this name in alluding to such a trade mark. In the case just cited, the plaintiffs had been in the habit of using the terms "Camel," "Camel Brand," and "Camel Hair," as descriptive of their woven belting, so that, as they alleged, belting so distinguished was known all over the world as the plaintiffs' manufacture, and no other. The defendants, who had not been long in business, began to use the same terms as descriptive of their belting, justifying their action by alleging that their belting was woven from woollen yarns known in the market as "Camel Hair yarn." At the Manchester Assizes, in May 1892, Cave, J., directed a verdict for the defendants. The plaintiffs

Common-law trade mark.

Example of common-law mark.

Reddaway v. Bentham.

moved for a new trial, and it was held in the Court of Appeal that there was evidence which ought to have been left to the jury. A new trial was therefore ordered, but before it took place the matter was arranged, the defendants submitting to an injunction. The result therefore was, that the plaintiffs established their right to the common-law trade mark constituted by the word "Camel," which was both an unregistered and an unregistrable word, seeing that the Comptroller had pointed out that it was not only a geographical name, but was also, strictly speaking, either descriptive or deceptive.

"Stone Ale" case. *Montgomery v. Thompson.*

Another instance of a common-law trade mark is to be found in the "Stone Ale" case (*Montgomery v. Thompson*, 8 P. O. R. 361), which was finally decided in the House of Lords in May 1891. The respondents and their predecessors had for many years carried on business as brewers at the town of Stone. Their ale had become well known in the market as "Stone Ale." Together with other labels, they had registered the words "Stone Ale" as a trade mark. The infringer, Montgomery, built a brewery at Stone, and began to sell his liquor as "Stone Ale." On an action being brought by Thompson, Montgomery applied to rectify the Register by cancelling the registration of the word "Stone." Chitty, J., held that Montgomery should be restrained from using "Stone Ale," and refused the motion to rectify.

Geographical name expunged from Register, but upheld as common-law trade mark.

On appeal it was held that the injunction against the defendant was properly granted, but that the registered mark "Stone Ale" must be removed from the Register (thus changing it from a registered into a common-law mark).

The defendant Montgomery appealed to the House of Lords, but without success, as the order of the Court of Appeal was affirmed. Thus it will be seen that even where a party has had the registration of his trade mark cancelled, as being at variance with the law which governs the registration of trade marks, he is not left defenceless, but may uphold his right to the exclusive use of the mark at common law.

Similar considerations weighed in deciding *Wotherspoon*

v. Currie (L. R. 5 H. L. 508), the "Glenfield Starch" case, and others which need not be referred to here.

Just as an imitation of a well-known trade mark or trade name, placed upon goods, becomes an instrument of fraud by leading the public to believe that they are buying the goods of one person, whereas the goods are really those of another person, so the trading name of an individual or company may be imitated, on a signboard for example, or in advertisements or circulars, in such a manner as to deceive the public into the belief that they are dealing with the individual or firm whose name has been imitated. Except under the terms of the Companies Act, 1862 (25 & 26 Vict., Cap. 89), there is no such thing as registration of a firm's name in the same sense as trade mark or design registration.

Trading and firm names.

25 & 26 Vict., cap. 89.

Suppose, therefore, a firm of cabinet makers consisting of less than seven members (this being the number entitling to registration under the Companies Act, 1862) were to launch a business under the title of "The London and Counties Furnishing Company," there are no means of registering such a name, and if another firm should assume the same or a deceptively similar name, the first company has only its common-law remedy. Where the name of the company is composed of words in ordinary use, the evidence as to deception or the probability of deception, through the assumption by another company of a similar name, requires to be very convincing, before a successful action can be maintained.

Examples of conflicting firm and company names.

For example, where a bill was filed by *The London and Provincial Life Assurance Society* seeking to restrain *The London and Provincial Joint Stock Life Assurance Company* an injunction was refused. In the same manner injunctions were refused in the following suits: viz.—*The Colonial Life Assurance Company v. Home and Colonial Assurance Company, Limited*, and *The London Assurance Company v. London and Westminster Assurance Corporation, Limited*. *The Guinea Coal Company* was successful in restraining a rival concern which had taken the name of *The Pall Mall Guinea Coal Company*. *The India and China Tea Company*, however, failed to get an injunction against *The India and China Packet Tea Company*, the Court holding that the name assumed by the defendant company was truthfully descriptive of their business, and referred to the countries from which the goods were actually derived.

Registration under the Companies Act, 1862.

As to registration under the Companies Act of 1862, Section 20 of the Act provides that "No company shall be registered under a name identical with that by which a subsisting company is already registered, or so nearly resembling the same as to be calculated to deceive, except in a case where such subsisting company is in the course of being dissolved, and testifies its consent in such manner as the Registrar requires."

A company cannot, however, under the Companies Acts, legally register and maintain a name similar to the name of an earlier unregistered company (*Hendriks v. Montague*, 17 Ch. D. 643).

Fancy business title.

Where the trading name is the name of an individual, and this is assumed by a person of a different name, the intention of fraud is so evident that redress is quickly obtained. Even where the plaintiff's name is itself assumed or is a fancy title, such as *The Christy Minstrels*, *The Oldfield Lane Doctor*, or *Madame Elise*, an injunction to restrain the use of such an assumed name by others is readily obtained.

Use of own name in deceptive manner.

Holloway v. Holloway (13 Beav. 209).

It has been held that a person might use his own name in such a manner as to deceive (*Churton v. Douglas*, Johns. 174; *Burgess v. Burgess*, 3 De G. M. & G. 896; *Holloway v. Holloway*, 13 Beav. 209), but in such a case the plaintiff's evidence as to fraudulent intent must be very clear and convincing. Mere liability to confusion between the names of two firms where *mala fides* cannot be shown will not suffice to obtain an injunction (*Turton v. Turton*, 42 Ch. D. 128).

Fraudulent collusion to create firm name similar to existing firm.

A partnership got up between persons of the requisite names, and intended to take fraudulent advantage of the reputation attaching to an old-established business, will not be permitted to take the name of the older business, although the partners may be of the same names. Thus a clerk named Day and a shopkeeper named Martin were restrained from carrying on the business of blacking manufacturers as "Day and Martin" in imitation of the well-known firm of that name.

PART III.

COPYRIGHT IN DESIGNS.

CHAPTER I.

DEFINITION AND NATURE OF DESIGNS.

Formerly designs separately classed as "Ornamental" and "Useful."

PRIOR to the Patents, Designs, and Trade Marks Acts of 1883 to 1888, there were two distinct forms of copyright in Designs—viz., "Ornamental" and "Useful." Ornamental designs referred solely to such designs as are used to beautify articles of manufacture, such as designs for printed calicoes, wall-papers, carpeting, and the like, or raised or flat ornaments upon all sorts of goods, or ornamental shapes of manufactured objects. Useful designs, on the other hand, referred to objects whose novel shape or configuration enabled them to fulfil a useful purpose, such, for example, as an ink-bottle moulded with a recess to fulfil the additional function of a pen tray; or a tool whose shape or configuration enabled it to be used for more than one purpose; or a pavement light or prism of such a shape or configuration as to enable it to divert light into cellars.

Now such distinction is abolished, and designs are registered for ornament or shape.

Now, however, under the present Act, this distinction between Ornamental and Useful Designs is abolished, and a design is registered for the ornament or pattern, or for the shape or configuration, the latter not necessarily meaning a beautiful or artistic shape or configuration.

Utility not considered.

As to any *useful effect* that may be brought about by the shape or configuration of a design, registration gives no claim in respect of this. The shape or design must appeal to and be judged by the eye alone, and the Court will discard all reference to the useful effect, if any such exists.

Thus in *The Hecla Foundry Co. v. Walker, Hunter & Co.* (6 P. O. R. 554), the lower Courts, hampered probably by some reminiscences of the extinct Useful Designs registration, instanced the useful effect of the registered design of a kitchen range fire-door as one of the reasons for recognising and maintaining the validity of the registration. But the Judges in the House of Lords, while upholding the decision of the Courts below, expressly pointed out that the *utility* of the design must not be allowed to influence the question in any respect.

Definition of the Term "Design."

"Design" defined.

The term "Design" is defined in Section 60 of the Act to mean any design applicable to any article of manufacture, or to any substance, artificial or natural, or partly artificial and partly natural, whether the design is applicable for the pattern, or for the shape or configuration, or for the ornament thereof, or for any two or more of such purposes, and by whatever means it is applicable, whether by printing, painting, embroidering, weaving, sewing, modelling, casting, embossing, engraving, stamping, or any other means whatever, manual, mechanical, or chemical, separate or combined, not being a design for sculpture or other thing within the protection of the Sculpture Copyright Act of the year 1814 (54 Geo. III., Cap. 56).

Thus a design, within the Act, may be some ornament printed or produced on the flat, such as woven or printed designs on textile fabrics, paper-hangings, floorcloths, or the like; or patterns or designs etched, or stamped, or cast, or embossed, or cut, or otherwise produced on metal articles, or glass, or plastic material, or furniture, or tiles, or worked or woven, as in lace; or it may be for artistic or beautiful shape or configuration, as in a lamp stand, or lamp shade, or iron railing, or gate; or for shape, in which no appeal is made to the sense of beauty, as in a new shape or configuration of grate-door, or oil-can, or cravat, &c. Or, as the Act says, the design might contain two or all of the foregoing elements—*i.e.*, ornament, pattern, shape, and configuration.

Design may combine ornament, pattern, and shape.

It will be noted that the section does not make the

smallest allusion to utility. It is the design, and the design alone, that is protected. The Court will not look beneath the surface, but must find the reasons for registration apparent to the eye. If a useful object is attained, well and good; but this consideration will not be allowed to obtrude itself as an element to be taken into account.

Hecla Foundry Co. v. Walker.

In the case of *The Hecla Foundry Co. v. Walker, Hunter & Co.*, already referred to, the design was applied to a kitchen range fire-door, and consisted in casting an "ogee" moulding upon the upper edge of the door, which moulding filled in the gap across the top of the grate when the door was closed, and practically continued the moulding of the same description which already extended along the front of the grate on each side of the fireplace. Its practical advantages were, that it did away with the usual hinged fall-bar which had before been used to bridge the gap, and also helped to exclude cold air from the top of the grate. The new door was not registered as part of the range, but as an object by itself, the short specification on the application form being, "Range fire-door, with moulding on top: *Shape* to be registered." The defendants (the appellants in the House of Lords) had infringed by using a similar fire-door.

Utility not a consideration in designs.

The eye to be the judge.

The Lord Ordinary, in giving judgment for the plaintiffs, and confirming the validity of the registration, laid stress upon the elements of utility; and on appeal the Inner House, confirming the Lord Ordinary, made the same mistake. Finally, on appeal to the House of Lords, the decisions of the lower Scotch Courts were affirmed, but their error in allowing the question of utility to influence them was strongly insisted upon, and it was laid down that the eye alone must be the judge in dealing with a design. The defendants' fire-door had also a moulding along the top, and that being the plaintiffs' registered design, judgment was given accordingly. As Lord Fitzgerald said towards the conclusion of the case, "In the course of the discussion at the Bar, one of the learned counsel asked us to put the two things (*i.e.* the two fire-doors) side by side, and said that we should see by a look that the article produced by the appellants was an obvious imitation of the registered design of the respondents. My Lords, I looked at the two things then, and I came to the conclusion that the door of the appellants was clearly an obvious imitation of the registered design of the respondents, and from that moment I thought that the argument was at an end."

Walker v. Scott.

The case of *Walker v. Scott* (9 P. O. R. 482) is another instance in which a design, while conforming to the requirements of the section, yet had wrapped up in it an essentially useful purpose or result. The design was applicable to a cyclist's oil-can, and consisted in rounding the edges of the can, so that when carried on the person there was no danger of its catching or cutting the clothes or person. Although the validity of the registration was not questioned by the defendant, Chitty, J., in giving judgment for the plaintiff, did not seem to doubt its fitness as subject-matter. The design was practically a modified shape of oil-can. It was a change of shape apparent to the eye, and that satisfied the Court. The fact that the change did not mean any added beauty, and that it undoubtedly did enlarge the usefulness of the can, had nothing to do with the question.

Mere change of old shape may constitute design.

While thus showing that *utility* does not form a recognised element in a design, it may be advisable at this point to go a step further and glance at a possible confusion between patentable inventions and designs. It may well be that something which is perfectly fit subject-matter as a design might also be fit subject-matter for a patent. For example, the range-door already referred to, by virtue of its useful functions, and in combination with the range, would undoubtedly have constituted a patentable invention, and yet it has been seen that the registration of the door as a design was upheld by the highest authority.

Patentable inventions and designs.

Nevertheless, such an instance is likely to be rare, and it may be instructive to notice an example where the registration of a design was held to fail on the ground that it was not properly a design, but trenched upon the domain of patentable inventions. In *Moody v. Tree* (9 P. O. R. 333) a design of basket was registered, the basket being woven in such a manner that the osiers were

Conception not capable of registration as design may be patentable as invention.

worked in singly, the butt-ends showing outside; the whole, on being finished off, presenting a very pretty appearance. The jury in the County Court found that the basket was a novelty, but the judge, doubting whether it was fit subject-matter for registration as a design, granted an appeal to the Divisional Court. There it was held that the so-called design was really a method of manufacture, and should have been patented. Again, in *Cooper v. Symington* (10 P. O. R. 264) the plaintiff had registered as a design a corset, in which the busks in front, although really fastened together by eyes and studs, had yet, when secured upon the wearer, the appearance of having been laced together. This appearance was obtained by the arrangement and display of certain diagonal lacing which confined the busks in their sheaths. The general appearance was similar to the admittedly more becoming appearance of a laced-up corset. But then, to lace up a corset was a tedious operation, whereas in the plaintiff's corset the busks were secured at once by means of the eyes and studs. It was held by the Court that in a design the eye must be the judge, and although in the registered corset there was undoubtedly something new which might have been patented, nevertheless the *appearance* to the eye was not new, but was precisely the same as the old laced-up corset, which indeed it was designed and intended to imitate. Accordingly, Chitty, J., refused the plaintiff's motion for an injunction.

Moody v. Tree.

Cooper v. Symington.

A new combination of two or more old patterns or designs might form good subject-matter for registration as a new and original design. There is a case under the old Act of 5 & 6 Vict., Cap. 100, that of *Harrison v. Taylor* (4 H. & N. 815), decided on appeal from the Court of Exchequer, in which it was held that the plaintiff's design, which related to a species of double honeycomb fabric, was new and original and formed good subject-matter. The design was formed by combining a large honeycomb fabric with a small honeycomb fabric, the small honeycomb fabric serving as a ground upon which the large honeycomb was displayed. Both the large and the small honeycomb patterns were old, but their combination

Combination of old patterns may form new design.

Harrison v. Taylor.

had not been carried out before. It is, however, certain that, under present practice, combination designs are narrowly scrutinised.

An example of the treatment usually accorded to designs which consist of combinations of old elements, too obvious to be upheld as novel and original, is to be found in the case of *Hothersall v. Moore* (9 P. O R. 27). Here the plaintiff registered, as a design for dusters, the combination of an old and well-known border with an equally old and well-known fabric as centre-piece. Bristowe, V.C., held that this did not constitute a registrable design, and dismissed the action with costs.

Hothersall v. Moore. Obvious combination of old materials not design.

In *Le May v. Welch* (28 Ch. D. 24) a registered design of a collar contained three characteristics which it was admitted had *separately* appeared in collars prior to the date of the plaintiff's registration. The combination was considered too narrow or trifling to constitute a new design, and in the Court of Appeal, Lord Justice Bowen, in delivering his judgment, very properly drew attention to one of the reasons of the Court for declining to maintain the validity of such a registration. "We must not," said his Lordship, "allow industry to be oppressed. It is not every mere difference of cut, every change of outline, every change of length or breadth or configuration, in a simple and familiar article of dress like this, which constitutes novelty of design. To hold that, would be to paralyse industry, and make the Patents, Designs, and Trade Marks Acts a trap to catch honest traders."

Combination of separately old characteristics not a new design.

Bowen, L J., on limits of registration.

In the last case quoted, not only the fitness or unfitness of a combination design as subject-matter for registration, but also the amount of invention or fancy displayed, was inferentially considered. As Lord Justice Bowen said, "there must be a substantial novelty in the design, having regard to the nature of the article." Thus in *Smith v. Hope Bros.* (6 P. O. R. 200) the plaintiff had registered a design for application to a scarf. At the hearing it became apparent that the sole advance upon what was acknowledged to be an old shape of scarf was the introduction of one or two folds or pleats in the body of the scarf. Mr. Justice Stirling dismissed the plaintiff's motion

Design must display some substantial novelty.

for injunction with costs, and directed that the design should be struck from the Register. The learned judge referred to the case of *Le May v. Welch*, and quoted with approval the remarks of Lord Justices Baggallay and Bowen. It should, however, be mentioned here that, just as the commercial success of an apparently obvious or simple invention has been considered an additional reason for maintaining a somewhat doubtful patent, so the commercial success of a registered design has been allowed to weigh with the Court in upholding the registration, even where the subject-matter has been somewhat narrow. In *Tyler v. Sharpe* (11 P. O. R. 35), Romer, J., in upholding the plaintiff's design of a watercloset basin, said that, although the design was somewhat slight, he could not help being favourably impressed by the immediate popularity and large sale of the article to which the design was applied.

Commercial success of design will influence Court.

The question of what constitutes good subject-matter for registration as a design would be incomplete without a reference to the adaptation of existing and well-known things, such as famous objects or buildings, to the purposes of design, as applied to manufactured objects. It seems only reasonable to suppose that if someone adapts a view or picture of some thing, or some personality, whether it be a flower or landscape, a building, or a statesman, and applies that representation or picture to some article of manufacture, he should be allowed to register it as a new design, and should be protected in such a specific adaptation. His right may perhaps be open to cavil if the representation he made use of was common and well known, such as a well-known photograph or engraving, although even this might not affect his right. But suppose the particular representation or view he uses is one produced or procured by himself, it might be asked why such adaptation should not be fit subject-matter for registration as a design for application to certain specified manufactured goods, according to the Act. It has been said, in text-books upon the subject of designs copyright, that the copy of a photograph of a well-known public character is not a new or original design within the meaning of the Act. The decision

Adaptation of pictures of well-known objects and persons as designs.

Adams v. Clementson.

Saunders v. Wiel.

upon which this assertion is based occurred in the case of *Adams v. Clementson* (12 Ch. D. 714). But this case turned on the old Act of 5 and 6 Vict., Cap. 100, Section 3, which is differently worded from the corresponding sections of the Act of 1883, and it has been thought by a high authority (Lindley, L.J., in *Saunders v. Wiel*, 10 P. O. R. 29) that the variation in the language of the Act of 1883 was influenced or caused by this very decision of *Adams v. Clementson.* In the latter case the dispute was between two earthenware manufacturers, the plaintiff, Adams, seeking to restrain the defendant by injunction from infringing the plaintiff's registered design which he applied to plates and other articles of earthenware. The design consisted of a portrait of General Martinez de Campos, copied from a photograph which had been sent to the plaintiff from Cuba. The defendant had received a similar photograph and was applying it to similar goods. In both cases the goods were produced almost entirely for export to Cuba.

Vice-Chancellor Malins decided that this was not fit subject-matter for a registrable design, because the plaintiff had simply taken the photograph and copied it, and the defendant had done the same thing. Accordingly the injunction was refused. It is, however, submitted that this decision has since been subjected to such destructive criticism that there is but little fear of its being repeated or having henceforth any weight as a precedent. A more correct interpretation of the law as it now stands is to be found in the case of *Saunders v. Wiel* (*supra*). Here the plaintiff, a silversmith, had registered, in Class 1, a design applicable to the handles of spoons and forks. The design consisted of a view of Westminster Abbey, modelled in relief on the spoon or fork handle. The nature of the design as stated in the application was for the "pattern and shape of spoon or fork handle in metal." The defendants had infringed, and, relying in their defence upon the decision in *Adams v. Clementson*, contended that the design was not one that could be registered. Cave, J., dissented from the judgment in *Adams v. Clementson*, and held that the design was proper subject-matter for registration, and that the defendants had infringed.

Held in *Saunders v. Wiel* that a modelled view of Westminster Abbey on spoon-handle good as design.

In the Court of Appeal the decision of the lower Court was upheld, and the adverse remarks of Cave, J., upon the decision in *Adams v. Clementson* were strongly endorsed by Lindley and Bowen, L.JJ.

Design must be new or original.

Novelty is also essential to the valid registration of a design. The design must at the date of application be "a new or original design not previously published in the United Kingdom."

Limited disclosure not usually publication of design.

Where a design has been freely exhibited, and sold prior to registration, of course novelty has been destroyed and cannot be revived. But there are many instances where a species of *quasi*-disclosure has taken place, in respect of which the question has to be debated whether or not such disclosure amounts to publication. Confidential disclosure to a partner, servant, agent, customer, or friend, for the purpose of obtaining an opinion on the merits of a design, is not publication, so long as it goes no further, and so long as actual business is not done in the goods bearing the design.

***Heinrichs v. Bastendorff.* Example of limited disclosure held not to be publication.**

***Blank v. Footmann.* Example of limited disclosure held to be publication.**

In *Heinrichs v. Bastendorff* (10 P. O. R. 160), the defendant pleaded that a sample of the writing-table which embodied the design had, before registration, been submitted by the plaintiff to a customer, who had altered and returned it. It was held by Day, J., that this did not constitute publication. But where, as in *Blank v. Footmann* (5 P. O. R. 653), the inventor of a new lace design had shown and handed a sample of the lace to his agent, and the agent had in turn shown the sample in a confidential manner to two selected customers, who gave orders and kept cuttings from the lace, it was held that publication had taken place. It would seem that the mere confidential exhibition of the lace to the three indicated persons would not of itself have constituted publication, but the concluding of an order, and the leaving of the cuttings or samples in the customers' hands, went beyond mere confidential disclosure. An examination of the report of the more recent and very similar case of *Winfield v. Snow* (8 P. O. R. 15), and a consideration of the remarks of Hawkins, J., will also help to show how far confidential communication of this description may go without con-

Winfield v. Snow.

Selling goods bearing design before date of registration is publication.

stituting publication. In *re Sherwood's Design* (9 P. O. R. 268) the proprietor of the design supplied a customer with two globes in accordance with the design, three days before registration was effected. There was a slight difference between the design of globe as registered and the globes as supplied; but it was held that publication had taken place, and the design was ordered to be expunged from the Register.

Substitution of one material for another (design remaining the same) not registrable.

It has also been laid down that the mere substitution of one material for another, where the object is the same and to be used for a similar purpose, does not constitute a registrable new design. Thus in *re Bach's Design* (6 P. O. R. 376) Bach registered, in Class 4, a fairy lamp-shade produced in the form of a rose and made of vitreous material. It was shown that lamp-shades of a similar design, but made of linen, had been manufactured and sold prior to the registration of Bach's design, and as a result the motion to expunge the design was successful.

Design published in one class, published in a similar class.

The same design may be registered in more than one class; but a design already registered in one class, and put on the market and made public, cannot afterwards be properly registered in another class as a new design. In *Hothersall v. Moore* (*supra*) the plaintiff had registered his design in Class 13 instead of in Class 14, which was the proper class. His after registration in Class 14 was held not to retrieve his error, and the registration in Class 14 was held invalid from publication, although such publication took place after registration in Class 13.

Marking Registered Designs.

Goods must be marked.

Section 51 of the Act provides that before delivery or sale of any articles to which a registered design has been applied, the proprietor of the design shall cause each such article to be marked with the prescribed mark or with the prescribed word or words or figures denoting that the design is registered; and if he fails to do so the copyright in the design shall cease, unless the proprietor shows that he took all proper steps to ensure the marking of the article.

In pursuance of this section, the Board of Trade Rules under the Act provide that all goods in Classes 1 to 12 shall during the period of copyright bear the abbreviation "R[D]" and (except in the case of lace) the number appearing on the certificate of registration. All goods in Classes 13 and 14 (printed or woven designs on textile piece goods and on handkerchiefs and shawls) shall be marked "REG[D]" without the number. Specified markings.

The object of the section being to protect the unwary by making it plain what goods are and what are not registered, a slight deviation from the strict letter of the Rules will not matter, so long as the goods are marked so as to make it plainly apparent that they are registered. In *Heinrichs v. Bastendorff* (*supra*) the plaintiff had marked his tables "REG[D]" instead of "R[D]". The defendant pleaded that registration was invalid on that account, but Day, J., brushed this contention aside, saying, "I am of opinion that does not vitiate registration at all" It is better, however, to adhere strictly to the Rules.

When it is impossible or inconvenient to place the mark actually on the goods, it may be placed on the case, or wrapping, or card. In *Blank v. Footmann* (*supra*), Kekewich, J., decided that the plaintiff had complied sufficiently with the Act in marking his trimming, when made up in bundles, with the abbreviation "R[D]" and the number printed on a paper band surrounding the goods. Made-up goods of certain nature may be marked in bulk.

But failure to mark the goods at all will undoubtedly vitiate registration, and the same may be said where the failure is only partial. For example, should a dozen dusters of a registered design be woven in a piece of, say, twelve dusters, it would not be sufficient to affix the mark "REG[D]" to the piece alone, since that would be marking one only of the twelve dusters comprising the piece. When the piece is cut up, eleven dusters would go forth to the public, perhaps in different directions, without any indication of the design having been registered. This was held, *inter alia*, to vitiate registration in *Hothersall v. Moore* (*supra*).

It will be noted that Section 51 concludes with a saving clause, giving relief in case of error if the proprietor can show that he took all proper steps to ensure the marking of the articles. Thus mere inadvertence or Relief in case of inadvertence.

blundering on the part of those over whom the proprietor of the design had no immediate control will not vitiate the registration of the design.

Wittmann v. Oppenheim.

In *Wittmann v. Oppenheim* (27 Ch. D. 260), a manufacturer employed by the proprietor of a design to make the articles for him, and to whom the proprietor had supplied a correct stamping die, used by mistake an old die, which related to an expired design of the same proprietor. Several articles were sold before the proprietor detected the blunder, but it was held that this did not vitiate his registration, it having been made apparent that he had done all in his power to ensure the correct marking of the articles. The question of what constitutes the taking of "all proper steps to ensure the marking" was also considered in the more recent case of *Johnson v. Bailey* (11 P. O. R. 21). Here a manufacturer who had registered the design of a teapot, and had prepared moulds and given his workmen injunctions to see that each pot was properly marked, lost his copyright because the workmen allowed the mould to become so worn that the registration mark on the goods was illegible. The Lord Ordinary (Low) decided that such general instructions as the plaintiff had given, when not followed up by personal supervision, did not constitute the taking of "all proper steps to ensure the marking."

Johnson v. Bailey.

Negligence in properly marking.

There is a penalty for marking designs as having been registered when such is not the case.

Penalty for Piracy.

Section 58.

Section 58 of the Act provides that during the existence of copyright in any design—

"(*a*) It shall not be lawful for any person without the licence or written consent of the registered proprietor to apply or cause to be applied such design, or any fraudulent or obvious imitation thereof, in the class or classes of goods in which such design is registered, for purposes of sale, to any article of manufacture, or to any substance, artificial or natural, or partly artificial and partly natural; and "(*b*) It shall not be lawful for any person to publish or expose for sale any article of manufacture, or any substance, to which such design, or any fraudulent or obvious imitation thereof, shall have been so applied, knowing that the same has been so applied without the consent of the registered proprietor.

"Any person who acts in contravention of this section shall be liable for every offence to forfeit a sum not exceeding fifty pounds to the registered proprietor of the design, who may recover such sum as a simple contract debt by action in any court of competent jurisdiction, provided that the total sum forfeited in respect of any one design shall not exceed one hundred pounds."

Penalties for infringement of registration.

Under the old Act, the onus of proof that the offender knew that the design had been applied without the consent of the registered proprietor lay upon the plaintiff. This difficult provision was modified in 5 & 6 Vict., Cap. 100, by virtue of which the proprietor, by giving notice in writing, laid the onus of proving *bona fides* on the defendant.

Under the present Act it is not necessary to serve even an innocent infringer of a registered design with notice, except in the case of an innocent retailer of the infringing goods.

Innocent retailer only entitled to notice before action.

The cases that have already been cited, and the remarks upon what constitutes a design, will show how unprofitable it would be to enter into a discussion upon what would be considered a "fraudulent" or an "obvious" imitation of a registered design. As has already been said, the eye is in the main the judge as to what is and what is not an obvious imitation. It is conceivable that a design might be held to be an obvious imitation of a registered design, even although in arrangement and detail it is, when narrowly inspected, different, so long as the general effect, seen at a short distance, is the same. *A fortiori*, the defendant will not be allowed to shelter himself behind trifling distinctions and variations from the registered design.

"Obvious" or "fraudulent" imitation.

In *Sherwood v. Decorative Tile Co.* (4 P. O. R. 207), Manisty, J., says, "Upon the question of *obvious* imitation, you must to a great extent (I do not say entirely)

Manisty, J., compares an "obvious" with

a "fraudulent" imitation.

be guided by the eye." And again the same learned judge remarks, "It may not be easy, I do not say it is impossible, to define in words exactly what is meant by a *fraudulent* imitation. I think the word was introduced for the very purpose of meeting the case of an imitation, not an *obvious* imitation, but an imitation varied for the purpose really of perpetrating what is a legal fraud. For instance, having before your mind and before your eye the design of another, and introducing into your design some differences, in order if possible to avoid coming within the Act of Parliament."

In the case last quoted the same learned judge came to the conclusion that the defendants' design, although not an "obvious," was on the other hand a "fraudulent" imitation.

Course to be adopted by innocent retailer of goods wrongfully bearing registered design.

It will be seen from Section 58, Sub-section *b*, that an innocent retailer of the infringing goods is not treated in the same manner as an infringer having full knowledge of what he is doing. Such innocent retailer may prove—

(*a*) That he sold without knowledge that the design was registered, or

(*b*) Without knowledge that it had been applied without the consent of the registered proprietor.

An innocent infringer who *manufactures* goods without the knowledge that he is trespassing upon a registered design may be made to pay the costs of a motion for an injuction to restrain him from continuing the infringement. even although he has had no prior notice from the plaintiff warning him that he is infringing. But with the innocent *retailer* of infringing goods the case is different. As Vice-Chancellor Bristowe said in *Smith v. Lewis Roberts & Co.* (5 P. O. R. 611), "I think that the intention of the Act, Section 58, Sub-section *b*, is to protect a retail dealer, or dealer selling goods and not being himself the manufacturer of them, from pains and penalties in respect of that which he does not himself know; and if the retail dealer is selling goods as to which he has no knowledge that there is any registration, he is doing that which is no wrong: the wrong is in doing it after having knowledge brought home to him that protection by registration has been given to the goods

Bristowe, V.C., on the innocent retailer.

which he is seeking to sell." In this action it was held that the defendants had not sold with knowledge that the designs were registered, and that there was no intention to sell after acquiring such knowledge. The action was accordingly dismissed, with costs against the plaintiff.

In the case of *Sherwood v. Decorative Tile Co.* (*supra*), where the sale of one hundred infringing tiles was proved, a penalty of £50 was imposed, although under the Act as it then stood a penalty of £5,000 might have been adjudged. In view of this and similar cases, to prevent the possibility of ruinous penalties being imposed, in the Amending Act of 1888 the total amount of penalties to be forfeited in respect of any one design was limited to a maximum of £100.

Limitation of penalty.

It is an offence under the Act (Section 105) to describe an article as "registered" where no registration has been effected. A person is deemed to represent a design as registered if he sells the article bearing any word or mark expressing or implying that registration has been obtained. The penalty for such misrepresentation is that the offender is liable for each offence on summary conviction to a fine not exceeding £5.

Wrongfully marking goods as registered.

Penalty.

Duration of Copyright.

The Duration of Copyright is limited to five years from the date of registration, and there is no provision for extension of this time. An unusual clause for the fostering of native industry occurs in Section 54 of the Act, which provides that if a registered design is used in manufacture in any foreign country, and is not used in this country within six months of its registration here, the copyright in the design shall cease. This clause is akin to the condition of "working" attached to the grant of many foreign patents.

Registration lasts five years.

Foreign owner of registered design not using same in this country forfeits copyright.

It might be thought needless to say that the protection accorded to designs by the Patents, Designs, and Trade Marks Acts, 1883 to 1888, does not extend beyond the limits of the United Kingdom.

Copyright extends only to United Kingdom

Reference, however, may be made to a case (*Potter & Co. v. Braco de Prata Co.*, 8 P. O. R. 218), in which the plaintiffs, who were a British firm, sought to make the defendants (also British subjects) liable for the infringement of certain calico-printers' designs. It was admitted that the designs of the plaintiffs were being copied and sold, but the defendants pleaded that the goods bearing the designs were manufactured and sold in Portugal and Brazil—countries which were not subject to the operations of the Act. The judgment of the Lord President was to the effect that an infringement of a design registered under the Act consists in the production of goods in this country, where they are protected, and nowhere else. No right is secured to a registered design in a foreign country by registration here, except the right under the International Convention.

Isle of Man.

The Acts of 1883 to 1888 extend to the Isle of Man, but nothing in the Acts is to affect the jurisdiction of the Courts in the Isle in proceedings for infringement or in any action or proceeding respecting a design competent in those Courts (see Section 112 of the Act).

Persons Entitled to Register.

Person entitled to register may be either designer or purchaser.

The author of a new and original design is entitled to register himself as the "proprietor." But if he has executed the work on behalf of another person for a consideration, then his employer or the purchaser of his work shall be entitled to have himself registered as the proprietor. A body corporate, or a firm, or a company incorporated under the Companies Acts, may be the registered proprietors of a design. Aliens are also entitled to registration. A copyright in a design is personal property, and may be bequeathed, assigned, and dealt with at the owner's pleasure. The proprietor may license another to use the design. It may devolve by intestacy or by operation of law upon the proprietor's personal representative or trustee in bankruptcy.

Design copyright is personal property.

CHAPTER II.

PROCEDURE IN REGISTERING DESIGNS.

THE procedure in registering designs is simplicity itself, and the scope of this chapter will be limited to bringing together, condensing, and classifying the information scattered throughout the Act, the Board of Trade Rules, and the Comptroller's instructions.

Application forms.

Stamped forms of application to register, price 10s. in Classes 1 to 12 (except for lace), and 1s. in classes 13 and 14, and also for lace designs, can be obtained at the chief post-offices of most important towns. Examples of these forms are to be found in the Appendix. By following the marginal instructions on the application form, "E," no mistake need be made by the applicant in filling in the particulars. The only part of the form that calls for the exercise of judgment is that where the applicant is directed to state the nature of the design, and "whether it is applicable for the pattern or for the shape." The latest instructions issued by the Patent Office require that the statement of the nature of the design shall particularise whether it is applicable for "the pattern" or for "the shape or configuration" or for "the ornament," these more extended terms being drawn from Section 60 of the Act. It may be taken that the terms "pattern" and "ornament" are practically synonymous. If any difference is to be recognised, "pattern" may be taken to refer to a simple repeat design, such as checks, stripes, or combinations of that description; while "ornament" would more fitly apply to the ornate floral or other devices which are usually employed to decorate window-curtains, calicoes, carpets, and the like. Lace designs (in Class 9) are classified as "patterns," and the lace design application forms, E^1 and O^1, which appear in the set of Rules which came into operation on the 30th

Statement of nature of design.

November, 1893, contain a statement that "the nature of the design is the pattern." It may be noted that these latest application forms for lace request the Comptroller to register the accompanying design "without search." "Shape or configuration" evidently refers more particularly to manufactured objects and articles in the round, and relates to general outline rather than to surface decoration. The term would properly describe a design for a tombstone, or a chair, or a lamp-stand, and each of these might combine ornament with it, as set forth in Section 60.

When thought to be necessary, a short technical description of the article may be added, with the part or parts which are claimed as new or original specifically defined. The form is signed by the applicant or his authorised agent and dated, and is then ready for filing. The application form should be accompanied by three exactly similar drawings, photographs, or specimens of the design. The drawings, photographs, tracings, or specimens should be mounted on foolscap sheets of paper of the same size as Form E (13 in. by 8 in.). Rough sketches or unfixed pencil drawings will not be accepted. When the design refers to the shape or configuration, two views of the object may be given, if such should be necessary, to convey a correct impression of the design. Both views should be on the same half-sheet of foolscap. Each drawing or specimen of a design in Classes 13 and 14 should show the complete pattern and a portion of the repeat, and ought not to be of less size than 7in. by 3in. When specimen cuttings of the design are furnished instead of drawings, they must be of a nature that will permit of their being pasted into books. The drawings or mounted specimens should be signed by the applicant or his agent.

Drawings, photographs, or specimens.

When the papers have been thus completed they should be delivered or sent by post to—

The Comptroller,
Patent Office (Designs Branch),
25 Southampton Buildings,
Chancery Lane,
London, W.C.

The goods to which designs are applicable are divided into fourteen classes. The following is a list of the classes:— Classes of goods.

1. Articles composed wholly or chiefly of metal not included in Class 2.
2. Jewellery.
3. Articles composed wholly or chiefly of wood, bone, ivory, papier mâché, or other solid substances not included in other classes.
4. Articles composed wholly or chiefly of glass, earthenware or porcelain, bricks, tiles, or cement.
5. Articles composed wholly or chiefly of paper (except hangings).
6. Articles composed wholly or chiefly of leather, including bookbinding of all materials.
7. Paper-hangings.
8. Carpets and rugs in all materials, floorcloths, and oilcloths.
9. Lace, hosiery.
10. Millinery and wearing apparel, including boots and shoes.
11. Ornamental needlework in muslin or other textile fabrics.
12. Goods not included in other classes.
13. Printed or woven designs on textile piece-goods.
14. Printed or woven designs on handkerchiefs and shawls.

By Section 58 of the Act, the protection afforded to a registered design is restricted to the particular class or classes of goods in which the design is registered.

The same design may be registered in more than one class, but for each class a separate application, each with its annexed three representations, will be required. Design may be registered in more than one class.

When the design is to be applied to a set, each of the drawings accompanying the application should show all the various arrangements in which it is proposed to apply the design to the articles included in the set. Registration in "sets."

There is a special form, "O," for applications of this nature, and the stamp is £1. For sets of lace designs in Class 9 a special form, O^1, is provided.

Caveat applications.

Should an applicant be desirous of losing no time in making his application, he may send up the application forms, accompanied by a single sketch, instead of the three careful drawings or photographs required. This fixes the date of the application, and the finished drawings may then be made at greater leisure, and afterwards filed. The sketch and the drawings must, however, agree in showing the nature of the design.

Acceptance.

On receipt of an application, the Comptroller considers the design, and if he decides to register it he sends a certificate of registration to the applicant, sealed with the seal of the Patent Office.

Objection.

Hearing.

The Comptroller might, however, decline to register, and in that case, before exercising the discretionary power given to him by the Acts, adversely to the applicant, the Comptroller shall, if so required by the applicant, within one month from the date of the Comptroller's objection, give the applicant an opportunity of being heard personally or by his agent, by sending the applicant ten days' notice of a time when he may be so heard. Within five days from the receipt of this notice, the applicant must notify the Comptroller whether or not he intends to be heard.

The decision of the Comptroller consequent upon the hearing is then notified to the applicant.

Refusal.

Appeal to Board of Trade.

Final decision.

If this decision is a refusal to register, the applicant may still appeal to the Board of Trade. If he intends to do so, he should, within one month from the adverse decision, leave at the Patent Office a notice of his intention to appeal. The form of this notice (Form F) will be found in the Appendix. The notice is to be accompanied by a statement of the grounds of appeal and of the applicant's case in support thereof. A copy of the notice should at the same time be sent to the Secretary of the Board of Trade, 7 Whitehall Gardens, London. The Board of Trade will then appoint a hearing, and a notice of the time and place of hearing is sent to the Comptroller and to the applicant. After the hearing, the Board of Trade gives its decision, and this is final.

When registration of a design is refused on the ground of identity with a design already registered, the applicant for registration shall be entitled to inspect the design so registered. During the existence of the copyright in a design, the design shall not be open to inspection except by the proprietor, or by a person authorised by him, or by the Comptroller, or by the Court, and then only in presence of the Comptroller or his representative, and upon payment of the prescribed fee. The person making the inspection is not allowed to make any copy of the design.

Inspection of registered designs.

When the copyright in the design has ceased, the design is open to inspection by anyone paying the prescribed fee, and copies may be freely made.

Searches.

Any person wishing to know whether the registration of a particular design marked as "registered" is still in force, and when and by whom it was registered, may obtain the information he requires by producing or sending the design, with its mark and number, to the Comptroller, and paying the prescribed fee. The request for search should be made on Form "N," stamped with five shillings.

Searches by Comptroller.

A still more valuable provision in the Rules empowers the Comptroller, on payment of the same fee, to make a search among the registered designs for the purpose of finding whether a design produced by the person requesting the search is identical with, or an obvious imitation of, any registered design still in force.

This is a precautionary measure that might be recommended to manufacturers who contemplate the production of a design concerning which they may have any doubt. It must, however, be said that if, even after receiving the Comptroller's certificate that it is *not* an obvious imitation, the owner of a registered design should take action on the ground that it *is* an obvious imitation, the Comptroller's certificate is not admitted as evidence on the defendant's behalf, and has no weight with the Court.

Comptroller's certificate not evidence.

Register of Designs.

Upon the issue of the certificate of registration, the name, address, and description of the proprietor of the

Proprietor entered on Register.

design, together with the date and number of registration, are entered in the Register of Designs by the Comptroller.

Assignee or licensee entered on Register.

When a person becomes entitled to the copyright in a registered design, or to any share or interest therein, by assignment, transmission, or other operation of law, or where a person acquires any right to apply the design, either exclusively or otherwise, a request for the entry of his name in the Register as such proprietor, or as having acquired such right, should be addressed to the Comptroller, and left at the Patent Office, Designs Branch. This request, which is made on Form "K" (see Appendix), is stamped with ten shillings in the case of designs in Classes 1 to 12, and with one shilling in the case of designs in Classes 13 and 14.

The request should state the name, address, and description of the claimant, and give particulars, with dates and names of the assignment, transmission, or licence, by virtue of which the request is made.

The request concludes with a statutory declaration, signed by the claimant, verifying and declaring the truth of the several statements made and particulars given in the request. The Comptroller will then alter the Register in accordance with the request.

When the request is made on behalf of a firm or partnership, it should be signed by some one or more members of the firm or partnership, or by his or their duly authorised agent. A body corporate can be registered as proprietors by its corporate name, and the request may be signed by a director or by the secretary, or by the duly authorised agent of the body corporate.

Rectification of Register by Court.

When an order has been made by the Court to rectify the Register, the person in whose favour the order has been made should forthwith leave at the Patent Office an office copy of such order, whereupon the Register will be rectified, or the purport of the order duly entered in the Register, as the case may be. Four clear days' notice of every application to the Court for rectification of the Register should be given to the Comptroller.

Register of Designs *primâ facie* evidence.

The Register of Designs shall be *primâ facie* evidence of any matters directed or ordered by the Act to be entered therein.

A certificate of any entry on the Register of Designs, for use in legal proceedings, may be had from the Comptroller by making a request on Form "I," which is stamped with five shillings.

Industrial and International Exhibitions.

Exhibition of unregistered designs.

Any person desirous of exhibiting an unregistered design at an industrial or international exhibition, certified so to be by the Board of Trade or by an Order in Council made in pursuance of Section 57 of the Act, should give the Comptroller seven days' notice of his intention to exhibit, and such notice must be given upon form "L," stamped with five shillings. This notice preserves his prior right to make application for registration of the design during six months from the opening of the exhibition. The notice to the Comptroller should include a brief description of the design, and be accompanied by a sketch or specimen.

CHAPTER III.

LEGAL PROCEEDINGS FOR INFRINGEMENT OF REGISTERED DESIGNS.

No common-law right in unregistered designs.

Proprietor of design only person entitled to sue.

Remedies.

Licensee cannot sue.

There is no common-law right in unregistered designs, such as may exist in unregistered common-law trade marks or trading names. The right to sue for the infringement of a design rests only in the registered proprietor of the copyright. Apart from the remedy given under Section 58 of the Act, in virtue of which a registered proprietor may recover penalties for the infringement of his design, the proprietor, if he elects not to proceed for a penalty, may bring an action in the Queen's Bench Division for the recovery of damages, or in the Chancery Division for damages or an account of profits, and for an injunction to restrain further infringement. There are cases under patent practice which give some authority for believing that an exclusive licensee may in certain circumstances sue alone and in his own name for the infringement of a patent of which he has an exclusive licence, but the case of *Woolley v. Broad* (9 P. O. R. 208) shows good grounds for stating authoritatively that the exclusive licensee of a registered design has not by himself any such right of action.

Criminal prosecution.

When an infringement of a registered design comes to the knowledge of the proprietor, and he decides to take action, he has a choice of remedy. In the case of an aggravated infringement, where the offence is very glaring, and can be proved to have been committed with full knowledge of registration, it would not be improper to select the police court as the proper tribunal before which to bring the offender. The promptness and cheapness of the remedy is a consideration to the prosecutor, while the stigma of conviction, and the infliction of penalties, might act as more stringent deterrents than would be the case if the infringer were merely made a defendant in a civil action.

Queen's Bench Division.

As a rule, however, the superior courts are chosen, and action may be taken either in the Queen's Bench or in the Chancery Division. If the penalty is sued for under Section 58 of the Act, or if the plaintiff seeks damages, as he is entitled to do under Section 59, the action should be entered in the Queen's Bench Division. But if, in addition to or apart from damages or an account of profits, an injunction is sought to restrain the defendant from infringing, the action will go to the Chancery Division. This convenient means of restraining an infringer by injunction, apart from other advantages, has rendered the Chancery Division the most popular Court for settling design copyright disputes.

Chancery Division.

In cases of copyright in the Chancery Division, the action is usually brought in respect of an alleged infringement of the copyright, with claims for an injunction, and either damages or an account of profits, as may be selected by the plaintiff.

Statement of Claim.

The statement of claim should be drawn with careful reference to the sections under which the claims are made. For example, if for a penalty, the wording of Section 58 should be carefully studied; if for damages, the terms of Section 59 must be adopted.

Although the Designs portion of the Act is much less

minute in its directions as to the preparation of pleadings than is the portion referring to Patent litigation, nevertheless, it was held by Mr. Justice North, in *Morris, Wilson & Co. v. Coventry Machine Co.* (8 P. O. R. 353), that it is convenient to follow the practice in patent actions. Therefore, particulars of breaches may be delivered by the plaintiff, and particulars of objections by the defendant, and those particulars may be made subject to amendment, upon the usual terms, just as in pleadings under patent practice. **Patent practice followed.**

The statement of claim should, together with the usual essentials, aver that the plaintiff is the registered proprietor of the design; that the design was new and original at the date of registration; that the defendant had applied (or caused to be applied), during the existence of the copyright, the said design, or an obvious or fraudulent imitation thereof, in the class of goods for which the design was registered, for purposes of sale, and without the licence or written consent of the registered proprietor. **Features of Statement of Claim.**

If action is taken against the retailer, the statement of claim should be modified to allege that the article to which the design has been applied has been published or exposed for sale by the defendant, knowing that the design has been applied without the consent of the registered proprietor. **Action against retailer.**

In the case of a retailer of infringing goods, whether innocent or not, it is preferable to give him notice of the infringement before taking action. **Notice to retailer.**

In an action under Section 58, the sum recoverable being in the form of a penalty, the plaintiff is not entitled to administer interrogatories to the defendant (*Saunders v. Weil, supra*). **In action for penalty interrogatories not allowed.**

For the purpose of comparison, the infringing articles should, if possible, be produced in court, and, if not admitted, the proofs should be clear that they have actually been made or sold by the defendant. This being established, the Court or jury will then be able to decide whether the design applied to the defendant's goods is or is not a piracy of the plaintiff's registered design. **Comparison and proofs.**

Although the conducting of design cases has been held to be governed, where permissible, by the practice in patent actions, the judge nevertheless has complete discretion as **Judge has complete discretion.**

Terms of amendment of pleadings.

to the amendment of the pleadings and as to costs. Where fresh evidence is discovered, for example by the defendant, and leave is sought to amend particulars so as to include such evidence, permission would no doubt be granted as is ordinarily the case in patent actions, but upon the usual terms—viz., that the plaintiff may discontinue if he pleases, defendant bearing the costs subsequent to the delivery of his first particulars (*Morris, Wilson & Co. v. Coventry Machine Co.*, 8 P. O. R. 353).

Onus on defendant who questions title.

If a defendant calls in question (as he is entitled to do) the right of the plaintiff to be on the Register, the *onus probandi* is on the party questioning the title of the registered proprietor.

Apportionment of costs.

Again, agreeing with the practice in patent and trade mark actions, the costs in designs cases are often split up and apportioned to the different issues. The practice of thus apportioning costs was originally intended to discourage the introduction into the pleadings of anything except the issues vitally material to the matter. Therefore when either of the parties raises an unnecessary issue, or one in which he is unsuccessful, the other side will, subject to the discretion of the judge, have the costs of that issue. In patent cases the principle of apportionment of costs has been applied not only where a plaintiff has established the validity of his patent, while failing to prove infringement (*Needham v. Johnson*, 1 P. O. R. 49), but also where a defendant, while failing on the issue of infringement, has succeeded on the question of validity (*Hocking v. Fraser*, 3 P. O. R. 7), and it may safely be presumed that the same principles would apply in actions for infringement of design copyright. Thus, in *Sherwood v. Decorative Art Tile Co.* (4 P. O. R. 207), the plaintiffs put in evidence which the Court considered unnecessary, and as a result, although successful in their action, the plaintiffs were awarded two-thirds only of their costs.

Threats.

There is no provision in the Designs portion of the Act giving a remedy in the case of threats of legal proceedings issued by the proprietor of a registered design, such as exists in the Patents portion relative to threats emanating from the proprietor of Letters Patent.

PART IV.

FOREIGN AND COLONIAL PATENTS.

GENERAL REMARKS.

Prior publication a bar to obtaining patents in some countries.

It frequently happens that an inventor who has protected or patented his invention in this country desires also to obtain patents abroad. It is necessary, therefore, to point out that certain foreign countries will not grant a valid patent in the face of prior publication in this, or in the particular country in which protection is sought. As a rule publication may be said to take place when a complete and full description and illustration of the invention has been placed before readers here or in such foreign countries.

Therefore, an invention which has been fully described during the period of provisional protection in some widely circulated technical paper, such, for example, as *The Engineer* or *Engineering*, which papers are as a rule posted immediately upon publication to subscribers in various foreign countries, would be considered as published here and in such countries.

If, however, no such publication should have been allowed to take place during provisional protection, the publication of the British Complete Specification, which would follow in due course after filing and acceptance, would amount to the same thing. It may be taken for granted that the Patent Office copies of the Complete Specifications are to be seen in most foreign countries of any industrial importance within a week or two after publication in London. The British Government presents complete sets of the Patent Office publications to certain

English Specifications sent abroad as soon as published.

British Colonies and Foreign States, including Austria, Belgium, France, Germany, Italy, Japan, Russia, Spain, Sweden, and the United States of America. The agents in London, through whom the published Specifications are transmitted to the respective countries, call for fresh consignments weekly as a rule, in one or two cases monthly, and the parcel for Austria is despatched on an average about once in six weeks. It appears, therefore, that publication of the Complete Specification here is followed so swiftly by publication abroad that, although of course such publication always remains a matter of proof, it would be, generally speaking, unsafe to delay filing the application in those foreign countries which are affected by publication.

The chief Continental States in which valid patents cannot be obtained after the invention has thus been published are Austria, France, Germany, and Switzerland.

In Austria and France, and generally in Switzerland, a patent would be issued to the applicant without objection, even after such publication; but of course, if publication has actually taken place, such a patent would only remain good so long as it was unattacked. In Germany, however, patents are rigidly refused if it can be shown that the British Specification was published in London even a day before the date of application in Germany.

It will, therefore, be evident that if valid patents are desired in those countries, application should be made if possible before publication of the invention takes place here, and certainly before any publication within the States named. As a rule it is sufficient to make application before publication of the Complete Specification in this country. France and Switzerland are both adherents to the International Convention, and in their case, if any doubt exists, it is advisable to make application in those countries under the Convention. The provisions of the Convention are, that if a subject of any one of the subscribing countries who has made application for a patent at home should make application in any of the other countries within six months (and in countries beyond the sea within seven months) of his original application, then the foreign application will receive the same date as the original home application. But Austria and Germany are not members of the Convention, and with them there is therefore no such mutual arrangement. France and Switzerland are members, so that the above arrangements would apply to them. As a matter of fact, the privileges of the Convention are very little taken advantage of, and for every hundred applications for foreign patents by British subjects, scarcely five are made under the terms of the Convention.

Austria and Germany not members of the International Convention.

In certain foreign countries, as for example in Germany, the United States of America, Switzerland, &c., applications for patents are subjected to a stringent examination both as to novelty and patentability, and the results of these examinations, especially in Germany, are sometimes surprising, and not always satisfactory to the inventor.

Duration of foreign patents.

The duration of foreign patents varies with the different countries, but in very few cases is the foreign patent allowed to run for a longer term than the full period of the original home grant. Thus the term of a United States patent is seventeen years, but when founded upon a prior British patent, for example, it will expire at the end of the British term of fourteen years. At one time it was thought that the premature lapsing of the mother patent in Great Britain, by the non-payment of the renewal fees for example, also voided the United States patent for the same invention. But the decision of Judge Wallace in *Paillard v. Bruno* (38 O. G. 900), affirmed by the more recent finding of Justice Bradley, of the United States Supreme Court, in *The Bate Refrigerating Co. v. Gillett et al.*, establishes the conclusion that such premature failure of the mother patent does not involve the expiry of the United States patent for the same invention.

As a natural corollary to what has been said, it follows that no United States patent can be granted to the inventor upon a previous foreign patent which has expired, from whatever cause, even when such cause has been the mere non-payment of the taxes. This was established in the United States Supreme Court in 1892 in the case of *Hubner v. Nelson*, the Court deciding that the delay in applying for the United States patent until after the foreign patent had expired amounted to an abandonment of the right to a United States patent.

Difficulty of obtaining full term of patent right in all countries.

The differences of duration of patents in different countries suggest that an inventor who had thoroughly made up his mind concerning the world-wide value of his invention, and who was desirous of obtaining the full term of patent right in each country, might elect to secure his patent first in the countries which grant the longest term of all, and next and successively in the countries which grant shorter terms. For example, the first patents might be taken out in Belgium and Spain, which grant twenty years; the next in the United States, which grants seventeen; the next in France, Germany, Italy, &c., which grant fifteen; the next in Great Britain and the Colonies, granting fourteen; the next in Russia, where the grant might be for ten; and after these in countries where the duration of grant would be uncertain. It would not be impossible to carry out such a plan, but it is submitted that the suggestion is more theoretically interesting than practically useful, as unavoidable delays in obtaining the issues of the respective patents might either wreck the whole scheme or exhaust the patience of the applicant.

Annual taxes.

In most important foreign countries, with the notable exception of the United States, annual taxes are payable upon existing patents, and certain countries require the patent to be "worked" at intervals or continuously. These and other requirements are, however, so various that it will be safer for the reader to refer to each particular country in the alphabetically arranged pages which follow.

Algeria.

ALGERIA.

This is a French colony, and is covered by the French patent law.

America (United States).

AMERICA (United States).

(Revised Statute, 1874: Title XI.)

Patentee.

Patentee.—Anyone, of any age, sex, or nationality, who is the true and first inventor, or the executor or administrator of a deceased inventor, can obtain a patent. A patent may be issued to the inventor, or to and in the name of an assignee of the inventor, or jointly to the inventor and his assignee, but in all cases the *actual inventor* must make the application and sign the papers. When it is desired to issue the patent to the inventor's assignee, or to the inventor jointly with the assignee, an assignment should be filed *before the issue of the patent*, containing a request to that effect. A mere importer who is not the inventor, but who has introduced the invention for the first time from another country, is not entitled to apply for a patent. No official of the Patent Office can obtain a patent.

America (United States).

Duration of Patent.

Duration of Patent.—United States patents are granted for seventeen years, but in the case of British and other foreign patentees, the United States patent is limited by the full term for which the prior mother patent was granted. Premature lapse of the mother patent by non-payment of taxes, &c., does not affect the United States patent, which runs for the full term for which the mother patent was granted. To have a limiting effect, the foreign patent must have been in force or published as a patent before the issue of the American patent. It has been decided by the United States Courts that a patent applied for in the United States *after* the date of a British Provisional application, and issued in America *before* the filing of the British Complete, is not limited by the duration of the subsequently issued British patent, notwithstanding that the British patent is dated as of the date of the Provisional application. The term of a United States patent cannot be extended except by a special Act of Congress. Such extensions are costly, and are very seldom granted.

What is Patentable.

What is Patentable.—The subject-matter of patents in the United States of America is of the same nature as the subject-matter of British patents. Section 4,886 specifies "any new and useful art, machine, manufacture, or composition of matter, or any new and useful improvements thereon." This includes chemical and mechanical processes, combinations in machinery, and other features common to British practice.

America (United States).

Novelty of Invention: Effect of Prior Patent or Publication.

Novelty of Invention: Effect of Prior Patent or Publication.—Although the Act says that, to obtain a valid patent, the invention should not have been publicly known to or used by others in the United States before its *discovery* by the inventor, the real test of novelty lies in the further provision that the invention shall not have been in public use or on sale for more than two years prior to the date of *application* for a patent. An invention which has been patented in another country may be patented in America at any time during the existence of the foreign patent, if the inventor has not introduced it into public use in the United States for more than two years prior to the application there.

Taxes.

Taxes.—There are no taxes or renewal fees payable after the issue of the patent.

Working.

Working.—It is not necessary to "work" the invention in the United States.

Procedure.

Procedure.—The application must be accompanied by a Complete Specification and drawings. There is no such thing as provisional protection, and the nearest approach, which consists in filing a *caveat*, is available only to citizens of the United States, or residents about to become citizens. The examination of applications is conducted by a staff of thirty-two principal examiners, and about one hundred and seventy assistant examiners, divided into first, second, third, and fourth grades, with a host of clerks and copyists. The applications are arranged in order as received, each being taken in its turn. The time during which an application may be awaiting examination varies from one to six months. Inventions are classified into two hundred and three general classes, which are again split up into more than four thousand sub-classes. The examination is very careful and thorough, and the applicant is allowed to reply to all references and objections advanced by the examiner. If the result of the examination proves the applicant to be entitled to a patent, the allowance is granted. The final fee may then be paid, and the patent is printed and issued. All patents are issued upon the third Tuesday after the first Thursday following the day upon which the final fee is received at the Patent Office. In the event of a patent being refused, the applicant may appeal to the examiners-in-chief; from them to the Commissioner of Patents; and from the Commissioner to the Supreme Court of Columbia.

America (United States).

Models.—It was formerly the custom to require a model or sample of the invention in all cases, but these are now only rarely required. The Commissioner, however, retains the power to call for a working model, if the specifications and drawings fail to make the invention clear, or if the examiner thinks the invention would be practically inoperative.

Models.

Assignments and Licences.—An invention may be assigned wholly or in part, and the assignment recorded at any time, either simultaneously with or after application for a patent is made or the patent granted. The assignment may be for the whole or for any specified part of the States. All assignments should be recorded in the Patent Office within three months from date: otherwise they will be void against a subsequent purchaser or mortgagee without notice. The assignment may be drawn in any convenient form so long as the patent or application is identified by description, number, and date. *Licences* relating to patents may be granted, and such licences may be exclusive, general, or restricted. Licences need not be recorded.

Assignments and Licences.

Marking Patented Articles. — According to the Act, patented articles should be distinctly marked "Patented," together with the date. Where action is taken for the infringement of an invention not so marked "Patented," the plaintiff cannot recover damages except upon proof that the defendant knew he was infringing a patent, or continued to infringe after having been notified of the existence of a patent.

Marking Patented Articles.

Importation of Patented Articles.—The patented articles may be imported into the United States without affecting the patent.

Importation of Patented Articles.

Government Fees.—The fee on application for a patent is fifteen dollars, and on allowance twenty dollars.

Government Fees.

Argentine Republic.

ARGENTINE REPUBLIC.

(Law of 11th October, 1864.)

Patentee.

Patentee.—The actual inventor or his assignee, or a foreign patentee (if the inventor) or his assignee, may obtain a patent in the Argentine Republic.

Description and Duration of Patents.

Description and Duration of Patents.—Patents are granted for five, ten, or fifteen years, according to the merit of the invention or the wish of the applicant. A fifteen years' patent can be obtained only for an invention which has not been previously patented elsewhere. When a patent has been previously obtained in another country, the duration of the Argentine patent is limited to the duration of the foreign patent, but is restricted to ten years at most. Patents of addition may from time to time be obtained, and these expire with the original patent. Inventions may be protected by provisional patents, which are kept secret, and may be extended from year to year. They act as a species of caveat. There is an official examination as to novelty and patentability. The term of a patent once granted cannot be extended.

Unpatentable Inventions.

Unpatentable Inventions.—Pharmaceutical compositions, financial schemes, principles or inventions of a theoretical nature, or contrary to law and morals.

Novelty of Invention Effect of Prior Patent or Publication.

Novelty of Invention: Effect of Prior Patent or Publication.—To obtain a valid patent the invention should be novel, and should not have received such wide and full publicity in Argentina, or in other countries, as to place the public in full possession of the invention. A foreign patentee may apply for and obtain an Argentinian patent at any time during the existence of his foreign patent. A rigid interpretation of Article 4 of the Act would suggest that it would be safer for a foreign patentee to file his application in the Argentine Republic before the publication of his Specification abroad.

Taxes.

Taxes.—There are no annual taxes to pay after the issue of the patent, but one half of the application fees is usually paid in successive yearly instalments after the grant of the patent. **Argentine Republic.**

Working.—To keep the patent in force, the invention must be worked in the Republic within two years from the date of issue of grant, nor must the working be thereafter interrupted for a longer period than two years, unless under excusable circumstances, which should be reported to the Patent Office. It is advisable, although not obligatory, to obtain a legalised certificate of each working as it is effected. **Working.**

Marking and Importation.—There are no provisions regulating the marking or importation of patented articles, but anyone falsely marking his goods "Patented," or otherwise fraudulently representing himself to be a patentee, is liable to a penalty. **Marking and Importation.**

Assignments and Licences.—Assignments can only be made by notarial act, and after payment of the full amount of fees still due on the patent. An assignment should be registered in the Patent Office to preserve the assignee's rights against third parties. Licences may also be issued under the patent. **Assignments and Licences.**

Government Fees.—The fees on a new patent are 80, 200, or 350 piastres, according as the patent is taken for five, ten, or fifteen years. Patents of importation are assessed on a similar scale, according to the term granted. A provisional patent for one year is rated at 50 piastres. **Government Fees.**

AUSTRALIA.

The Australasian Colonies of New South Wales, Queensland, South Australia, Tasmania, Victoria, Western Australia, and New Zealand, have in each case separate patent laws, and these will be found under their separate headings. **Australia.**

Austria.

AUSTRIA.

(Including Bohemia, Bosnia, Herzegovina, and Lichtenstein.)

LAW OF 15TH AUGUST, 1852; TREATY OF COMMERCE, 24TH DECEMBER, 1867, EXTENDING PATENT TO HUNGARY; LAW OF 27TH DECEMBER, 1893, SEPARATING AUSTRIAN AND HUNGARIAN PATENTS.)

Under Article 14 of the reciprocal Treaty of Commerce of 1867 between Austria and Hungary, a common Austro-Hungarian patent was formerly granted covering both countries. Now, however, according to the new law of 27th December, 1893, which came into operation on the 1st January, 1894, separate and independent patents are granted in Austria and Hungary.

Patentee.

Patentee.—The inventor or his assignee, or the first importer (except where the invention has already been patented abroad). Where a prior patent exists in another country, an Austrian patent for the same invention can only be obtained validly by the foreign patentee or his legal representative or assignee. A firm or corporation may be the grantee of a patent.

Duration of Patent.

Duration of Patent.—Patents are granted for fifteen years, but if based upon a prior patent in another country, the Austrian patent is limited by the term of such prior patent.

Novelty: Effect of Prior Patent or Publication.

Novelty: Effect of Prior Patent or Publication.—Prior to the date of application in Austria, the invention must not have been described in a printed publication in Austria, nor must it have been publicly worked in the Empire. British inventors who have applied for a patent at home, and who wish to obtain an Austrian patent, would do well to refrain from giving premature descriptions of their inventions in the leading English technical papers, and to make the Austrian application before the publication of the British Complete Specification. Presentation copies of all published Specifications are sent from the Patent Office in London to Austria at short intervals of time, so that publication in Austria may always be relied upon to take place very shortly after publication in this country. Nevertheless, the fact of publication in Austria is always a matter for proof. As far as copies of German Patent Office prints are concerned, valid patents may be obtained in Austria, irrespective of publication there, if applied for within three months from the issue of the German print. **Austria.**

Taxes.—Although the aggregate of taxes for the whole term may be paid in a lump sum, patentees as a rule prefer to pay the taxes in annual instalments—*i.e.* 20 florins per annum for the first five years, and for the remaining ten years, 30, 35, 40, 45, 50, 60, 70, 80, 90, and 100 florins. **Taxes.**

Working.—The invention must be worked within a year from the date of grant, and the working must not be discontinued for any two years during the term of patent right. The working should be *bonâ fide.* Proof of each working should be entered upon the Patent Register. **Working.**

Assignments.—When made in England the assignments (prepared in German) should be executed by the assignee before a notary public, whose signature in turn requires to be legalised by an Austrian consul. The assignment must be registered in Austria, and to effect this the *assignee* should sign a notarial power, also legalised by the consul, authorising an attorney in Austria to effect the registration of the assignment. **Assignments**

BAHAMA ISLANDS.

Bahama Islands.

(COLONIAL ACT 52 VICT., CAP. 23: 23RD MAY, 1889.)

Patentee.—Strictly the true and first inventor, but practically the first importer also, may obtain a valid patent. **Patentee.**

Duration of Patent.—Patents are granted for seven years, but extensions can be easily obtained up to a maximum period of twenty-one years. **Duration of Patent.**

N

Bahama Islands.

Novelty: Effect of Prior Patent

Novelty: Effect of Prior Patent.—The invention must not have been publicly known or used within the Bahama Islands. The fact of prior patents having been obtained in other countries will not affect the granting of a perfectly valid patent in the Bahamas, so long as the invention is not public property there at the time of application being made.

Taxes.

Taxes.—No taxes are due after issue of seven years' patents. But in the event of extensions being sought, the Government fee is £10 for the second term of seven years, and £20 for the third term of seven years.

Working.

Working.—Under the original Act it was necessary to work the patent in the Bahamas within three years from date. Now, however, under Section 6 of 53 Vict., Cap. 2, an Amending Act (assented to in March, 1890) repealed the working clause, so that there is now no obligation to work the invention within the colony during the term of patent right.

Assignments and Licences.

Assignments and Licences.—Assignments require to be in duplicate and in the English language. Any form will serve, and, although not obligatory under present practice, it is desirable to have assignments acknowledged before a notary public whenever possible. Assignments must be recorded in the office of the Registrar of Records. Licences can be granted as in other countries.

General

General.—When a prior British patent exists, a certified copy of such patent should accompany the application papers. A printed copy of the Specification, certified by the Comptroller, will do. No formal "Letters Patent" are at present issued by the authorities in the Bahamas, the only documents confirming title being the Registrar's certificate of filing and the Official Gazette containing a notice of the application. A certified copy of the patent can, however, be obtained for about £6. There are no provisions as to importing or marking patented articles.

Government Fees.

Government Fees.—£3 on original grant; £10 for first extension of seven years; £20 for second extension of seven years.

BARBADOES.

Barbadoes.

(Act of 12th December, 1883.)

Patentee.—The true and first inventor or the first importer may obtain a valid patent.

Patentee.

Duration of Patent.—The duration and description of patents are the same as in the Bahamas. Patents are granted for seven years, but they may be extended for two successive terms of seven years each.

Duration of Patent.

Novelty: Effect of Prior Patent or Publication.—The invention must be new in Barbadoes—*i.e.* must not have been published nor be in general use before the date of application. The fact of the invention having been patented or published elsewhere will not prevent the grant of a valid patent in Barbadoes.

Novelty: Effect of Prior Patent or Publication.

Taxes.—There are no taxes on the seven years' patent. If the patent is extended for the further second and third terms of seven years, the fees on such extensions are £10 and £20 respectively.

Taxes.

Working.—The invention must be worked in Barbadoes within three years from the date of the patent. In practice, the working requirement can be validly met by importing and offering the patented articles for sale in the colony. A patent for a process should, however, actually be put in operation.

Working.

Assignments and Licences.—Assignments should be prepared in duplicate in the English language, attested before a notary, and legalised. Licences may be granted. There are no provisions for the registration of either assignments or licences.

Assignments and Licences.

General.—No formal Letters Patent are issued, and the patentee must be content with the certificate of filing and the notice in the Official Gazette, unless he cares to pay an extra fee of from £5 to £10 for a certified copy of the patent. The patented goods may be imported in

General.

Barbadoes.

any quantity, and there are no provisions to compel the marking of the goods with the word "Patented."

Government Fees.

Government Fees.—On original grant three pounds six shillings and eightpence; on first extension for seven years ten pounds; on second extension for seven years twenty pounds.

Belgium.

BELGIUM.

(Law of 24th May, 1854.)

Patentee.

Patentee.—The true and first inventor, or his assignee, or anyone authorised by the inventor, or the first importer, or a firm or a corporation, may obtain a valid patent so long as no fraud has been exercised in procuring the patent.

Duration and Description of Patents.

Duration and Description of Patents.—Belgian Patents are of two kinds—viz., Patents of Invention and Patents of Importation. *Patents of Invention* are granted to applicants who apply for a patent in Belgium before a patent has been issued to them for the same invention in another country. This patent is granted for twenty years. *Patents of Importation* are granted to an importer, or to an inventor who has already obtained a patent or patents in other countries. Such patents are limited to expire with the prior foreign patent having the longest term, so long as this does not exceed twenty years. *Patents of Addition* for improvements on the original invention may from time to time be tacked on to the original patent, whether of Invention or Importation, and become part of the original patent, and expire with it.

Novelty: Effect of Prior Patent or Publication.

Novelty: Effect of Prior Patent or Publication.—As far as *Patents of Invention* are concerned, the invention must not have been published or openly used in Belgium, nor must a patent for the same have been actually obtained in any other country before the date of the Belgian application. Therefore, a patent applied for in Belgium after the date of the British provisional protection, but before actual issue of the British Letters Patent, or at least before the

Belgium.

filing of the British Complete, would be lawfully a patent of invention lasting for twenty years. *Patents of Importation* can be applied for at any time during the term of the foreign patent, granted that it has not meanwhile come into public and commercial use in Belgium, and also granted that it has not been described in a printed or published work in that country. The official publication of the Complete Specification in those countries where such publication takes place does not affect the validity of Patents of Importation in Belgium.

Taxes.

Taxes.—Belgian patents are subject to increasing annual taxes. The first tax of ten francs is paid with the application; the second annuity is increased to twenty francs; and so on, the tax increasing ten francs annually. If, by inadvertence, the tax should not be paid at the proper time, one month's grace is allowed without fine, and six months' grace may be obtained by payment of a fine of ten francs in addition to the tax.

Working.

Working.—The invention must be worked in Belgium within one year from the date of the patent, or within one year of its having been practically or commercially worked in any other country, and so long as the working in any other country continues to be carried on, the working in Belgium must not cease for an entire year at a time. Where the Belgian patent has been taken out *after* the invention has been practically worked abroad, the invention should be worked in Belgium within one year from the date of the patent. The working should be *bonâ fide.* If the invention relates to a marketable article, the article should be made and offered for sale in reasonable quantity; if to a process, the process should be carried out in some manufactory in Belgium. In all cases a certificate of working should be obtained from the proper authorities. The question of "working" patented inventions in Belgium and in one or two other European States is full of uncertainty, expense, and annoyance. The usual course that inventors take is to effect some kind of nominal or perfunctory working of their inventions at the lowest cost possible, and then, having received the certificate,

Belgium.

they feel at ease. But this compliance with the letter of the law and evasion of the spirit, although it may serve to keep the patent in force, yet leaves it seriously open to attack. The Belgian Courts have declined to pronounce on such matters, and leave it to the Government to annul or maintain a patent according as it may think a patent has or has not been sufficiently worked. However, in the few cases which the Government authorities have taken into consideration, the opinion has been expressed that working cannot be effected by importation, although importation is not prohibited; also that a strictly legal working consists in manufacturing the patented articles in Belgium, in sufficient quantity to meet the commercial demand. The Government, however, seldom or never interferes to annul a patent or question its validity on account of insufficient working, unless called upon to do so by an interested party, and even then reasons for insufficient working might exist which would be held to form a good and sufficient excuse.

Working.

Assignments and Licences.

Assignments and Licences.—Assignments must be in French, executed in duplicate before a notary public, whose signature, when out of Belgium, must be legalised by a Belgian consul. Assignments must be registered. Licences can also be granted to work the patent in Belgium.

Government Fees.

Government Fees.—First tax on application ten francs; second year, twenty francs; and so on to the twentieth year, for which the tax is two hundred francs. Patents of Addition become incorporated with the original patent, and no taxes are payable in respect of them except the fees on application. This, however, only applies to patents of addition granted to the original patentee.

Bolivia.

BOLIVIA.

(Law of 8th May, 1858.)

Patentee.

Patentee.—The actual inventor or the true and first importer from abroad.

Duration and Description of Patent.

Duration and Description of Patent.—There are two kinds of Patents—viz., *Patents of Invention* (that is, when the original patent is obtained in Bolivia), and *Patents of Importation* granted to a foreign patentee or to an importer. Patents of Invention are granted for not less than ten nor more than fifteen years. The term of Patents of Importation is subject to a curious qualification. If the establishment of the industry would involve an outlay of 20,000 pesos, the patent is granted for three years; if the outlay would amount to 50,000 pesos, the term is six years; if to 100,000 pesos, the patent right is for ten years. **Bolivia.**

Novelty: Effect of Prior Patent or Publication.—The invention must not have been widely or generally published in the press, or have come into general use, either in Bolivia or elsewhere. An invention already patented in another country may be validly patented in Bolivia, even after the publication of the foreign Specification. **Novelty: Effect of Prior Patent or Publication.**

Taxes.—None after issue of the patent. **Taxes.**

Working.—Patents must be worked in Bolivia within a year and a day from date. A certificate of the working should be obtained from the proper authorities. **Working.**

Assignments and Licences.—Assignments must be in duplicate, in the Spanish language, legalised by a Bolivian consul when executed out of Bolivia. A power of attorney, also legalised by the consul, is required to authorise the recording of the assignment, a step which is absolutely necessary to avoid forfeiture. Licences can be issued. **Assignments and Licences.**

BRAZIL.

Brazil.

(Law of 14th October, 1892.)

Patentee.—The true and first inventor may obtain a patent, or a foreign patentee may have his rights confirmed in Brazil. Joint inventors may obtain a joint patent. **Patentee.**

Duration of Patent.—Patents are granted for fifteen years, but they expire with a prior foreign patent for the same invention, if such has been obtained. Patents of addition to the original patent may be obtained during **Duration of Patent.**

Brazil.

the first year by the original patentee or his legal representative only; after that time patents of addition may be obtained by other inventors.

Novelty: Effect of Prior Patent or Publication.

Novelty: Effect of Prior Patent or Publication.—The invention must not be known or publicly used in Brazil at the time of application. An inventor who has already obtained a patent elsewhere is protected from the consequences of publication, or use or attempted appropriation of the invention by another applicant in Brazil, if he makes his application within seven months from the date of his foreign patent. If an inventor wishes to use or exhibit his invention in Brazil before applying for a patent there, he may do so with safety on obtaining an official permit to that effect.

Taxes.

Taxes.—Patents are subject to annual and increasing taxes, commencing with twenty dollars for the first year, increasing to thirty dollars for the second, forty dollars for the third, and so on, at the rate of ten dollars per annum until the full term is reached. No extension of the time for payment is allowed.

Working.

Working.—The working of the invention must be effected, proved, and a certificate obtained, before the end of the third year, and such working must not be at any time suspended for a greater period than one year. If the working should be prevented by any circumstances over which the patentee has no control, the Government will condone the omission on proper proof being shown. Importation of the patented goods is not prohibited. The fraudulent marking of patented articles is punishable by a fine of from one hundred to five hundred dollars.

Assignments and Licences.

Assignments and Licences may be prepared in any convenient form, and must be in the Spanish language. No assignment will take effect until registered in the Bureau of Agriculture, Commerce, and Public Works.

Government Fees.

Government Fees.—The actual Government fees, apart from other unfixed expenses, are represented by the amounts under the head of "Taxes."

BRITISH GUIANA.

British Guiana.

(ORDNANCE NO. 13 OF 1861.)

Patentee.

Patentee.—Patents are granted to the true and first inventor, which term includes the first importer of the invention to the colony.

Duration of Patent.

Duration of Patent.—Patents are granted for fourteen years, subject to the limiting effect of any prior foreign patent. It is, however, not difficult to obtain the extension of a patent for a further term of seven years.

Novelty: Effect of Prior Patent or Publication.

Novelty: Effect of Prior Patent or Publication.—To obtain a valid patent the invention must not, prior to the date of application, have been publicly known or used in the colony. A prior patent in another country, even when published there, will not affect the validity of a subsequent patent in British Guiana, so long as the invention is not publicly known or used there at the date of application.

Taxes.

Taxes.—A renewal fee of one hundred dollars is due before the expiry of the seventh year of the patent right. No extension of the time for payment is obtainable.

Working.

Working.—There is no compulsory working of the invention, and the patented articles may be imported to the colony. The marking of the goods is left to the discretion of the patentee.

Assignments and Licences.

Assignments and Licences.—These should be in the English language, and assignments should be made in duplicate in any suitable form. When made in a foreign country they should be legalised by a British consul. Both assignments and licences must be entered in the Register of Patents.

BRITISH HONDURAS.

British Honduras.

(LAW OF 10TH SEPTEMBER, 1862.)

Patentee.

Patentee.—The true and first inventor, or the first importer, may obtain a valid patent.

Duration of Patent.

Duration of Patent.—Fourteen years, subject to the limit of any prior patent for the same invention obtained elsewhere. Extensions may sometimes be obtained.

Novelty: Effect of Prior Patent or Publication.

Novelty: Effect of Prior Patent or Publication.—The invention must not be published or publicly known, or used in the colony, before the date of application. The existence of a prior home or foreign patent, so long as it is not publicly known in British Honduras, will not affect the validity of a patent there.

Taxes.

Taxes.—A tax of fifty dollars is due before the end of the third year of the patent, and a further tax of one hundred dollars is due before the expiry of the seventh year. The time for making these payments cannot be extended.

Assignments and Licences.

Assignments and Licences.—These should be in the English language, and should be entered in the Register of Patents to have effect against third parties.

British North Borneo.

BRITISH NORTH BORNEO.

(PROCLAMATION NO. 1 OF 1887.) See **Straits Settlements.**

Burmah.

BURMAH.

Burmah is a province of British India, and is covered by the Indian patent.

Canada.

CANADA.

(COLONIAL ACT OF 1886, CAP. 61.)

Patentee.

Patentee.—A patent may be obtained by the true and first inventor or inventors, or by his or their assigns or legal representatives. As in the United States, the actual inventor, or, if deceased, his legal representative, must in all cases sign the papers and make the application, but the patent may issue to the inventor alone, or jointly to the inventor and his assignee, or to the assignee alone, a proper assignment and request being filed before the issue. **Canada.**

Duration of Patent.—Patents are granted for eighteen years, subject to the conditions as to payment of taxes and working, but where a prior patent exists in another country, the Canadian patent will expire with the said prior patent. A special legislative Act is required to obtain an extension. A caveat, which is a species of provisional application, may be filed by an intending applicant so as to secure a date, and such a caveat will remain good for a year, but cannot be renewed.

Duration of Patent.

Novelty: Effect of Prior Patent or Publication.—For the purposes of a valid patent, an invention is considered new in Canada if the invention has not been in public use or on sale in the Dominion for more than one year, without the consent of the inventor. It will be remembered that similar latitude, extending to two years, exists in the United States. If a home or foreign patent exists for the same invention, the Canadian application must be made before the expiry of twelve months from the date of such prior patent.

Novelty: Effect of Prior Patent or Publication.

Taxes.—The taxes for the full term of eighteen years may be paid before the issue of the patent. This, however, is very rarely done. The better plan is to pay the amount of twenty dollars for the first six years only at the time of making application, then to pay the renewal tax of twenty dollars before the end of the sixth year, and twenty dollars before the end of the twelfth year. There are no means of prolonging the time for making these payments.

Taxes.

Working.—The invention must be worked or commenced to be worked in Canada within two years from the date of the patent. The working must not be of a perfunctory nature, but must be sufficiently real and extensive to place goods on the market and supply any demand that may exist for the patented article. If two years should prove too short a period in which to effect this, an enlargement of the time of from six to twelve months may be obtained by presenting a petition for such enlarge-

Working.

Canada.

ment. This petition must not be made more than three months before the expiry of the term of two years. After working has been commenced, it must not be discontinued. In order to work an invention continuously, so as to comply with the law, it is a common practice with patentees to arrange with some manufacturer to make or to be ready to make the patented articles, and then to advertise that the goods may be had from this manufacturer or agent. Such an arrangement is held by authorities in Canada to constitute a perfectly legal working of the invention within the provisions of the Act.

Assignments and Licences.

Assignments and Licences may be prepared in any manner acceptable to English practice. Every assignment must be registered in the office of the Commissioner of Patents.

Marking Patented Articles.

Marking Patented Articles.—All patented articles must be marked "Patented," together with the date of the patent. Penalties are exacted from those who fraudulently mark their goods "Patented" where no patent exists.

Importation of Patented Goods.

Importation of Patented Goods.—No patented goods must be imported by the patentee, or with his knowledge or consent, into Canada, at any time after twelve months from the date of the patent. The effect of such importation would be to make the patent void. An extension of the term within which importing may be carried on may usually be had by filing a petition to that effect.

Models.

Models.—Before the Canadian patent is issued, it is usual to demand a model, which should to some extent be a working model of the invention. The size should not exceed twelve inches on the longest side. Compositions (except explosive compounds) should be explained by the production of samples of their ingredients.

Canary Islands.

CANARY ISLANDS.

(Covered by Spanish Patent.)

CAPE OF GOOD HOPE.

Cape of Good Hope.

(Act No. 17 of 1860.)

Patentee.—Patents are granted to the true and first inventor, or to the person who first imports an invention into the colony.

Patentee.

Duration of Patent.—Patents are granted for fourteen years, but where a prior home or foreign patent exists the term expires with such prior patent.

Duration of Patent.

Novelty of Invention: Effect of Prior Patent.—To obtain a valid patent in the Cape, the only requirement is that application should be made before publication or public use of the invention has taken place within the colony. The existence of a prior patent, or the fact of the invention having been published in another country, does not injure the validity of the grant in the Cape.

Novelty of Invention: Effect of Prior Patent.

Taxes.—Ten pounds is due to be paid before the end of the third year of the term of the patent right, and a further sum of ten pounds before the expiry of the seventh year.

Taxes.

Working.—There is no obligation to work the invention in the colony.

Working.

Assignments and Licences.—These may be prepared in any suitable form, and must be entered in the Register of Proprietors.

Assignments and Licences.

CEYLON.

Ceylon.

(Act No. 16 of 1892.)

Patentee.—Patents are issued to the actual inventor or to his legal representative or assign. A first importer is not entitled to a patent.

Patentee.

Duration of Patent.—Patents are granted for fourteen years, and are capable of extension if sufficiently good grounds can be shown. When prior patents exist, the

Duration of Patent.

Ceylon.

patent in Ceylon is limited by the term of the mother patent.

Novelty of Invention Effect of Prior Patent.

Novelty of Invention: Effect of Prior Patent.—When the original application is made in Ceylon, the invention must be new and unpublished in Ceylon or in the United Kingdom. If a British patent has been obtained, application in Ceylon should be made within twelve months from the date of the *actual sealing* of the British Letters Patent, and a valid patent will be issued for Ceylon, granted that the invention has not become publicly known in the colony before the date of application. Where application only has been made for a British patent, the applicant may take out a patent in Ceylon if he makes application there within twelve months from the date of his British application, and the validity of such a patent will not be affected by the fact that the invention has, within such period of twelve months, become publicly known in the United Kingdom and in Ceylon. The Specification can, from time to time, be amended as in Great Britain.

Taxes.

Taxes.—An annual tax of fifty rupees is payable before the expiry of the fourth, fifth, sixth, seventh, and eighth years; and a tax of one hundred rupees before the expiry of the ninth, tenth, eleventh, twelfth, and thirteenth years.

Working.

Working.—There is no requirement as to working the invention, and no prohibition upon importation.

Assignments.

Assignments.—These may be prepared in any suitable form, and should be entered in the Register of Inventions. The new proprietor's name should also be entered in the address book kept in the office of the Colonial Secretary for the purposes of service.

Channel Islands.

CHANNEL ISLANDS.

These islands are no longer covered by the British patent, but a species of protection may be obtained by enrolling a certified copy of the British patent in the Rolls of the Royal Court in Jersey and Guernsey.

CHILI.

Chili.

(Law of 9th September, 1840; Amended 20th January, 1883).

Patentee.

Patentee.—The actual author, or inventor, or first importer.

Duration of Patent.

Duration of Patent.—The duration of patents was fixed by the law of 1840 at ten years, but by the Amending Act of 1883 power was given to the President to extend this term up to twenty years, and, as a matter of fact, in practice, this latter term is usually granted. The term of a patent commences at the expiry of the term fixed within which it must be worked.

Novelty: Effect of Prior Patent or Publication.

Novelty: Effect of Prior Patent or Publication.—The invention must be new to, or not known or published in, Chili at the date of application. With this proviso, inventions already patented and published abroad may be validly patented in Chili. A regulation exists, whereby, in the case of an invention which has been patented abroad, the Chilian application is advertised in the Official Gazette, so as to give any person who has begun to practise the invention in Chili an opportunity of opposing the grant.

Examination.

Examination.—The application is subject to examination as to novelty and utility by a committee of experts.

Taxes.

Taxes.—None.

Working.

Working.—In granting the patent the Government fixes and endorses on the grant a period of time within which the invention must be put to work in Chili. The manufacture should be actually established or taken in hand by that time, and it is submitted that a mere perfunctory working would scarcely avail. The term of the patent commences on the expiry of the time allotted for working it. The working must not at any time be discontinued for more than one year.

Assignments &c.

Assignments, &c.—These should be in the Spanish language, executed in duplicate, and legalised, when signed

Chili.

abroad, by a Chilian consul. The Minister of the Interior should be advised of the completion of an assignment, and, if he is satisfied that it is a *bonâ fide* transaction, he will enter the assignment on the transfer book.

Government Fees.

Government Fees.—A fee of fifty dollars is payable upon application.

CHINA.

China.

The Empire of China has no law for the protection of inventions. It is, however, possible to obtain protection by securing a special grant or monopoly from the national authorities, the average cost of which has been estimated at about £500. Another method is to register certified copies of the Specification in the Chinese Foreign Office, and also at the consulate of the country to which the applicant belongs, and thereafter to advertise full particulars of the invention, together with a notification of the inventor's right of property, in the principal Chinese official newspapers. This latter method is said to confer quite as much protection as the first, and is greatly less expensive, as it may be done for about £50.

Cochin China.

COCHIN CHINA.

(Included under the French Patent.)

Columbia.

COLUMBIA.

(Law No. 35, 13th May, 1869.)

Patentee.

Patentee.—The true inventor, first importer, or the owner of a prior foreign patent, may obtain a valid patent in Columbia.

Duration of Patent.

Duration of Patent.—Patents are granted for five, ten, fifteen, or twenty years, at the option of the applicant. A Columbian patent will expire with a prior foreign patent.

Novelty: Effect of Prior Publication.

Novelty: Effect of Prior Publication.—To be validly patentable the invention should not be known or published in Columbia. Inventions patented abroad may be patented in Columbia at any time during the existence of the prior patent, but not if the invention has in the meantime become known in Columbia. **Columbia.**

Examination.—There is no preliminary examination. Examination.

Taxes.—None after the issue of the patent. Taxes.

Working.—The patent must be worked within a year from date, and must not be discontinued during the entire year. There is nothing to prohibit importation. Working.

Assignments &c. should be prepared in Spanish and be made in duplicate. They should be legalised by a Columbian consul. There being no provision in the law for the assignment of patent rights, it is not the practice to register them; but, as a patent is now everywhere recognised as constituting property, it would be quite a proper step to seek registration for documents which deal with such rights. Assignments &c.

Government Fees.—Ten dollars on application. On grant of a patent a fee is paid, which is arrived at by assessing from five to ten dollars for each year of the term for which the patent is issued. Government Fees.

CONGO FREE STATES.

Congo Free States.

(Law of 29th October, 1886; Decree of 30th October, 1886.)

Patentee.—Anyone may obtain a patent in Congo, whether the inventor or not. Patentee.

Duration and Description of Patent.—Patents are classified as "Patents of Invention" and "Patents of Importation." Patents of Invention are granted for twenty years. A Patent of Importation expires with the prior foreign patent upon which it is usually founded. Patents of Addition are also granted, which become a part of and expire with the original patent. Duration and Description of Patent.

Novelty: Effect of Prior Patent or Publication.—The law Novelty.

Congo Free States.

Effect of Prior Patent or Publication.

says nothing as to the effect of prior use or publication upon patents in Congo. The practice is, however, grounded upon that of Belgium, so that it may be taken that inventions which are known or published in Congo at the date of application are not patentable there unless the invention is patented abroad, and even then only upon the conditions annexed to the Belgian law.

Examination.

Examination.—There is no examination.

Taxes.

Taxes.—None after issue of patent.

Working.

Working.—Working is not compulsory. Patented articles may be imported, and there is no obligation to mark them as such.

Assignments.

Assignments.—These must be notified to the Department of Foreign Affairs, and the assignment is advertised in the *Bulletin Officiel* in the same manner as patent grants.

Government Fees.

Government Fees.—One hundred francs on application.

Corsica.

CORSICA.

(Included in French Patent.)

Costa Rica.

COSTA RICA.

There is no patent law in this country, but protection for inventions which are likely to prove of advantage to the country is granted by special Act of the Constitutional Congress. The average cost is from £60 to £70.

Cuba.

CUBA.

Official registration for this and other Spanish colonies can be effected in virtue of the Spanish patent.

Cyprus.

CYPRUS.

(No Patent Law.)

DENMARK.

Denmark.

(Law of 28th March, 1894.)

Prior to the 28th March, 1894, no statutory provision existed in Denmark for the protection of inventors. The Ministry of the Interior had powers to grant equivalent privileges, which were perhaps sufficiently adequate for national industries, but which adopted a harsh attitude towards foreign inventors. Now, however, Danish patents are granted by virtue of an Act passed by the Danish Parliament on the above date, and taking effect from July, 1894. The chief provisions are as follows:—

Patentee.

Patentee.—Any person, whether native or alien, may obtain a patent, provided he is the true inventor or the legal assignee of the true inventor.

Duration of Patent.

Duration of Patent.—Patents are granted for fifteen years from the date of application, and are not subject to limitation by prior patents for the same invention in other countries. Patents of Addition are granted for improvements on the original invention, and these expire with the original patent. The grant of a patent may be opposed by an interested or aggrieved person.

Novelty: Effect of Prior Patent or Publication.

Novelty: Effect of Prior Patent or Publication.—At the date of application the invention must be new and unpublished in Denmark; but the fact of publication in another country—for example, the publication of the British Complete Specification—will not cause the refusal of the Danish application, provided such publication has not been circulated in Denmark. All applications are subject to examination as to novelty and patentability.

Taxes.

Taxes.—Patents, to be kept in force, must be sustained by the payment of annual taxes, amounting for the first, second, and third years respectively to £1 8s. 2d. in English money, and thereafter doubling in amount every third year until the end of the twelfth year, when the tax is £16 18s. for each of the last three years. An extension of time of three months within which to pay any overlooked

Denmark. tax may be had on payment of a fine amounting to one-fifth of the tax due.

Working.

Working.—The invention protected by the patent must be worked in Denmark within three years from date of patent. Under special circumstances, the term for working the patent may be prolonged, or exemption from working may be obtained. At this date it is impossible to say what will be held a legal working of the invention. It seems that the importation of the patented goods into Denmark is prohibited.

Assignments and Licences.

Assignments and Licences.—These may be prepared in any suitable terms, and should be registered.

Government Fees.

Government Fees.—Represented in English money, these amount to £3 3s. on application, and consist of the application fee, 20 crowns; the issuing fee, 10 crowns; and the first annual tax, 25 crowns. The succeeding annual taxes have already been detailed.

Ecuador.

ECUADOR.

(Law of 18th October, 1890.)

Patentee.

Patentee.—The true inventor or the first importer.

Duration and Description of Patent.

Duration and Description of Patent.—There are two kinds of patents—viz., *Patents of Invention*, that is when the original patent is obtained in Ecuador; and *Patents of Importation*, granted to a foreign patentee or to an importer. Patents of Invention are granted for not less than ten or more than fifteen years. If the establishment of the industry constituting the subject-matter of a Patent of Importation involves an outlay of twenty thousand pesos, the patent is granted for three years; if the outlay would amount to fifty thousand pesos, the term is six years; if to one hundred thousand pesos, the patent right is for ten years.

Novelty:

Novelty: Effect of Prior Patent or Publication.—The invention must not have been widely or generally published in the press in Ecuador or elsewhere before the date of application. An invention patented in another country may be validly patented in Ecuador even after publication of the Specification abroad.

Ecuador.

Effect of Prior Patent or Publication.

Taxes.—None after issue of patent.

Taxes.

Working.—Patents must be worked in Ecuador within a year and a day from date. An official certificate of the working should be obtained.

Working.

Assignments and Licences.—Assignments should be in duplicate, in the Spanish language. When executed out of Ecuador they should be legalised by a consul of Ecuador. The assignment should be recorded, or it will be of no effect. Licences and assignments can be prepared in any convenient form.

Assignments and Licences.

EGYPT.

Egypt.

The Egyptian Government has a patent law under consideration, but at present nothing of the sort exists except the nominal and wholly ineffectual protection supposed to be given in Egypt under the Turkish patent.

FIJI ISLANDS.

Fiji Islands.

(ORDNANCE No. 3 OF 1889.)

Patentee.—Patents are granted to the true and first inventor or importer.

Patentee.

Duration of Patent.—Patents are granted for fourteen years, limited to expire with any prior patent in another country.

Duration of Patent.

Novelty: Effect of Prior Patent or Publication.—The fact of the invention having been already patented or published in other countries will not prejudice the validity of a patent obtained in Fiji, if unknown there at the date of application.

Novelty: Effect of Prior Patent or Publication.

Fiji Islands.

Working.

Government Fees.

Taxes.—None.

Working.—None.

Government Fees.—On application, £5 5s.; on issue of patent, £10 10s.

Finland.

FINLAND.

(Decree of 30th March, 1876.)

Patentee.

Patentee.—The inventor only can obtain a valid patent.

Duration of Patent.

Duration of Patent.—The duration is fixed by the Government at from three to twelve years, limited by any prior foreign patent for the same invention.

Novelty: Effect of Prior Patent or Publication.

Novelty: Effect of Prior Patent or Publication.—The owner of a prior foreign patent, even when this has been published and used, may also obtain a valid patent in Finland. When the Finnish application is the original, the invention must be unknown in Finland.

Taxes.

Taxes.—None after issue.

Working.

Working.—The invention should be worked in Finland within two years from date of the patent, and thereafter from year to year. The practice is loose, and it is considered a valid working to import a machine (if this is the invention) and operate it in Finland. A process must, however, be put in use. Proof of the working should be obtained, and delivered to the Government.

Assignments and Licences.

Assignments and Licences.—Patents may be transferred and dealt with as in most other countries. The documents must be legalised by a Russian consul, and these, as well as the fact of working, be notified to the *Manufacturers' Direction.*

France (and Colonies).

FRANCE (and Colonies).

(Law of 5th July, 1844; Decree of 21st October, 1848.)

Patentee.

Patentee.—Although, strictly speaking, only the true inventor or his assignee is legally entitled to a patent, practically anyone, whether the inventor or not, or the first importer, or a firm, or a corporation, may obtain a patent in France. In any case where the patentee is not the inventor, his title to the patent is unquestionable, if he can show that he made the application in his own name with the consent of the inventor.

Duration of Patent.

Duration of Patent.—Patents are granted for five, ten, or fifteen years at the option of the applicant. In almost all cases the fifteen years' term is asked for. Patents of Importation for inventions already patented abroad expire with the prior foreign patent which is the first to lapse. Patents of Addition are granted, and become part of the original patent, and expire with it.

Unpatentable Inventions.

Unpatentable Inventions.—Pharmaceutical compositions and medicines of all kinds, and also financial schemes, cannot be patented in France.

Novelty: Effect of Prior Patent or Publication.

Novelty: Effect of Prior Patent or Publication.—The invention must be novel, and Article 31 of the French Law says, "No discovery, invention, or application shall be considered as new which in France *or abroad*, and before the date of the deposit of the application, has received sufficient publicity to enable the same to be worked." It is clear, therefore, that to enable a British applicant to obtain a valid French patent he must make his application in France before the publication of his Specification *in this country*. It must be understood that the French authorities make no examination into the novelty of an invention, and a patent for anything will be granted to any applicant; but of course a patent which did not possess the legal essentials would be of but little value to its owner. The mere fact of a prior foreign patent being in existence for the same invention will not invalidate the French patent so long as the invention has not been published, or used, or otherwise made publicly known, before application for a patent in France.

Taxes.

Taxes.—French patents are subject to the payment of an annual tax of one hundred francs. No extension of time for the payment of the tax can be obtained.

France (and Colonies).

Working.

Working.—A French patent must be worked within two years from the date of the *actual signature or issue of the Letters Patent*, and must not cease during any two consecutive years thereafter. Failure to fulfil this condition will render the patent liable to be declared void, unless such failure was caused by circumstances which were beyond the patentee's control. Sickness, poverty, political disturbance, the difficulty of getting the invention taken up by reason of the limited field of use, all of these have been held good as excuses to prevent forfeiture. There are several cases which show that the French Courts are becoming more and more unwilling to accept the mere pretence of working which is common in the case of most patents. It has been held, for example, that a single act of manufacture of the invention is not enough. No doubt the expense of working is a severe tax upon patentees, but if the patent is at all likely to be of value, proper working should not be neglected. The mere sending of the parts of a machine into France and fitting them together there would not, according to the Courts, be a sufficient working. The whole or a portion of the parts should be made in France, and the readiness of the patentee to supply a demand should be advertised in a French newspaper of standing. The patentee might sometimes find a manufacturer or agent to undertake the working of the invention on reasonable terms. It is advisable in all cases when the working is effected, to obtain a certificate to that effect from the proper authorities. So long, however, as it is possible to prove afterwards *that the invention actually was worked*, the mere omission to obtain a certificate will not matter.

Assignments.

Assignments.—According to the French law (Section 4, Article 20) no assignment can be recorded until all the future annual taxes are paid for the full term of the patent. This immediate expense can, however, be avoided by preparing an irrevocable power of attorney, authorising a notary to effect the assignment, and the name of the notary may be left blank. This power is signed by the vendor, legalised by a French consul, and may then be kept by the purchaser. If circumstances should require registration, he has only to fill in a notary's name, who will then be empowered to have the assignment made and recorded.

France (and Colonies).

Marking and Importing Patented Articles.—In France a patentee is not obliged to mark patented articles as such; but if he do so, he must add the words "*Sans Garantie du Gouvernement*," or the initial letters of the phrase, "S. G. D. G." The penalty for omitting this is from 50 to 1,000 francs. France being a member of the International Convention, the patented articles may be imported freely from other countries which are also members of the Union, as is, for example, the case with Great Britain. But the denizens of other countries which are not members of the Union are not allowed this privilege, and importation by a citizen of such a country would involve the forfeiture of his patent.

Marking and Importing Patented Articles.

Government Fees.—These are represented by the annual taxes already set forth.

Government Fees.

(*N.B. The French patent covers the colonies of Algeria, Cambodia, Cochin China, French Guiana, Guadaloupe, La Ré-Union, Loyalty Islands, Marquesas Islands, Martinique, Micquelon, New Caledonia, St. Pierre, Senegambia, and Tahiti.*)

FRENCH INDO-CHINA.

French Indo-China.

(Decree of 24th June, 1893.)

Under this Decree patents are issued in Indo-China upon conditions similar to those set forth in the French law.

GAMBIA (British).

Gambia (British).

This colony has no patent law, but protection for a meritorious invention can easily be obtained by special Legislative Act, at a cost of about £50.

German Empire.

GERMAN EMPIRE.

(LAW OF 1ST JULY, 1877.)

Patentee.

Patentee.—Whoever first applies for a patent is entitled to the grant. Patents are granted to a single applicant, to joint applicants, to a firm, or to a corporation. But if a person who is not the inventor has his application opposed by the true inventor, and the latter succeeds in showing that the applicant obtained the invention from him, the patent will be refused to the fraudulent applicant and granted to the true inventor.

Duration of Patent.

Duration of Patent.—Patents are granted for fifteen years from the day following the date of application, and the lapse of a prior foreign patent does not affect the German patent. Patents of Addition are granted, which expire with the original patent.

Unpatentable Inventions.

Unpatentable Inventions.—Articles of food, pharmaceutical compositions, and the products of chemical processes. But chemical processes apart from the products are patentable.

Novelty: Effect of Prior Patent or Publication.

Novelty: Effect of Prior Patent or Publication.—The German law is very severe in respect to novelty. An application for a patent must be filed before the invention has been described in any printed publication, either in Germany or elsewhere. For example, German applications by British inventors, even when made before the publication of the British Complete Specification, have been refused, because of short descriptions of the invention which have been incautiously published in some English technical paper. Therefore, whoever wishes to secure a German patent must see to it that no publication of his invention shall be allowed to take place until after the deposit of his German application.

Examination.

Examination.—All applications are subject to a very strict and thorough examination as to novelty, utility, and patentability. The patent records and technical publications of every country are examined carefully, and any

German Empire.

anticipatory matter which can be found is quickly brought to the notice of the applicant. Patentability is also a feature which the examiners take upon themselves to decide. Although not so drastic in their decisions as they formerly were, the conclusions of the German examiners are not always of a satisfactory nature. An appeal may be had from the decision of the first examiner to the Board of Examiners-in-Chief.

Taxes.

Taxes.—Annual progressive taxes are payable on German patents. The first annuity amounts to thirty marks, the second to fifty marks, and thereafter the tax increases at the rate of fifty marks per annum.

Working.

Working.—Patents must be put to work within three years from the date of the grant of the patent. If this working is not effected in due time, the Act says, not that the patent therefore *becomes void*, but that *it may be declared void*. There are, therefore, many cases where failure to work within the appointed time has not been followed by any annulment of the patent. But this depends upon the circumstances. For example, the patentee of a new manufacture of armour-plate was excused because of the difficulty and cost of working such an invention, and in view of the fact that he had offered to license certain makers in Germany. But the patentee of an automatic pencil was deprived of his patent because the Court held that the invention could have been easily worked in Germany. Besides, it was shown that a large demand existed in Germany for the pencil, which was proved by the fact that the patentee had imported enormous quantities of the pencils into Germany. The decisions all show that the provision for working is intended to be met by a real manufacture of the invention being carried on in Germany; that the working should be actual and thorough; and that a mere scamped pretence of working would not satisfy requirements. Therefore, when a patentee cannot himself establish such a manufacture, he should try to arrange with a German manufacturer or agent to make or put himself in a position to make the patented article, and to advertise

German Empire.

that fact in the public press. Importation of the patented goods is not prohibited, and there is no obligation to mark the articles as "Patented," although this should always be done.

Models.

Models.—Models and samples are required in the following classes of invention:—Firearms, spools, spindles and shuttles (in the case of spindles a sectional model should also be supplied), skates, chemicals (except explosives), and dyes.

Assignments and Licences.

Assignments and Licences.—To enable an assignment of a German patent to be properly registered at the Patent Office, the assignment should be in German, signed by the assignor before a notary, whose signature should be attested by a German consul. No consideration need be expressed. The assignment should be accompanied by a power of attorney, signed by the assignee, and authorising an agent or attorney in Berlin to register the assignment on behalf of the assignee. This power should also be attested by a notary and consul, as in the case of the assignment. Licences may also be granted in respect of German patents, and there is a provision in the German law whereby a patentee who refuses to grant licences on reasonable terms, when such licences seem to be demanded in the public interest, may be deprived of his patent.

Useful Design Patents.

Useful Design Patents.

An Act for the protection of useful designs in Germany came into effect on the 1st of October, 1891. Such design patents are granted without any examination. For many articles and novelties which would not warrant the expense of a patent, or which do not possess the elements of patentability, the Designs Act will suit admirably. The full period of protection is six years. Where a Patent of Invention is wished for, but where the chance of obtaining it seems slight, applicants sometimes file an application for a patent and an application under the Designs Act *simultaneously*, including under the latter application a request that the office will grant the design protection only in case of the rejection of the patent

German Empire.

application. If the patent is refused, all is not lost, as the applicant has the design application to fall back upon. If the patent is granted, then the design application can be withdrawn. There is no obligation to work a patented design in Germany, as must be done in the case of ordinary patents. The design must be new in Germany.

(Baden, Bavaria, Prussia, Saxony, and Wurtemberg are covered by the German patent.)

GIBRALTAR.

Gibraltar.

Gibraltar has no patent law, but British patentees may have their patents extended to cover the dependency for the unexpired term of the British patent.

GOLD COAST COLONY.

Gold Coast Colony.

This colony has no patent law, but protection may be obtained by way of special Legislative Act at a cost of about fifty pounds.

GREECE.

Greece.

Greece has no patent law, but a private Act can be obtained for the protection of a meritorious invention.

GUADELOUPE.

Guadeloupe.

Covered by French patent.

Guatemala.

GUATEMALA.

(LAW OF 21ST MAY, 1886.)

Patentee.

Patentee.—Under present conditions the applicant for a patent must be—

(*a*) A citizen of Guatemala;

(*b*) A foreigner domiciled there; or

(*c*) A person who has already applied for a patent in a country which is a party to the International Convention.

An applicant not coming under one of these descriptions must authorise a native attorney to obtain a patent on his behalf.

Duration of Patent.

Duration of Patent.—From five to fifteen years, limited by the term of a prior foreign patent when such exists.

Novelty: Effect of Prior Patent or Publication.

Novelty: Effect of Prior Patent or Publication.—The invention must not be publicly known or used in Guatemala. Publication or use elsewhere does not matter.

Taxes.

Taxes.—The taxes are variable at the pleasure of the Government, but are fixed at the time of issuing the patent. The tax varies from five to fifty pesos, payable annually in advance. In practice the larger amounts are seldom imposed.

Working.

Working.—The invention should be worked within one year from the date of the patent, and should not cease for a year. Importation, against which there is no prohibition, usually suffices for working.

Assignments.

Assignments.—These should be in the Spanish language, prepared in duplicate, and legalised by a Guatemalan consul when the documents are signed abroad.

Hawaii.

HAWAII.

(LAW OF 29TH AUGUST, 1884.)

Patentee.

Patentee.—Only the true and first inventor is entitled to a patent.

Hawaii.

Duration of Patent.—Ten years from date of issue, but limited by the term of any existing prior foreign patent. Duration of Patent.

Novelty: Effect of Prior Patent or Publication.—The invention should not have been publicly used or published either in Hawaii or elsewhere. But where an invention has been patented elsewhere, a valid patent can be obtained in Hawaii for the invention, granted that it has not been in public use in Hawaii for more than one year. Novelty: Effect of Prior Patent or Publication.

Taxes.—None after issue of patent. Taxes.

Working.—The patentee is not obliged to work the invention in Hawaii. Working.

Assignments.—Assignments should be acknowledged before a notary public, and must be recorded within three months from date of execution. Assignments.

Government Fees.—On application five dollars are payable. The Commissioner of Patents is paid a fee of twenty dollars for examination, and a tax of five dollars is payable on the issue of the patent. No further payments are required. Government Fees.

HOLLAND.

Holland.

Holland has no patent law; but it is probable that in the near future a law will be passed.

HONDURAS (Republic).

Honduras (Republic).

Honduras has no patent law; but the Government will protect inventions of special utility by introducing and carrying a Bill to that effect. The cost of such a grant necessarily varies, but the average expense is about £80.

HONG KONG.

Hong Kong.

(Ordnance of 1892.)

Patentee.—The patentee, inventor, or proprietor, by assignment or otherwise, of an invention which has already Patentee.

Hong Kong. been patented in Great Britain, is alone entitled to obtain a patent for the same invention in Hong Kong.

Duration of Patent. *Duration of Patent.*—The term is limited to expire with that of the British patent. If the British patent is extended, the Hong Kong patent may be similarly extended.

Novelty: Prior Publication. *Novelty: Prior Publication.*—The form of petition (Schedule A) requires the applicant to declare that the invention is not now and has not been publicly used in the colony, but the Act says nothing about novelty, and it may be taken that, whether so used or not, the proprietor of a British patent has a right to a patent in Hong Kong.

Taxes. *Taxes.*—None after issue.

Working. *Working.*—No requirements.

Hungary.

HUNGARY.

As already explained under the heading "Austria," the arrangement whereby an Austro-Hungarian patent was granted, covering both States, came to an end on the 31st of December, 1893. A separate patent is now granted for Hungary, the law and practice being precisely the same as in Austria. In fact, the Act under which Hungarian patents are granted is the Austrian Act of 1852. Readers are, therefore, referred to the heading "Austria."

Iceland.

ICELAND.

Iceland (which is a Danish possession) has no patent law, but patents are granted in the same manner and upon the same terms and conditions as in Denmark. (See "Denmark.")

India.

INDIA.

(Act No. 5 of 1888.)

Patentee. *Patentee.*—Patents are granted only to the true inventor, his assignee, or legal representative. The term "inventor" does not include the first importer.

Duration of Patent. *Duration of Patent.*—Patents are granted for fourteen years, and are limited by the duration of any prior foreign patent. Thus an Indian patent founded on a prior British patent will expire with the British patent. **India.**

Novelty: Effect of Prior Patent or Publication.—When a British patent has already been applied for or obtained, an application by the inventor for an Indian patent may be filed at any time within one year from the *actual sealing* of the British Letters Patent. But in such a case the invention must not have been known or publicly used *in India* before the date of the British application. Use or publication in India between the date of the British application and the expiry of one year from the sealing of the British patent will not prejudice the Indian patent, whether such use or publication takes place in India or in the United Kingdom. But in the case of an original Indian application the invention must be absolutely new and unknown in India; and in the case of an application by a foreign patentee, *i.e.* a patentee other than British, his application in India must be made within one year from the *actual date* of his prior foreign patent, and before any use or publication of the invention in India. **Novelty: Effect of Prior Patent or Publication.**

Taxes.—As is the case in Great Britain, the Indian patent remains untaxed until the end of the fourth year of its existence, when annual taxes of fifty rupees from the fourth to the eighth year, and one hundred rupees from the eighth to the thirteenth year, fall due to be paid. **Taxes.**

Working.—There are no requirements as to working, nor as to importation or marking. **Working.**

Assignments.—Assignments may be drawn in any usual form, and must be registered at the office of the Secretary of the Government of India. Compulsory licences may in certain cases be applied for and enforced. **Assignments.**

ITALY.

Italy.

(Law of 31st January, 1864, whereby the Sardinian Law of 30th October, 1859, was extended to the Whole Kingdom.)

Patentee.—In original applications by subjects, the applicant must be the true and first inventor. In the **Patentee.**

Italy.

case of inventions already patented abroad, the true inventor or his assignee (which term includes an individual, a firm, or a corporation) may obtain a valid patent.

Duration of Patent.

Duration of Patent.—Patents are granted for from one to fifteen years, as desired by the applicant. In most cases it is advisable to apply in the first instance for a six years' patent, because in that case *two* years are granted within which to work the invention, whereas for a less term *one* year only is allowed. The six years' patent can afterwards be prolonged to the full term of fifteen years, either annually or by terms of years as desired. An Italian patent for an invention which has been already patented abroad expires with the foreign prior patent which has been granted for the longest term. Patents of Addition are granted, to expire with the original patent, of which they form a part.

Novelty: Effect of Prior Patent or Publication.

Novelty: Effect of Prior Patent or Publication.—When a foreign patent has been already applied for or obtained, a valid patent may be had in Italy for the same invention at any time during the existence of the said foreign patent, even when published and in general use. But in that case the Italian application should be made before the invention has become publicly known or been put to public use in Italy by persons *other than the inventor or patentee.* When an original application is made in Italy, the invention must not have been known or publicly used in the kingdom before the date of application.

Taxes.

Taxes.—When the patent is applied for and the term of grant fixed, a proportional tax on the number of years agreed upon is calculated and paid, at the rate of 10 lire per annum. In addition to this there are annual taxes of 40 lire for each of the first three years; 65 lire for each of the following three years; 90 lire for the next three years; 115 lire for the tenth, eleventh, and twelfth years; and 140 lire for each of the three last years. Three months' grace without fine is allowed within which to pay these taxes. Patents of Addition are subject only to the payment in advance of a fee of 20 lire.

Italy.

Working.

Working.—If the term of patent right is less than six years, the patent must be worked in Italy before the expiry of one year from the date of the patent, and must not cease during any one year thereafter. If the term of the patent is for six years or more, then two years are allowed within which to work the patent, and the working must not cease during any two years thereafter. Where the working has been omitted, owing to causes which were beyond the patentee's control, his failure to work may be condoned so as not to entail forfeiture of his patent rights. As a rule the Italian Courts have shown themselves inclined to favour patentees, but it may be said that lack of means has not been held to constitute a good excuse. When the patent is for a machine, the best plan is to import the machine, preferably in parts, and put it together and operate it in Italy. But a process patent should be worked by going through the process there. In all cases a properly attested certificate of the working should be obtained and filed by the patentee. Importation is allowed, and there are no provisions as to marking patented articles.

Assignments.

Assignments.—When a patent is assigned *in toto* the assignee becomes bound to pay the taxes or renewal fees. When only partly assigned, or when assigned in distinct shares or to separate individuals, not having common interests, registration can only be effected upon payment of the whole of the taxes still due in the future upon the remainder of the term of the patent right. It will be remembered that a provision similar to the latter, but applicable to all forms of assignment, exists in the French law.

JAMAICA.

Jamaica.

(Law No. 15 of 27th May, 1891.)

Patentee.

Patentee.—The intention of the Act is evidently to confine the grant of letters patent to the true and first inventor or his authorised attorney. But, with the widening of the meaning of the term "inventor," it is the

Jamaica.

custom for assignees and first importers to apply for patents of which they are in no sense the authors. There is, however, no decision to the effect that letters patent so granted are invalid.

Duration of Patent.

Duration of Patent.—Patents are granted for fourteen years, and when prior foreign patents exist the patent in Jamaica expires with the foreign patent having the shortest term. As is the case in the United States and in most other countries, a valid patent cannot be obtained for an invention the foreign patent for which has expired. Patents of Addition are granted, which expire with the original patent.

Novelty: Effect of Prior Patent or Publication.

Novelty: Effect of Prior Patent or Publication.—The invention should not, at the date of application, have been introduced into public and common use in Jamaica. With this proviso, inventions patented and published in other countries may be validly patented in Jamaica at any time during the term of the foreign mother patent.

Taxes.

Taxes.—No taxes are due after issue.

Working.

Working.—The invention must be worked within two years from the date of the patent. Importation and operation of a patented apparatus have been held sufficient to fulfil the requirements of working in Jamaica. The goods need not be marked.

Assignments.

Assignments.—These should be registered in the office of the Colonial Secretary.

Japan.

JAPAN.

The new Japanese Patent Law, which was passed in December, 1888, and which came into operation on 1st February, 1889, provides for the granting of patents to *natives* of Japan only. Foreigners do not, therefore, participate in the benefits of this law. All that can be done at present is to make application for a special grant, the response to which is uncertain, while the cost is considerable.

LEEWARD ISLANDS.

Leeward Islands.

(Antigua, Anguilla, Dominica, Montserrat, Nevis, St. Christopher, and Virgin Islands.)

(Act No. 12 of 1876, and No. 16 of 1878.)

Patentee.—The true and first inventor or first importer. Patentee.

Duration of Patent.—Patents are granted for fourteen years, expiring with any prior foreign patents. Extensions may sometimes be obtained. Duration of Patent.

Novelty: Effect of Prior Patent or Publication.—Prior publication or patents in another country will not prevent the grant of a valid patent in the Leewards, if the invention is not known or used in the colonies at the time of application being made. Novelty: Effect of Prior Patent or Publication.

Taxes.—Before the end of the third year a tax of £10 is payable, and before the end of the seventh year a further tax of £20. No prolongation of time is obtainable if these taxes should be missed. Taxes.

Working.—No working is necessary. Working.

Assignments.—These may be in any suitable form, and should be recorded in the Register of Proprietors. Assignments.

Government Fees.—In addition to the taxes already mentioned, the fees payable on application and issue of the patent amount to £15, and those to the Attorney-General to about £20. Government Fees.

LIBERIA.

Liberia.

(Act of 23rd December, 1864.)

Patentee.—The true and first inventor, his legal representatives or assigns. Patentee.

Duration of Patent.—Twenty years. Duration of Patent.

Novelty: Effect of Prior Patent or Publication.—The invention, whether sought to be protected by a citizen of Novelty: Effect of Prior

Liberia.

Patent or Publication.

Liberia or a foreigner, must not be known or published within the limits of the Republic at the date of application. A prior patent in another country will not prevent the same inventor from obtaining a valid patent in Liberia.

Taxes.

Taxes. None after issue.

Working.

Working. Patents granted to aliens must be worked within three years of date.

Assignments.

Assignments.—By Section 8 patents are assignable in law.

Government Fees.

Government Fees.—Fifty dollars are payable on application.

Luxemburg.

LUXEMBURG.

(Law of 30th June, 1880.)

Patentee.

Patentee.—The first applicant or applicants. A firm or corporation may be the grantee of a patent. A patent may, however, be revoked if it can be proved that the grantee has procured the patent in fraud of another person.

Duration of Patent.

Duration of Patent.—Patents are granted for fifteen years. Patents of Addition are also granted, which expire with the original patent.

Novelty: Effect of Prior Patent or Publication.

Novelty: Effect of Prior Patent or Publication.—The patent must not be known or publicly used in Luxemburg at the date of application. Neither must it have been published or openly worked in any one of the States of the German Customs Union. If these conditions as to novelty hold good, the existence of prior foreign patents will not prejudice the Luxemburg grant.

Taxes.

Taxes.—There are annual taxes of ten francs for the first year, twenty francs for the second year, and so on, increasing ten francs per annum during the term of the patent. Three months' grace is allowed for making payment.

Luxemburg.

Working.

Working.—The patent should be worked within three years from date. Importation and operation of a patented machine will satisfy requirements.

N.B.—The patent lapses if a patent for the same invention has not been applied for, or is not within three months applied for, in the States with which the Grand Duchy may be connected by treaties of Customs Union; and if such collateral patent expires from any cause, the Luxemburg patent also expires. At present the German patent is the only one answering to the indicated description, so that unless the inventor possesses or intends to apply for a German patent the Luxemburg grant would be of no use to him.

MADEIRA ISLANDS.

Madeira Islands.

(Covered by Portuguese Patent.)

MALTA.

Malta.

(Ordnance No. 13 of 1889.)

Patentee.

Patentee.—The true and first inventor or his authorised attorney.

Duration of Patent.

Duration of Patent.—Patents are granted for fourteen years, limited by the term of any prior patent in another country.

Novelty: Effect of Prior Patent or Publication.

Novelty: Effect of Prior Patent or Publication.—The invention must not have been published or openly used either in Malta or elsewhere. A patent in another country will not prejudice the Maltese grant if the invention has not been made publicly known. The publication of the British, American, or German Specification would prevent the obtaining of a valid Maltese patent.

Taxes.

Taxes.—There is a tax of £1 payable every two years during the term of the patent right, and, in addition to

Malta.

the said fixed tax, the patentee is required to pay five per cent. of the profits he may have made from the manufacture under the patent in Malta.

Working.

Working.—If the invention is not worked in Malta within twelve months, or if the working is thereafter suspended for a continuous period of twelve months, the patentee may be required to assign his rights, or grant the use of the patent to some competent manufacturer, for a consideration to be determined by a Civil Court. Inquiry from those competent to give an opinion points to the conclusion that importation and sale of the patented articles would satisfy working requirements.

Assignments.

Assignments.—There are no provisions as to assignments, but it may be assumed that these may be prepared in the usual form in the English language.

Government Fees.

Government Fees.—£1 is payable on application, in addition to the taxes and percentage of profits as set forth.

Martinique.

MARTINIQUE.

(Covered by French Patent.)

Mauritius.

MAURITIUS.

(Ordnance No. 16 of 1875.)

Patentee.

Patentee.—Patents are granted to the actual inventor, whether native or alien, and to the representative or assigns of the actual inventor. A mere importer cannot obtain a valid patent.

Duration of Patent.

Duration of Patent.—Patents are granted for a term of fifteen years, but this term is limited by the duration of any prior patent, whether British or foreign. Extension of the term may be obtained if the Governor in Council thinks that such extension is called for.

Mauritius.

Novelty: Effect of Prior Patent or Publication.

Novelty: Effect of Prior Patent or Publication.—An inventor who has obtained a British patent may take out a patent in Mauritius within one year from the date of the British patent, although the invention is publicly known and used in Mauritius at the date of application there. But such publication in Mauritius must not have taken place prior to the date of the British patent. There is no examination.

Taxes.

Taxes.—None after issue of patent.

Working.

Working.—There are no requirements as to working, and no provisions as to importation and marking.

Assignments.

Assignments may be in any usual form, and must be registered and transcribed at the Mortgage Office.

Government Fees.

Government Fees.—Ten pounds on issue of the Procureur Général's certificate of protection, and two pounds on the sealing of the patent.

MEXICO.

Mexico.

(Law of 7th June, 1890.)

Patentee.

Patentee.—Patents are granted to inventors, or to the improvers of any manufacture or branch of industry, or to their lawful representatives.

Duration of Patent.

Duration of Patent.—Patents are granted for twenty years, but where prior foreign patents exist, the Mexican patent expires with the first or mother patent of the series. Extensions for five years are sometimes granted if the executive thinks fit. Existing ten years' patents, under the old Act, may be extended to the new term of twenty years.

Novelty: Effect of Prior Patent or Publication.

Novelty: Effect of Prior Patent or Publication.—The application must be made before the invention has been publicly worked in Mexico or elsewhere. Publication of the Specifications of prior patents by foreign patent offices, or publicity given by international or other exhibitions, is not considered to constitute publication. Apart from this

Mexico.

requirement as to novelty, the existence of prior foreign patents is no bar to the granting of a valid Mexican patent. Patents are granted without examination.

Taxes. *Taxes.*—None after issue.

Working. *Working.*—The patent dates from its *issue*, and the patentee must prove that within five years from this date the patented articles are made and used in the Republic: otherwise the patent becomes forfeited. The wording of the Article seems to point to importation and sale as being sufficient to satisfy the requirements. Patented articles must bear the date and number of the patent.

Assignments. *Assignments.*—A Mexican patent may be assigned at any time and place and in any language, although preferably in Spanish. The documents should be executed before a notary, legalised by a Mexican consul, and must be registered in the Mexican Patent Office.

Morocco.

MOROCCO.

(MOROCCO HAS NO PATENT LAW.)

Natal.

NATAL.

(LAWS NO. 4 OF 1870, NO. 5 OF 1871, AND NO. 32 OF 1884.)

Patentee. *Patentee.*—Patents are granted to the true and first inventor. The Act provides that the word "inventor" shall bear the same interpretation which is put upon it in British practice. Therefore it is submitted that the true and first inventor includes the true and first importer to the colony.

Duration of Patent. *Duration of Patent.*—Patents are granted for fourteen years from the date of application. If prior foreign patents exist, the patent in Natal will expire with that foreign patent which first expires. Extensions of patents may, in some cases, be obtained.

Natal.

Novelty: Effect of Prior Patent or Publication.—The sole essential is that the invention should not be publicly known or publicly used in Natal at the date of application. Prior patenting, or publication, or use elsewhere, will have no prejudicial effect upon the validity of the Natal patent. There is no preliminary examination. Novelty; Effect of Prior Patent or Publication.

Taxes.—Before the expiry of the third year of the patent, a tax of £5 is due; and before the expiry of the seventh year, a tax of £10. Taxes.

Working.—There is no obligation to work the patent in the colony, and no provision as to importation or marking. Working.

Assignments.—These may be prepared in any usual form, in duplicate, and must be entered in the Register of Proprietors. Assignments.

NEWFOUNDLAND.

Newfoundland.

(Consolidated Statutes, Title XV., Cap. 54, Sec. 1.)

Patentee.—The true inventor or the representative or assignee of the inventor. Patentee.

Duration of Patent.—Patents run for fourteen years, but are limited by the term of any prior foreign patent. Duration of Patent.

Novelty: Effect of Prior Patent or Publication.—A patent may be obtained in Newfoundland for an invention already patented and published abroad, but it must not be publicly known or used in the island. There is no examination as to novelty. Novelty Effect of Prior Patent or Publication.

Taxes.—There are no taxes payable after issue. Taxes.

Working.—The invention should be brought into operation in Newfoundland within two years from date of patent. It is understood that importation and sale of the patented goods will constitute a valid working. There is no obligation to mark the goods. Working.

Models and Specimens.—When the invention relates to a machine, the patent authorities are empowered to demand a model; and in compositions of matter (except explosives) Models and Specimens.

Newfoundland.

specimens of the ingredients and of the composition may be required. In practice neither models nor specimens are often asked for.

New South Wales.

NEW SOUTH WALES.

(ACT 24 OF 6TH DECEMBER, 1852; ACT 3 OF 8TH JULY, 1887.)

Patentee.

Patentee.—The inventor, or his assignee, or nominee, or agent, or the first importer, or a firm or corporation.

Duration of Patent.

Duration of Patent.—Patents are granted for fourteen years from the date of the filing of the application.

Novelty: Effect of Prior Patent or Publication.

Novelty: Effect of Prior Patent or Publication.—The invention should not at the time of application have been published, made, sold, or used in New South Wales. Publication abroad, or the issue of prior foreign patents, will not prevent the obtaining of a valid patent in New South Wales. A preliminary examination is not usual, but it is provided in the Act that it may be ordered.

Taxes.

Taxes.—There are no taxes after the issue of the patent.

Working.

Working.—There are no requirements as to working, importation, or marking.

Assignments and Licences.

Assignments and Licences.—These must be registered in the office of the Examiner of Patents: otherwise they are null and void. The periods within which registration must be effected are as follows:—When executed within the colony, fourteen days; within any of the other Australian colonies, thirty days; other places, ninety days. The documents are prepared in the English language, in any suitable form, and must be in duplicate.

New Zealand.

NEW ZEALAND.

(ACT NO. 12 OF 1889.)

Patentee.

Patentee.—Patents are granted to the true inventor, or his nominee or assignee, or to the authorised first importer.

A company or corporation may be the assignees, but cannot be the grantees of letters patent. **New Zealand.**

Duration of Patent.—Patents are granted for fourteen years from the date of the acceptance of the specification. The Act makes provision for the extension of a patent for seven, and in exceptional cases, for fourteen years. **Duration of Patent.**

Novelty: Effect of Prior Patent or Publication.—To obtain a valid patent the invention must not have been published or made publicly known or openly used in New Zealand before the date of application. Subject to this condition, the existence and publication of British or foreign patents will not militate against the validity of the New Zealand patent. The application is not subject to any examination as to novelty or utility. **Novelty; Effect of Prior Patent or Publication.**

Taxes.—A tax of five pounds is payable before the expiration of the fourth year of patent right, and a further sum of ten pounds is payable before the expiry of the seventh year. An extension of time for three months for the payment of these taxes may be had on payment of a fine of four pounds. **Taxes.**

Working.—There are now, since January 1st, 1890, no requirements as to working, and none as to importation and marking. **Working.**

Assignments.—These may be drawn in the same form as British assignments. The documents are prepared in duplicate, and should be accompanied by a request for entry in the Register of Patents, signed by the assignee. **Assignments.**

NICARAGUA.

Nicaragua.

There is no patent law in Nicaragua, but inventions are protected by special legislative grant if they promise to be of practical utility to the country. The cost of such grant averages from £50 to £60. The terms usually granted are ten years for a patent of invention; seven years for a patent of improvement; and five years for a patent of importation.

Norway.

NORWAY.

(Law of 16th June, 1885.)

Patentee.

Patentee.—Patents are granted to the actual inventor only, or to some one directly deriving his rights from the inventor. Patents of Addition are granted up to within two years from the date of the original grant, and then only to the original patentee.

Duration of Patent.

Duration of Patent.—Patents are granted for fifteen years. Such Patents of Addition as may be granted expire with the original patent.

Novelty: Effect of Prior Patent or Publication.

Novelty: Effect of Prior Patent or Publication.—A valid patent cannot be obtained for an invention sufficiently well known in Norway to be put in practice by other persons. But publication in print, or the exhibition of the invention in Norway, will not prevent the grant of a valid patent, if the application is made within six months of such publication or exhibition. But notice of such publication or exhibition should be given to the Patent Office. The existence of a foreign patent will be no bar to the grant of a Norwegian patent. There is no preliminary examination as to novelty.

Taxes.

Taxes.—Annual taxes are payable of 10 kroner for the second year, 15 kroner for the third, and so on, increasing 5 kroner per annum. Three months' grace may be obtained to make these payments, but under a fine of one-fifth of the tax sought to be paid.

Working.

Working.—Inventions are required to be worked in Norway within three years from date of patent, and must not at any time thereafter be discontinued for an entire year. No proof of working is required by the authorities, but it is advisable to obtain a certificate of working on each occasion. In practice, importation and exposure for sale are considered to meet requirements.

Assignments.

Assignments may be prepared in accordance with the law of the country where the contracting parties are domiciled. They should be legalised by a Norwegian consul, and must be registered at the Patent Office in Norway.

ORANGE FREE STATE.

Orange Free State.

(ORDNANCE No. 10 OF 1888.)

Patentee.

Patentee. Patents are granted to the actual inventors, whether citizens or foreigners, or to their authorised representatives or assignees. With the inventor there may be associated another or other applicants who are not inventors, or a firm or corporation may be associated with the inventor. In all cases, however, the inventor must join in the application, and must be indicated as such in the application form. Depending upon the liberal interpretation of the word "inventor," patents have in many cases been granted to first importers, but in the absence of any judicial decision on this point it is impossible to say whether such grants would be valid or not, although Article 43 does not read very favourably to the suppositious rights of a mere importer.

Duration of Patent.

Duration of Patents.—Patents are granted for fourteen years, but this term is limited by the duration of any prior foreign patent having the shortest term.

Novelty: Effect of Prior Patent or Publication.

Novelty: Effect of Prior Patent or Publication.—The grant of prior foreign patents, or the publication of the invention in other countries, will not prevent the obtaining of a valid patent in the Orange Free State, provided the invention is still new and unpublished in the State at the time of application. By Article 45 of the Ordnance, the exhibition, or publication, or use of the invention in or in connection with an international or industrial exhibition in the State, will not constitute publication in the eye of the law, granted that before such exhibition or publication the inventor has given written notice of his intention to exhibit, to the Attorney-General, and makes application for a patent within six months after the opening of the exhibition. There is no examination as to utility or novelty.

Taxes.

Taxes.—On or before the expiration of the third year of the patent a renewal tax of £5 is due to be paid, and a similar tax of £10 on or before the expiry of the seventh year. An enlargement of the time for making this payment

Orange Free State.

may be had for three months, subject to a fine of £5 in addition to the tax.

Working.

Working.—No requirements. There are also no provisions as to importation or marking.

Assignments and Licences.

Assignments and Licences.—Assignments should be in duplicate, signed by the assignor and legalised by a consul of the Orange Free State. For the purposes of registration, the assignment should be accompanied by a power of attorney, signed by the *assignee* and legalised by the consul, empowering the attorney to record the assignment and pay the fees. Licences may be granted and recorded in a similar manner, and by Article 21, on the petition of any party who has been refused a licence and who is able to show that (*a*) the patent is not being used in the State, or that (*b*) the reasonable requirements of the public are not being served, or that (*c*) a person is being prevented from using another invention to the best advantage, then the authorities may compel the patentee to grant licences on reasonable terms.

Government Fees.

Government Fees.—On depositing application, £1 1s. On certificate of allowance, £1 1s. On sealing letters patent the President fixes a sealing fee, which shall not be less than £10 nor more than £50. In practice this sealing fee is almost invariably fixed at £25. The schedule says that the amount is fixed "according to the importance of the grant."

Paraguay.

PARAGUAY.

Paraguay has no patent law, but inventions may be protected by special Act, the cost of which is usually about from £80 to £100. The documents are in form similar to those employed for Chili.

Peru

PERU.

(LAW OF 28TH JANUARY, 1869.)

Patentee.

Patentee.—The actual inventor only.

Duration of Patent.

Duration of Patent.—Patents are granted for ten years.

Novelty

Novelty : Effect of Prior Patent.—The invention must be

new and unpublished, not only in Peru, but in any other country. It is submitted that publication abroad of a foreign Specification would destroy the validity of a subsequent Peruvian application.

Peru.

Effect of Prior Patent.

Taxes.—An annual tax of 100 dollars is payable on a patent.

Taxes.

Working.—The patent must be worked in a serious and commercial fashion within two years from grant: otherwise it becomes void. The importation of the patented articles is absolutely prohibited. Infraction of this rule will render the patent void. Marking the patented goods is not obligatory.

Working.

Assignments &c.—Assignments and licences of Peruvian patents may be validly made. They should be executed before a notary public, and legalised by a Peruvian consul. No provision is made for registration.

Assignments &c.

PHILIPPINE ISLANDS and PORTO RICO.

Philippine Islands and Porto Rico.

Both of these colonies are covered by the Spanish patent. Registration for the colonies and provinces beyond the seas is usually effected at the time of obtaining the Spanish patent; but if not, such registration can be effected at a small cost at any time during the existence of the Spanish patent. Such registration is necessary before legal proceedings, or transfer, or licence under the patent could be carried out in Porto Rico or the Philippines.

PORTUGAL.

Portugal.

(CIVIL CODE, CHAPTER 3, SECTIONS 1 TO 7; LAW RE PORTUGUESE DEPENDENCIES, 21st MAY, 1892.)

Patentee.—The law says that patents are granted to "anyone who invents, perfects, or improves any manufacture, product, or article"; but in practice patents are granted to anyone who may make the application. Nevertheless, an applicant who gets a patent in fraud of the

Patentee.

Portugal.

real inventor could not maintain such a patent. Grants of patents are issued to firms or corporations.

Duration of Patent.

Duration of Patent.—Portuguese patents date from the issue, and are granted for from one to fifteen years at the option of the applicant. When granted for a shorter term than fifteen years, a patent may be prolonged from year to year or for any term of years within the maximum period. Where a prior patent exists in another country, the Portuguese patent will cease with the expiry of such prior patent. Patents of Addition to the original patent may be had.

Novelty Effect of Prior Patent or Publication.

Novelty: Effect of Prior Patent or Publication.—To obtain a valid patent the invention should be novel and not in public use in Portugal. Section 5 says that the invention should not be "known to the public practically or theoretically through any technical description divulged in home or foreign documents, or by any other means." It would seem, therefore, that publication abroad will not prejudice the obtaining of a valid patent in Portugal, so long as such publication has not circulated in Portugal. There is no examination as to novelty or utility.

Taxes.

Taxes.—None after issue of patent.

Working.

Working.—The invention must be worked in Portugal within two years from the date of issue, and must not be discontinued for any consecutive two years thereafter. At each working a properly legalised certificate should be obtained. It is the custom to consider the mere importation and operation of patented apparatus as constituting working. An advertisement of the working, coupled with an offer of sale, should also be inserted in the public press, as an evidence of the wish of the patentee to introduce the invention. The goods may be imported in any quantity, and need not be marked.

Colonies and Dependencies.

Colonies and Dependencies.—The Portuguese patent only extends to the Azores, but, to encourage the extension of inventions among the Portuguese colonies and provinces beyond the sea, such as Angola, Cape Verde, Guinea, Mozambique, Macao and Timor, Portuguese Indies, and

St. Thomas and Prince, a special Act was passed on the 21st May, 1892, allowing patents of invention for twenty years, and patents of importation for twelve years, to be independently taken out in such colonies and dependencies. Provisions as to working, taxes, &c., are embodied in regulations formulated in consequence of the law. **Portugal.**

Assignments.—Transfer of patents is specially provided for in the Portuguese law. It should be effected by notarial deed. Where two foreigners are concerned, the proper plan is for assignor and assignee respectively to authorise two attorneys in Lisbon—the one, on the part of the assignor, to sell, and the other, on the part of the assignee, to accept the sale of the patent. This formality is gone through before a notary public in Lisbon, who notes the deeds, and gives two attested copies to the parties—one for the assignee, the other for filing in the Patent Office. The Letters Patent are at the same time handed in and endorsed with an abstract of the deed of purchase. Licences not affecting the proprietorship of the patent need not be notified to the Patent Office. **Assignments.**

Government Fees.—For the full term, a fee of about £26 is payable on the grant of the patent. **Government Fees.**

QUEENSLAND.

Queensland.

(Act No. 13 of 13th October, 1884; Act No. 5 of 4th September, 1886.)

Patentee.—The "Patentee" is defined as the person for the time being entitled to the benefit of a patent. Accordingly, in practice, patents are granted to the inventor alone or in conjunction with a capitalist, or to the inventor's assignee, or to the legal representative of a deceased inventor, provided the application is made within six months from the death of the inventor. **Patentee.**

Duration of Patent.—Patents are granted for fourteen years. Preliminary provisional protection for twelve **Duration of Patent.**

Queensland.

months (limited to nine months for the time for filing the Complete) may be had in Queensland as in Great Britain.

Novelty Effect of Prior Patent and Publication.

Novelty: Effect of Prior Patent and Publication.—The invention should not, prior to the date of application, have been published or openly used in Queensland. With this proviso, the patenting or publication of the invention in another country will not bar the grant of a patent in Queensland. There is a preliminary examination. Publication of an unpatented invention in an industrial exhibition held in the colony will have no hurtful effect, provided that notice is given to the Registrar of the intention to exhibit, and application for a patent is made within six months from the opening of the exhibition.

Taxes.

Taxes.—A tax of £5 is due before the expiry of the fourth year of the patent, and £10 before the expiry of the eighth year. In lieu of these amounts, the taxes may be paid annually as follows:—£1 before the expiry of the fourth, fifth, sixth, and seventh years; £1 10s. before the expiry of the eighth and ninth years; £2 before the expiry of the tenth, eleventh, twelfth, and thirteenth years.

Working.

Working.—There is no obligation to work the patent.

Assignments.

Assignments.—These may be prepared in any usual form, and should be registered in the Patent Office. The Registrar will not record the assignment until the letters patent are produced, so that he may endorse the assignment on the back thereof.

Russia.

RUSSIA.

(Code of Laws, Vol. II., Part 2, Section 3.)

Patentee.

Patentee.—The inventor, or his assignee, or a firm or corporation may obtain a valid patent in Russia. A first importer who is not the inventor is entitled to a "Patent of Importation."

Duration and Description of Patent.

Duration and Description of Patent.—There are two kinds of patents—viz., Patents of Invention and Patents of

Importation. A Patent of Invention is granted to the actual inventor or his assignee for a term of three, five, or ten years at the option of the applicant. When the patent has been once issued the term fixed upon cannot be extended. But if an application to extend the shorter period originally applied for is made before the actual issue of the patent, or within six months after the filing of the application, such extension will be granted upon payment of the difference in the amount of taxes. A Patent of Importation is granted to an importer for any desired term from one up to six years, subject to expiry by the lapse of any prior foreign patent. Caveats may be filed, but the application for a patent must follow within three months. **Russia.**

Novelty: Effect of Prior Patent or Publication.—The application should be made before the invention has been made publicly known or worked in Russia. A valid patent can be obtained where the invention has already been patented and published in other countries, so long as it has not been practised in Russia. There is no examination as to novelty and utility, and if a refusal takes place the Government returns the bulk of the application fees. The Russian Patent Office is unique in this particular. **Novelty: Effect of Prior Patent or Publication.**

Taxes.—There are no annual or other taxes payable after issue of the patent. **Taxes.**

Working and Importation.—The patentee is bound to put the invention into practice during the first quarter of the duration of the patent, and, within six months after, to present to the department of the Ministry from which the patent is issued a certificate of working from the local authorities. No extension of time is allowed within which to work the patent. One working within the allotted time suffices to keep the patent in force during the whole of its term. Importation is allowed, and does not affect the validity of the patent. **Working and Importation.**

Assignments and Licences.—In assigning a patent, if both parties are resident abroad, the transfer may be made by deed in the country of residence, and in the language of that country. The deed should be legalised after execution by a Russian consul, who will certify that **Assignments and Licences.**

Russia.

the transfer has been made in accordance with the laws of the country in which it was executed. The deed should then be sent, together with a power of attorney, to some agent in St. Petersburg, authorising him to effect record in Russia. If the transfer is executed before the issue of the patent, the latter may be issued to and in the name of the assignee. No patentee is allowed to form a joint-stock company in Russia to exploit his patent, and he cannot sell his patent to such a company without special permission from the Government. Licences are granted by deed in the same way as transfers.

Government Fees.

Government Fees.—On "Patents of Invention," for three years, 90 silver roubles; for five years, 150 silver roubles; for ten years, 450 silver roubles. On "Patents of Importation," for one year, 60 silver roubles; for two years, 120 silver roubles; for three years, 180 silver roubles; for four years, 240 silver roubles; for five years, 300 silver roubles; for six years, 360 silver roubles.

(N.B.—Medicines are not patentable in Russia. Patents are also refused for heavy munitions of war; but small firearms and hand weapons are patentable, on condition that the military and naval forces of the Czar may have free use of such inventions.)

St. Helena.

ST. HELENA.

(Ordnance No. 3 of 1872.)

Patentee

Patentee.—The grantee of a British patent, his executors, administrators, and assigns, may obtain letters of registration in St. Helena at any time during the existence of the British patent.

Duration of Patent.

Duration of Patent.—The patent expires with the British patent, or with any extension thereof that may be granted.

Novelty Effect of Prior Patent or Publication.

Novelty: Effect of Prior Patent or Publication.—So long as a British patent has been obtained, a patent in St. Helena is granted as a matter of course, and without regard to publication or public use.

Taxes.

Taxes.—None.

St. Helena.

Working.—No requirements.

Assignments are made in the usual English form.

Government Fees.—One guinea is payable to the Registrar on filing the Specification.

ST. LUCIA, ST. VINCENT, SAMOA, SAN DOMINGO, and SAN SALVADOR.

These countries have no patent law, but in all of them protection for an invention can be obtained by special Legislative Act, the expense varying from £25 to £200.

SERVIA.

Although Servia is a member of the International Union, she has no patent law. It is expected, however, that a law will be passed shortly, as the Legislature is at present engaged on the preparation of a Bill.

SIAM.

There is no available mode of protecting inventions in Siam.

SIERRA LEONE.

Sierra Leone has no patent law, but inventions may be protected under special grant.

SOUTH AFRICAN REPUBLIC (Transvaal).

(LAW OF 1ST JUNE, 1887.)

The patent law of this Republic is very similar to that of the Orange Free State.

South African Republic (Transvaal).

Patentee.

Patentee.—Patents are granted to the true inventor or to joint inventors, either alone or in conjunction with another not responsible for the invention. The inventor may join in an application with a firm or corporation, but in any case the inventor must be a party, and must be pointed out as such in the application documents.

Duration of Patent.

Duration of Patent.—Patents are granted for fourteen years; but where foreign patents exist, the South African patent will expire with the original or mother patent. Provisional protection for six months is obtainable, but is seldom applied for, except by residents. The legal representative of a deceased inventor may obtain a patent if application be made within six months from the death of the inventor.

Novelty Effect of Prior Patent or Publication.

Novelty: Effect of Prior Patent or Publication.—The invention must not have been published or publicly used in the South African Republic prior to the application. The fact of a prior patent having been obtained, and the invention having been published in another country, will not prevent the obtaining of a valid patent in the Republic. Disclosure of the invention in an industrial exhibition will not amount to legal publication if prior notice of the intention to exhibit is served on the Attorney-General. and application for a patent made within six months from the opening of the exhibition.

Taxes.

Taxes.—A tax of £5 is due before the expiry of the third year, and £10 before the expiry of the seventh year. The time for payment of these taxes may be extended for three months upon payment of a fine of £5 in addition to the tax.

Working.

Working.—There is no obligation to work the patent within the Republic.

Assignments.

Assignments.—These may be prepared in any convenient form. They must be made in duplicate and legalised by a consul of the South African Republic. Under certain circumstances compulsory licences may be ordered to be granted by the Government.

SOUTH AUSTRALIA.

South Australia.

(Act No. 78 of 21st December, 1877; Act No. 201 of 1881; Patents Amendment Act, 1887.)

Patentee.—The true and first inventor or his representative. There is no decision as to whether "true and first inventor" includes the true and first importer, but in accordance with British practice many patents are taken out by first importers. **Patentee.**

Duration of Patent.—Patents are granted for fourteen years, limited to expire with the original or mother patent, in those cases where prior patents for the same invention exist in other countries. Provisional protection for twelve months may be obtained, and caveats may be filed by intending applicants, such caveats remaining in force for one year. **Duration of Patent.**

Novelty: Prior Patent or Publication.—To ensure a valid patent, the invention should not at the time of application be known or publicly used in South Australia. Inventions already patented abroad or in the mother country, but not publicly known in the Colony, may be validly patented there. **Novelty: Prior Patent or Publication.**

Taxes.—Before the end of the third year a tax of £2 10s. falls due, and before the end of the seventh year a further tax of £2 10s. No prolongation for making these payments is obtainable. **Taxes.**

Working.—Under Clause 43 of the principal Act, patents are liable, upon the application of an interested party, to be revoked by the Governor, if the invention has not been worked before the expiry of three years from date. In practice the working of South Australian patents is generally disregarded, and so far no case exists in which the power of revocation has been exercised upon this ground. Nevertheless, in the case of valuable inventions it would be wiser for the inventor to comply with the clause. **Working.**

Assignments.—These may be in any convenient form, and must be filed in duplicate. Stamp duty is payable on **Assignments.**

South Australia.

the amount of the consideration money at the rate of five shillings per £100. Assignments must be endorsed as "certified as correct for the purposes of the Patent Acts of 1877 to 1887." This may be signed by one of the parties or by the local attorney or agent acting for the parties. A nominal consideration is professedly not allowed. The actual consideration should be stated, but a nominal consideration of £10 is not questioned. The assignment is registered in the Register of Proprietors.

Spain.

SPAIN.

(LAW OF 30TH JULY, 1878.)

Patentee.

Patentee.—Patents are granted to any individual, firm, or corporation making application, whether originators of the invention or not.

Duration and Description of Patent.

Duration and Description of Patent.—Patents are of two kinds—*i.e.* "Patents of Invention" and "Patents of Importation." Original applicants in Spain can obtain a patent for twenty years. If the invention has been already patented abroad, the patent in Spain is granted for ten years, but application must be made in Spain within two years from the date of the first foreign patent. If the applicant is merely an importer, the patent term is for five years only. Patents of Addition are granted, which expire with the original patent.

Novelty: Prior Patent or Publication.

Novelty: Prior Patent or Publication.—The Spanish application should be made before the invention has come into public use in the Spanish dominions. The existence, publication or working of patents for the same invention in other countries is no hindrance to the obtaining of a perfectly valid patent in Spain, so long as it is new there. The Spanish patent is, however, limited by the duration of the prior foreign mother patent.

Taxes.

Taxes.—Patents are subject to the payment of annual taxes amounting to ten pesetas for the first year, twenty pesetas for the second, thirty pesetas for the third, and so on, increasing at the rate of ten pesetas per annum. The peseta is equivalent to tenpence of English money. **Spain.**

Working.—The invention must be worked in Spain within two years from the issue of the patent, and must not be discontinued for a year and a day thereafter. The owners of patents are required to prove the working before the Director of the Conservatory of Arts. A merely perfunctory pretence of working, such as might serve in certain other countries, will not suffice in Spain. The patented articles should be actually made in Spain. Mere importation and working will not do. The working in Spain covers the working in her colonies, and the properly proved working in one of the colonies would cover the working in Spain. The goods may be imported for sale in Spain in any quantity. **Working.**

Assignments.—All assignments made out of Spain must be executed before a notary public, whose signature must be legalised by a Spanish consul. Assignments are registered in the Spanish Patent Office. **Assignments.**

Colonial Registration.—Article 8 of the Law says that all patents shall be considered as granted not only for the Peninsula and adjacent islands, but also for the provinces beyond the sea. Under this Article the Spanish patent theoretically covers all of the colonies, including Cuba, Porto Rico, the Philippines, the Balearic and Canary Islands, Marianas Islands, Caroline Islands, Palaos, Fernando Po, Annabom, Corises, and the Settlement of Rio de Oro on the West Coast of Africa. But practically the patent requires to be registered for the colonies in the Colonial Department in Madrid, which can be done at a slight expense. Most attorneys do this without specific instructions, but patentees should make sure that it has been done, because without such registration no legal proceedings could be taken in the colonies or dependencies under the patent, nor can the patent be assigned or licensed there. **Colonial Registration.**

Straits Settlements.

STRAITS SETTLEMENTS.

(Ordnance No. 12 of 1871.)

Patentee.

Patentee.—Patents are granted to the actual inventor or his assignee, to the first importer, or to the patentee or proprietor of a British patent or invention patented in any British possession.

Duration of Patent.

Duration of Patent.—Fourteen years is the term for which patents are granted, but this term is limited by the duration of any prior patent in another country.

Novelty: Prior Patent or Publication.

Novelty: Prior Patent or Publication.—The invention is deemed to be new and patentable if not "publicly used" in the United Kingdom or in any British possession prior to the date of application in the colony. The use of the term "public use" would seem to point to the conclusion that publication of the specification in Great Britain, or publication in a newspaper or book, would not vitiate the claim of the patentee to a patent in the Straits Settlements, provided no public use had taken place. There is no examination as to novelty or utility.

Taxes.

Taxes.—None after issue of patent.

Working.

Working.—None required.

Assignments.

Assignments.—Assignments must be prepared in duplicate and registered in the Register of Proprietors.

Sweden.

SWEDEN.

(Law of 16th May, 1884.)

Patentee.

Patentee.—Inventors only or the legal representatives of inventors are entitled to obtain patents.

Duration of Patent.

Duration of Patent.—Patents are granted for fifteen years. Patents of Addition to existing Swedish patents may be obtained, such Patents of Addition expiring with the original patent.

Sweden.

Novelty: Effect of Prior Patent or Publication.—The publication of a prior foreign specification, for example of the British specification, or the showing of the invention in an exhibition, will not prevent the obtaining of a valid Swedish patent, provided the application is made within six months from the said publication, or within six months from the opening of the exhibition. In the case of an original Swedish application, the invention must not be known or publicly used in Sweden. Applications are subject to a preliminary examination as to novelty. Novelty: Effect of Prior Patent or Publication.

Taxes.—An annual tax of twenty-five crowns is payable on the first, second, third, fourth, and fifth years; fifty crowns on the sixth, seventh, eighth, ninth, and tenth years; and seventy-five crowns for each of the five following years. Three months' extension of time within which to pay these taxes may be had, subject to a fine amounting to one-fifth of the amount of the tax due. Taxes.

Working.—The invention should be worked within three years from date of patent, and thereafter the working must not be entirely discontinued for a year. The rules regulating the working are not very stringent. The time may sometimes be extended to four years in difficult cases. In practice it is considered sufficient to import and operate a machine or patented article, at the same time advertising and inviting inquiries for it. It is better, however, not to rely too much upon this laxity. Working.

Assignments.—These should be executed in duplicate and legalised by a Swedish consul. The registration is effected on the request of the assignee. Assignments.

SWITZERLAND.

Switzerland.

(Law of 15th November, 1888.)

Patentee.—Patents are granted to the inventor or to his legal successors or assigns only. Patentee.

Duration and Description of Patent.—The Swiss Patent Office makes it a rule that it will grant no patents for Duration and Description of Patent.

Switzerland.

inventions which do not in themselves represent a visible and tangible marketable article. It follows from this short-sighted policy that patents cannot be obtained for mere new processes or methods of manufacture, although new products of new processes may be protected. To give time for the production of a specimen, or proof of the actual existence of the newly invented thing or machine, the custom is to make provisional application for a patent in the first instance, which application must contain a full description and illustration of the invention, but need not be accompanied by specimens or proofs of actual existence. This provisional patent lasts for three years. During this term, or at the end of the three years, a definitive patent is granted upon the payment of the tax and on the production of the specimen of the invention, or, in the case of large objects, of photographs of the invention. The specimen might either be the actual thing itself, or it might assume the form of a scale model of the invention. In the case of large apparatus or articles not easy of transport, and where a model would be difficult or expensive to make, photographs of the invention will suffice. These photographs must show, as far as practicable, the parts which are claimed. For example, if the invention is a boiler, or a gas-making apparatus, containing arrangements of tubes, partitions, and parts which are essential to the invention, a mere outside view of the boiler or the apparatus will not do. The claimed arrangements of the tubes or parts should be apparent in the photograph, or it will not be accepted as a proof of existence. Models must be deposited of all inventions relating to the cases or movements of watches, all inventions relating to portable firearms, and for all patented articles composed of combinations of substances which it is difficult to determine. Swiss patents are granted for fifteen years from the date of application.

Novelty: Effect of Prior Patent or Publication.

Novelty: Effect of Prior Patent or Publication.—The invention must be new and unpublished in Switzerland at the time of application. Proof of the published British specification having been at the disposal of the public in

Switzerland would probably act as a bar to novelty. Switzerland is, however, a member of the International Convention, so that even after publication of a British specification the Swiss application would be valid if made within six months from the date of the application in England. An examination as to novelty and utility is held upon all applications for patents. **Switzerland.**

Taxes.—Patents are subject to the payment of annual taxes of twenty francs for the first year, thirty francs for the second, forty francs for the third, and so on, increasing at the rate of ten francs per annum as in Belgium. **Taxes.**

Working.—The invention must be worked within three years from the date of application. The amount of working which will satisfy requirements has not been fixed by any judicial decision, but it would be unsafe to count upon anything less than a real and commercial carrying into effect of the invention. Importation of the patented goods is not prohibited, but if importation alone is carried on, the patentee cannot refuse licences on reasonable terms to Swiss manufacturers: otherwise his patent is forfeited. All articles protected by a Swiss patent and sold in Switzerland must be marked with the Federal Cross and the number of the patent. **Working.**

Assignments and Licences.—If a patent is sold wholly or partly, or if a licence is granted after the filing of the application or after the grant of the patent, such assignment or licence must be registered at the Federal Office of Industrial Property. **Assignments and Licences.**

TASMANIA.

Tasmania.

(ACT NO. 6 OF 1893.)

Patentee.—The true and first inventor, which is assumed to include the first importer. Patents are granted to the inventor in conjunction with others who are not inventors. The legal representative of a deceased inventor may obtain **Patentee.**

Tasmania. a patent if application is made within six months of the inventor's decease.

Duration of Patent.

Duration of Patent.—Patents are granted for fourteen years from the date of acceptance of the application.

Novelty: Effect of Prior Patent or Publication.

Novelty: Effect of Prior Patent or Publication.—The invention must not at the time of application have been "publicly manufactured, used, or sold within Tasmania." Therefore prior publication or use of an invention abroad, and apparently even prior publication alone in Tasmania, will not prevent the grant of a valid patent. Subject to notice given to the Registrar, exhibition of an invention at an "industrial exhibition" within or beyond the Colony will not amount to public use, if the application for a patent be made within six months from the opening of the exhibition.

Taxes.

Taxes.—At or before the expiration of the third year from date, a tax of £15 falls due, and a tax of £20 at or before the expiration of the seventh year. Three months extension of time for paying these taxes may be had, subject to payment of £1 on the application form, and £3 on the grant of extension.

Working.

Working.—No requirements.

Assignments.—Assignments and licences may be granted for the whole or a part of the colony. These should be entered on the register.

Tobago.

TOBAGO.

(Covered by Patent in Trinidad.)

Tonquin.

TONQUIN.

(Covered by French Patent.)

TRINIDAD.

Trinidad.

(Ordnance No. 25, 2nd September, 1867.)

Patentee.—The true and first inventor or his representative or assignee, or the first importer, may obtain a valid patent. Patentee.

Duration of Patent.—Patents are granted for fourteen years. Duration of Patent.

Novelty: Effect of Prior Patent or Publication.—The essential is that the invention should be new and not in public use in Trinidad at the time of application. A prior patent or prior publication abroad will not prejudice the validity of a patent subsequently obtained in Trinidad if the invention is unknown there. Novelty Effect of Prior Patent or Publication.

Taxes.—None after issue of patent. Taxes.

Working.—There are no conditions as to working. Working.

Assignments.—These should be in duplicate, and should be registered. Assignments.

TUNIS.

Tunis.

(Law of 22nd Rabia-et-Tani, 1306: 26th December, 1888.)

Patentee.—Patents are granted to whomsoever may apply, or to a firm or corporation. Patentee.

Duration of Patent.—Five, ten, or fifteen years, at the option of the applicant. Duration of Patent.

Novelty: Effect of Prior Patent or Publication.—An application for a Tunisian patent should be filed before the invention is generally known or in public use either in the Regency or elsewhere. Novelty Effect of Prior Patent or Publication.

Taxes.—Patents are subject to an annual tax of one hundred piastres. No enlargement of time for paying this annuity can be obtained. Taxes.

Working.—The invention should be put in practice before the expiry of two years from the date of the patent, and the working must not thereafter be interrupted Working.

Tunis.

for any two years in succession. Tunis being a member of the International Convention, the prohibition against importation of the patented goods is inoperative against patentees who are citizens of States also in the Union, such as Great Britain for example. All patented goods should be marked with the number of the patent and the words "Sans Garantie du Gouvernement."

Assignments.

Assignments.—As is the case in France, an assignment can only be recorded by paying the full amount of taxes for the complete term of patent right. This immediate expense may, however, be obviated by adopting the plan advised with reference to the French assignment—viz., leaving the assignment unregistered *pro tem.*, and causing the parties to the assignment to execute a blank power authorising a notary (whose name can afterwards be filled in) to effect the registration and pay the fees. This power should be legalised by a French consul, and can afterwards be used by the assignee if required.

Turkey.

TURKEY.

(Law of 18th February, 1879.)

Patentee

Patentee.—Patents are granted to the first inventor or first importer. A firm or corporation may be the grantee of a patent.

Duration of Patent.

Duration of Patent.—The term of grant is for five, ten, or fifteen years, as the applicant may elect.

Novelty Effect of Prior Patent or Publication.

Novelty: Effect of Prior Patent or Publication.—The invention, to form the subject-matter of a valid patent, should not have been published or worked in Turkey, and, strictly speaking, should not have been made public abroad. It is, however, the usually accepted opinion that the mere official publication of the specification of a prior foreign patent would not injure the validity of a subsequent Turkish patent.

Taxes.

Taxes.—Patents are subject to an annual tax of two Turkish pounds.

Turkey.

Working.

Working.—The invention must be worked in Turkey within two years from the date of issue, and the working must not thereafter cease for any two successive years, on pain of forfeiture of the patent rights. Importation of patented goods is strictly prohibited, under penalty of forfeiture of the patent. Even the introduction of models of the invention or samples of the goods for exhibition, trial, or other purposes, must take place only under permission from the Government.

Assignments.

Assignments.—When a Turkish patent is assigned, all the taxes due on the unexpired term of patent right require to be paid in advance before the assignment can be recorded. This necessity is sometimes evaded by the plan frequently resorted to in the case of French assignments. (See "France.") Assignments should be by notarial deed, and must, when made abroad, be legalised by a Turkish consul.

URUGUAY.

Uruguay.

(Law of 12th November, 1885.)

Patentee.

Patentee.—Patents are granted to the inventor, or to his attorney or assignee.

Duration of Patent.

Duration of Patent.—Patents are issued for terms of three, six, or nine years, at the option of the applicant.

Novelty Effect of Prior Patent or Publication.

Novelty: Effect of Prior Patent or Publication.—To constitute a valid patent, the subject-matter should not be publicly known in Uruguay or elsewhere. When prior foreign patents have been obtained, the owner may, irrespective of publication or public use, obtain a valid patent in Uruguay if he files his application within one year from the date of the first prior foreign patent. Patents of Addition may be obtained.

Taxes.

Taxes.—Patents are subject to an annual tax of twenty-five pesos. Patents of Addition are subject to an annual tax of one-third of this amount.

Working.

Working.—On the grant of the patent, the authorities

Uruguay. specify what is, in their estimation, a reasonable time within which the invention must be worked. This may vary from one to three years, according to the nature of the invention. Once commenced, the working must not be interrupted for any one year at a time.

Assignments. *Assignments.*—These must be in duplicate in the Spanish language, and must be legalised by a Uruguayan consul.

Venezuela.

VENEZUELA.

(Law of 25th May, 1882.)

Patentee. *Patentee.*—Patents are granted to the actual inventor, or to a patentee who has already patented the invention in a foreign country.

Duration of Patent. *Duration of Patent.*—Patents are granted for five, ten, or fifteen years, at the option of the applicant, and when a foreign patent exists, then for the unexpired term of the foreign patent.

Novelty: Effect of Prior Patent or Publication. *Novelty: Effect of Prior Patent or Publication.*—A valid patent may be had only in cases where the invention is not publicly known or used in Venezuela, or has not been patented in another country to an inventor other than the applicant. But in the case of an inventor and owner of a foreign patent, he may at any time during the existence of the foreign patent protect his invention in Venezuela for a period coterminous with that of the foreign patent.

Taxes. *Taxes.*—There are no taxes payable after issue.

Working. *Working.*—A five years' patent must be worked within six months of grant; a ten years' patent within one year; and a fifteen years' patent within two years of grant. In the case of patented apparatus it is usual to consider the importation and operation of a machine as sufficient to constitute working; but this is only presumed, and is not based upon any judicial decision.

Assignments. *Assignments.*—Patents may be assigned. The documents should be in Spanish and legalised by a Venezuelan Consul Licences may be in any form, so long as the existence of the permit is apparent.

VICTORIA.

Victoria.

(Act No. 1034 of 25th November, 1889.)

Patentee.

Patentee.—Patents are granted to the actual inventor, or to his assignee, or to an importer who has had the invention communicated to him from abroad by the inventor. A corporation may be the grantee of a patent for an invention communicated to them by the inventor. The legal representative of a deceased inventor may obtain a patent, if application is made within twelve months from the death of the inventor.

Duration of Patent.

Duration of Patent.—Patents are granted for fourteen years. Inventions may be provisionally protected as in Great Britain, the provisional being followed up in nine months by a Complete Specification.

Novelty: Effect of Prior Patent or Publication.

Novelty: Effect of Prior Patent or Publication.—The invention must not be a matter of public knowledge in the Colony. But in the case of an applicant who is the owner of a foreign patent, publication or public use prior to application in Victoria will not matter, if the Victorian application is made within one year from the date of the prior foreign patent.

Taxes.

Taxes.—Before the expiry of the third year a tax of £2 10s. is payable, and a further tax of £2 10s. before the expiry of the seventh year. An extension of time for making these payments (in no case exceeding six months) may be had on showing sufficient cause and on payment of a fine of £1 in addition to the tax.

Working.

Working.—Patentees are not required to work their inventions in the Colony, and may import the patented goods at pleasure.

Assignments.

Assignments.—These are prepared in the form customary in England, and should be entered upon the Register of Patents.

WESTERN AUSTRALIA.

Western Australia.

(Act No. 5 of 26th November, 1888; Act No. 15 of 1892.)

Patentee.

Patentee.—Patents are granted to the true and first inventor or inventors, either alone or in conjunction with

Western Australia.

another, or with others not inventors. *Letters of Registration*, having the same force as letters patent, are issued to the *bonâ fide* holder or assignee of letters patent granted in Great Britain or elsewhere.

Description and Duration of Patent.

Description and Duration of Patent.—Patents issued to actual inventors are granted for fourteen years. *Letters of Registration*, issued to owners of prior patents elsewhere, expire with the original foreign or other patent upon which the Letters of Registration are based.

Novelty; Effect of Prior Patent or Publication.

Novelty: Effect of Prior Patent or Publication.—To obtain valid *Letters Patent* the application should be filed before any publication or public use of the invention has taken place in the Colony. As in most other British Colonies, the showing of an invention in an industrial exhibition does not for six months constitute publication, if notice has previously been given the Registrar. *Letters of Registration* can be obtained at any time during the continuance of the prior foreign or other patent upon which the Letters of Registration are based.

Taxes.

Taxes.—There are no taxes payable upon Letters of Registration. Letters Patent are subject to a tax of £4 before the expiry of the fourth year, and a further tax of £4 before the expiry of the seventh year.

Working.

Working. — There are no provisions as to working, importing, or marking the patented goods in Western Australia.

Assignments and Licences.

Assignments and Licences.—These are prepared as in England, and should be entered in the Register of Patents.

FOREIGN TRADE MARKS AND DESIGNS.

Trade marks, and in some instances designs also, can be protected in many of the foregoing countries and colonies. In most cases registration or protection is effected under existing statutes, but where these do not exist special Legislative Acts may be furthered to obtain the same results.

THE PATENTS, DESIGNS, AND TRADE MARKS ACTS, 1883 to 1888 (Consolidated).

THE ACTS CONTAIN 117 SECTIONS WITH SCHEDULES, AND THE RESPECTIVE SECTIONS ARE TO THE FOLLOWING EFFECT :—

PART I.—PRELIMINARY.

Section
1. Short title.
2. Division of Act into parts.
3. Commencement of Acts.

PART II.—PATENTS.

Application for and Grant of Patent.

4. Persons entitled to apply for patent.
Power to grant patents to several persons jointly.
5. Application and specification.
6. Reference of application to examiner.
7. Power for comptroller to refuse application or require amendment.
8. Time for leaving complete specification.
9. Comparison of provisional and complete specification.
10. Advertisement on acceptance of complete specification.
11. Opposition to grant of patent.
12. Sealing of patent.
13. Date of patent.
Specifications &c. not to be published unless application accepted.

Provisional Protection.

14. Provisional protection.

PART II.—PATENTS (*continued*).

Protection by Complete Specification.

Patent.

Amendment of Specification.

Compulsory Licences.

Register of Patents.

Fees

Extension of Term of Patent.

Revocation.

Crown.

Legal Proceedings.

Miscellaneous.

PART II.—PATENTS (*continued*).

PART V.—GENERAL.

Patent Office and Proceedings thereat.

International and Colonial Arrangements.

Offences.

Scotland, Ireland, &c.

PART V.—GENERAL (*continued*).

Repeal, Transitional Provisions, Savings.

General Definitions.

Register of Patent Agents.

The Patents, Designs, and Trade Marks Acts, 1883 to 1888 (Consolidated).

[THE REPEALED PORTIONS OF THE ACT OF 1883 ARE PRINTED IN *italics*. THE AMENDMENTS EFFECTED BY THE SUCCEEDING ACTS ARE IN **heavy type.** THE AMENDING ACT AND SECTIONS ARE CITED IN THE MARGIN.]

(46 & 47 VICTORIA, CHAPTER 57.)

An Act to amend and consolidate the Law relating to Patents for Inventions, Registration of Designs, and of Trade Marks. [25th August, 1883.

48 & 49 Vict. c. 63.—An Act to amend the Patents, Designs, and Trade Marks Act, 1883. [14th August, 1885.

49 & 50 Vict. c. 37.—An Act to remove certain doubts respecting the construction of the Patents, Designs, and Trade Marks Act, 1883, so far as respects the drawings by which specifications are required to be accompanied, and as respects exhibitions. [25th June, 1886.

51 & 52 Vict. c. 50.—An Act to amend the Patents, Designs, and Trade Marks Act, 1883. [24th December, 1888.

BE IT ENACTED by the Queen's most Excellent Majesty, by and with the advice and consent of the Lords Spiritual and Temporal, and Commons, in this present Parliament assembled, and by the authority of the same, as follows:

PART I.

PRELIMINARY.

Short title.

1. This Act may be cited as The Patents, Designs, and Trade Marks Act, 1883.

Division of Act into parts.

2. This Act is divided into parts, as follows:—

Part I.—PRELIMINARY.
II.—PATENTS.
III.—DESIGNS.
IV.—TRADE MARKS.
V.—GENERAL.

Commencement of Act.

3. This Act, except where it is otherwise expressed, shall commence from and immediately after the Thirty-first day of December, One thousand eight hundred and eighty-three.

Act 1888, s. 28.

The Act of 1888 shall, except so far as is thereby otherwise specially provided, commence and come into operation on the First day of January, One thousand eight hundred and eighty-nine.

PART II.

PATENTS.

Application for and Grant of Patent.

Persons entitled to apply for Patent.

4. (1) Any person, whether a British subject or not, may make an application for a patent.

(2) Two or more persons may make a joint application for a patent, and a patent may be granted to them jointly.

Act 1885, s. 5. Power to

Whereas doubts have arisen whether under the principal Act a patent may lawfully be granted to

several persons jointly, some or one of whom only are or is the true and first inventors or inventor; be it therefore enacted and declared that it has been and is lawful under the principal Act to grant such a patent. grant Patents to several persons jointly.

5. (1) An application for a patent must be made in the form set forth in the First Schedule to this Act, or in such other form as may be from time to time prescribed; and must be left at, or sent by post to, the Patent Office in the prescribed manner. Application and Specification.

(2) An application must contain a declaration to the effect that the applicant is in possession of an invention, whereof he, or in the case of a joint application, one or more of the applicants, claims or claim to be the true and first inventor or inventors, and for which he or they desires or desire to obtain a patent; and must be accompanied by either a provisional or complete specification.

The declaration may be either a statutory declaration under the Statutory Declarations Act, 1835, or not, as may be from time to time prescribed. **Act 1885, s. 2.** 5 & 6 Will. 4, c. 62.

(3) A provisional specification must describe the nature of the invention, and be accompanied by drawings, if required.

(4) A complete specification, whether left on application or subsequently, must particularly describe and ascertain the nature of the invention, and in what manner it is to be performed, and must be accompanied by drawings, if required.

The requirement of this sub-section as to drawings shall not be deemed to be insufficiently complied with by reason only that instead of being accompanied by drawings the complete specification refers to the drawings which accompanied the provisional specification. And no patent heretofore sealed shall be invalid by reason only that the complete specification was not accompanied by drawings, but referred to those which accompanied the provisional specification. The same drawings may accompany both Specifications. **Act 1886, s. 2.**

(5) A specification, whether provisional or complete, must commence with the title, and in the case of a complete

specification must end with a distinct statement of the invention claimed.

Reference of application to Examiner.

6. The comptroller shall refer every application to an examiner, who shall ascertain and report to the comptroller whether the nature of the invention has been fairly described, and the application, specification, and drawings (if any) have been prepared in the prescribed manner, and the title sufficiently indicates the subject-matter of the invention.

Power for Comptroller to refuse application or require amendment.

[**7.** (1) *If the examiner reports that the nature of the invention is not fairly described, or that the application, specification, or drawings has not or have not been prepared in the prescribed manner, or that the title does not sufficiently indicate the subject-matter of the invention, the comptroller may require that the application, specification, or drawings be amended before he proceeds with the application.*

Repealed by **Act 1888, s. 2.**

(2) *Where the comptroller requires an amendment, the applicant may appeal from his decision to the law officer.*

(3) *The law officer shall, if required, hear the applicant and the comptroller, and may make an order determining whether and subject to what conditions, if any, the application shall be accepted.*

(4) *The comptroller shall, when an application has been accepted, give notice thereof to the applicant.*

(5) *If after an application has been made, but before a patent has been sealed, an application is made, accompanied by a specification bearing the same or a similar title, it shall be the duty of the examiner to report to the comptroller whether the specification appears to him to comprise the same invention; and, if he reports in the affirmative, the comptroller shall give notice to the applicant that he has so reported.*

(6) *Where the examiner reports in the affirmative, the comptroller may determine, subject to an appeal to the law officer, whether the invention comprised in both applications is the same, and if so he may refuse to seal a patent on the application of the second applicant.*]

Act 1888, s. 2. Power of

7. (1) If the examiner reports that the nature of the invention is not fairly described, or that the

application, specification, or drawings has not, or have not, been prepared in the prescribed manner, or that the title does not sufficiently indicate the subject-matter of the invention, the comptroller may refuse to accept the application, or require that the application, specification, or drawings be amended before he proceeds with the application; and in the latter case the application shall, if the comptroller so directs, bear date as from the time when the requirement is complied with.

Comptroller to refuse application or require amendment.

(2) Where the comptroller refuses to accept an application or requires an amendment, the applicant may appeal from his decision to the law officer.

(3) The law officer shall, if required, hear the applicant and the comptroller, and may make an order determining whether, and subject to what conditions (if any), the application shall be accepted.

(4) The comptroller shall, when an application has been accepted, give notice thereof to the applicant.

(5) If, after an application for a patent has been made, but before the patent thereon has been sealed, another application for a patent is made, accompanied by a specification bearing the same or a similar title, the comptroller, if he thinks fit, on the request of the second applicant, or of his legal representative, may, within two months of the grant of a patent on the first application, either decline to proceed with the second application or allow the surrender of the patent, if any, granted thereon.

8. (1) If the applicant does not leave a complete specification with his application, he may leave it at any subsequent time within nine months from the date of application.

Time for leaving complete specification.

A complete specification may be left within such extended time, not exceeding one month after the said nine months, as the comptroller may on payment of the prescribed fee allow.

Act 1885, s. 3.

(2) Unless a complete specification is left within that time, the application shall be deemed to be abandoned.

Comparison of provisional and complete specification.

9. (1) Where a complete specification is left after a provisional specification, the comptroller shall refer both specifications to an examiner for the purpose of ascertaining whether the complete specification has been prepared in the prescribed manner, and whether the invention particularly described in the complete specification is substantially the same as that which is described in the provisional specification.

(2) If the examiner reports that the conditions hereinbefore contained have not been complied with, the comptroller may refuse to accept the complete specification unless and until the same shall have been amended to his satisfaction; but any such refusal shall be subject to appeal to the law officer.

(3) The law officer shall, if required, hear the applicant and the comptroller, and may make an order determining whether and subject to what conditions, if any, the complete specification shall be accepted.

(4) Unless a complete specification is accepted within twelve months from the date of application, then (save in the case of an appeal having been lodged against the refusal to accept) the application shall, at the expiration of those twelve months, become void.

Act 1885, s. 3.

A complete specification may be accepted within such extended time, not exceeding three months after the said twelve months, as the comptroller may on payment of the prescribed fee allow.

(5) Reports of examiners shall not in any case be published or be open to public inspection, and shall not be liable to production or inspection in any legal proceeding [*other than an appeal to the law officer under this Act*], unless the Court or officer having power to order discovery in such legal proceeding shall certify that such production or inspection is desirable in the interests of justice, and ought to be allowed.

Repealed by Act 1888, s. 3.

Advertisement on acceptance of complete specification.

10. On the acceptance of the complete specification the comptroller shall advertise the acceptance; and the application and specification or specifications with the drawings (if any) shall be open to public inspection.

11. (1) Any person may at any time within two months from the date of the advertisement of the acceptance of a complete specification give notice at the Patent Office of opposition to the grant of the patent on the ground of the applicant having obtained the invention from him, or from a person of whom he is the legal representative, or on the ground that the invention has been patented in this country on an application of prior date [*or on the ground of an examiner having reported to the comptroller that the specification appears to him to comprise the same invention as is comprised in a specification bearing the same or a similar title, and accompanying a previous application*], **or on the ground that the complete specification describes or claims an invention other than that described in the provisional specification, and that such other invention forms the subject of an application made by the opponent in the interval between the leaving of the provisional specification and the leaving of the complete specification,** but on no other ground. Opposition to grant of patent. Repealed by Act 1888, s. 4. Act 1888, s. 4.

(2) Where such notice is given the comptroller shall give notice of the opposition to the applicant, and shall, on the expiration of those two months, after hearing the applicant and the person so giving notice, if desirous of being heard, decide on the case, but subject to appeal to the law officer.

(3) The law officer shall, if required, hear the applicant and any person so giving notice and being, in the opinion of the law officer, entitled to be heard in opposition to the grant, and shall determine whether the grant ought or ought not to be made.

(4) The law officer may, if he thinks fit, obtain the assistance of an expert, who shall be paid such remuneration as the law officer, with the consent of the Treasury, shall appoint.

12. (1) If there is no opposition, or, in case of opposition, if the determination is in favour of the grant of a patent, the comptroller shall cause a patent to be sealed with the seal of the Patent Office. Sealing of patent.

(2) A patent so sealed shall have the same effect as if it were sealed with the great seal of the United Kingdom.

(3) A patent shall be sealed as soon as may be, and not after the expiration of fifteen months from the date of application, except in the cases hereinafter mentioned, that is to say—

(*a*) Where the sealing is delayed by an appeal to the law officer, or by opposition to the grant of the patent, the patent may be sealed at such time as the law officer may direct.

(*b*) If the person making the application dies before the expiration of the fifteen months aforesaid, the patent may be granted to his legal representative, and sealed at any time within twelve months after the death of the applicant.

Act 1885, s. 3.

A complete specification may be left and accepted within such extended times, not exceeding one month and three months respectively after the said nine and twelve months respectively as the comptroller may on payment of the prescribed fee allow, and where such extension of time has been allowed, a further extension of four months after the said fifteen months shall be allowed for the sealing of the patent; and the principal Act shall have effect as if any time so allowed were added to the said periods specified in the principal Act.

Date of patent.

13. Every patent shall be dated and sealed as of the day of the application: Provided that no proceedings shall be taken in respect of an infringement committed before the publication of the complete specification: Provided also, that in case of more than one application for a patent for the same invention, the sealing of a patent on one of those applications shall not prevent the sealing of a patent on an earlier application.

Specifications &c. not to be published unless

Where an application for a patent has been abandoned, or become void, the specification or specifications and drawings (if any) accompanying or left in con-

nection with such application, shall not at any time be open to public inspection or be published by the comptroller. application accepted. Act 1885, s. 4.

Provisional Protection.

14. Where an application for a patent in respect of an invention has been accepted, the invention may during the period between the date of the application and the date of sealing such patent be used and published without prejudice to the patent to be granted for the same; and such protection from the consequences of use and publication is in this Act referred to as provisional protection. Provisional protection.

Protection by Complete Specification.

15. After the acceptance of a complete specification and until the date of sealing a patent in respect thereof, or the expiration of the time for sealing, the applicant shall have the like privileges and rights as if a patent for the invention had been sealed on the date of the acceptance of the complete specification: Provided that an applicant shall not be entitled to institute any proceeding for infringement unless and until a patent for the invention has been granted to him. Effect of acceptance of complete specification.

Patent.

16. Every patent when sealed shall have effect throughout the United Kingdom and the Isle of Man. Extent of patent.

17. (1) The term limited in every patent for the duration thereof shall be fourteen years from its date. Term of patent.

(2) But every patent shall, notwithstanding anything therein or in this Act, cease if the patentee fails to make the prescribed payments within the prescribed times.

(3) If, nevertheless, in any case, by accident, mistake, or inadvertence, a patentee fails to make any prescribed payment within the prescribed time, he may apply to the comptroller for an enlargement of the time for making that payment.

(4) Thereupon the comptroller shall, if satisfied that the failure has arisen from any of the above-mentioned causes, on receipt of the prescribed fee for enlargement, not exceeding ten pounds, enlarge the time accordingly, subject to the following conditions:—

(*a*) The time for making any payment shall not in any case be enlarged for more than three months.

(*b*) If any proceeding shall be taken in respect of an infringement of the patent committed after a failure to make any payment within the prescribed time, and before the enlargement thereof, the Court before which the proceeding is proposed to be taken may, if it shall think fit, refuse to award or give any damages in respect of such infringement.

Amendment of Specification.

Amendment of specification.

18. (1) An applicant or a patentee may, from time to time, by request in writing left at the Patent Office, seek leave to amend his specification, including drawings forming part thereof, by way of disclaimer, correction, or explanation, stating the nature of such amendment and his reasons for the same.

(2) The request and the nature of such proposed amendment shall be advertised in the prescribed manner, and at any time within one month from its first advertisement any person may give notice at the Patent Office of opposition to the amendment.

(3) Where such notice is given the comptroller shall give notice of the opposition to the person making the request, and shall hear and decide the case subject to an appeal to the law officer.

(4) The law officer shall, if required, hear the person making the request and the person so giving notice, and being in the opinion of the law officer entitled to be heard in opposition to the request, and shall determine whether and subject to what conditions, if any, the amendment ought to be allowed.

(5) Where no notice of opposition is given, or the

person so giving notice does not appear, the comptroller shall determine whether and subject to what conditions, if any, the amendment ought to be allowed.

(6) When leave to amend is refused by the comptroller, the person making the request may appeal from his decision to the law officer.

(7) The law officer shall, if required, hear the person making the request and the comptroller, and may make an order determining whether, and subject to what conditions, if any, the amendment ought to be allowed.

(8) No amendment shall be allowed that would make the specification, as amended, claim an invention substantially larger than or substantially different from the invention claimed by the specification as it stood before amendment.

(9) Leave to amend shall be conclusive as to the right of the party to make the amendment allowed, except in case of fraud; and the amendment shall in all courts and for all purposes be deemed to form part of the specification.

[(10) *The foregoing provisions of this section do not apply when and so long as any action for infringement or other legal proceeding in relation to a patent is pending.*] Repealed by Act 1888, s. 5.

(10) The foregoing provisions of this section do not apply when and so long as any action for infringement or proceeding for revocation of a patent is pending. Act 1885, s. 5.

Power to disclaim part of invention during action &c.

19. In an action for infringement of a patent, and in a proceeding for revocation of a patent, the Court or a judge may at any time order that the patentee shall, subject to such terms as to costs and otherwise as the Court or a judge may impose, be at liberty to apply at the Patent Office for leave to amend his specification by way of disclaimer, and may direct that in the meantime the trial or hearing of the action shall be postponed.

Restriction on recovery of damages.

20. Where an amendment by way of disclaimer, correction, or explanation, has been allowed under this Act, no damages shall be given in any action in respect of the use of the invention before the disclaimer, correction, or explanation, unless the patentee establishes to the satisfaction of the Court that his original claim was framed in good faith and with reasonable skill and knowledge.

Advertisement of amendment.

21. Every amendment of a specification shall be advertised in the prescribed manner.

Compulsory Licences.

Power for Board to order grant of licences.

22. If on the petition of any person interested it is proved to the Board of Trade that by reason of the default of a patentee to grant licences on reasonable terms—

(*a*) The patent is not being worked in the United Kingdom; or

(*b*) The reasonable requirements of the public with respect to the invention cannot be supplied; or

(*c*) Any person is prevented from working or using to the best advantage an invention of which he is possessed,

the Board may order the patentee to grant licences on such terms as to the amount of royalties, security for payment or otherwise, as the Board, having regard to the nature of the invention and the circumstances of the case, may deem just, and any such order may be enforced by mandamus.

Register of Patents.

Register of Patents.

23. (1) There shall be kept at the Patent Office a book called the Register of Patents, wherein shall be entered the names and addresses of grantees of patents, notifications of assignments and of transmissions of patents, of licences under patents, and of amendments, extensions, and revocations of patents, and such other matters affecting the validity or proprietorship of patents as may from time to time be prescribed.

(2) The Register of Patents shall be *primâ facie* evidence of any matters by this Act directed or authorised to be inserted therein.

(3) Copies of deeds, licences, and any other documents affecting the proprietorship in any letters patents or in any licence thereunder, must be supplied to the comptroller in the prescribed manner for filing in the Patent Office.

Fees.

24. (1) There shall be paid in respect of the several instruments described in the Second Schedule to this Act the fees in that schedule mentioned, and there shall likewise be paid, in respect of other matters under this part of the Act, such fees as may be from time to time, with the sanction of the Treasury, prescribed by the Board of Trade; and such fees shall be levied and paid to the account of her Majesty's Exchequer in such manner as the Treasury may from time to time direct. Fees in Schedule.

(2) The Board of Trade may from time to time, if they think fit, with the consent of the Treasury, reduce any of those fees.

Extension of Term of Patent.

25. (1) A patentee may, after advertising in manner directed by any rules made under this section his intention to do so, present a petition to her Majesty in Council, praying that his patent may be extended for a further term; but such petition must be presented at least six months before the time limited for the expiration of the patent. Extension of term of patent on petition to Queen in Council.

(2) Any person may enter a caveat, addressed to the registrar of the Council at the Council Office, against the extension.

(3) If her Majesty shall be pleased to refer any such petition to the Judicial Committee of the Privy Council, the said Committee shall proceed to consider the same, and the petitioner and any person who has entered a caveat shall be entitled to be heard by himself or by counsel on the petition.

(4) The Judicial Committee shall, in considering their decision, have regard to the nature and merits of the invention in relation to the public, to the profits made by the patentee as such, and to all the circumstances of the case.

(5) If the Judicial Committee report that the patentee has been inadequately remunerated by his patent, it shall be lawful for her Majesty in Council to extend the term of the patent for a further term not exceeding seven, or in

exceptional cases fourteen, years; or to order the grant of a new patent for the term therein mentioned, and containing any restrictions, conditions, and provisions that the Judicial Committee may think fit.

(6) It shall be lawful for her Majesty in Council to make, from time to time, rules of procedure and practice for regulating proceedings on such petitions, and subject thereto such proceedings shall be regulated according to the existing procedure and practice in patent matters of the Judicial Committee.

(7) The costs of all parties of and incident to such proceedings shall be in the discretion of the Judicial Committee; and the orders of the Committee respecting costs shall be enforceable as if they were orders of a Division of the High Court of Justice.

Revocation.

Revocation of patent.

26. (1) The proceeding by *scire facias* to repeal a patent is hereby abolished.

(2) Revocation of a patent may be obtained on petition to the Court.

(3) Every ground on which a patent might, at the commencement of this Act, be repealed by *scire facias* shall be available by way of defence to an action of infringement, and shall also be a ground of revocation.

(4) A petition for revocation of a patent may be presented by—

(*a*) The Attorney-General in England or Ireland, or the Lord Advocate in Scotland:

(*b*) Any person authorised by the Attorney-General in England or Ireland, or the Lord Advocate in Scotland:

(*c*) Any person alleging that the patent was obtained in fraud of his rights, or of the rights of any person under or through whom he claims:

(*d*) Any person alleging that he, or any person under or through whom he claims, was the true inventor of any invention included in the claim of the patentee:

(*e*) Any person alleging that he, or any person under or through whom he claims an interest in any trade, business, or manufacture, had publicly manufactured, used, or sold, within this realm, before the date of the patent, anything claimed by the patentee as his invention.

(5) The plaintiff must deliver with his petition particulars of the objections on which he means to rely, and no evidence shall, except by leave of the Court or a judge, be admitted in proof of any objection of which particulars are not so delivered.

(6) Particulars delivered may be from time to time amended by leave of the Court or a judge.

(7) The defendant shall be entitled to begin, and give evidence in support of the patent, and if the plaintiff gives evidence impeaching the validity of the patent the defendant shall be entitled to reply.

(8) Where a patent has been revoked on the ground of fraud, the comptroller may, on the application of the true inventor made in accordance with the provisions of this Act, grant to him a patent in lieu of and bearing the same date as the date of revocation of the patent so revoked, but the patent so granted shall cease on the expiration of the term for which the revoked patent was granted.

Crown.

27. (1) A patent shall have to all intents the like effect as against her Majesty the Queen, her heirs and successors, as it has against a subject. Patent to bind Crown.

(2) But the officers or authorities administering any department of the service of the Crown may, by themselves, their agents, contractors, or others, at any time after the application, use the invention for the services of the Crown on terms to be before or after the use thereof agreed on, with the approval of the Treasury, between those officers or authorities and the patentee, or, in default of such agreement, on such terms as may be settled by the Treasury after hearing all parties interested.

Legal Proceedings.

Hearing with assessor.

28. (1) In an action or proceeding for infringement or revocation of a patent, the Court may, if it thinks fit, and shall, on the request of either of the parties to the proceeding, call in the aid of an assessor specially qualified, and try and hear the case wholly or partially with his assistance; the action shall be tried without a jury unless the Court shall otherwise direct.

(2) The Court of Appeal or the Judicial Committee of the Privy Council may, if they see fit, in any proceeding before them respectively, call in the aid of an assessor as aforesaid.

(3) The remuneration, if any, to be paid to an assessor under this section shall be determined by the Court or the Court of Appeal or Judicial Committee, as the case may be, and be paid in the same manner as the other expenses of the execution of this Act.

Delivery of particulars.

29. (1) In an action for infringement of a patent the plaintiff must deliver with his statement of claim, or by order of the Court or the judge, at any subsequent time, particulars of the breaches complained of.

(2) The defendant must deliver with his statement of defence, or, by order of the Court or a judge, at any subsequent time, particulars of any objections on which he relies in support thereof.

(3) If the defendant disputes the validity of the patent, the particulars delivered by him must state on what grounds he disputes it, and if one of those grounds is want of novelty, must state the time and place of the previous publication or user alleged by him.

(4) At the hearing no evidence shall, except by leave of the Court or a judge, be admitted in proof of any alleged infringement or objection of which particulars are not so delivered.

(5) Particulars delivered may be from time to time amended, by leave of the Court or a judge.

(6) On taxation of costs regard shall be had to the particulars delivered by the plaintiff and by the defendant;

and they respectively shall not be allowed any costs in respect of any particular delivered by them unless the same is certified by the Court or a judge to have been proven or to have been reasonable and proper, without regard to the general costs of the case.

30. In an action for infringement of a patent, the Court or a judge may on the application of either party make such order for an injunction, inspection or account, and impose such terms and give such directions respecting the same and the proceedings thereon as the Court or a judge may see fit. Order for inspection &c. in action.

31. In an action for infringement of a patent, the Court or a judge may certify that the validity of the patent came in question; and if the Court or a judge so certifies, then in any subsequent action for infringement, the plaintiff in that action on obtaining a final order or judgment in his favour shall have his full costs, charges and expenses, as between solicitor and client, unless the Court or judge trying the action certifies that he ought not to have the same. Certificate of validity questioned, and costs thereon.

32. Where any person claiming to be the patentee of an invention, by circulars, advertisements, or otherwise, threatens any other person with any legal proceedings or liability in respect of any alleged manufacture, use, sale, or purchase of the invention, any person or persons aggrieved thereby may bring an action against him, and may obtain an injunction against the continuance of such threats, and may recover such damage (if any) as may have been sustained thereby, if the alleged manufacture, use, sale, or purchase to which the threats related was not in fact an infringement of any legal rights of the person making such threats: Provided that this section shall not apply if the person making such threats with due diligence commences and prosecutes an action for infringement of his patent. Remedy in case of groundless threats of legal proceedings.

Miscellaneous.

33. Every patent may be in the form in the First Schedule to this Act, and shall be granted for one invention Patent for one invention only.

only, but may contain more than one claim; but it shall not be competent for any person in an action or other proceeding to take any objection to a patent on the ground that it comprises more than one invention.

Patent on application of representative of deceased inventor.

34. (1) If a person possessed of an invention dies without making application for a patent for the invention, application may be made by, and a patent for the invention granted to, his legal representative.

(2) Every such application must be made within six months of the decease of such person, and must contain a declaration by the legal representative that he believes such person to be the true and first inventor of the invention.

Patent to first inventor not invalidated by application in fraud of him.

35. A patent granted to the true and first inventor shall not be invalidated by an application in fraud of him, or by provisional protection obtained thereon, or by any use or publication of the invention subsequent to that fraudulent application during the period of provisional protection.

Assignment for particular places.

36. A patentee may assign his patent for any place in or part of the United Kingdom, or Isle of Man, as effectually as if the patent were originally granted to extend to that place or part only.

Loss or destruction of patent.

37. If a patent is lost or destroyed, or its non-production is accounted for to the satisfaction of the comptroller, the comptroller may at any time cause a duplicate thereof to be sealed.

Proceedings and costs before law officer.

38. The law officers may examine witnesses on oath and administer oaths for that purpose under this part of this Act, and may from time to time make, alter, and rescind rules regulating references and appeals to the law officers and the practice and procedure before them under this part of this Act; and in any proceeding before either of the law officers under this part of this Act, the law officer may order costs to be paid by either party, and any such order may be made a rule of the Court.

39. The exhibition of an invention at an industrial or international exhibition, certified as such by the Board of Trade, or the publication of any description of the invention during the period of the holding of the exhibition, or the use of the invention for the purpose of the exhibition in the place where the exhibition is held, or the use of the invention during the period of the holding of the exhibition by any person elsewhere, without the privity or consent of the inventor, shall not prejudice the right of the inventor or his legal personal representative to apply for and obtain provisional protection and a patent in respect of the invention or the validity of any patent granted on the application, provided that both the following conditions are complied with, namely,— Exhibition at industrial or international exhibition not to prejudice patent rights.

(*a*) The exhibitor must, before exhibiting the invention, give the comptroller the prescribed notice of his intention to do so; and

(*b*) The application for a patent must be made before or within six months from the date of the opening of the exhibition.

Whereas it is expedient to provide for the extension of this section to industrial and international exhibitions held out of the United Kingdom, be it therefore enacted as follows:

It shall be lawful for Her Majesty, by Order in Council, from time to time to declare that sections thirty-nine and fifty-seven of the Patents, Designs, and Trade Marks Act, 1883, or either of those sections, shall apply to any exhibition mentioned in the Order in like manner as if it were an industrial or international exhibition certified by the Board of Trade, and to provide that the exhibitor shall be relieved from the conditions, specified in the said sections, of giving notice to the comptroller of his intention to exhibit, and shall be so relieved either absolutely or upon such terms and conditions as to Her Majesty in Council may seem fit. Protection of Patents and Designs exhibited at international exhibitions. **Act 1886, s. 3.**

40. (1) The comptroller shall cause to be issued periodically an illustrated journal of patented inventions, as well as reports of patent cases decided by courts of law, and Publication of illustrated journal, indexes &c.

any other information that the comptroller may deem generally useful or important.

(2) Provision shall be made by the comptroller for keeping on sale copies of such journal, and also of all complete specifications of patents for the time being in force, with their accompanying drawings, if any.

(3) The comptroller shall continue, in such form as he may deem expedient, the indexes and abridgments of specifications hitherto published, and shall from time to time prepare and publish such other indexes, abridgments of specifications, catalogues, and other works relating to inventions, as he may see fit.

Patent Museum.

41. The control and management of the existing Patent Museum and its contents shall from and after the commencement of this Act, be transferred to and vested in the Department of Science and Art, subject to such directions as her Majesty in Council may see fit to give.

Power to require models on payment.

42. The Department of Science and Art may at any time require a patentee to furnish them with a model of his invention on payment to the patentee of the cost of the manufacture of the model; the amount to be settled, in case of dispute, by the Board of Trade.

Foreign vessels in British waters.

43. (1) A patent shall not prevent the use of an invention for the purposes of the navigation of a foreign vessel within the jurisdiction of any of her Majesty's Courts in the United Kingdom, or Isle of Man, or the use of an invention in a foreign vessel within that jurisdiction, provided it is not used therein for or in connection with the manufacture or preparation of anything intended to be sold in or exported from the United Kingdom or Isle of Man.

(2) But this section shall not extend to vessels of any foreign state of which the laws authorise subjects of such foreign state, having patents or like privileges for the exclusive use or exercise of inventions within its territories, to prevent or interfere with the use of such inventions in British vessels while in the ports of such foreign state, or in

the waters within the jurisdiction of its courts, where such inventions are not so used for the manufacture or preparation of anything intended to be sold in or exported from the territories of such foreign state.

Assignment to Secretary for War of certain inventions.

44. (1) The inventor of any improvement in instruments or munitions of war, his executors, administrators, or assigns (who are in this section comprised in the expression the inventor), may (either for or without valuable consideration) assign to her Majesty's Principal Secretary of State for the War Department (hereinafter referred to as the Secretary of State), on behalf of her Majesty, all the benefit of the invention and of any patent obtained or to be obtained for the same; and the Secretary of State may be a party to the assignment.

(2) The assignment shall effectually vest the benefit of the invention and patent in the Secretary of State for the time being on behalf of her Majesty, and all covenants and agreements therein contained for keeping the invention secret and otherwise shall be valid and effectual (notwithstanding any want of valuable consideration), and may be enforced accordingly by the Secretary of State for the time being.

(3) Where any such assignment has been made to the Secretary of State, he may at any time before the application for a patent for the invention, or before publication of the specification or specifications, certify to the comptroller his opinion that, in the interest of the public service, the particulars of the invention and of the manner in which it is to be performed should be kept secret.

(4) If the Secretary of State so certifies, the application and specification or specifications with the drawings (if any), and any amendment of the specification or specifications, and any copies of such documents and drawings, shall, instead of being left in the ordinary manner at the Patent Office, be delivered to the comptroller in a packet sealed by authority of the Secretary of State.

(5) Such packet shall until the expiration of the term or extended term during which a patent for the invention may be in force, be kept sealed by the comptroller, and shall

not be opened save under the authority of an order of the Secretary of State, or of the law officers.

(6) Such sealed packet shall be delivered at any time during the continuance of the patent to any person authorised by writing under the hand of the Secretary of State to receive the same, and shall if returned to the comptroller be again kept sealed by him.

(7) On the expiration of the term or extended term of the patent, such sealed packet shall be delivered to any person authorised by writing under the hand of the Secretary of State to receive it.

(8) Where the Secretary of State certifies as aforesaid, after an application for a patent has been left at the Patent Office, but before the publication of the specification or specifications, the application, specification, or specifications, with the drawings (if any), shall be forthwith placed in a packet sealed by authority of the comptroller, and such packet shall be subject to the foregoing provisions respecting a packet sealed by authority of the Secretary of State.

(9) No proceeding by petition or otherwise shall lie for revocation of a patent granted for an invention in relation to which the Secretary of State has certified as aforesaid.

(10) No copy of any specification or other document or drawing, by this section required to be placed in a sealed packet, shall in any manner whatever be published or open to the inspection of the public, but, save as in this section otherwise directed, the provisions of this part of this Act shall apply in respect of any such invention and patent as aforesaid.

(11) The Secretary of State may, at any time, by writing under his hand, waive the benefit of this section with respect to any particular invention, and the specifications, documents, and drawings shall be thenceforth kept and dealt with in the ordinary way.

(12) The communication of any invention for any improvement in instruments or munitions of war to the Secretary of State, or to any person or persons authorised by him to investigate the same or the merits thereof,

shall not, nor shall anything done for the purposes of the investigation, be deemed use or publication of such invention so as to prejudice the grant or validity of any patent for the same.

Existing Patents.

45. (1) The provisions of this Act relating to applications for patents and proceedings thereon shall have effect in respect only of applications made after the commencement of this Act. **Provisions respecting existing patents.**

(2) Every patent granted before the commencement of this Act, or on an application then pending, shall remain unaffected by the provisions of this Act relating to patents binding the Crown, and to compulsory licences.

(3) In all other respects (including the amount and time of payment of fees) this Act shall extend to all patents granted before the commencement of this Act, or on applications then pending, in substitution for such enactments as would have applied thereto if this Act had not been passed.

(4) All instruments relating to patents granted before the commencement of this Act required to be left or filed in the Great Seal Patent Office shall be deemed to be so left or filed if left or filed before or after the commencement of this Act in the Patent Office.

Definitions.

46. In and for the purposes of this Act— **Definitions of "patent," "patentee," and "invention."**

"Patent" means letters patent for an invention:

"Patentee" means the person for the time being entitled to the benefit of a patent:

"Invention" means any manner of new manufacture the subject of letters patent and grant of privilege within section six of the Statute of Monopolies (that is, the Act of the twenty-first year of the reign of King James the First, chapter three, intituled "An Act concerning monopolies and dispensations with penal laws and the forfeiture thereof"), and includes an alleged invention.

In Scotland "injunction" means "interdict."

PART III.

DESIGNS.

Registration of Designs.

Application for registration of designs.

47. (1) The comptroller may, on application by or on behalf of any person claiming to be the proprietor of any new or original design not previously published in the United Kingdom, register the design under this part of this Act.

(2) The application must be made in the form set forth in the First Schedule to this Act, or in such other form as may be from time to time prescribed, and must be left at, or sent by post to, the Patent Office in the prescribed manner.

(3) The application must contain a statement of the nature of the design, and the class or classes of goods in which the applicant desires that the design be registered.

(4) The same design may be registered in more than one class.

(5) In case of doubt as to the class in which a design ought to be registered, the comptroller may decide the question.

(6) The comptroller may, if he thinks fit, refuse to register any design presented to him for registration, but any person aggrieved by any such refusal may appeal therefrom to the Board of Trade.

(7) The Board of Trade shall, if required, hear the applicant and the comptroller, and may make an order determining whether, and subject to what conditions, if any, registration is to be permitted.

Drawings, &c. to be furnished on application.

48. (1) On application for registration of a design the applicant shall furnish to the comptroller the prescribed number of copies of drawings, photographs, or tracings of the design sufficient, in the opinion of the comptroller, for enabling him to identify the design; or the applicant may, instead of such copies, furnish exact representations or specimens of the design.

(2) The comptroller may, if he thinks fit, refuse any drawing, photograph, tracing, representation, or specimen which is not, in his opinion, suitable for the official records.

49. (1) The comptroller shall grant a certificate of registration to the proprietor of the design when registered Certificate of registration.

(2) The comptroller may, in case of loss of the original certificate, or in any other case in which he deems it expedient, grant a copy or copies of the certificate.

Copyright in Registered Designs.

50. (1) When a design is registered, the registered proprietor of the design shall, subject to the provisions of this Act, have copyright in the design during five years from the date of registration. Copyright on registration.

(2) Before delivery on sale of any articles to which a registered design has been applied, the proprietor must (if exact representations or specimens were not furnished on the application for registration), furnish to the comptroller the prescribed number of exact representations or specimens of the design; and if he fails to do so, the comptroller may erase his name from the register, and thereupon his copyright in the design shall cease.

51. Before delivery on sale of any articles to which a registered design has been applied, the proprietor of the design shall cause each such article to be marked with the prescribed mark, or with the prescribed word or words or figures, denoting that the design is registered; and if he fails to do so, the copyright in the design shall cease, unless the proprietor shows that he took all proper steps to ensure the marking of the article. Marking registered designs.

52. (1) During the existence of copyright in a design, the design shall not be open to inspection except by the proprietor, or a person authorised in writing by the proprietor, or a person authorised by the comptroller or by the Court, and furnishing such information as may enable the comptroller to identify the design, nor except in the Inspection of registered designs.

presence of the comptroller, or of an officer acting under him, nor except on payment of the prescribed fee; and the person making the inspection shall not be entitled to take any copy of the design, or of any part thereof.

Act 1888, s. 6.

Provided that where registration of a design is refused on the ground of identity with a design already registered, the applicant for registration shall be entitled to inspect the design so registered.

(2) When the copyright in a design has ceased, the design shall be open to inspection, and copies thereof may be taken by any person on payment of the prescribed fee.

Information as to existence of copyright.

53. On the request of any person producing a particular design, together with its mark of registration, or producing only its mark of registration, or furnishing such information as may enable the comptroller to identify the design, and on payment of the prescribed fee, it shall be the duty of the comptroller to inform such person whether the registration still exists in respect of such design, and if so, in respect of what class or classes of goods, and stating also the date of registration, and the name and address of the registered proprietor.

Cesser of copyright in certain events.

54. If a registered design is used in manufacture in any foreign country and is not used in this country within six months of its registration in this country, the copyright in the design shall cease.

Register of Designs.

Register of Designs.

55. (1) There shall be kept at the Patent Office a book called the Register of Designs, wherein shall be entered the names and addresses of proprietors of registered designs, notifications of assignments and of transmissions of registered designs, and such other matters as may from time to time be prescribed.

(2) The register of designs shall be prima facie evidence of any matters by this Act directed or authorised to be entered therein.

Fees.

56. There shall be paid in respect of applications and registration and other matters under this part of this Act such fees as may be from time to time, with the sanction of the Treasury, prescribed by the Board of Trade; and such fees shall be levied and paid to the account of her Majesty's Exchequer in such manner as the Treasury shall from time to time direct.

Fees on registration &c.

Industrial and International Exhibitions.

57. The exhibition at an industrial or international exhibition certified as such by the Board of Trade, or the exhibition elsewhere during the period of the holding of the exhibition, without the privity or consent of the proprietor, of a design, or of any article to which a design is applied, or the publication, during the holding of any such exhibition, of a description of a design, shall not prevent the design from being registered, or invalidate the registration thereof, provided that both the following conditions are complied with; namely,—

Exhibition at industrial or international exhibition not to prevent or invalidate registration

(*a*) The exhibitor must, before exhibiting the design or article, or publishing a description of the design, give the comptroller the prescribed notice of his intention to do so; and

(*b*) The application for registration must be made before or within six months from the date of the opening of the exhibition.

And whereas it is expedient to provide for the extension of this section to industrial and international exhibitions held out of the United Kingdom, be it therefore enacted as follows:

Protection of patents and designs exhibited at international exhibitions. **Act 1886, s. 3.**

It shall be lawful for her Majesty, by Order in Council, from time to time to declare that sections thirty-nine and fifty-seven of the Patents, Designs, and Trade Marks Act, 1883, or either of those sections, shall apply to any exhibition mentioned in the Order in like manner as if it were an industrial or international exhibition certified by the Board of

Trade, and to provide that the exhibitor shall be relieved from the conditions, specified in the said sections, of giving notice to the comptroller of his intention to exhibit, and shall be so relieved either absolutely or upon such terms and conditions as to her Majesty in Council may seem fit.

Legal Proceedings.

Penalty on piracy of registered design. **Act 1888, s. 7.**

58. During the existence of copyright in any design—

(*a*) It shall not be lawful for any person without the license or written consent of the registered proprietor to apply **or cause to be applied** such design or any fraudulent or obvious imitation thereof, in the class or classes of goods in which such design is registered, for purposes of sale to any article of manufacture or to any substance artificial or natural or partly artificial and partly natural; and

(*b*) It shall not be lawful for any person to publish or expose for sale any article of manufacture or any substance to which such design or any fraudulent or obvious imitation thereof shall have been so applied, knowing that the same has been so applied without the consent of the registered proprietor.

Any person who acts in contravention of this section shall be liable for every offence to forfeit a sum not exceeding fifty pounds to the registered proprietor of the design, who may recover such sum as a simple contract debt by action in any court of competent jurisdiction: **Provided that the total sum forfeited in respect of any one design shall not exceed one hundred pounds.**

Act 1888, s. 7.

Action for damages.

59. Notwithstanding the remedy given by this Act for the recovery of such penalty as aforesaid, the registered proprietor of any design may (if he elects to do so) bring an action for the recovery of any damages arising from the application of any such design, or of any fraudulent or obvious imitation thereof for the purpose of sale, to any article of manufacture or substance, or from the publication, sale or exposure for sale by any person of any article or substance to which such design or any fraudulent or obvious imitation thereof shall have been so applied, such person knowing that the proprietor had not given his consent to such application.

Definitions.

Definition of "design," "copyright."

60. In and for the purposes of this Act—

"Design" means any design applicable to any article of manufacture, or to any substance artificial or natural, or partly artificial and partly natural, whether the design is applicable for the pattern, or for the shape or configuration, or for the ornament thereof, or for any two or more of such purposes, and by whatever means it is applicable, whether by printing, painting, embroidering, weaving, sewing, modelling, casting, embossing, engraving, staining, or any other means whatever, manual, mechanical, or chemical, separate or combined, not being a design for a sculpture, or other thing within the protection of the Sculpture Copyright Act of the year 1814 (fifty-fourth George the Third, chapter fifty-six).

"Copyright" means the exclusive right to apply a design to any article of manufacture or to any such substance as aforesaid in the class or classes in which the design is registered.

Definition of "proprietor."

61. The author of any new and original design shall be considered the "proprietor" thereof, unless he executed the work on behalf of another person for a good or valuable consideration, in which case such person shall be considered the proprietor, and every person acquiring for a good or valuable consideration a new and original design, or the right to apply the same to any such article or substance as aforesaid, either exclusively of any other person or otherwise, and also every person on whom the property in such design or such right to the application thereof shall devolve, shall be considered the proprietor of the design in the respect in which the same may have been so acquired, and to that extent, but not otherwise.

PART IV.

TRADE MARKS.

Registration of Trade Marks.

Application for registration.

62. (1) The comptroller may, on application by or on behalf of any person claiming to be the proprietor of a trade mark, register the trade mark.

Act 1888, s. 8.

(2) The application must be made in the form set forth in the First Schedule to this Act, or in such other form as may be from time to time prescribed, and must be left at, or sent by post to [*the Patent Office in the prescribed manner*] **such place and in such manner as may be prescribed.**

(3) The application must be accompanied by the prescribed number of representations of the trade mark, and must state the particular goods or classes of goods in connexion with which the applicant desires the trade mark to be registered.

(4) The comptroller may, if he thinks fit, refuse to register a trade mark, but any such refusal shall be subject to appeal to the Board of Trade, who shall, if required, hear the applicant and the comptroller, and may make an order determining whether, and subject to what conditions, if any, registration is to be permitted.

(5) The Board of Trade may, however, if it appears expedient, refer the appeal to the Court; and in that event the Court shall have jurisdiction to hear and determine the appeal and may make such order as aforesaid.

Act 1888, s. 8.

(6.) Where an applicant for the registration of a trade mark otherwise than under an international convention is out of the United Kingdom at the time of making the application he shall give the comptroller an address for service in the United Kingdom, and if he fails to do so the application shall not be proceeded with until the address has been given.

Limit of time for proceeding

63. Where registration of a trade mark has not been or shall not be completed within twelve months from the date of the application, by reason of default on the part of the applicant [*the application shall be deemed to be abandoned*], **the comptroller shall give notice of the non-completion to the agent employed on behalf of the applicant, and, if at the expiration of fourteen days from that notice the registration is not completed, shall give the like notice to the applicant, and if at the expiration of the latter fourteen days, or such further time as the comptroller may in special cases permit, the registration is not completed, the application shall be deemed to be abandoned.** with application. Act 1888, s. 9.

[64. (1) *For the purposes of this Act, a trade mark must consist of or contain at least one of the following essential particulars:* Conditions of registration of trade mark.

(*a*) *A name of an individual or firm printed, impressed, or woven in some particular and distinctive manner; or* Repealed by Act 1888, s. 10.

(*b*) *A written signature or copy of a written signature of the individual or firm applying for registration thereof as a trade mark; or*

(*c*) *A distinctive device, mark, brand, heading, label, ticket, or fancy word or words not in common use.*

(2) *There may be added to any one or more of these particulars any letters, words, or figures, or combination of letters, words, or figures, or of any of them.*

(3) *Provided that any special and distinctive word or words, letter, figure, or combination of letters or figures or of letters and figures, used as a trade mark before the Thirteenth day of August, One thousand eight hundred and seventy-five, may be registered as a trade mark under this part of this Act.*]

64. (1) For the purposes of this Act, a trade mark must consist of or contain at least one of the following essential particulars: Conditions of registration of trade mark. Act 1888, s. 10.

(*a*) **A name of an individual or firm printed, impressed, or woven in some particular and distinctive manner; or**

(b) A written signature or copy of a written signature of the individual or firm applying for registration thereof as a trade mark; or

(c) A distinctive device, mark, brand, heading, label, or ticket; or

(d) An invented word or invented words; or

(e) A word or words having no reference to the character or quality of the goods, and not being a geographical name.

(2) There may be added to any one or more of the essential particulars mentioned in this section any letters, words, or figures, or combination of letters, words, or figures, or of any of them; but the applicant for registration of any such additional matter must state in his application the essential particulars of the trade mark, and must disclaim in his application any right to the exclusive use of the added matter, and a copy of the statement and disclaimer shall be entered on the register.

(3) Provided as follows:

(i.) A person need not under this section disclaim his own name or the foreign equivalent thereof, or his place of business, but no entry of any such name shall affect the right of any owner of the same name to use that name or the foreign equivalent thereof:

(ii.) Any special and distinctive word or words, letter, figure, or combination of letters or figures, or of letters and figures, used as a trade mark before the Thirteenth day of August, One thousand eight hundred and seventy-five, may be registered as a trade mark under this part of this Act.

Connection of trade mark with goods.

65. A trade mark must be registered for particular goods or classes of goods.

Registration of a series of marks.

66. When a person claiming to be the proprietor of several trade marks which, while resembling each other in the material particulars thereof, yet differ in respect of (*a*) the statement of the goods for which they are respectively used or proposed to be used, or (*b*) statements of numbers, or (*c*) statements of price, or (*d*) statements of quality, or (*e*) statements of names of places, seeks to register such trade marks, they may be registered as a series in one registration. A series of trade marks shall be assignable and transmissible only as a whole, but for all other purposes each of the trade marks composing a series shall be deemed and treated as registered separately.

Trade marks may be registered in any colour. Act 1888, s. 11.

67. A trade mark may be registered in any colour **or colours,** and such registration shall (subject to the provisions of this Act) confer on the registered owner the exclusive right to use the same in that or any other colour **or colours.**

Advertisement of application. Act 1888, s. 12.

68. Every application for registration of a trade mark under this part of this Act shall as soon as may be after its receipt be advertised by the comptroller, **unless the comptroller refuse to entertain the application.**

Opposition to registration. Act 1888, s. 13, sub-ss. 1, 2.

69. (1) Any person may within [*two months*] **one month or such further time, not exceeding three months, as the comptroller may allow,** of the [*first*] advertisement of the application, give notice in duplicate at the Patent Office of opposition to registration of the trade mark, and the comptroller shall send one copy of such notice to the applicant.

Act 1888, s. 13, sub-s. 3.

(2) Within [*two months*] **one month** after receipt of such notice, or such further time as the comptroller may allow, the applicant may send to the comptroller a counter statement in duplicate of the grounds on which he relies for his application, and if he does not do so, shall be deemed to have abandoned his application.

Repealed by Act 1888, s. 13, sub-s. 4.

[(3) *If the applicant sends such counter statement, the comptroller shall furnish a copy thereof to the person who gave notice of opposition, and shall require him to give security in such manner and to such amount as the comptroller may require for such costs as may be awarded in respect of such opposition; and if such security is not given within fourteen days after such requirement was made or such further time as the comptroller may allow, the opposition shall be deemed to be withdrawn.*

(4) *If the person who gave notice of opposition duly gives such security as aforesaid, the comptroller shall inform the applicant thereof in writing, and thereupon the case shall be deemed to stand for the determination of the Court.*]

Act 1888, s. 13, sub-s. 4.

(3) If the applicant sends such counter statement, the comptroller shall furnish a copy thereof to the person who gave notice of opposition, and shall, after hearing the applicant and the opponent, if so required, decide whether the trade mark is to be registered, but his decision shall be subject to appeal to the Board of Trade, who shall, if required, hear the applicant and the opponent and the comptroller, and may make an order determining whether, and subject to what conditions (if any), registration is to be permitted.

(4) The Board of Trade may, however, if it appears expedient, refer the appeal to the Court, and in that event the Court shall have jurisdiction to hear and determine the appeal, and may make such order as aforesaid.

(5) If the applicant abandons his application after notice of opposition in pursuance of this section, he shall be liable to pay to the opponent such costs in respect of the opposition as the comptroller may determine to be reasonable.

(6) Where the opponent is out of the United Kingdom, he shall give the comptroller an address for service in the United Kingdom.

Assignment and transmission of trade mark.

70. A trade mark, when registered, shall be assigned and transmitted only in connection with the goodwill of the business concerned in the particular goods or classes of goods for which it has been registered, and shall be determinable with that goodwill.

Conflicting claims to registration.

71. Where each of several persons claims to be registered as proprietor of the same trade mark, the comptroller may refuse to register any of them until their rights have been determined according to law, and the comptroller may himself submit or require the claimants to submit their rights to the Court.

72. (1) Except where the Court has decided that two or more persons are entitled to be registered as proprietors of the same trade mark, the comptroller shall not register in respect of the same goods or description of goods a trade mark identical with one already on the register with respect to such goods or description of goods. **Restrictions on registration.**

(2) **Except as aforesaid** the comptroller shall not register with respect to the same goods or description of goods a trade mark [*so nearly resembling*] **having such resemblance to** a trade mark already on the register with respect to such goods or description of goods as to be calculated to deceive. **Act 1888, s. 14.**

73. It shall not be lawful to register as part of or in combination with a trade mark any words the [*exclusive*] use of which would by reason of their being calculated to deceive or otherwise, be deemed disentitled to protection in a court of justice, or any scandalous design. **Further restriction on registration. Act 1888, s. 15.**

74. (1) Nothing in this Act shall be construed to prevent the comptroller entering on the register, in the prescribed manner, and subject to the prescribed conditions, as an addition to any trade mark— **Saving for power to provide for entry on register of common marks as additions to trade marks.**

(*a*) In the case of an application for registration of a trade mark used before the thirteenth day of August one thousand eight hundred and seventy-five—

Any distinctive device, mark, brand, heading, label, ticket, letter, word, or figure, or combination of letters, words, or figures, though the same is common to the trade in the goods with respect to which the application is made;

(*b*) In the case of an application for registration of a trade mark not used before the Thirteenth day of

August, One thousand eight hundred and seventy-five

Any distinctive word or combination of words, though the same is common to the trade in the goods with respect to which the application is made;

Repealed by Act 1888, s. 16.

[(2) *The applicant for entry of any such common particular or particulars must, however, disclaim in his application any right to the exclusive use of the same, and a copy of the disclaimer shall be entered on the register.*]

Act 1888, s. 16.

(2) The applicant for registration of any such addition must, however, state in his application the essential particulars of the trade mark, and must disclaim in his application any right to the exclusive use of the added matter, and a copy of the statement and disclaimer shall be entered on the register.

Provided that a person need not under this section disclaim his own name or the foreign equivalent thereof, or his place of business, but no entry of any such name shall affect the right of any owner of the same name to use that name or the foreign equivalent thereof.

(3) Any device, mark, brand, heading, label, ticket, letter, word, figure, or combination of letters, words, or figures, which was or were, before the Thirteenth day of August, One thousand eight hundred and seventy-five, publicly used by more than three persons on the same or a similar description of goods shall, for the purposes of this section, be deemed common to the trade in such goods.

Effect of Registration.

Registration equivalent to public use. Act 1888, s. 17.

75. [*Registration of a trade mark shall be deemed to be equivalent to public use of the trade mark.*]

Application for registration of a trade mark shall be deemed to be equivalent to public use of the trade mark, and the date of the application shall for the purposes of this Act be deemed to be, and as from the First day of January, One thousand eight

hundred and seventy-six to have been, the date of the registration.

76. The registration of a person as proprietor of a trade mark shall be primâ facie evidence of his right to the exclusive use of the trade mark, and shall, after the expiration of five years from the date of the registration, be conclusive evidence of his right to the exclusive use of the trade mark, subject to the provisions of this Act. Right of first proprietor to exclusive use of trade mark.

77. A person shall not be entitled to institute any proceeding to prevent or to recover damages for the infringement of a trade mark unless, in the case of a trade mark capable of being registered under this Act, it has been registered in pursuance of this Act, or of an enactment repealed by this Act, or, in the case of any other trade mark in use before the Thirteenth of August, One thousand eight hundred and seventy-five, registration thereof under this part of this Act, or of an enactment repealed by this Act, has been refused. The comptroller may, on request, and on payment of the prescribed fee, grant a certificate that such registration has been refused. Restrictions on actions for infringement, and on defence to action in certain cases.

77a. In an action for infringement of a registered trade mark the Court or a judge may certify that the right to the exclusive use of the trade mark came in question, and if the Court or a judge so certifies, then in any subsequent action for infringement the plaintiff in that action, on obtaining a final order or judgment in his favour, shall have his full costs, charges, and expenses as between solicitor and client, unless the Court or judge trying the subsequent action certifies that he ought not to have the same. Certificate as to exclusive use, and costs thereon. Act 1888, s. 18.

Register of Trade Marks.

78. There shall be kept at the Patent Office a book called the Register of Trade Marks, wherein shall be entered the names and addresses of proprietors of registered trade marks, notifications of assignments and of transmissions of trade marks, and such other matters as may be from time to time prescribed. Register of Trade Marks.

Removal of trade mark after fourteen years unless fee paid.

79. (1) At a time not being less than two months nor more than three months before the expiration of fourteen years from the date of the registration of a trade mark, the comptroller shall send notice to the registered proprietor that the trade mark will be removed from the register unless the proprietor pays to the comptroller before the expiration of such fourteen years (naming the date at which the same will expire) the prescribed fee: and if such fee be not previously paid, he shall at the expiration of one month from the date of the giving of the first notice send a second notice to the same effect.

(2) If such fee be not paid before the expiration of such fourteen years, the comptroller may after the end of three months from the expiration of such fourteen years remove the mark from the register, and so from time to time at the expiration of every period of fourteen years.

(3) If before the expiration of the said three months the registered proprietor pays the said fee, together with the additional prescribed fee, the comptroller may without removing such trade mark from the register accept the said fee as if it had been paid before the expiration of the said fourteen years.

(4) Where after the said three months a trade mark has been removed from the register for non-payment of the prescribed fee, the comptroller may, if satisfied that it is just so to do, restore such trade mark to the register on payment of the prescribed additional fee.

(5) Where a trade mark has been removed from the register for non-payment of the fee or otherwise, such trade mark shall nevertheless, for the purpose of any application for registration during [*the five years*] **one year** next after the date of such removal, be deemed to be a trade mark which is already registered, **unless it is shown to the satisfaction of the comptroller that the non-payment of the fee arises from the death or bankruptcy of the registered proprietor, or from his having ceased to carry on business, and that no person claiming under that proprietor or under his bankruptcy is using the trade mark.**

Act 1888, s. 19, sub-s. 1.

Act 1888, s. 19, sub-s. 2.

Fees.

80. There shall be paid in respect of applications and registration and other matters under this part of this Act, such fees as may be from time to time, with the sanction of the Treasury, prescribed by the Board of Trade; and such fees shall be levied and paid to the account of Her Majesty's Exchequer in such manner as the Treasury may from time to time direct. Fees for registration &c.

Sheffield Marks.

81. With respect to the master, wardens, searchers, assistants, and commonalty of the Company of Cutlers in Hallamshire, in the county of York (in this Act called the Cutlers' Company), and the marks or devices (in this Act called Sheffield marks) assigned or registered by the master, wardens, searchers, and assistants of that company, the following provisions shall have effect: Registration by Cutlers' Company of Sheffield marks

(1) The Cutlers' Company shall establish and keep at Sheffield a new register of trade marks (in this Act called the Sheffield register):

[(2) *The Cutlers' Company shall enter in the Sheffield register, in respect of cutlery, edge tools, or raw steel, and the goods mentioned in the next sub-section, all the trade marks entered before the commencement of this Act in respect of cutlery, edge tools, or raw steel, and such goods in the register established under the Trade Marks Registration Act,* 1875, *belonging to persons carrying on business in Hallamshire, or within six miles thereof, and shall also enter in such register, in respect of the same goods, all the trade marks which shall have been assigned by the Cutlers' Company and actually used before the commencement of this Act, but which have not been entered in the register established under the Trade Marks Registration Act,* 1875 :] Repealed by Act 1888, s. 20, sub-s. 1.

(2) The Cutlers' Company shall enter in the Sheffield register, in respect of metal goods as defined in this section, all the trade marks entered Act 1888, s. 20, sub-s. 1.

before the First day of January, One thousand eight hundred and eighty-nine, in respect of metal goods either in the register established under the Trade Marks Registration Act, 1875, or in the register of trade marks under this Act, belonging to persons carrying on business in Hallamshire or within six miles thereof. The Cutlers' Company shall also, on request made in the prescribed manner, enter in the Sheffield register, in respect of metal goods, all the trade marks which shall have been assigned by the Cutlers' Company and actually used before the First day of January, One thousand eight hundred and eighty-four, but which have not been entered in either of the said other registers:

38 & 39 Vict. c. 91.

(3) An application for registration of a trade mark used [*on cutlery, edge tools, or on raw steel, or on goods made of steel, or of steel and iron combined, whether with or without a cutting edge*] **on metal goods** shall, if made after the commencement of this Act by a person carrying on business in Hallamshire, or within six miles thereof, be made to the Cutlers' Company:

Act 1888, s. 20, sub-s. 2.

(4) Every application so made to the Cutlers' Company shall be notified to the comptroller in the prescribed manner, and unless the comptroller within the prescribed time gives notice to the Cutlers' Company that he objects to the acceptance of the application, it shall be proceeded with by the Cutlers' Company in the prescribed manner:

(5) If the comptroller gives notice of objection as aforesaid, the application shall not be proceeded with by the Cutlers' Company, but any person aggrieved may appeal to the Court:

(6) Upon the registration of a trade mark in the Sheffield register the Cutlers' Company shall give notice thereof to the comptroller, who shall thereupon enter the mark in the register of trade

marks; and such registration shall bear date as of the day of application to the Cutlers' Company, and have the same effect as if the application had been made to the comptroller on that day:

[(7) *The provisions of this Act, and of any general rules made under this Act, with respect to application for registration in the register of trade marks, the effect of such registration, and the assignment and transmission of rights in a registered trade mark shall apply in the case of applications aad registration in the Sheffield register; and notice of every entry made in the Sheffield register must be given to the comptroller by the Cutlers' Company, save and except that the provisions of this sub-section shall not prejudice or affect any life estate and interest of a widow of the holder of any Sheffield mark which may be in force in respect of such mark at the time when it shall be placed upon the Sheffield register:*] Repealed by Act 1888, s. 20, sub-s. 3.

(7) **The provisions of this Act and of any general rules made under this Act with respect to the registration of trade marks, and all matters relating thereto, shall, subject to the provisions of this section, apply to the registration of trade marks on metal goods by the Cutlers' Company, and to all matters relating thereto; and this Act and any such general rules shall, so far as applicable, be construed accordingly, with the substitution of the Cutlers' Company, the office of the Cutlers' Company, and the Sheffield register, for the comptroller, the Patent Office, and the Register of Trade Marks respectively; and notice of every entry, cancellation, or correction made in the Sheffield register shall be given to the comptroller by the Cutlers' Company: provided that this section shall not affect any life estate and interest of a widow of the holder of any Sheffield mark which may be in force in respect of such mark at the time when it shall be placed upon the Sheffield register:** Act 1888, s. 20, sub-s. 3.

(8) Where the comptroller receives from any person not carrying on business in Hallamshire or within six miles thereof an application for registration of a trade mark used [*on cutlery, edge tools, or on raw steel, or on goods made of steel, or of steel and iron combined, whether with or without a cutting edge*] **on metal goods,** he shall in the prescribed manner notify the application and proceedings thereon to the Cutlers' Company:

Act 1888, s. 20, sub-s. 2.

(9) At the expiration of five years from the commencement of this Act the Cutlers' Company shall close the Cutlers' register of corporate trade marks. and thereupon all marks entered therein shall, unless entered in the Sheffield register, be deemed to have been abandoned:

(10) A person may (notwithstanding anything in any Act relating to the Cutlers' Company) be registered in the Sheffield register as proprietor of two or more trade marks:

(11) A body of persons, corporate or not corporate, may (notwithstanding anything in any Act relating to the Cutlers' Company) be registered in the Sheffield register as proprietor of a trade mark or trade marks:

(12) Any person aggrieved by a decision of the Cutlers' Company in respect of anything done or omitted under this Act may, in the prescribed manner, appeal to the comptroller, who shall have power to confirm, reverse, or modify the decision, but the decision of the comptroller shall be subject to a further appeal to the Court:

(13) So much of the Cutlers' Company's Acts as applies to the summary punishment of persons counterfeiting Sheffield corporate marks, that is to say, the fifth section of the Cutlers' Company's Act of 1814, and the provisions in relation to the recovery and application of the penalty imposed by such last-mentioned section contained in the Cutlers' Company's Act of 1791, shall apply to any mark entered in the Sheffield register:

(14) For the purposes of this section the expression "metal goods" means all metals, whether wrought, unwrought, or partly wrought, and all goods composed wholly or partly of any metal: Act 1888, s. 20, sub-s. 4.

(15) For the purpose of legal proceedings in relation to trade marks entered in the Sheffield register a certificate under the hand of the master of the Cutlers' Company shall have the same effect as the certificate of the comptroller.

PART V.

General.

Patent Office and Proceedings thereat.

82. (1) The Treasury may provide for the purposes of this Act an office with all requisite buildings and conveniences, which shall be called, and is in this Act referred to as, the Patent Office. Patent Office.

(2) Until a new Patent Office is provided, the offices of the Commissioners of Patents for inventions and for the registration of designs and trade marks existing at the commencement of this Act shall be the Patent Office within the meaning of this Act.

(3) The Patent Office shall be under the immediate control of an officer called the comptroller-general of patents, designs, and trade marks, who shall act under the superintendence and direction of the Board of Trade.

(4) Any act or thing directed to be done by or to the comptroller may, in his absence, be done by or to any officer for the time being in that behalf authorised by the Board of Trade.

83. (1) The Board of Trade may at any time after the passing of this Act, and from time to time, subject to the approval of the Treasury, appoint the comptroller-general Officers and clerks.

of patents, designs, and trade marks, and so many examiners and other officers and clerks with such designations and duties as the Board of Trade think fit, and may from time to time remove any of those officers and clerks.

(2) The salaries of those officers and clerks shall be appointed by the Board of Trade, with the concurrence of the Treasury, and the same and the other expenses of the execution of this Act shall be paid out of money provided by Parliament.

Seal of Patent Office.

84. There shall be a seal for the Patent Office, and impressions thereof shall be judicially noticed and admitted in evidence.

Trust not to be entered in registers.

85. There shall not be entered in any register kept under this Act, or be receivable by the comptroller, any notice of any trust, expressed, implied, or constructive.

Refusal to grant patent &c. in certain cases.

86. The comptroller may refuse to grant a patent for an invention, or to register a design or trade mark, of which the use would, in his opinion, be contrary to law or morality.

Entry of assignments and transmissions in registers.

Act 1888, s. 21.

87. Where a person becomes entitled by assignment, transmission, or other operation of law to a patent, or to the copyright in a registered design, or to a registered trade mark, the comptroller shall on request, and on proof of title to his satisfaction, cause the name of such person to be entered as proprietor of the patent, copyright in the design, or trade mark, in the register of patents, designs, or trade marks, as the case may be. The person for the time being entered in the register of patents, designs, or trade marks, as proprietor of a patent, copyright in a design, or trade mark as the case may be, shall, subject to **the provisions of this Act and to** any rights appearing from such register to be vested in any other person, have power absolutely to assign, grant licences as to, or otherwise deal with, the same and to give effectual receipts for any consideration for such assignment, licence, or dealing. Provided that any equities in respect of such patent, design, or trade mark may be enforced in like manner as in respect of any other personal property.

88. Every register kept under this Act shall at all convenient times be open to the inspection of the public, subject to **the provisions of this Act and to** such regulations as may be prescribed; and certified copies, sealed with the seal of the Patent Office, of any entry in any such register shall be given to any person requiring the same on payment of the prescribed fee. Inspection of and extracts from registers. **Act 1888, s. 22.**

89. Printed or written copies or extracts, purporting to be certified by the comptroller and sealed with the seal of the Patent Office, of or from patents, specifications, disclaimers, and other documents in the Patent Office, and of or from registers and other books kept there, shall be admitted in evidence in all Courts in Her Majesty's dominions, and in all proceedings, without further proof or production of the originals. Sealed copies to be received in evidence.

90. (1) The Court may on the application of any person aggrieved by the omission without sufficient cause of the name of any person **or of any other particulars** from any register kept under this Act, or by any entry made without sufficient cause in any such register, make such order for making, expunging, or varying the entry as the Court thinks fit; or the Court may refuse the application; and in either case may make such order with respect to the costs of the proceedings as the Court think fit. Rectification of registers by Court. **Act 1888, s. 23.**

(2) The Court may in any proceeding under this section decide any question that it may be necessary or expedient to decide for the rectification of a register, and may direct an issue to be tried for the decision of any question of fact, and may award damages to the party aggrieved.

(3) Any order of the Court rectifying a register shall direct that due notice of the rectification be given to the comptroller.

91. The comptroller may, on request in writing, accompanied by the prescribed fee,— Power for comptroller to correct clerical errors.

(*a*) Correct any clerical error in or in connection with an application for a patent, or for registration of a design or trade mark; or (*b*) Correct any clerical error in the name, style, or address of the registered proprietor of a patent, design, or trade mark.

(*c*) Cancel the entry or part of the entry of a trade mark on the register: provided that the applicant accompanies his request by a statutory declaration, made by himself, stating his name, address, and calling, and that he is the person whose name appears on the register as the proprietor of the said trade mark.

Act 1888, s. 24.

(*d*) **Permit an applicant for registration of a design or trade mark to amend his application by omitting any particular goods or classes of goods in connection with which he has desired the design or trade mark to be registered.**

Alteration of registered mark.

92. (1) The registered proprietor of any registered trade mark may apply to the Court for leave to add to or alter such mark in any particular, not being an essential particular within the meaning of this Act, and the Court may refuse or grant leave on such terms as it may think fit.

(2) Notice of any intended application to the Court under this section shall be given to the comptroller by the applicant, and the comptroller shall be entitled to be heard on the application.

(3) If the Court grants leave, the comptroller shall, on proof thereof and on payment of the prescribed fee, cause the register to be altered in conformity with the order of leave.

Falsification of entries in registers.

93. If any person makes or causes to be made a false entry in any register kept under this Act, or a writing falsely purporting to be a copy of an entry in any such register, or produces or tenders or causes to be produced or tendered in evidence any such writing, knowing the entry or writing to be false, he shall be guilty of a misdemeanour.

Exercise of discretionary

94. Where any discretionary power is by this Act given to the comptroller, he shall not exercise that power adversely to the applicant for a patent, or for amendment of a specification, or for registration of a trade mark or design, without (if so required within the prescribed time by the applicant) giving the applicant an opportunity of being heard personally or by his agent. power by comptroller.

95. The comptroller may, in any case of doubt or difficulty arising in the administration of any of the provisions of this Act, apply to either of the law officers for directions in the matter. Power of comptroller to take directions of law officers.

96. A certificate purporting to be under the hand of the comptroller as to any entry, matter, or thing which he is authorised by this Act, or any general rules made thereunder, to make or do, shall be primâ facie evidence of the entry having been made, and of the contents thereof, and of the matter or thing having been done or left undone. Certificate of comptroller to be evidence.

97. (1) Any application, notice, or other document authorised or required to be left, made, or given at the Patent Office or to the comptroller, or to any other person under this Act, may be sent by a prepaid letter through the post; and if so sent shall be deemed to have been left, made, or given respectively at the time when the letter containing the same would be delivered in the ordinary course of post. Applications and notices by post.

(2) In proving such service or sending, it shall be sufficient to prove that the letter was properly addressed and put into the post.

98. Whenever the last day fixed by this Act, or by any rule for the time being in force, for leaving any document or paying any fee at the Patent Office shall fall on Christmas Day, Good Friday, or on a Saturday or Sunday, or any day observed as a holiday at the Bank of England, or any day observed as a day of public fast or thanksgiving, herein referred to as excluded days, it shall be lawful to leave such document or to pay such fee on the day next following such excluded day, or days, if two or more of them occur consecutively. Provision as to days for leaving documents at office.

Declaration by infant, lunatic &c.

99. If any person is, by reason of infancy, lunacy, or other inability, incapable of making any declaration or doing anything required or permitted by this Act or by any rules made under the authority of this Act, then the guardian or committee (if any) of such incapable person, or, if there be none, any person appointed by any Court or judge possessing jurisdiction in respect of the property of incapable persons, upon the petition of any person on behalf of such incapable person, or of any other person interested in the making such declaration or doing such thing, may make such declaration or a declaration as nearly corresponding thereto as circumstances permit, and do such thing in the name and on behalf of such incapable person, and all acts done by such substitute shall for the purposes of this Act be as effectual as if done by the person for whom he is substituted.

Transmission of certified printed copies of specifications &c.

100. Copies of all specifications, drawings, and amendments left at the Patent Office after the commencement of this Act, printed for and sealed with the seal of the Patent Office, shall be transmitted to the Edinburgh Museum of Science and Art, and to the Enrolments Office of the Chancery Division in Ireland, and to the Rolls Office in the Isle of Man, within twenty-one days after the same shall respectively have been accepted or allowed at the Patent Office; and certified copies of or extracts from any such documents shall be given to any person requiring the same on payment of the prescribed fee; and any such copy or extract shall be admitted in evidence in all Courts in Scotland and Ireland and in the Isle of Man without further proof or production of the originals.

Power for Board of Trade to make general rules for classifying goods and regulating business of Patent Office.

101. (1) The Board of Trade may from time to time make such general rules and do such things as they think expedient, subject to the provisions of this Act—

(*a*) For regulating the practice of registration under this Act:

(*b*) For classifying goods for the purposes of designs and trade marks:

(*c*) For making or requiring duplicates of specifications, amendment, drawings, and other documents:

(*d*) For securing and regulating the publishing and selling of copies, at such prices and in such manner as the Board of Trade think fit, of specifications, drawings, amendments, and other documents:

(*e*) For securing and regulating the making, printing, publishing, and selling of indexes to, and abridgments of, specifications and other documents in the Patent Office; and providing for the inspection of indexes and abridgments and other documents:

(*f*) For regulating (with the approval of the Treasury) the presentation of copies of Patent Office publications to patentees and to public authorities, bodies, and institutions at home and abroad:

(*g*) Generally, for regulating the business of the Patent Office, and all things by this Act placed under the direction or control of the comptroller, or of the Board of Trade.

(2) Any of the forms in the First Schedule to this Act may be altered or amended by rules made by the Board as aforesaid.

(3) General rules may be made under this section at any time after the passing of this Act, but not so as to take effect before the commencement of this Act, and shall (subject as hereinafter mentioned) be of the same effect as if they were contained in this Act, and shall be judicially noticed.

(4) Any rules made in pursuance of this section shall be laid before both Houses of Parliament, if Parliament be in session at the time of making thereof, or, if not, then as soon as practicable after the beginning of the then next session of Parliament, and they shall also be advertised twice in the official journal to be issued by the comptroller.

(5) If either House of Parliament, within the next forty days after any rules have been so laid before such House, resolve that such rules or any of them ought to be annulled, the same shall after the date of such resolution be of no

effect, without prejudice to the validity of anything done in the meantime under such rules or rule or to the making of any new rules or rule.

Annual reports of comptroller.

102. The comptroller shall, before the first day of June in every year, cause a report respecting the execution by or under him of this Act to be laid before both Houses of Parliament, and therein shall include for the year to which each report relates all general rules made in that year under or for the purposes of this Act, and an account of all fees, salaries, and allowances, and other money received and paid under this Act.

Proceedings of Board of Trade. **Act 1888, s. 25.**

102a. (1) All things required or authorised under this Act to be done by, to, or before the Board of Trade, may be done by, to, or before the President or a secretary or an assistant secretary of the Board.

(2) All documents purporting to be orders made by the Board of Trade and to be sealed with the seal of the Board, or to be signed by a secretary or assistant secretary of the Board, or by any person authorised in that behalf by the President of the Board, shall be received in evidence, and shall be deemed to be such orders without further proof, unless the contrary is shown.

(3) A certificate, signed by the President of the Board of Trade, that any order made or act done is the order or act of the Board, shall be conclusive evidence of the fact so certified.

International and Colonial Arrangements.

International arrangements for protection of inventions, designs, and trade marks.

103. (1) If her Majesty is pleased to make any arrangement with the government or governments of any foreign state or states for mutual protection of inventions, designs, and trade marks, or any of them, then any person who has applied for protection for any invention, design, or trade mark in any such state shall be entitled to a patent for his invention or to registration of his design or trade mark (as the case may be) under this Act, in priority to other applicants; and such patent or registration shall have the same date as the [*date of the protection obtained*] **date of the application** in such foreign state. Act 1885, s. 6.

Provided that his application is made, in the case of a patent within seven months, and in the case of a design or trade mark within four months, from his applying for protection in the foreign state with which the arrangement is in force.

Provided that nothing in this section contained shall entitle the patentee or proprietor of the design or trade mark to recover damages for infringements happening prior to the date of the actual acceptance of his complete specification, or the actual registration of his design or trade mark in this country, as the case may be.

(2) The publication in the United Kingdom, or the Isle of Man, during the respective periods aforesaid, of any description of the invention, or the use therein during such periods of the invention, or the exhibition or use therein during such periods of the design, or the publication therein during such periods of a description or representation of the design, or the use therein during such periods of the trade mark, shall not invalidate the patent which may be granted for the invention, or the registration of the design or trade mark.

(3) The application for the grant of a patent, or the registration of a design, or the registration of a trade mark under this section, must be made in the same manner as an ordinary application under this Act: provided that, in the case of trade marks, any trade mark the registration of which has been duly applied for in the country of origin may be registered under this Act:

(4) The provisions of this section shall apply only in the case of those foreign states with respect to which her Majesty shall from time to time by Order in Council declare them to be applicable, and so long only in the case of each state as the Order in Council shall continue in force with respect to that state.

104. (1) Where it is made to appear to her Majesty that the legislature of any British possession has made Provision for colonies and India.

satisfactory provision for the protection of inventions, designs, and trade marks, patented or registered in this country, it shall be lawful for her Majesty from time to time by Order in Council to apply the provisions of the last preceding section, with such variations or additions, if any, as to her Majesty in Council may seem fit, to such British possession.

(2) An Order in Council under this Act shall, from a date to be mentioned for the purpose in the Order, take effect as if its provisions had been contained in this Act; but it shall be lawful for her Majesty in Council to revoke any Order in Council made under this Act.

Offences.

Penalty on falsely representing articles to be patented.

105. (1) Any person who represents that any article sold by him is a patented article, when no patent has been granted for the same, or describes any design or trade mark applied to any article sold by him as registered which is not so, shall be liable for every offence on summary conviction to a fine not exceeding five pounds.

(2) A person shall be deemed, for the purposes of this enactment, to represent that an article is patented or a design or a trade mark is registered, if he sells the article with the word "patent," "patented," "registered," or any word or words expressing or implying that a patent or registration has been obtained for the article stamped, engraved, or impressed on, or otherwise applied to, the article.

Penalty on unauthorised assumption of Royal arms.

106. Any person who, without the authority of her Majesty, or any of the Royal Family, or of any Government Department, assumes or uses in connection with any trade, business, calling, or profession, the Royal arms, or arms so nearly resembling the same as to be calculated to deceive, in such a manner as to be calculated to lead other persons to believe that he is carrying on his trade, business, calling, or profession by or under such authority as aforesaid, shall be liable on summary conviction to a fine not exceeding twenty pounds.

Scotland, Ireland, &c.

107. In any action for infringement of a patent in Scotland the provisions of this Act, with respect to calling in the aid of an assessor, shall apply, and the action shall be tried without a jury, unless the Court shall otherwise direct, but otherwise nothing shall affect the jurisdiction and forms of process of the Courts in Scotland in such an action or in any action or proceeding respecting a patent hitherto competent to those Courts. Saving for Courts in Scotland.

For the purposes of this section "Court of Appeal" shall mean any Court to which such action is appealed.

108. In Scotland any offence under this Act declared to be punishable on summary conviction may be prosecuted in the Sheriff Court. Summary proceedings in Scotland.

109. (1) Proceedings in Scotland for revocation of a patent shall be in the form of an action of reduction at the instance of the Lord Advocate, or at the instance of a party having interest with his concurrence, which concurrence may be given on just cause shown only. Proceedings for revocation of patent in Scotland.

(2) Service of all writs and summonses in that action shall be made according to the forms and practice existing at the commencement of this Act.

110. All parties shall, notwithstanding anything in this Act, have in Ireland their remedies under or in respect of a patent as if the same had been granted to extend to Ireland only. Reservation of remedies in Ireland.

111. (1) The provisions of this Act conferring a special jurisdiction on the Court as defined by this Act, shall not, except so far as the jurisdiction extends, affect the jurisdiction of any Court in Scotland or Ireland in any proceedings relating to patents or to designs or to trade marks; and with reference to any such proceedings in Scotland, the term "the Court" shall mean any Lord Ordinary of the Court of Session, and the term "Court of Appeal" shall mean either division of the said Court; and with reference to any such proceedings in Ireland, the terms "the Court" and "the Court of Appeal" respectively mean the High General saving for jurisdiction of Courts.

Court of Justice in Ireland and Her Majesty's Court of Appeal in Ireland.

(2) If any rectification of a register under this Act is required in pursuance of any proceeding in a Court in Scotland or Ireland, a copy of the order, decree, or other authority for the rectification shall be served on the comptroller, and he shall rectify the register accordingly.

Isle of Man.

112. This Act shall extend to the Isle of Man, and—

(1) Nothing in this Act shall affect the jurisdiction of the Courts in the Isle of Man, in proceedings for infringement or in any action or proceeding respecting a patent, design, or trade mark competent to those Courts;

(2) The punishment for a misdemeanour under this Act in the Isle of Man shall be imprisonment for any term not exceeding two years, with or without hard labour, and with or without a fine not exceeding one hundred pounds, at the discretion of the Court;

(3) Any offence under this Act committed in the Isle of Man which would in England be punishable on summary conviction may be prosecuted, and any fine in respect thereof recovered, at the instance of any person aggrieved, in the manner in which offences punishable on summary conviction may for the time being be prosecuted.

Jurisdiction of Lancashire Palatine Court. Act 1888, s. 26.

112a. The Court of Chancery of the County Palatine of Lancaster shall, with respect to any action or other proceeding in relation to trade marks the registration whereof is applied for in the Manchester Office, have the like jurisdiction under this Act as Her Majesty's High Court of Justice in England, and the expression "the Court" in this Act shall be construed and have effect accordingly.

Provided that every decision of the Court of Chancery of the County Palatine of Lancaster in pursuance of this section shall be subject to the like appeal as decisions of that Court in other cases.

Repeal; Transitional Provisions; Savings.

113. The enactments described in the Third Schedule to this Act are hereby repealed. But this repeal of enactments shall not— **Repeal and saving for past operation of repealed enactments &c.**

(*a*) Affect the past operation of any of those enactments, or any patent or copyright or right to use a trade mark granted or acquired, or application pending, or appointment made, or compensation granted, or order or direction made or given, or right, privilege, obligation, or liability acquired, accrued, or incurred, or anything duly done or suffered under or by any of those enactments before or at the commencement of this Act; or

(*b*) Interfere with the institution or prosecution of any action or proceeding, civil or criminal, in respect thereof, and any such proceeding may be carried on as if this Act had not been passed; or

(*c*) Take away or abridge any protection or benefit in relation to any such action or proceeding.

114. (1) The registers of patents and of proprietors kept under any enactment repealed by this Act shall respectively be deemed parts of the same book as the register of patents kept under this Act. **Former registers to be deemed continued.**

(2) The registers of designs and of trade marks kept under any enactment repealed by this Act shall respectively be deemed parts of the same book as the register of designs and the register of trade marks kept under this Act.

115. All general rules made by the Lord Chancellor or by any other authority under any enactment repealed by this Act, and in force at the commencement of this Act, may at any time after the passing of this Act be repealed, altered, or amended by the Board of Trade, as if they had been made by the Board under this Act, but so that no such repeal, alteration, or amendment shall take effect before the commencement of this Act; and, subject as aforesaid, such general rules shall, so far as they are consistent with **Saving for existing rules.**

and are not superseded by this Act, continue in force as if they had been made by the Board of Trade under this Act.

Saving for prerogative.

116. Nothing in this Act shall take away, abridge, or prejudicially affect the prerogative of the Crown in relation to the granting of any letters patent or to the withholding of a grant thereof.

General Definitions.

General definitions.

117. (1) In and for the purposes of this Act, unless the context otherwise requires,—

"Person" includes a body corporate:

"The Court" means (subject to the provisions for Scotland, Ireland, and the Isle of Man) Her Majesty's High Court of Justice in England:

"Law officer" means Her Majesty's Attorney-General or Solicitor-General for England:

"The Treasury" means the Commissioners of Her Majesty's Treasury:

"Comptroller" means the Comptroller General of Patents, Designs, and Trade Marks:

"Prescribed" means prescribed by any of the Schedules to this Act, or by general rules under or within the meaning of this Act:

"British possession" means any territory or place situate within her Majesty's dominions, and not being or forming part of the United Kingdom, or of the Channel Islands, or of the Isle of Man, and all territories and places under one legislature, as hereinafter defined, are deemed to be one British possession for the purposes of this Act:

"Legislature" includes any person or persons who exercise legislative authority in the British possession; and where there are local legislatures as well as a central legislature, means the central legislature only.

In the application of this Act to Ireland, "summary conviction" means a conviction under the Summary Jurisdiction Acts, that is to say, with reference to the Dublin

Metropolitan Police District the Acts regulating the duties of justices of the peace and of the police for such district, and elsewhere in Ireland the Petty Sessions (Ireland) Act, 1851, and any Act amending it.

Register of Patent Agents.
Act 1888, s. 1.

(1) After the First day of July, One thousand eight hundred and eighty-nine, a person shall not be entitled to describe himself as a patent agent, whether by advertisement, by description on his place of business, by any document issued by him, or otherwise, unless he is registered as a patent agent in pursuance of this Act.

(2) The Board of Trade shall, as soon as may be after the passing of this Act, and may from time to time, make such general rules as are in the opinion of the Board required for giving effect to this section, and the provisions of Section One hundred and one of the principal Act shall apply to all rules so made as if they were made in pursuance of that section.

(3) Provided that every person who proves to the satisfaction of the Board of Trade that prior to the passing of this Act he had been bona fide practising as a patent agent shall be entitled to be registered as a patent agent in pursuance of this Act.

(4) If any person knowingly describes himself as a patent agent in contravention of this section he shall be liable on summary conviction to a fine not exceeding twenty pounds.

(5) In this section "patent agent" means exclusively an agent for obtaining patents in the United Kingdom.

SCHEDULES.

THE FIRST SCHEDULE.

FORMS OF APPLICATION, &c.

Section 5.

FORM A.

[£1 Stamp.] FORM OF APPLICATION FOR PATENT.

See *Forms A and A1, Patents Rules*, 1885.

FORM B.

FORM OF PROVISIONAL SPECIFICATION.

See *Form B, Patents Rules*, 1885.

FORM C.

[£3 Stamp.] FORM OF COMPLETE SPECIFICATION.

See *Form C, Patents Rules*, 1885.

Section 33.

FORM D.

FORM OF PATENT.

Form of Letters Patent.

VICTORIA, by the grace of God, of the United Kingdom of Great Britain and Ireland Queen, Defender of the Faith: To all to whom these presents shall come greeting:

Whereas *John Smith*, of 29 *Perry Street, Birmingham*, in the county of *Warwick, Engineer*, hath by his solemn

Form of Letters Patent.

declaration represented unto us that he is in possession of an invention for "*Improvements in Sewing Machines*," that he is the true and first inventor thereof, and that the same is not in use by any other person to the best of his knowledge and belief:

And whereas the said inventor hath humbly prayed that we would be graciously pleased to grant unto him (hereinafter together with his executors, administrators, and assigns, or any of them, referred to as the said patentee) our Royal Letters Patent for the sole use and advantage of his said invention:

And whereas the said inventor hath by and in his complete specification particularly described the nature of his invention:

And whereas we, being willing to encourage all inventions which may be for the public good, are graciously pleased to condescend to his request:

Know ye, therefore, that We, of our especial grace, certain knowledge, and mere motion do by these presents, for us, our heirs and successors, give and grant unto the said patentee our especial licence, full power, sole privilege, and authority, that the said patentee by himself, his agents or licensees, and no others, may at all times hereafter during the term of years herein mentioned, make, use, exercise, and vend the said invention within our United Kingdom of Great Britain and Ireland, and Isle of Man, in such manner as to him or them may seem meet, and that the said patentee shall have and enjoy the whole profit and advantage from time to time accruing by reason of the said invention, during the term of fourteen years from the date hereunder written of these presents: And to the end that the said patentee may have and enjoy the sole use and exercise and the full benefit of the said invention, We do by these presents, for us our heirs and successors, strictly command all our subjects whatsoever within our United Kingdom of Great Britain and Ireland, and the Isle of Man, that they do not at any time during the continuance of the said term of fourteen

Form of Letters Patent.

years either directly or indirectly make use of or put in practice the said invention, or any part of the same, nor in anywise imitate the same, nor make or cause to be made any addition thereto or subtraction therefrom, whereby to pretend themselves the inventors thereof, without the consent, licence, or agreement of the said patentee in writing under his hand and seal, on pain of incurring such penalties as may be justly inflicted on such offenders for their contempt of this our Royal command, and of being answerable to the patentee according to law for his damages thereby occasioned: Provided that these our letters patent are on this condition, that, if at any time during the said term it be made to appear to us, our heirs or successors, or any six or more of our Privy Council, that this our grant is contrary to law, or prejudicial or inconvenient to our subjects in general, or that the said invention is not a new invention as to the public use and exercise thereof within our United Kingdom of Great Britain and Ireland, and Isle of Man, or that the said patentee is not the first and true inventor thereof within this realm as aforesaid, these our letters patent shall forthwith determine, and be void to all intents and purposes, notwithstanding anything hereinbefore contained: Provided also, that if the said patentee shall not pay all fees by law required to be paid in respect of the grant of these letters patent, or in respect of any matter relating thereto, at the time or times, and in manner for the time being by law provided; and also if the said patentee shall not supply or cause to be supplied, for our service, all such articles of the said invention as may be required by the officers or commissioners administering any department of our service in such manner, at such times, and at and upon such reasonable prices and terms as shall be settled in manner for the time being by law provided, then, and in any of the said cases, these our letters patent, and all privileges and advantages whatever hereby granted shall determine and become void notwithstanding anything hereinbefore contained: Provided also that nothing herein contained shall prevent the granting of licences in such manner and for such considerations as they may by law be granted: And, lastly, we do by these presents, for us, our heirs and successors, grant unto the said patentee that these our letters patent shall be construed in the most beneficial sense for the advantage of the said patentee. In witness whereof we have caused these our letters to be made patent this One thousand eight hundred and and to be sealed as of the One thousand eight hundred and

Form of Letters Patent.

Seal of Patent Office.

FORM E.

Section 47.

FORM OF APPLICATION FOR REGISTRATION OF DESIGN.

See *Form E*, *Designs Rules*, 1883.

FORM F.

Section 62.

FORM OF APPLICATION FOR REGISTRATION OF TRADE MARK.

See *Form F*, *Trade Marks Rules*, 1883.

THE SECOND SCHEDULE.

FEES ON INSTRUMENTS FOR OBTAINING PATENTS AND RENEWAL.

[ALTERED IN ACCORDANCE WITH THE PATENTS RULES, 1892, SECOND SET.]

(a) *Up to Sealing.*

	£	s.	d.	£	s.	d.
On application for provisional protection ...	1	0	0			
On filing complete specification	3	0	0			
				4	0	0

Or

On filing complete specification at first application ...	4	0	0

(b) *Further Annual Renewal Fees, beginning before End of Four Years from Date of Patent.*

	£	s.	d.
Before the expiry of the fourth year from the date of the patent, and in respect of the fifth year ..	5	0	0
Before the expiry of the fifth year from the date of the patent, and in respect of the sixth year ...	6	0	0
Before the expiry of the sixth year from the date of the patent, and in respect of the seventh year ...	7	0	0
Before the expiry of the seventh year from the date of the patent, and in respect of the eighth year ...	8	0	0
Before the expiry of the eighth year from the date of the patent, and in respect of the ninth year ...	9	0	0
Before the expiry of the ninth year from the date of the patent, and in respect of the tenth year ...	10	0	0
Before the expiry of the tenth year from the date of the patent, and in respect of the eleventh year ...	11	0	0
Before the expiry of the eleventh year from the date of the patent, and in respect of the twelfth year ...	12	0	0
Before the expiry of the twelfth year from the date of the patent, and in respect of the thirteenth year...	13	0	0
Before the expiry of the thirteenth year from the date of the patent, and in respect of the fourteenth year	14	0	0

THE THIRD SCHEDULE.

Enactments Repealed. (*See Section* 113.)

21 James 1, c. 3. [1623.]	The Statute of Monopolies. In part; namely,— Sections ten, eleven, and twelve.
5 & 6 Will. 4, c. 62. [1835.] In part.	The Statutory Declarations Act, 1835. In part; namely,— Section eleven.
5 & 6 Will. 4, c. 83. [1835.]	An Act to amend the law touching letters patent for inventions.
2 & 3 Vict. c. 67. [1839.]	An Act to amend an Act of the fifth and sixth years of the reign of King William the Fourth, intituled "An Act to amend the law touching letters patent for inventions."
5 & 6 Vict. c. 100. [1842.]	An Act to consolidate and amend the laws relating to the copyright of designs for ornamenting articles of manufacture.
6 & 7 Vict. c. 65. [1843.]	An Act to amend the laws relating to the copyright of designs.
7 & 8 Vict. c. 69 (*a*) [1844.] In part.	An Act for amending an Act passed in the fourth year of the reign of his late Majesty, intituled "An Act for the better administration of justice in his Majesty's Privy Council, and to extend its jurisdiction and powers." In part; namely,— Sections two to five, both included.
13 & 14 Vict. c. 104 [1850.]	An Act to extend and amend the Acts relating to the copyright of designs.
15 & 16 Vict. c. 83. [1852.]	The Patent Law Amendment Act, 1852.
16 & 17 Vict. c. 5. [1853.]	An Act to substitute stamp duties for fees on passing letters patent for inventions, and to provide for the purchase for the public use of certain indexes of specifications.

(*a*) *Note.*—Sections Six and Seven of this Act are repealed by the Statute Law Revision (No. 2) Act, 1874.

16 & 17 Vict. c. 115 [1853.]	An Act to amend certain provisions of the Patent Law Amendment Act, 1852, in respect of the transmission of certified copies of letters patent and specifications to certain offices in Edinburgh and Dublin, and otherwise to amend the said Act.
21 & 22 Vict. c. 70. [1858.]	An Act to amend the Act of the fifth and sixth years of her present Majesty, to consolidate and amend the laws relating to the copyright of designs for ornamenting articles of manufacture.
22 Vict. c. 13. [1859.]	An Act to amend the law concerning patents for inventions with respect to inventions for improvements in instruments and munitions of war.
24 & 25 Vict. c. 73. [1861.]	An Act to amend the law relating to the copyright of designs.
28 & 29 Vict. c. 3. [1865.]	The Industrial Exhibitions Act, 1865.
33 & 34 Vict. c. 27. [1870.]	The Protection of Inventions Act, 1870.
33 & 34 Vict. c. 97. [1870.]	The Stamp Act, 1870. In part; namely,— Section sixty-five, and in the Schedule the words and figures "Certificate of the registration of a design...£5 0 0 And see section 65."
38 & 39 Vict. c. 91. [1875.]	The Trade Marks Registration Act, 1875.
38 & 39 Vict. c. 93. [1875.]	The Copyright of Designs Act, 1875.
39 & 40 Vict. c. 33. [1876.]	The Trade Marks Registration Amendment Act, 1876.
40 & 41 Vict. c. 37. [1877.]	The Trade Marks Registration Extension Act, 1877.
43 & 44 Vict. c. 10. [1880.]	The Great Seal Act, 1880. In part; namely,— Section five.
45 & 46 Vict. c. 72. [1882.]	The Revenue, Friendly Societies, and National Debt Act, 1882. In part; namely,— Section sixteen.

PATENTS RULES, 1890 TO 1892 (CONSOLIDATED).

NOTE.—THE RULES REPEALED ARE PRINTED IN ITALICS. THE SUBSTITUTED MATTER FROM THE RULES OF 1892 IS IN HEAVIER TYPE.

BY VIRTUE of the provisions of the Patents, Designs, and Trade Marks Acts, 1883 to 1888, the Board of Trade do hereby make the following Rules:—

SHORT TITLE.

1. These Rules may be cited as the Patents Rules, 1890. Short Title.

Note.—The Rules of 1892, incorporated herewith, are to be cited as the Patents Rules, 1892 (Second Set).

COMMENCEMENT.

2. These Rules shall come into operation from and immediately after the 31st day of March, 1890. Commencement.

Note.—The Rules of 1892 came into operation from the 30th September, 1892.

INTERPRETATION.

3. In the construction of these Rules, any words herein used defined by the said Acts shall have the meanings thereby assigned to them respectively. Interpretation.

FEES.

Fees.

4. The fees to be paid under the above-mentioned Acts shall be those specified in the list of fees in the First Schedule to these Rules.

Note.—Meaning now the fees in the Schedule substituted by the Rules of 1892.

FORMS.

Forms. Alterations.

5. The Forms A, B, and C in the First Schedule to the Act of 1883 shall be altered or amended by the substitution therefor of the Forms A, A1, A2, B, and C in the Second Schedule to these Rules.

Application.

6. (1) An application for a patent containing the declaration mentioned in Sub-section 2 of Section 5 of the Act of 1883 and Section 2 of the Act of 1885 shall be made either in the Form A, or the Form A1, or the Form A2, set forth in the Second Schedule to these Rules, as the case may be.

Specification.

(2) The Form B in such Schedule of provisional specification and the Form C of complete specification shall respectively be used.

Other forms.

(3) The remaining forms other than A, A1, A2, B, and C, set forth in the Second Schedule to these Rules, may, as far as they are applicable, be used in any proceedings under these Rules.

GENERAL.

Hours of business.

7. The Patent Office shall be open to the public every weekday between the hours of ten and four, except on the days and times following:—

Christmas Day.

Good Friday.

The day observed as her Majesty's birthday.

The days observed as days of public fast or thanksgiving, or as holidays at the Bank of England.

Agency.

8. An application for a patent must be signed by the applicant, but all other communications between the applicant and the Comptroller and all attendances by the

applicant upon the Comptroller may be made by or through an agent duly authorised to the satisfaction of the Comptroller, and if he so require resident in the United Kingdom.

Statement of address.

9. The application shall be accompanied by a statement of an address to which all notices, requisitions, and communications of every kind may be made by the Comptroller or by the Board of Trade, and such statement shall thereafter be binding upon the applicant unless and until a substituted statement of address shall be furnished by him to the Comptroller. He may in any particular case require that the address mentioned in this Rule be in the United Kingdom.

Size &c. of documents.

10. All documents and copies of documents, except statutory declarations and affidavits, sent to or left at the Patent Office or otherwise furnished to the Comptroller or to the Board of Trade shall be written or printed in large and legible characters, and unless otherwise directed in the English language, upon strong wide-ruled paper (on one side only), of a size of 13 inches by 8 inches, leaving a margin of 2 inches on the left-hand part thereof, and the signature of the applicants or agents thereto must be written in a large and legible hand. Duplicate documents shall at any time be left, if required by the Comptroller.

Exercise of discretionary power by Comptroller. Notice of hearing.

11. Before exercising any discretionary power given to the Comptroller by the said Acts adversely to the applicant for a patent or for amendment of a specification, the Comptroller shall give ten days' notice, or such longer notice as he may think fit, to the applicant, of the time when he may be heard personally or by his agent before the Comptroller. Statutory declarations and affidavits shall be in the form for the time being in use in the High Court of Justice.

Notice by applicant.

12. Within five days from the date when such notice would be delivered in the ordinary course of post, or such longer time as the Comptroller may appoint in such notice, the applicant shall notify in writing to the Comptroller whether or not he intends to be heard upon the matter.

Comptroller may require statement &c.

13. Whether the applicant desires to be heard or not, the Comptroller may at any time require him to submit a

statement in writing within a time to be notified by the Comptroller, or to attend before him and make oral explanations with respect to such matters as the Comptroller may require.

Decision to be notified to parties.

14. The decision or determination of the Comptroller in the exercise of any such discretionary power as aforesaid shall be notified by him to the applicant, and any other person affected thereby.

Industrial or international exhibitions.

15. Any person desirous of exhibiting an invention at an industrial or international exhibition, or of publishing any description of the invention during the period of the holding of the exhibition, or of using the invention for the purpose of the exhibition in the place where the exhibition is held, shall, after the Board of Trade have issued a certificate that the exhibition is an industrial or international one, give to the Comptroller notice, in writing, of his intention to exhibit, publish, or use the invention, as the case may be.

For the purpose of identifying the invention in the event of an application for a patent being subsequently made, the applicant shall furnish to the Comptroller a brief description of his invention, accompanied, if necessary, by drawings, and such other information as the Comptroller may in each case require.

Power of amendment &c.

16. Any document for the amending of which no special provision is made by the said Acts may be amended, and any irregularity in procedure, which in the opinion of the Comptroller may be obviated without detriment to the interests of any person, may be corrected, if and on such terms as the Comptroller may think fit.

16A. Any application, notice, or other document authorised or required to be left, made, or given at the Patent Office, or to the Comptroller, or to any other person under these Rules, may be sent by a prepaid letter through the post, and if so sent shall be deemed to have been left, made, or given at the time when the letter containing the same would be delivered in the ordinary course of post. In proving such service or sending, it shall be sufficient to prove that the letter was properly addressed and put into the post.

17. The statutory declarations required by the said Acts and these Rules, or used in any proceedings thereunder, shall be made and subscribed as follows:—

Manner in which, and persons before whom, declaration is to be taken.

(a) In the United Kingdom, before any justice of the peace, or any commissioner or other officer authorised by law in any part of the United Kingdom to administer an oath for the purpose of any legal proceeding;

(b) In any other part of Her Majesty's dominions, before any court, judge, justice of the peace, or any officer authorised by law to administer an oath there for the purpose of a legal proceeding; and

(c) If made out of Her Majesty's dominions, before a British Minister, or person exercising the functions of a British Minister, or a Consul, Vice-Consul, or other person exercising the functions of a British Consul, or a notary public, or before a judge or magistrate.

17A. Statutory declarations and affidavits shall be headed in the matter or matters to which they relate. They shall be divided into paragraphs consecutively numbered, and each paragraph shall so far as possible be confined to one subject.

Note.—All statutory declarations under the Patents Acts now require a 2/6 impressed Revenue stamp.

APPLICATION WITH PROVISIONAL OR COMPLETE SPECIFICATION.

18. Applications for patents sent through the post shall, as far as may be practicable, be opened and numbered in the order in which the letters containing the same have been respectively delivered in the ordinary course of post.

Order of recording applications.

Applications left at the Patent Office otherwise than through the post shall be in like manner numbered in the order of their receipt at the Patent Office.

19. Where a person making application for a patent includes therein, by mistake, inadvertence, or otherwise, more than one invention, he may, after the refusal of the

Application for separate patents by way of

amendment. Comptroller to accept such application, amend the same so as to apply to one invention only, and may make application for separate patents for each such invention accordingly.

Every such application shall, if the applicant notify his desire to that effect to the Comptroller, bear the date of the first application, and shall, together therewith, be proceeded with in the manner prescribed by the said Acts and by these Rules, as if every such application had been originally made on that date.

Application by representative of deceased inventor

20. An application for a patent by the legal representative of a person who has died possessed of an invention shall be accompanied by an official copy of or extract from his will, or the letters of administration granted of his estate and effects, in proof of the applicant's title as such legal representative, and must be supported by such further evidence as the Comptroller may require.

Notice and advertisement of acceptance.

21 On the acceptance of a provisional or complete specification the Comptroller shall give notice thereof to the applicant, and shall advertise such acceptance in the official journal of the Patent Office.

Inspection on acceptance of complete specification.

22. Upon the publication of such advertisement of acceptance in the case of a complete specification, the application and specification or specifications with the drawings (if any) may be inspected at the Patent Office upon payment of the prescribed fee.

Application on Communication from Abroad.

Communication from abroad.

23. An application for a patent for an invention communicated from abroad shall be made in the form A1 set forth in the Second Schedule to these Rules.

International and Colonial Arrangements.

24. The term "foreign application" shall mean an application by any person for protection of his invention in a Foreign State or British Possession to which by any Order of Her Majesty in Council for the time being in force the provisions of Section 103 of the Patents, Designs, and Trade Marks Act, 1883, have been declared applicable.

25. An application in the United Kingdom for a patent for any invention in respect of which a foreign application has been made shall contain a declaration that such foreign application has been made, and shall specify all the Foreign States or British Possessions in which foreign applications have been made, and the official date or dates thereof respectively. The application must be made within seven months from the date of the first foreign application, and must be signed by the person or persons by whom such first foreign application was made. If such person, or any of such persons, be dead, the application must be signed by the legal personal representative of such dead person, as well as by the other applicants, if any.

26. The application in the United Kingdom shall be made in the Form A in the Second Schedule to these Rules, and, in addition to the specification, provisional or complete, left with such application, must be accompanied by

(1) A copy or copies of the specification, and drawings or documents corresponding thereto, filed or deposited by the applicant in the Patent Office of the Foreign State or British Possession in respect of the first foreign application, duly certified by the official chief or head of the Patent Office of such Foreign State or British Possession as aforesaid, or otherwise verified to the satisfaction of the Comptroller;

(2) A statutory declaration as to the identity of the invention in respect of which the application is made with the invention in respect of which the said first foreign application was made, and if the specification or document corresponding thereto be in a foreign language, a translation thereof shall be annexed to and verified by such statutory declaration.

27. On receipt of such application, together with the prescribed specification and the other document or documents accompanying the same, required by the last preceding Rule, and with such other proof (if any) as the Comptroller

may require of or relating to such foreign application or of the official date thereof, the Comptroller shall make an entry of the applications in both countries and of the official dates of such applications respectively.

28. All further proceedings in connection with such application shall be taken within the times and in the manner prescribed by the Acts or Rules for ordinary applications.

29. The patent shall be entered in the Register of Patents as dated of the date on which the first foreign application was made, and the payment of renewal fees, and the expiration of the patent, shall be reckoned as from the date of the first foreign application.

SIZES AND METHODS OF PREPARING DRAWINGS ACCOMPANYING PROVISIONAL OR COMPLETE SPECIFICATIONS.

Drawings for specifications.

30. The provisional or complete specification need not be accompanied by drawings if the specification sufficiently describes the invention without them, but if drawings are furnished, they should accompany the provisional or complete specification to which they refer, except in the case provided for by Rule 33. No drawing or sketch such as requires a special engraving for letterpress should appear in the specification itself.

31. Drawings (if any) must be delivered at the Patent Office either in a flat state or on rollers, so as to be free from folds, breaks, or creases.

Requirements as to paper &c.

They must be made on pure white, hot-pressed, rolled, or calendered drawing paper of smooth surface and good quality, and where possible without colour or Indian-ink washes.

Size of drawings.

They must be on sheets of one of the two following sizes (the smaller being preferable), 13 inches at the sides by 8 inches at the top and bottom, or 13 inches at the sides by 16 inches at the top and bottom, including margin, which must be half an inch wide. If there are more figures than can be shown on one of the smaller sized sheets, two or more of these sheets should be used in preference to employing the larger size. When an exceptionally large drawing is required, it should be *continued* on subsequent sheets. There is no limit to the number of sheets that may be sent in.

Quality of ink.

To ensure their satisfactory reproduction, the drawings must be executed with absolutely black Indian ink; the same strength and colour of fine and shade lines to be maintained throughout. Section lines, and lines for effect, or shading lines, must not be closely drawn. Reference figures and letters must be bold, distinct, not less than one-eighth of an inch in height, and the same letters should be used in different views of the same parts. In cases of complicated drawings, the reference letters must be shown outside the figure, and connected with the part referred to by a fine line.

Scale of drawings.

The scale adopted should be large enough to show clearly wherein the invention consists, and only so much of the apparatus, machine, &c., need be shown as effects this purpose. When the scale is shown on the drawing it should be denoted not by words, but by a drawn scale.

Drawings to bear name of applicant &c.

Drawings must bear the name of the applicant (and in the case of drawings left with a complete specification after a provisional specification, the number and year of the application) in the left-hand top-corner; the number of sheets of drawings sent, and the number of each sheet in the right-hand top corner; and the signature of the applicant or his agent in the right-hand bottom corner.

No written description of the invention should appear on the drawings.

Restrictions as to wood engravings.

Wood engravings, or representations of the invention, other than the drawings prepared as above described, will not be received, unless of such a character as to be suitable for reproduction by the process of photo-lithography.

Copies of drawings.

32. A facsimile of the original drawings, but without colour or Indian ink washes, and prepared strictly in accordance with the regulations prescribed in Rule 31, must accompany the originals, and be marked "true copy."

Provisional drawings used for complete specification.

33. If an applicant desires to adopt the drawings lodged with his provisional specification as the drawings for his complete specification, he should refer to them as those "left with the provisional specification."

OPPOSITION TO GRANTS OF PATENTS.

Notice of opposition.

34. A notice of opposition to the grant of a patent shall be on Form D, and shall state the ground or grounds on which the person giving such notice (hereinafter in Rules 37, 38, 41, and 43 called the opponent) intends to oppose the grant, and must be signed by him Such notice shall state his address for service in the United Kingdom, and shall be accompanied by an unstamped copy.

Copy for applicant.

35. On receipt of such notice the copy thereof shall be transmitted by the Comptroller to the applicant.

Particulars of prior patent.

36. Where the ground or one of the grounds of opposition is that the invention has been patented in this country on an application of prior date, the number and date of such prior application shall be specified in the notice.

Opponent's evidence.

37. Within 14 days after the expiration of two months from the date of the advertisement of the acceptance of a complete specification, the opponent may leave at the Patent Office statutory declarations in support of his opposition, and on so leaving shall deliver to the applicant a list thereof.

Applicant's evidence.

38. Within 14 days from the delivery of such list the applicant may leave at the Patent Office statutory declarations in answer, and on so leaving shall deliver to the opponent a list thereof, and within 14 days from such delivery the opponent may leave at the Patent Office his statutory declarations in reply, and on so leaving shall deliver to the applicant a list thereof. Such last-mentioned declarations shall be confined to matters strictly in reply.

Evidence in reply.

Copies of the declarations mentioned in this and the last preceding Rule may be obtained either from the Patent Office or from the opposite party.

39. No further evidence shall be left on either side except by leave of the Comptroller upon the written consent of the parties duly notified to him, or by special leave of the Comptroller on application in writing made to him for that purpose. Closing of evidence.

40. Either party making such application shall give notice thereof to the opposite party, who shall be entitled to oppose the application.

41. On completion of the evidence, or at such other time as he may see fit, the Comptroller shall appoint a time for the hearing of the case, and shall give the parties ten days' notice at the least of such appointment. If the applicant or opponent desires to be heard, he must forthwith send the Comptroller an application on Form E. The Comptroller may refuse to hear either party who has not sent such application for hearing. If neither party applies to be heard, the Comptroller shall decide the case and notify his decision to the parties. Notice of hearing.

42. On the hearing of the case no opposition shall be allowed in respect of any ground not stated in the notice of opposition, and where the ground or one of the grounds is that the invention has been patented in this country on an application of prior date, the opposition shall not be allowed upon such ground unless the number and date of such prior application shall have been duly specified in the notice of opposition. Disallowance of opposition in certain cases.

43. Where the ground of an opposition is that the applicant has obtained the invention from the opponent, or from a person of whom such opponent is the legal representative, unless evidence in support of such allegation be left at the Patent Office within the time prescribed by these Rules, the opposition shall be deemed to be abandoned, and a patent shall be sealed forthwith.

44. The decision of the Comptroller, after hearing any party who applies under Rule 41, shall be notified by him to the parties. Decision to be notified to parties.

Repealed.

[*Certificates of Payment or Renewal.*

[45. *If a patentee intends at the expiration of the fourth or eighth year from the date of his patent to keep the same in force, he shall, before the expiration of such fourth or eighth year, as the case may be, subject as hereinafter provided, pay the prescribed fee of £50 or £100, as the case may be.*

46. *In the case of patents granted before the commencement of the said Acts, the above Rule shall be read as if the words "seventh year" were therein written instead of the words "eighth year."*

47. *If the patentee intends to pay annual fees in lieu of the above-mentioned fees of £50 and £100, he shall, before the expiration of the fourth and each succeeding year during the term of the patent, until and inclusive of the thirteenth year thereof, pay the prescribed fee.*

The Form J in the Second Schedule, duly stamped, should be used for the purpose of this and the payment referred to in Rule 45.]

PAYMENT OF ANNUAL FEES FOR CONTINUANCE OF PATENT.

Patents Rules 1892. (Second Set). Rules 4 and 5.

If a patentee intends at the expiration of the fourth year from the date of his patent to keep the same in force, he shall, before the expiration of the fourth and each succeeding year during the term of the patent, pay the prescribed fee. The patentee may pay the whole or any portion of the aggregate of such prescribed annual fees in advance.

The form J in the Second Schedule, duly stamped, should be used for the purpose of this payment.

FEES.

For the fees specified in the First Schedule to the Patents Rules, 1890, shall be substituted the fees specified in the Schedule hereto.

Certificate of payment.

48. On due compliance with these Rules, and as soon as may be after such respective periods as aforesaid, or any enlargement thereof respectively duly granted, the Comptroller shall issue a certificate that the prescribed payment has been duly made.

ENLARGEMENT OF TIME.

49. An application for an enlargement of the time for making a prescribed payment shall state in detail the circumstances in which the patentee by accident, mistake, or inadvertance has failed to make such payment, and the Comptroller may require the patentee to substantiate by such proof as he may think necessary the allegations contained in the application for enlargement. Enlargement of time for payments.

50. An application for enlargement of time for leaving or accepting a complete specification shall state in detail in what circumstances and upon what grounds such extension is applied for, and the Comptroller may require the applicant to substantiate such allegations by such proof as the Comptroller may think necessary. Extension of time for leaving and accepting complete specification.

51. The time prescribed by these Rules for doing any act, or taking any proceeding thereunder, may be enlarged by the Comptroller if he think fit, and upon such notice to other parties, and proceedings thereon, and upon such terms, as he may direct. In other cases

AMENDMENT OF SPECIFICATION.

52. A request for leave to amend a specification must be signed by the applicant or patentee (hereinafter, in Rules 54, 55, and 58, called the applicant), and accompanied by a duly certified printed copy of the original specification and drawings, showing in red ink the proposed amendment, and shall be advertised by publication of the request and the nature of the proposed amendment in the official journal of the Patent Office, and in such other manner (if any) as the Comptroller may in each case direct. Request for leave to amend. Advertisement.

53. A notice of opposition to the amendment shall state the ground or grounds on which the person giving such notice (hereinafter called the opponent) intends to oppose the amendment, and must be signed by him. Such notice shall state his address for service in the United Kingdom, and shall be accompanied by an unstamped copy. Notice of opposition.

Copy for the applicant.

54. On receipt of such notice the copy thereof shall be transmitted by the Comptroller to the applicant.

Opponent's evidence.

55. Within 14 days after the expiration of one month from the first advertisement of the application for leave to amend, the opponent may leave at the Patent Office statutory declarations in support of his opposition, and on so leaving shall deliver to the applicant a list thereof.

Further proceedings.

56. Upon such declarations being left, and such list being delivered, the provisions of Rules 38, 39, 40, 41, and 44 shall apply to the case, and the further proceedings therein shall be regulated in accordance with such provisions as if they were here repeated.

Requirements thereon.

57. Where leave to amend is given, the applicant shall, if the Comptroller so require, and within a time to be limited by him, leave at the Patent Office a new specification and drawings as amended, to be prepared in accordance with Rules 10, 30, and 31.

Leave by order of Court.

58. Where a request for leave to amend is made by or in pursuance of an order of the Court or a judge, an official or verified copy of the order shall be left with the request at the Patent Office.

Advertisement of amendment.

59. Every amendment of a specification shall be forthwith advertised by the Comptroller in the official journal of the Patent Office, and in such other manner (if any) as the Comptroller may direct.

COMPULSORY LICENCES.

Petition for compulsory grant of licences.

60. A petition to the Board of Trade for an order upon a patentee to grant a licence shall show clearly the nature of the petitioner's interest, and the ground or grounds upon which he claims to be entitled to relief, and shall state in detail the circumstances of the case, the terms upon which he asks that an order may be made, and the purport of such order.

To be left with evidence at Patent Office.

61. The petition and an examined copy thereof shall be left at the Patent Office, accompanied by the affidavits, or statutory declarations, and other documentary evidence (if

any) tendered by the petitioner in proof of the alleged default of the patentee.

62. Upon perusing the petition and evidence, unless the Board of Trade shall be of opinion that the order should be at once refused, they may require the petitioner to attend before the Comptroller, or other person or persons appointed by them, to receive his or their directions as to further proceedings upon the petition. Directions as to further proceedings unless petition refused.

63. If and when a primâ facie case for relief has been made out to the satisfaction of the Board of Trade, the petitioner shall upon their requisition, and on or before a day to be named by them, deliver to the patentee copies of the petition and of the affidavits or statutory declarations and other documentary evidence (if any) tendered in support thereof. Procedure. Petitioner's evidence.

64. Within 14 days after the day of such delivery the patentee shall leave at the Patent Office his affidavits or statutory declarations in opposition to the petition, and deliver copies thereof to the petitioner. Patentee's evidence.

65. The petitioner within 14 days from such delivery shall leave at the Patent Office his affidavits, or statutory declarations in reply, and deliver copies thereof to the patentee; such last-mentioned affidavits or declarations shall be confined to matters strictly in reply. Evidence in reply.

66. Subject to any further directions which the Board of Trade may give, the parties shall then be heard at such time, before such person or persons, in such manner, and in accordance with such procedure as the Board of Trade may, in the circumstances of the case, direct, but so that full opportunity shall be given to the patentee to show cause against the petition. Further proceedings.

Register of Patents.

67. Upon the sealing of a patent the Comptroller shall cause to be entered in the Register of Patents the name, address, and description of the patentee as the grantee thereof, and the title of the invention. Entry of grant.

Request for entry of subsequent proprietorship.

68. Where a person becomes entitled to a patent or to any share or interest therein, by assignment either throughout the United Kingdom and the Isle of Man, or for any place or places therein, or by transmission or other operation of law, a request for the entry of his name in the register as such complete or partial proprietor of the patent, or of such share or interest therein, as the case may be, shall be addressed to the Comptroller, and left at the Patent Office.

Signature of request.

69. Such request shall in the case of individuals be made and signed by the person requiring to be registered as proprietor, or by his agent duly authorised to the satisfaction of the Comptroller, and in the case of a body corporate by their agent, authorised in like manner.

Particulars to be stated in request.

70. Every such request shall state the name, address, and description of the person claiming to be entitled to the patent, or to any share or interest therein, as the case may be (hereinafter called the claimant), and the particulars of the assignment, transmission, or other operation of law, by virtue of which he requires to be entered in the register as proprietor, so as to show the manner in which, and the person or persons to whom, the patent, or such share or interest therein as aforesaid, has been assigned or transmitted.

Production of documents of title and other proof.

71. Every assignment and every other document containing, giving effect to, or being evidence of the transmission of a patent or affecting the proprietorship thereof as claimed by such request, except such documents as are matters of record, shall be produced to the Comptroller, together with the request above prescribed, and such other proof of title as he may require for his satisfaction.

As to a document which is a matter of record, an official or certified copy thereof shall in like manner be produced to the Comptroller.

Copies for Patent Office.

72. There shall also be left with the request an attested copy of the assignment or other document above required to be produced.

As to a document which is a matter of record, an official

or certified copy shall be left with the request in lieu of an attested copy.

73. A body corporate may be registered as proprietor by its corporate name. Body corporate.

74. Where an order has been made by her Majesty in Council for the extension of a patent for a further term or for the grant of a new patent, or where an order has been made by the Court for the revocation of a patent or the rectification of the register under Section 90 of the Act of 1883, or otherwise affecting the validity or proprietorship of the patent, the person in whose favour such order has been made shall forthwith leave at the Patent Office an office copy of such order. The register shall thereupon be rectified, or the purport of such order shall otherwise be duly entered in the register, as the case may be. Entry of Orders of the Privy Council or of the Court.

75. Upon the issue of a certificate of payment under Rule 48, the Comptroller shall cause to be entered in the Register of Patents a record of the amount and date of payment of the fee on such certificate. Entry of payment of fees on issue of certificate.

76. If a patentee fails to make any prescribed payment within the prescribed time, or any enlargement thereof duly granted, such failure shall be duly entered in the register. Entry of failure to pay fees.

77. An attested copy of every licence granted under a patent shall be left at the Patent Office by the licensee, with a request that a notification thereof may be entered in the register. The licensee shall cause the accuracy of such copy to be certified as the Comptroller may direct, and the original licence shall at the same time be produced and left at the Patent Office if required for further verification. Entry of licences.

78. The Register of Patents shall be open to the inspection of the public on every week-day between the hours of ten and four, except on the days and the times following:— Hours of inspection of register.

(*a*) Christmas Day, Good Friday, the day observed as her Majesty's birthday, days observed as days of public fast or thanksgiving, and days observed as holidays at the Bank of England; or

(b) Days which may from time to time be notified by a placard posted in a conspicuous place at the Patent Office;

(c) Times when the register is required for any purpose of official use.

Certified copies of documents.

79. Certified copies of any entry in the register, or certified copies of, or extracts from, patents, specifications, disclaimers, affidavits, statutory declarations, and other public documents in the Patent Office, or of or from registers and other books kept there, may be furnished by the Comptroller on payment of the prescribed fee.

POWER TO DISPENSE WITH EVIDENCE, &c.

80. Where, under these Rules, any person is required to do any act or thing, or to sign any document, or to make any declaration on behalf of himself or of any body corporate, or any document or evidence is required to be produced to or left with the Comptroller, or at the Patent Office, and it is shown to the satisfaction of the Comptroller that from any reasonable cause such person is unable to do such act or thing, or to sign such document, or make such declaration, or that such document or evidence cannot be produced or left as aforesaid, it shall be lawful for the Comptroller, with the sanction of the Board of Trade, and upon the production of such other evidence and subject to such terms as they may think fit, to dispense with any such act or thing, document, declaration, or evidence.

REPEAL.

Repeal.

81. All general Rules heretofore made by the Board of Trade under the Patents Designs and Trade Marks Acts, 1883 to 1888, and in force on the 31st day of March, 1890, shall be and they are hereby repealed as from that date, without prejudice, nevertheless, to anything done under such Rules, or to any application then pending.

Dated the 31st day of March, 1890.

M. E. HICKS-BEACH,
President of the Board of Trade.

RULES REGULATING THE PRACTICE AND PROCEDURE ON APPEALS TO THE LAW OFFICERS.

I.—When any person intends to appeal to the law officer from a decision of the Comptroller in any case in which such appeal is given by the Acts, he shall within fourteen days from the date of the decision appealed against file in the Patent Office a notice of such his intention.

II.—Such notice shall state the nature of the decision appealed against, and whether the appeal is from the whole or part only, and, if so, what part of such decision.

III.—A copy of such notice of intention to appeal shall be sent by the party so intending to appeal to the law officers' clerk, at Room 549, Royal Courts of Justice, London; and when there has been an opposition before the Comptroller, to the opponent or opponents; and when the Comptroller has refused to seal a patent on the ground that a previous application for a patent for the same invention is pending, to the prior applicant.

IV.—Upon notice of appeal being filed, the Comptroller shall forthwith transmit to the law officers' clerk all the papers relating to the matter of the application in respect of which such appeal is made.

V.—No appeal shall be entertained of which notice is not given within 14 days from the date of the decision appealed against, or such further time as the Comptroller may allow, except by special leave upon application to the law officer.

VI.—Seven days' notice, at least, of the time and place appointed for the hearing of any appeal, shall be given by the law officers' clerk, unless special leave be given by the law officer that any shorter notice be given.

VII.—Such notice shall in all cases be given to the Comptroller and the appellant; and, when there has been an opposition before the Comptroller, to the opponent or opponents; and, when the Comptroller has refused to seal a patent on the ground that an application for a patent for the same invention is pending, to the prior applicant.

VIII.—The evidence used on appeal to the law officer shall be the same as that used at the hearing before the Comptroller; and no further evidence shall be given, save as to matters which have occurred or come to the knowledge of either party, after the date of the decision appealed against, except with the leave of the law officer upon application for that purpose.

IX.—The law officer shall, at the request of either party, order the attendance at the hearing on appeal, for the purpose of being cross-examined, of any person who has made a declaration, in the matter to which the appeal relates, unless in the opinion of the law officer there is good ground for not making such order.

X.—Any person requiring the attendance of a witness for cross-examination shall tender to the witness whose attendance is required a reasonable sum for conduct money.

XI.—Where the law officer orders that costs shall be paid by any party to another, he may fix the amount of such costs, and if he shall not think fit to fix the amount thereof, he shall direct by whom and in what manner the amount of such costs shall be ascertained.

XII.—If any costs so ordered to be paid be not paid within fourteen days after the amount thereof has been so fixed or ascertained, or such shorter period as shall be directed by the law officer, the party to whom such costs are to be paid may apply to the law officer for an order for payment under the provisions of Section 38 of the Act.

XIII.—All documentary evidence required, or allowed by the law officer to be filed, shall be subject to the same regulations, in all respects, as apply to the precedure before the Comptroller, and shall be filed in the Patent Office, unless the law officer shall order to the contrary.

XIV.—Any notice or other document required to be given to the law officers' clerk, under these Rules, may be sent by a prepaid letter through the post.

HENRY JAMES, A.G.

FARRER HERSCHELL, S.G.

FIRST SCHEDULE.

(AMENDED IN CONFORMITY WITH THE PATENTS RULES, 1892.)

LIST OF FEES PAYABLE ON AND IN CONNECTION WITH LETTERS PATENT.

Up to Sealing.

		£ s. d.	£ s. d.
1.	On application for provisional protection ...	1 0 0	
2.	On filing complete specification ..	3 0 0	
			4 0 0
	or		
3.	On filing complete specification with first application		4 0 0
4.	On appeal from Comptroller to Law Officer. By appellant		3 0 0
5.	On notice of opposition to grant of patent. By opponent		0 10 0
6.	On hearing by Comptroller. By applicant and by opponent respectively		1 0 0
	On application to amend specification :—		
7.	Up to sealing. By applicant		1 10 0
8.	After sealing. By patentee		3 0 0
9.	On notice of opposition to amendment. By opponent		0 10 0
10.	On hearing by Comptroller. By applicant and by opponent respectively		1 0 0
11.	On application to amend specification during action or proceeding. By patentee		3 0 0
12.	On application to the Board of Trade for a compulsory licence. By person applying		5 0 0
13.	On opposition to grant of compulsory licence. By patentee		5 0 0
	On certificate of renewal :—		
14.	Before the expiration of the fourth year from the date of the patent, and in respect of the fifth year		5 0 0

		£	s.	d.
15.	Before the expiration of the fifth year from the date of the patent, and in respect of the sixth year	6	0	0
16.	Before the expiration of the sixth year from the date of the patent, and in respect of the seventh year	7	0	0
17.	Before the expiration of the seventh year from the date of the patent, and in respect of the eighth year	8	0	0
18.	Before the expiration of the eighth year from the date of the patent, and in respect of the ninth year	9	0	0
19.	Before the expiration of the ninth year from the date of the patent, and in respect of the tenth year	10	0	0
20.	Before the expiration of the tenth year from the date of the patent, and in respect of the eleventh year	11	0	0
21.	Before the expiration of the eleventh year from the date of the patent, and in respect of the twelfth year	12	0	0
22.	Before the expiration of the twelfth year from the date of the patent, and in respect of the thirteenth year	13	0	0
23.	Before the expiration of the thirteenth year from the date of the patent, and in respect of the fourteenth year	14	0	0
	On enlargement of time for payment of renewal fees :—			
24.	Not exceeding one month	1	0	0
25.	,, two months	3	0	0
26.	,, three months	5	0	0
27.	For every entry of an assignment, transmission, agreement, licence, or extension of patent ...	0	10	0
28.	For duplicate of letters patent ... . each	2	0	0

		£	s.	d.
29.	On notice to Comptroller of intended exhibition of a patent under Section 39	0	10	0
30.	Search or inspection fee ... . each	0	1	0
31.	For office copies ... ... every 100 words (but never less than one shilling)	0	0	4
32.	For office copies of drawings, cost according to agreement.			
33.	For certifying office copies, MSS. or printed, each	0	1	0
34.	On request to Comptroller to correct a clerical error			
	up to sealing	0	5	0
	after sealing	1	0	0
35.	For certificate of Comptroller under Section 96 ...	0	5	0
36.	For altering address in register	0	5	0
37.	For enlargement of time for filing complete specification, not exceeding one month	2	0	0
38.	For enlargement of time for acceptance of complete specification:—			
	Not exceeding one month	2	0	0
	,, two months	4	0	0
	,, three months	6	0	0

M. E. HICKS-BEACH,
President of the Board of Trade.

4th July 1892.

Approved:—SIDNEY HERBERT,

HERBERT EUSTACE MAXWELL,
Lords Commissioners of Her Majesty's Treasury.

SECOND SCHEDULE.

FORMS.

A.—Form of Application for Patent.
A1.— " " " communicated from abroad.
B.— " Provisional Specification.
C.— " Complete "
D.— " Opposition to Grant of Patent.
E.— " Application for Hearing by Comptroller.
F.— " " to Amend Specification or Drawings.
G.— " Opposition to Amendment of Specification or Drawings.
H.— " Application for Compulsory Grant of Licence.
H1.— " Petition for Compulsory Grant of Licences.
I.— " Opposition to Compulsory Grant of Licence.
J.— " Application for Certificate of Payment or Renewal.
K.— " Application for Enlargement of Time for Payment of Renewal Fee.
L.— " Request to Enter Name upon the Register of Patents.
M.— " Request to Enter Notification of Licence in Register.
N.— " Application for Duplicate of Letters Patent.
O.— " Notice of Intended Exhibition of Unpatented Invention.
P.— " Request for Correction of Clerical Error.
Q.— " Certificate of Comptroller.
R.— " Notice for Alteration of an Address in Register.
S.— " Application for Entry of Order of Privy Council in Register.
T.— " Appeal to Law Officer.
U.— " Application for Extension of Time for Leaving a Complete Specification.
V.— " Application for Extension of Time for Acceptance of Complete Specification.

PATENTS, DESIGNS, AND TRADE MARKS ACTS, 1883 TO 1888.

(N.B.—THIS HEADING SHOULD APPEAR AT THE TOP OF EACH OF THE FOLLOWING FORMS.)

FORM A.

(To be accompanied by two copies of Form B or of Form C.)

APPLICATION FOR PATENT.

I (*or* We) [here insert name and full address and calling of applicant or applicants] do hereby declare that I am [*or* we are] in possession of an invention the title of which is [here insert title of invention]; that [in the case of more than one applicant state whether all, or if not, who is or are the inventor or inventors] I am [*or* we are] the true and first inventor [*or* inventors] thereof; and that the same is not in use by any other person or persons to the best of my [*or* our] knowledge and belief; and I [*or* we] humbly pray that a Patent may be granted to me [*or* us] for the said invention.

Dated ________ day of ________ 18__

[To be signed by applicant or applicants. In the case of a firm, each member of the firm must sign.]

To the Comptroller,
Patent Office, 25 Southampton Buildings,
Chancery Lane, London, W.C.

NOTE.—Where application is made through an Agent (Rule 8), an authorisation to the following effect should be signed by the applicant or applicants:—

I [*or* We] hereby appoint ____________ of ____________ to act as my [*or* our] Agent in respect of the accompanying application for a Patent, and request that all notices, requisitions, and communications relating thereto may be sent to such Agent at the above address.

Dated the ______ day of __________ 18____

[To be signed by applicant or applicants.]

To the Comptroller &c.

Where application is made without an Agent (Rule 9), a request to the following effect should accompany the application :—

I [*or* We] hereby request that all notices, requisitions, and communications in respect of the accompanying application for a Patent may be sent to me [*or* us] at ______

Dated the day of ______ 18___

[To be signed by applicant or applicants.]

To the Comptroller &c.

FORM A1.

(To be accompanied by two copies of Form B or Form C.)

APPLICATION FOR PATENT FOR INVENTIONS COMMUNICATED FROM ABROAD.

I (*or* We) [here insert name and full address and calling of applicant] of ______ ______ in the county of ______ do hereby declare that I am [*or* we are] in possession of an invention the title of which is [here insert title of invention], which invention has been communicated to me [*or* us] by [here insert name, address, and calling of communicant]; that I [*or* we] claim to be the true and first inventor thereof; and that the same is not in use within the United Kingdom of Great Britain and Ireland and the Isle of Man by any other person or persons to the best of my [*or* our] knowledge and belief; and I [*or* we] humbly pray that a Patent may be granted to me [*or* us] for the said invention.

Dated the ______ day of ___ 18___

[To be signed by applicant or applicants.]

To the Comptroller &c.

NOTE.—Where application is made through an Agent (Rule 8), an authorisation as above should be signed by the applicant or applicants.

FORM A2.

APPLICATION FOR PATENT UNDER INTERNATIONAL AND COLONIAL ARRANGEMENTS.

I (*or* We) [here insert name and full address and calling of applicant or of each of the applicants] do hereby declare that I [*or* we] have made foreign applications for protection of my [*or* our] invention of [here insert title of invention] in the following Foreign States and on the following official dates: viz. [here insert the names of each Foreign State, followed by the official date of the application in each respectively] and in the following British Possessions and on the following official dates: viz. [here insert the names of each British Possession, followed by the official date of the application in each respectively].

That the said invention was not in use within the United Kingdom of Great Britain and Ireland and the Isle of Man by any other person or persons before the [here insert the official date of the earliest foreign application] to the best of my [*or* our] knowledge, information, and belief; and I [*or* we] humbly pray that a Patent may be granted to me [*or* us] for the said invention in priority to other applicants, and that such Patent shall have the date [here insert the official date of the earliest foreign application].

[Signature of applicant or of each of the applicants.]

To the Comptroller &c.

FORM B.

(To be issued with **Form A, A1**, or **A2.**)

PROVISIONAL SPECIFICATION.

(To be furnished in duplicate.)

[Here insert title as in declaration.]

I (*or* We) [here insert name and full address and calling of applicant or applicants as in declaration] do hereby declare the nature of this invention to be as follows [here insert short description of invention].

NOTE.—No stamp is required on this document, which must form the commencement of the Provisional Specification; the continuation to be upon wide-ruled foolscap paper (but on one side only), with a margin of two inches on left hand of paper. The Provisional Specification and the "duplicate" thereof must be signed by the applicant, or his agent, on the last sheet, the date being first inserted as follows :—

"Dated this__________day of________ 18__"

To the Comptroller &c.

FORM C.

Where Provisional Specification has been left, quote number and date.

No.__________ Date__________

COMPLETE SPECIFICATION.

(To be furnished in duplicate, one unstamped.)

[Here insert title as in declaration.]

I (*or* We) [here insert name and full address and calling of applicant or applicants as in declaration] do hereby declare the nature of this invention and in what manner the same is to be performed to be particularly described and ascertained in and by the following statement: [here insert full description of invention, which must end with a distinct statement of claim or claims, in the following form :—"Having now particularly described and ascertained the nature of my (*or* our) said invention, and in what manner the same is to be performed, I (*or* we) declare that what I (*or* we) claim is]—

1.
2. } [Here state distinctly the features of novelty claimed.]
3.

NOTE.—This document must form the commencement of the Complete Specification; the continuation to be upon wide-ruled foolscap paper (but on one side only), with a margin of two inches on left hand of paper. The Complete Specification and the "duplicate" thereof must be signed by the applicant, or his agent, on the last sheet, the date being first inserted as follows :—

"Dated this__________day of__________18__"

To the Comptroller &c.

FORM D.

FORM OF OPPOSITION TO GRANT OF PATENT.

(To be accompanied by an unstamped copy.)

I (*or* We) [here state name and full address] hereby give notice of my [*or* our] intention to oppose the grant of Letters Patent upon application No.______of______, applied for by____________ upon the ground [here state upon which of the grounds of opposition permitted by Section 11 of the Act the grant is opposed].

Signed [here insert signature of opponent].

To the Comptroller &c.

FORM E.

FORM OF APPLICATION FOR HEARING BY THE COMPTROLLER.

(In Cases of Refusal to Accept, Opposition, or Applications for Amendments, &c.)

SIR,—I (*or* We), of [here insert address,] hereby apply to be heard in reference to____________________ and request that I [*or* we] may receive due notice of the day fixed for the hearing.

I am [*or* We are], Sir,
Your obedient Servant,

To the Comptroller &c.

FORM F.

FORM OF APPLICATION FOR AMENDMENT OF SPECIFICATION OR DRAWINGS.

I (*or* We) [here state name and full address of applicant or patentee] seek leave to amend the Specification of Letters Patent No.______ of 18 , as shown in red ink in the copy of the original Specification hereunto annexed.

My [*or* our] reasons for making this amendment are as follows [here state reasons for seeking amendment, and where the applicant is not the patentee state what interest he possesses in the letters patent].

Signed [to be signed by applicant or applicants].

To the Comptroller &c.

FORM G.

FORM OF OPPOSITION TO AMENDMENT OF SPECIFICATION OF DRAWINGS.

(To be accompanied by an unstamped copy.)

I (*or* We) [here state name and full address of opponent] hereby give notice of objection to the proposed amendment of the Specification or drawings of Letters Patent No.______ of 18______ for the following reason [here state reason of opposition].

(Signed)______________

To the Comptroller &c.

FORM H.

FORM OF APPLICATION FOR COMPULSORY GRANT OF LICENCE.

(To be accompanied by an unstamped copy.)

I (*or* We) [here state name and full address of applicant] hereby request you to bring to the notice of the Board of Trade the accompanying petition for the grant of a licence to me [*or* us] by [here state name and address of patentee, and number and date of his patent].

(Signed)______________

To the Comptroller &c.

NOTE.—The petition must clearly set forth the facts of the case and be accompanied by an examined copy thereof. (See Form H1.)

FORM H1.

FORM OF PETITION FOR COMPULSORY GRANT OF LICENCES.

To the LORDS of the COMMITTEE of PRIVY COUNCIL for Trade.

THE PETITION of [here insert name, full address, and description], of , in the county of , being a person interested in the matter of this petition as hereinafter described:

SHOWETH as follows:—

1. A patent dated____________No.________was duly granted to ________ for an invention of [here insert title of invention].

2. The nature of my interest in the matter of this petition is as follows:—[here state fully the nature of petitioner's interest].

3. [Here state in detail the circumstances of the case under Section 22 of the said Act, and show that it arises by reason of the default of the patentee to grant licences on reasonable terms. The statement of the case should also show as far as possible that the terms of the proposed order are just and reasonable. The paragraphs should be numbered consecutively.]

Having regard to the circumstances above stated, the petitioner alleges that by reason of the aforesaid default of the patentee to grant licences on reasonable terms [here state the ground or grounds on which relief is claimed in the language of Section 22, Sub-sections (*a*), (*b*), or (*c*), as the case may be].

Your petitioner therefore prays that an order may be made by the Board of Trade [here state the purport and effect of the proposed order and the terms as to the amount of royalties, security for payment, or otherwise, upon which the petitioner claims to be entitled to the relief in question], or that the petitioner may have such other relief in the premises as the Board of Trade may deem just.

FORM I.

FORM OF OPPOSITION TO COMPULSORY GRANT OF LICENCE.

I (*or* We) [here state name and full address] hereby give notice of objection to the application of____________________ for the compulsory grant of a licence under Patent No. of 18

(Signed)__________

To the Comptroller &c.

FORM J.

APPLICATION FOR CERTIFICATE OF PAYMENT OR RENEWAL.

I [*or* We] hereby transmit the fee prescribed for the continuation in force of [here insert name of patentee] Patent No.______, of 18__, for a further period of___

[Here insert name and full address.]

To the Comptroller &c.

(This part of the Form to be filled in at the Patent Office.)

CERTIFICATE OF PAYMENT OR RENEWAL.

Letters Patent No.__________of 18

____________________18____

This is to certify that____________________did this__________ day of____________________18__, make the prescribed payment of £__________in respect of a period of______________from__________ and that by virtue of such payment the rights of the patentee remain in force.*

Patent Office, London. Seal.

* See Section 17 of the Patents, Designs, and Trade Marks Act, 1883.

FORM K.

FORM OF APPLICATION FOR ENLARGEMENT OF TIME FOR PAYMENT OF RENEWAL FEE.

SIR,—I hereby apply for an enlargement of time for__________ month in which to make the____________________payment of £______________upon my Patent No.__________of 18__

The circumstances in which the payment was omitted are as follows. (See Rule 49.)

I am Sir,

Your obedient Servant,

[Here insert full address to which receipt is to be sent.]

To the Comptroller &c.

FORM L.

FORM OF REQUEST TO ENTER NAME UPON THE REGISTER OF PATENTS.

I (*or* We) [here insert name, full address, and description] hereby request that you will enter my name [*or* our names] in the Register of Patents.

I [*or* We] claim to be entitled [here insert the nature of the claim] of the Patent No.______of 18 , granted to [here give name and address &c. of patentee or patentees] for [here insert title of the invention], by virtue of [here specify the particulars of such document, giving its date, and the parties to the same, and showing how the claim here made is substantiated].

And in proof whereof I [*or* we] transmit the accompanying [here insert the nature of the document], with an attested copy thereof.

[Where any document which is a matter of record is required to be left, a certified or official copy in lieu of an attested copy must be left.]

I am [*or* We are], Sir,
Your obedient Servant.

To the Comptroller &c.

FORM M.

FORM OF REQUEST TO ENTER NOTIFICATION OF LICENCE IN THE REGISTER OF PATENTS.

SIR,—I hereby transmit an attested copy of a licence granted to me by________________________ ________________ under Patent No.________of 18 , as well as the original licence for verification, and I have to request that a notification thereof may be entered in the Register.

I am, Sir,
Your obedient Servant,
[Here insert full address.]

To the Comptroller &c.

FORM N.

APPLICATION FOR DUPLICATE OF PATENT.

Date____________________18_____

SIR,—I regret to have inform you that the Letters Patent dated [here insert date of Patent], No. [here insert number], granted to [here insert name and full address of patentee] for an invention of [here insert title of invention] have been [here insert the word "destroyed" or "lost" as the case may be].

I beg therefore to apply for the issue of a duplicate of such Letters Patent [here state interest possessed by applicant in the Letters Patent].

[Signature of Applicant.]

To the Comptroller &c.

FORM O.

Notice of Intended Exhibition of an Unpatented Invention.

I (*or* We) [here state name and full address of applicant] hereby give notice of my [*or* our] intention to exhibit a________ of__________ at the__________________ Exhibition, which [state "opened" or "is to open"] on the_______ day of __________ 18 , under the provisions of the Patents, Designs, and Trade Marks Act of 1883.

I (*or* We) herewith enclose [insert brief description of invention, with drawings if necessary].

(Signed)________________

To the Comptroller &c.

FORM P.

Form of Request for Correction of Clerical Error.

Sir,—I hereby request that the following clerical error [*or* errors] in the [here state whether in application, specification, or register] No._______ of 18____ may be corrected in the manner shown in red ink in the certified copy of the original [application, specification, or register] hereunto annexed.

Signature________________

Full Address____ ____ ____

To the Comptroller &c.

FORM Q.

Certificate of Comptroller-General.

Patent Office, London, 18

I, , Comptroller-General of Patents, Designs, and Trade Marks, hereby certify that &c.

To [name and full address of person requiring the information].

FORM R.

FORM OF NOTICE FOR ALTERATION OF AN ADDRESS IN REGISTER.

SIR,—I (*or* We) [here state name or names and full address of applicant or applicants] hereby request that__________address now upon the register may be altered as follows [here insert full address].

I am [*or* We are], Sir,

Your obedient Servant,

To the Comptroller &c.

FORM S.

FORM OF APPLICATION FOR ENTRY OF ORDER OF PRIVY COUNCIL IN REGISTER.

I (*or* We) [here state name and full address of applicant] hereby transmit an office copy of an Order in Council with reference to [here state the purport of the Order].

I am [*or* We are], Sir,

Your obedient Servant,

To the Comptroller &c.

FORM T.

FORM OF APPEAL TO LAW OFFICER.

I (*or* We) [here insert name and full address of appellant] hereby give notice of my [*or* our] intention to appeal to the Law Officer from [here insert "the decision" or "that part of the decision" as the case may be] of the Comptroller of the__________day of__________ 18 , whereby he [here insert "refused (or allowed) application for Patent," or "refused (or allowed) application for leave to amend Patent," or otherwise, as the case may be] No. [here insert number] of the year 18

Signature____________________

Date ____________________

N.B.—This notice has to be sent to the Comptroller-General at the Patent Office, London, W.C., and a copy of same to the Law Officers' Clerk at Room 549 Royal Courts of Justice, London.

FORM U.

FORM OF APPLICATION FOR EXTENSION OF TIME FOR LEAVING A COMPLETE SPECIFICATION.

SIR,—I (*or* We) hereby apply for extension of time for one month in which to leave a Complete Specification upon application.

No.__________ Dated____________________18

The circumstances in and grounds upon which this extension is applied for are as follows [see Rule 50].

I am [*or* We are], Sir,

Your obedient Servant,

[To be signed by applicant or applicants or his or their agent.]

To the Comptroller &c.

FORM V.

FORM OF APPLICATION FOR EXTENSION OF TIME FOR ACCEPTANCE OF A COMPLETE SPECIFICATION.

SIR,—I (*or* We) hereby apply for an extension of time for________ month for the acceptance of the Complete Specification upon application No.__________dated____________________

The circumstances in and grounds upon which this extension is applied for are as follows [see Rule 50].

I am [*or* We are], Sir,

Your obedient Servant,

[To be signed by applicant or applicants or his or their agent.]

To the Comptroller &c.

M. E. HICKS-BEACH,

31st *March*, 1890. President of the Board of Trade.

DESIGNS RULES, 1890 TO 1893 (CONSOLIDATED).

NOTE.—THE RULES REPEALED ARE PRINTED IN ITALICS. THE SUBSTITUTED MATTER FROM THE RULES OF 1893 IS IN HEAVIER TYPE.

BY VIRTUE of the provisions of the Patents, Designs, and Trade Marks Acts, 1883 to 1888, the Board of Trade do hereby make the following Rules:—

PRELIMINARY.

1. These Rules may be cited as the Designs Rules, 1890, and shall come into operation from and immediately after the 31st day of March, 1890.

Note.—The Designs Rules of 1893 are cited as such, and came into operation from the 30th November, 1893.

INTERPRETATION.

2. In the construction of these Rules any words herein used defined by the said Acts shall have the meanings thereby assigned to them respectively. Interpretation.

FEES.

3. The fees to be paid under the said Act, so far as it relates to applications for and registration of designs, shall be the fees specified in the First Schedule hereto. Fees.

Forms.

Repealed.

[4. *An application for the registration of a design shall be made in the Form E or Form O in the Second Schedule hereto. The remaining forms in such Schedule may be used in all cases to which they are applicable.*]

Forms.

Designs Rules 1893.

4. An application for the registration of a design for articles not being lace shall be made in the form E or form O in the Second Schedule hereto. An application for one design to be applied to lace shall be made in the form E1 in the Second Schedule hereto, and for one design to be applied to a set of lace articles shall be made in the form O1 in the Second Schedule hereto. A request for registration of the name of any subsequent proprietor of a lace design or set of lace designs shall be made in the form K1 in the Second Schedule hereto. The remaining forms in such Schedule may be used in all cases to which they are applicable.

Classification of Goods.

Classification of goods.

5. For the purposes of the registration of designs and of these Rules, goods are classified in the manner appearing in the Third Schedule hereto.

Application for Registration.

Agents.

6. All communications between an applicant for the registration of a design and the Comptroller or the Board of Trade, as the case may be, may be made by or through an agent duly authorised to the satisfaction of the Comptroller.

Address of Comptroller.

7. An application for the registration of a design shall, with the prescribed fee, be left at the Patent Office, Designs Branch, or be sent prepaid by post, addressed to the Comptroller at the Patent Office (Designs Branch), 25 Southampton Buildings, Chancery Lane, London.

Size of papers.

8. An application for the registration of a design, and all drawings, sketches, photographs, or tracings of a design,

and all other documents sent to or left at the Patent Office (Designs Branch), or otherwise furnished to the Comptroller or to the Board of Trade, shall be written, printed, copied, or drawn upon strong wide-ruled foolscap paper (on one side only), of the size of 13 inches by 8 inches, leaving a margin of not less than one inch and a half on the left-hand part thereof, and the signature of the applicants or agents thereto must be written in a large and legible hand.

The Comptroller may in any particular case vary the requirements of this rule as he may think fit.

Sketches and drawings.

Nature of design.

9. An application for the registration of a design shall be accompanied by a sketch or drawing, or by three exactly similar drawings, photographs, or tracings of the design, or by three specimens of the design, and shall, in describing the nature of the design, state whether it is applicable for the pattern or for the shape or configuration of the design, and the means by which it is applicable.

When sketches, drawings, or tracings are furnished they must be fixed.

When the articles to which designs are applied are not of a kind which can be pasted into books, drawings, photographs, or tracings of such designs shall be furnished.

Notice of registration.

10. If the Comptroller determines to register a design, he shall as soon as may be send to the applicant a certificate of such registration in the prescribed form, sealed with the seal of the Patent Office.

Applications may be sent by post.

11. Any application, notice, or other document authorised or required to be left, made, or given at the Patent Office or to the Comptroller or to any other person under these Rules may be sent by a prepaid letter through the post, and if so sent shall be deemed to have been left, made, or given respectively at the time when the letter containing the same would be delivered in the ordinary course of post.

In proving such service or sending, it shall be sufficient to prove that the letter was properly addressed and put into the post.

EXERCISE OF DISCRETIONARY POWERS.

Hearing by Comptroller.

12. Before exercising any discretionary power given to the Comptroller by the said Acts adversely to the applicant for registration of a design the Comptroller shall (if so required by the applicant within one month from the date of the Comptroller's objection) give the applicant an opportunity of being heard personally or by his agent by sending the applicant ten days' notice of a time when he may be so heard.

Hearing by Comptroller.

13. Within five days from the date when such notice would be delivered in the ordinary course of post, the applicant shall notify to the Comptroller whether or not he intends to be heard upon the matter.

Notification of Comptroller's decision.

14. The decision or determination of the Comptroller in the exercise of any such discretionary power as aforesaid shall be notified to the applicant.

APPEAL TO THE BOARD OF TRADE.

Notice of appeal to Board of Trade.

15. Where the Comptroller refuses to register a design, and the applicant intends to appeal to the Board of Trade from such refusal, he shall, within one month from the date of the decision appealed against, leave at the Patent Office, Designs Branch, a notice of such his intention.

Statement on appeal.

16. Such notice shall be accompanied by a statement of the grounds of appeal, and of the applicant's case in support thereof.

Notice to Secretary of Board of Trade.

17. The applicant shall forthwith, on leaving such notice, send a copy thereof to the Secretary of the Board of Trade, No. 7 Whitehall Gardens, London.

Directions by Board of Trade.

18. The Board of Trade may thereupon give such directions (if any) as they may think fit for the purpose of the hearing of the appeal for the Board of Trade.

Notice of time of hearing.

19. Seven days' notice, or such shorter notice as the Board of Trade may in any particular case direct, of the time and place appointed for the hearing of the appeal, shall be given to the Comptroller and the applicant.

REGISTER OF DESIGNS.

20. Upon the sealing of a certificate of registration the Comptroller shall cause to be entered in the Register of Designs the name, address, and description of the registered proprietor, and the date upon which the application for registration was received by the Comptroller, which day shall be deemed to be the date of the registration. Registering design.

21. Where a person becomes entitled to the copyright in a registered design, or to any share or interest therein, by assignment, transmission, or other operation of law, or where a person acquires any right to apply the design either exclusively or otherwise, a request for the entry of his name in the register as such proprietor of the design, or as having acquired such right, as the case may be (hereinafter called the claimant), shall be addressed to the Comptroller, and left at the Patent Office, Designs Branch. Subsequent proprietors.

22. Every such request shall, in the case of an individual, be made and signed by the person requiring to be registered as proprietor; and in the case of a firm or partnership, by some one or more members of such firm or partnership, or, in either case, by his or their agent respectively, duly authorised to the satisfaction of the Comptroller; and in the case of a body corporate, by their agent, authorised in like manner. Signature to request.

23. Every such request shall state the name, address, and description of the claimant, and the particulars of the assignment, transmission, or other operation of law by virtue of which the request is made, so as to show the manner in which and the person or persons to whom the design has been assigned or transmitted, or the person or persons who has or have acquired such right as aforesaid, as the case may be. Particulars in request.

24. Every such request shall be accompanied by a statutory declaration, to be thereunder written, verifying the several statements therein, and declaring that the particulars above described comprise every material fact and document affecting the proprietorship of the design or the right to Statutory declaration with request.

apply the same, as the case may be, as claimed by such request.

Proof of title if required.

25. The claimant shall furnish to the Comptroller such other proof of title as he may require for his satisfaction.

Corporate name.

26. A body corporate may be registered as proprietor by its corporate name.

Notice to Comptroller of application to rectify Register.

27. Four clear days' notice of every application to the Court under Section 90 of the Patents, Designs, and Trade Marks Acts, 1883 to 1888, for rectification of the Register of Designs, shall be given to the Comptroller.

Notice of order of Court.

28. Where an order has been made by the Court, under Section 90 of the said Acts, the person in whose favour such order has been made shall forthwith leave at the Patent Office an office copy of such order. The register shall thereupon be rectified, or the purport of such order shall otherwise be duly entered in the register, as the case may be.

POWER TO DISPENSE WITH EVIDENCE.

Comptroller's discretion as to evidence.

29. Where under these Rules any person is required to do any act or thing, or to sign any document, or make any declaration on behalf of himself or of any body corporate, or any document or evidence is required to be produced to or left with the Comptroller or at the Patent Office, and it is shown to the satisfaction of the Comptroller that from any reasonable cause such person is unable to do such act or thing, or to sign such document, or make such declaration, or that such document or evidence cannot be produced or left as aforesaid, it shall be lawful for the Comptroller, with the sanction of the Board of Trade, and upon the production of such other evidence and subject to such terms as they may think fit, to dispense with any such act or thing, document, declaration, or evidence.

AMENDMENTS.

Amendments.

30. Any document, drawings, sketches, or tracings for the amending of which no special provision is made by the said Act may be amended, and any irregularity in procedure

which, in the opinion of the Comptroller, may be obviated without detriment to the interests of any person may be corrected, if the Comptroller think fit, and upon such terms as he may direct.

ENLARGEMENT OF TIME.

31. The time prescribed by these Rules for doing any act or taking any proceeding thereunder may be enlarged by the Comptroller, if he think fit, and upon such terms as he may direct. Enlargement of time.

MARKING GOODS.

[32. *Before the delivery on sale of any article to which a registered design has been applied, the proprietor of such design shall, if such article is included in any of the classes one to twelve in the Third Schedule hereto, cause each such article to be marked with the abbreviation "R^D" and the number appearing on the certificate of registration, and shall, if such article is included in the classes thirteen or fourteen in the Third Schedule hereto, cause each such article to be marked with the abbreviation "REG^D."*] Registration marks. Repealed.

32. Before delivery on sale of any article to which a registered design has been applied, the proprietor of such design shall, if such article is included in Class 13 or Class 14 in the Third Schedule hereto, cause each such article to be marked with the abbreviation Regd., and shall, if such article is included in any of the Classes 1 to 12 in the Third Schedule hereto, cause each such article to be marked with the abbreviation Rd., and also, in the case of articles other than lace, with the number appearing on the certificate of registration. Registration mark. **Designs Rules 1893.**

INSPECTION.

33. On such days and during such hours as the Comptroller shall from time to time determine and notify by a placard posted at the Patent Office any person paying the prescribed fee may, on production of the number of any design of which the copyright has ceased, inspect such Office hours.

design, and any person paying the prescribed fee may take a copy or copies of such design.

Certificate by Comptroller.

Certificate in legal proceeding.

34. Where a certificate is required for the purpose of any legal proceeding or other special purpose as to any entry, matter, or thing which the Comptroller is authorised by the said Act or these Rules to make or do, the Comptroller may, on a request in writing and on payment of the prescribed fee, give such certificate, which shall also specify on the face of it the purpose for which it has been requested as aforesaid.

Searches on Production of Sketch of Design.

Search.

35. The Comptroller may, on receipt of the prescribed fee, make searches among the designs registered at the Patent Office, and inform any person requesting him so to do whether a particular design produced by such person, and to be applied to goods in any particular class, is or is not identical with or an obvious imitation of any registered design applied to such goods of which the copyright is still existing.

Industrial and International Exhibitions.

Notice of exhibition.

36. Any person desirous of exhibiting a design, or any article to which a design has been applied, at an industrial or international exhibition, or of publishing a description of a design during the period of the holding of the exhibition, shall, after having obtained from the Board of Trade a certificate that the exhibition is an industrial or international one, give to the Comptroller seven days' notice in writing of his intention to exhibit the design or article, or to publish a description of the design, as the case may be.

For the purpose of identifying the design in the event of an application to register the same being subsequently made, the applicant shall furnish to the Comptroller a brief description of the nature of the design, accompanied by a sketch or drawing thereof, and such other information as the Comptroller may in each case require.

REPEAL.

37. All general Rules as to the registration of Designs heretofore made by the Board of Trade under the Patents, Designs, and Trade Marks Acts, 1883 to 1888, and in force on the 31st day of March, 1890, shall be, and they are hereby, repealed, as from that date, without prejudice, nevertheless, to any proceeding which may have been taken under such Rules. Repeal of previous Rules.

M. E. HICKS-BEACH,
President of the Board of Trade.

31*st March*, 1890.

SCHEDULES.

FIRST SCHEDULE.

(Amended in conformity with the Designs Rules, 1893.)

Fees.

	£	s.	d.
1. On application to register one design to be applied to single articles in each class, not being lace, and except articles in Classes 13 and 14	0	10	0
2. On application to register one design to be applied to lace or to single articles in Classes 13 and 14 . .	0	1	0
3. On application to register one design to be applied to a set of articles, not being lace, for each class of registration	1	0	0
3*a*. On application to register one design to be applied to a set of lace articles	0	2	0
4. On notice of appeal to Board of Trade against refusal of Comptroller to register	1	0	0
5. Copy of certificate of registration, each copy	0	1	0
6. On request for Certificate of Comptroller for legal proceedings or other special purpose	0	5	0
7. On request to enter name of subsequent proprietor ...	same as registration fee.		
8. On notice to Comptroller of intended exhibition of an unregistered design	0	5	0
9. Inspection of design in any case in which inspection is permitted by the Patents, Designs, and Trade Marks Acts, 1883 to 1888, and the Designs Rules thereunder, for each quarter of an hour...	0	1	0

10. Copy of one such design . . .	cost according to agreement.		
	£	s.	d.
11. On request to correct clerical error	0	5	0
12. On request for search under Section 53	0	5	0
13. On request to enter new address	0	5	0
14. For office copy, every 100 words	0	0	4
	(but never less than 1*s*.)		
15. For certifying office copies, MSS. or printed	0	1	0

NOTE.—The term "set" to include any number of articles ordinarily on sale together, irrespective of the varieties of size and arrangement in which the particular design may be shown on each separate article.

M. E. HICKS-BEACH,
President of the Board of Trade.

Approved :—R. E. WELBY,
For the Lords Commissioners of Her Majesty's Treasury.

31*st March*, 1890.

SECOND SCHEDULE.

(Amended in conformity with the Designs Rules, 1893.)

FORMS.

Form of Application to Register.

" Appeal to Board of Trade.

" Certificate of Registration.

" Application for Copy of Certificate of Registration.

" Request for Certificate for use in Legal Proceedings.

" Certificate for use in Legal Proceedings.

" Request to enter Name of Subsequent Proprietor.

" Notice of intending Exhibition of Unregistered Design.

" Request for Correction of Clerical Error or for entry of New Address.

" Request for Search under Section 53.

" Application to Register for a set of Articles.

" Application for Registration of a Lace Design in Class 9.

" Application for Registration of a Lace Design to be applied to a set.

" Request to enter Name of Subsequent Proprietor of a Lace Design or set of Lace Designs.

PATENTS, DESIGNS, AND TRADE MARKS ACTS,
1883 TO 1888.

[N.B.—THIS HEADING SHOULD APPEAR AT THE TOP OF EACH OF THE FOLLOWING FORMS.]

FORM E.

APPLICATION FOR REGISTRATION OF DESIGN IN CLASSES ______.

You are hereby requested to register the accompanying design in Class______, in the name of [here insert legibly the name, address, and description of the individual or firm], who claims to be the proprietor thereof, and to return the same to______ ______.

Statement of nature of design [such as whether it is applicable for the pattern or for the shape].

(Signed)______________________

[To be signed by the applicant.]

Dated the______day of______________, 18 _

To the Comptroller &c.

FORM F.

APPEAL TO BOARD OF TRADE ON REFUSAL OF COMPTROLLER TO REGISTER A DESIGN.

(To be accompanied by an unstamped copy.)

SIR,—I hereby appeal against your decision upon my application to register______________ ____________, and beg to submit my case [the statement of the case to be written upon foolscap paper, on one side only, with a margin of two inches on the left-hand side thereof] for the decision of the Board of Trade.

I am, Sir,

Your obedient Servant,

To the Comptroller &c.

FORM G.

CERTIFICATE OF REGISTRATION OF DESIGN.

(Registered No.______.)

Patent Office, Designs Branch,
25 Southampton Buildings,
Chancery Lane, London, W.C.

This is to certify that the Design of which this is a copy was registered this________day of_______________18 , in pursuance of the Patents, Designs, and Trade Marks Acts, 1883 to 1888, in respect of the application of such Design to articles in Class______, for which a copyright of five years is granted.

FORM H.

APPLICATION FOR COPY OF CERTIFICATE OF REGISTRATION OF DESIGN.

SIR,—I hereby request you to furnish me with a copy Certificate of Registration of Design No.______in Class______

(Signed)____________________________

Dated the__________day of______________18__

To the Comptroller &c.

FORM I.

REQUEST FOR CERTIFICATE FOR USE IN LEGAL PROCEEDINGS.

SIR,—I hereby request you to send me for the purpose of use in the suit of [here state the title of the legal proceeding or the other purpose for which the certificate is required] a certificate that the design of which a copy is herein enclosed was [here state the entry, matter, or thing which the writer wishes certified].

(Signed)____________________________

Dated the ________day of_____________________18__

To the Comptroller &c.

FORM J.

CERTIFICATE FOR USE IN LEGAL PROCEEDINGS.

In the Matter of__________

No.

I,____________________Comptroller-General of Patents, Designs, and Trade Marks, hereby certify that &c.

Witness my hand and seal this_______day of_______18___

____

Comptroller.

Patent Office &c.

FORM K.

REQUEST TO ENTER NAME OF SUBSEQUENT PROPRIETOR OF DESIGN, WITH DECLARATION IN SUPPORT THEREOF.

I [here insert name, full address, and description] hereby request that you will enter my name in the Register of Designs as Proprietor of the Design No._______in Class_______

I am entitled as to the said Design [here state whether Design transmitted by death, marriage, bankruptcy, or other operation of law, and if entitled by assignment state the particulars thereof, as *e.g.* "by deed dated the_______day of_______18___made between so-and-so of the one part"].

And I do solemnly and sincerely declare that the above several statements are true, and the particulars above set out comprise every material fact and document affecting the proprietorship of the said Design as above claimed.

And I make this solemn declaration conscientiously believing the same to be true, and by virtue of the provisions of the Statutory Declarations Act, 1835. [This paragraph is not required when the declaration is made out of the United Kingdom.]

[To be signed here by the person making the declaration.]

Declared at____________this day of 18___ before me [signature and title of the authority before whom the declaration is made].

To the Comptroller &c.

FORM L.

NOTICE OF INTENDED EXHIBITION OF AN UNREGISTERED DESIGN.

I [here state name and address of applicant] hereby give notice of my intention to exhibit a________________
of________________________at the________ ____________
Exhibition, which [state "opened" or "is to open"] on__________
18_____, under the provisions of the Patents, Designs, and Trade Marks Acts of 1883 to 1888 [insert brief description of Design, with drawing], and I herewith enclose a______________________

Signed_________________________

Dated the __________day of______________18_____

To the Comptroller &c.

FORM M.

REQUEST FOR CORRECTION OF CLERICAL ERROR OR FOR ENTRY OF NEW ADDRESS.

SIR,—I hereby request that [state particulars].

(Signed)________________________

Dated the__________day of 18_____

To the Comptroller &c.

FORM N.

REQUEST FOR SEARCH UNDER SECTION 53.

SIR,—I hereby request that a search may be made in Class_____[state object of search].

(Signed)________________________

Dated the__________day of__________18_____

To the Comptroller &c.

FORM O.

APPLICATION FOR REGISTRATION OF DESIGN TO BE APPLIED TO A SET.

You are hereby requested to register the accompanying Design for [here set out the trade description of the articles in the set, as "a toilet set"], being a set of articles in Class_____in the name of [here insert legibly the name, address, and description of the individual or firm], who claims to be the proprietor thereof, and to return the same to____________________

Statement of nature of Design [such as whether it is applicable for the pattern or for the shape].

[To be signed by the applicant.]

Dated the__________day of__________18_____

To the Comptroller &c.

FORM E1.

APPLICATION FOR REGISTRATION OF A LACE DESIGN IN CLASS 9.

You are hereby requested to register, without search, the accompanying Design in Class 9 in the name of [here insert legibly the name, address, and description of the individual or firm], who claims to be the proprietor thereof, and to return the same to____________________

The nature of the design is the pattern.

Signed [To be signed by the Applicant or his Agent duly authorised. When signed by an Agent, there should be added to the signature "Agent duly authorised by authorisation dated the day of 18 "].

Dated the__________day of_______________18_____

To the Comptroller &c.

FORM O1.

APPLICATION FOR REGISTRATION OF A LACE DESIGN TO BE APPLIED TO A SET.

You are hereby required to register, without search, the accompanying Design for a Set of Lace Articles in Class 9 in the name of [here insert legibly the name, address, and description of the individual or firm], who claims to be the proprietor thereof, and to return the same to____________________

The nature of the design is the pattern.

Signed [to be signed by the Applicant or his Agent duly authorised. When signed by an Agent, there should be added to the signature " Agent duly authorised by authorisation dated the day of 18 "].

Dated the__________day of_______________18____

To the Comptroller &c.

FORM K1.

REQUEST TO ENTER NAME OF SUBSEQUENT PROPRIETOR OF A LACE DESIGN OR SET OF LACE DESIGNS.

The Comptroller is requested to enter the name of [here insert legibly the name, address, and description of the individual or firm] in respect of the proprietorship of the Registered Lace Design or Set of Lace Designs No.________in Class 9 in place of the name of__________________________at present appearing in the Register.

Signed [to be signed by the Registered Proprietor and by the Assignee].

Dated the__________day of_______________18____

To the Comptroller &c.

THIRD SCHEDULE.

CLASSIFICATION OF ARTICLES OF MANUFACTURE AND SUBSTANCES.

Classes.

1. Articles composed wholly or chiefly of metal, not included in Class 2.
2. Jewellery.
3. Articles composed wholly or chiefly of wood, bone, ivory, papier mâché, or other solid substances not included in other classes.
4. Articles composed wholly or chiefly of glass, earthenware, or porcelain, bricks, tiles, or cement.
5. Articles composed wholly or chiefly of paper (except hangings).
6. Articles composed wholly or chiefly of leather, including book-binding, of all materials.
7. Paper-hangings.
8. Carpets and rugs in all materials, floorcloths, and oilcloths.
9. Lace, hosiery.
10. Millinery and wearing apparel, including boots and shoes.
11. Ornamental needlework on muslin or other textile fabrics.
12. Goods not included in other classes.
13. Printed or woven designs on textile piece goods.
14. Printed or woven designs on handkerchiefs and shawls.

M. E. HICKS-BEACH,
President of the Board of Trade.

31*st March*, 1890.

TRADE MARKS RULES, 1890.

By virtue of the provisions of the Patents, Designs, and Trade Marks Acts, 1883 to 1888, the Board of Trade do hereby make the following Rules:—

Preliminary.

1. These Rules may be cited as the Trade Marks Rules, 1890, and shall come into operation from and immediately after the 31st day of December, 1889.

Interpretation.

Interpretation. 2. In the construction of these Rules any words herein used defined by the said Acts shall have the meanings thereby assigned to them respectively.

Fees.

Fees. 3. The fees to be paid in pursuance of the said Acts, so far as they relate to trade marks, shall be the fees specified in the First Schedule hereto.

Forms.

Forms. 4. The Form F in the First Schedule to the Patents, Designs, and Trade Marks Act, 1883, shall be altered or amended by the substitution therefor of the Form F in the Second Schedule to these Rules.

5. (1) An application for registration of a trade mark shall be made in the Form F in the Second Schedule to these Rules. (2) The remaining forms in such Schedule may be used in all cases to which they are applicable.

Classification of Goods.

6. For the purposes of trade marks registration and of these Rules goods are classified in the manner appearing in the Third Schedule hereto. Classification of goods.

If any doubt arises as to what class any particular description of goods belongs to, the doubt shall be determined by the Comptroller.

Application for Registration.

7. An application for registration of a trade mark, if made by any firm or partnership, may be signed by some one or more members of such firm or partnership, as the case may be. Application by firm.

If the application be made by a body corporate, it may be signed by the secretary or other principal officer of such body corporate.

8. Where a trade mark for registration of which application is made is in Classes 23, 24, or 25 of the Third Schedule to these Rules, the applicant shall address and send his application to the Manchester Trade Marks Branch, 48 Royal Exchange, Manchester. Other applications (except applications which under Section 81 of the said Acts should be made to the Cutlers' Company) shall be addressed and sent to the Patent Office, Trade Marks Branch, 25 Southampton Buildings, Chancery Lane, London, W.C. Address of application.

9. An application for registration and all other communications between the applicant and the Comptroller may be made by or through an agent duly authorised to the satisfaction of the Comptroller. Agency.

10. On receipt of the application the Comptroller shall furnish the applicant with an acknowledgment thereof. Acknowledgment of application.

11. Where application is made to register a trade mark which was used by the applicant or his predecessors in business before the 13th of August, 1875, the application shall contain a statement of the time during which and of the person by whom it has been so used in respect of the goods mentioned in the application. Contents of form of application.

Size &c. of documents.

12. Subject to any other directions that may be given by the Comptroller, all applications, notices, counter-statements, representations of marks, papers having representations affixed, or other documents required by the said Acts or by these Rules to be left with or sent to the Comptroller or to the Cutlers' Company shall be upon foolscap paper of a size of 13 inches by 8 inches, and shall have on the left-hand part thereof a margin of not less than one inch and a half.

Representations of trade mark.

13. Subject to any other directions that may be given by the Comptroller, three representations of each trade mark, except in the case of marks applied for in Classes 23 to 35 inclusive, must be supplied upon paper of the size aforesaid, and must be of a durable nature. One of such representations must be made upon or affixed to the form of application, the others upon separate half-sheets. In the case of trade marks exceeding the limits of the foolscap paper of the size aforesaid, such marks may be pasted and folded upon the sheets of foolscap.

In the case of marks applied for in Classes 23 to 35 inclusive, the applicant shall supply four representations of each mark for each class.

Where a drawing or other representation or specimen cannot be given in manner aforesaid, a specimen or copy of the trade mark may be sent either of full size or on a reduced scale, and in such form as the Comptroller may think most convenient.

The Comptroller may, if dissatisfied with the representation of a trade mark, require a fresh representation, either before he proceeds with the application or before he registers the trade mark.

The Comptroller may also, in exceptional cases, deposit in the Patent Office a specimen or copy of any trade mark which cannot conveniently be shown by a representation, and may refer thereto in the register in such manner as he may think fit.

Representations of a series of trade marks.

14. When an application relates to a series of trade marks differing from one another in respect of the particulars mentioned in Section 66 of the said Acts, a

representation of each trade mark of the series shall be made or affixed upon the form of application, and also upon each of the separate half-sheets of paper aforesaid.

15. Wherever a mark consists of or includes words printed in other than Roman character, there shall be given at the foot or on the back of each representation a translation of such words, signed by the applicant or his agent. Translation of foreign characters.

16. Any application, statement, notice, or other document authorised or required to be left, made, or given at the Patent Office, or to the Comptroller, or to any other person under these Rules, may be sent by a prepaid letter through the post, and if so sent shall be deemed to have been left, made, or given respectively at the time when the letter containing the same would be delivered in the ordinary course of post. Mode of sending notices &c.

In proving such service or sending, it shall be sufficient to prove that the letter was properly addressed and put into the post.

Exercise of Discretionary Powers.

17. Before exercising any discretionary power given to the Comptroller by the said Acts adversely to the applicant for registration of a trade mark, the Comptroller shall (if so required by the applicant within one month from the date of the Comptroller's objection) give the applicant an opportunity of being heard personally or by his agent by sending the applicant ten days' notice of a time when he may be so heard. Hearing by Comptroller.

18. Within five days from the date when such notice would be delivered in the ordinary course of post the applicant shall notify to the Comptroller whether or not he intends to be heard upon the matter. Notice of wish to be heard before Comptroller.

19. The decision of the Comptroller in the exercise of any such discretionary power as aforesaid shall be notified to the applicant. Notification of decision.

Appeal to the Board of Trade.

Notice of appeal.

20. When any person intends to appeal to the Board of Trade from a decision of the Comptroller in any case in which an appeal is given by the said Acts, he shall, within one month from the date of the decision appealed against, leave at the Patent Office, Trade Marks Branch, a notice of such his intention.

Grounds of appeal to be stated.

21. Such notice shall be accompanied by a statement in writing of the grounds of appeal, and of the appellant's case in support thereof.

Transmission of notice.

22. A copy of the notice of intention to appeal, accompanied by a statement of the case, shall also be forthwith sent to the Secretary of the Board of Trade, No. 7 Whitehall Gardens, London; and where there has been an opposition before the Comptroller to the opponent or applicant as the case may be.

Directions by Board.

23. The Board of Trade may thereupon give such directions (if any) as they may think fit with respect to evidence, or otherwise, for the purpose of the hearing of the appeal by the Board of Trade, or for the purpose of their referring the appeal to the Court to hear and determine the same.

Hearing of appeal.

24. Where the Board of Trade intend to hear the appeal, seven days' notice, or such shorter notice as the Board of Trade may in any particular case direct, of the time and place appointed for the hearing, shall be given to the Comptroller and to the appellant, and where there has been an opposition before the Comptroller to the opponent or applicant as the case may be.

No appeal unless notice duly given.

25. No appeal shall be entertained of which notice has not been given within one month from the date of the decision appealed against, or such further time as the Comptroller may allow, except by special leave of the Board of Trade.

Evidence on appeal.

26. Subject to the directions and leave of the Board of Trade, the evidence to be used on an appeal to the Board of Trade in the matter of an opposition shall be the same as that used at the hearing before the Comptroller.

Advertisement of Application.

27. Every application shall be advertised by the Comptroller in the official paper during such times and in such manner as the Comptroller may direct, unless he refuse to entertain the application. Advertisement of application.

If no representation of the trade mark be inserted in the official paper in connection with the advertisement of an application, the Comptroller shall refer in such advertisement to the place or places where a specimen or representation of the trade mark is deposited for exhibition.

28. The official paper for the purposes of these Rules shall be some paper published under the direction of the Board of Trade, or such other paper as such Board may from time to time direct. Definition of official paper.

29. For the purposes of such advertisement the applicant may be required to furnish a wood block or electrotype (or more than one, if necessary) of the trade mark, of such dimensions as may from time to time be directed by the Comptroller, or with such other information or means of advertising the trade mark as may be required by the Comptroller; and the Comptroller, if dissatisfied with the block or electrotype furnished by the applicant or his agent, may require a fresh block or electrotype before proceeding with the advertisement. Means of advertising trade mark to be supplied to official paper.

30. When an application relates to a series of trade marks differing from one another in respect of the particulars mentioned in Section 66 of the said Acts, the applicant may be required to furnish a wood block or electrotype (or more than one, if necessary) of any or of each of the trade marks constituting the series; and the Comptroller may, if he thinks fit, insert with the advertisement of the application a statement of the manner in respect of which the several trade marks differ from one another. Advertisement of series.

Opposition to Registration.

31. (1) A notice of opposition to the registration of a trade mark shall state the ground or grounds on which the Notice of opposition.

opponent intends to oppose the registration, and be signed by him or by his solicitor, and shall also contain an address for service in the United Kingdom, and shall be in the Form J in the Second Schedule to these Rules, with such variations as circumstances may require.

Opposition on the ground of trade mark already on the register.

(2) Where the ground, or one of the grounds, of opposition is that the applicant is applying for the registration of a trade mark identical with one already on the register with respect to the same goods or description of goods, or having such resemblance to a trade mark already on the register with respect to such goods or description of goods as to be calculated to deceive, the notice shall state the date of registration, and the number on the register of such trade mark already on the register.

Opponent's evidence.

(3) Within two months after the expiration of one month or such further time not exceeding three months as the Comptroller may allow from the date of the advertisement of the application the opponent shall leave at the Patent Office, Trade Marks Branch, such evidence by way of statutory declaration as he may desire to adduce in support of his opposition, and deliver to the applicant copies thereof.

Applicant's evidence.

(4) * Within one month from the delivery of the opponent's copies of his statutory declarations the applicant shall leave at the Patent Office, Trade Marks Branch, his evidence by way of statutory declaration in answer, and deliver to the opponent copies thereof, and within seven days from such delivery the opponent shall leave at the Patent Office, Trade Marks Branch, his evidence by way of statutory declaration in reply, and deliver to the applicant copies thereof. Such last-mentioned evidence shall be confined to matters strictly in reply.

Evidence in reply.

Closing of evidence.

(5) No further evidence shall be left on either side except by leave of the Comptroller upon the written consent of the parties duly notified to him, or by special leave of the Comptroller given on an application made to him.

Applications for leave to

(6) Either party making such application shall give

* The counter-statement required by the Acts must also be delivered by the applicant within one month from the date of the receipt of the opponent's notice of opposition.

notice thereof to the opposite party, who shall be entitled to oppose the application. adduce further evidence.

(7) On the completion of the evidence the Comptroller shall, upon application by either party, upon Form E in the Second Schedule to these Rules, and upon payment of the prescribed fee, appoint a time for the hearing of the case, and shall give the parties at least seven days' notice of such appointment. Appointment of time for hearing.

(8) On the hearing of the case no opposition shall be allowed in respect of any ground not stated in the notice of opposition, and where the ground or one of the grounds of opposition is that registration is being applied for in respect of a trade mark identical with one already on the register with respect to the same goods or description of goods, or having such resemblance to a trade mark already on the register with respect to such goods or description of goods as to be calculated to deceive, the opposition shall not be allowed upon such ground, unless the date of registration and the number on the register of the said trade mark already on the register have been duly specified in the notice of opposition. Disallowance of opposition in certain cases.

(9) The decision of the Comptroller in the case shall be notified to the parties. Decision to be notified to parties.

Register of Trade Marks.

32. As soon as may be after the expiration of one month from the date of the advertisement of the application, the Comptroller shall, subject to opposition to the application and the determination thereof, if he is satisfied that the applicant is entitled to registration, and on payment of the prescribed fee, enter the name, address, and description of the applicant in the Register of Trade Marks as the registered proprietor of the trade mark in respect of the particular goods or classes of goods described in his application. Time of registration of trade marks.

33. In case of the death of any applicant for a trade mark after the date of his application, and before the trade mark applied for has been entered on the register, the Comptroller, after the expiration of the prescribed period Where applicant dies before registration, the trade mark may be

registered for successor to goodwill of business.

of advertisement, may, on being satisfied of the applicant's death, enter on the register, in place of the name of such deceased applicant, the name, address, and description of the person owning the goodwill of the business, if such ownership be proved to the satisfaction of the Comptroller.

Entries to be made in register.

34. Upon registering any trade mark the Comptroller shall enter in the register the date on which the application for registration was received by the Comptroller, and such other particulars as he may think necessary.

Notice of registration.

35. The Comptroller shall send notice to the applicant of the registration of his trade mark, together with a reference to the advertisement of such trade mark in the official paper.

Request by subsequent proprietor.

36. Where a person becomes entitled to a registered trade mark by assignment, transmission, or other operation of law, a request for the entry of his name in the register as proprietor of the trade mark shall be addressed to the Comptroller, and left at the Patent Office, Trade Marks Branch.

Signature of request.

37. Such request shall in the case of an individual be made and signed by the person requiring to be registered as proprietor, and in the case of a firm or partnership by some one or more members of such firm or partnership, or in either case by his or their agent respectively, duly authorised to the satisfaction of the Comptroller, and in the case of a body corporate by their agent, authorised in like manner.

Contents of request.

38. Every such request shall state the name, address, and description of the person claiming to be entitled to the trade mark (hereinafter called the claimant), and the particulars of the assignment, transmission, or other operation of law, by virtue of which he requires to be entered in the register as proprietor, so as to show the manner in which, and the person or persons to whom, the trade mark has been assigned or transmitted, and so as to show further that it has been so assigned or transmitted in connection with the goodwill of the business concerned in the particular goods

or classes of goods for which the trade mark has been registered.

39. Every such request shall be accompanied by a statutory declaration, to be thereunder written, verifying the several statements therein, and declaring that the particulars above described comprise every material fact and document affecting the proprietorship of the trade mark as claimed by such request. Declaration to accompany request.

40. The claimant shall furnish to the Comptroller such other proof of title and of the existence and ownership of such goodwill as aforesaid as he may require for his satisfaction. Further proof of title if required.

41. A body corporate may be registered as proprietor by its corporate name. Body corporate.

42 The term "applicant" in Rules 17, 18, and 19 shall include each of several persons claiming to be registered as proprietor of the same trade mark. Definition of applicant.

43. Whether all such persons so claiming require to be heard before the Comptroller or not, he may, before exercising the discretion vested in him by Section 71 of the said Acts, require such persons, or any or either of them, to submit a statement in writing within a time to be notified by him, or to attend before him and make oral explanations with respect to such matters as the Comptroller may require. Comptroller may require statement from rival claimants.

44. Where each of several persons claims to be registered as proprietor of the same trade mark, and the Comptroller refuses to register any of them until their rights have been determined according to law, the manner in which the rights of such claimants may be submitted to the Court by the Comptroller, or, if the Comptroller so require, by the claimants, shall, unless the Court otherwise order, be by a special case; and such special case shall be filed and proceeded with in like manner as any other special case submitted to the Court, or in such other manner as the Court may direct. Submission to Court of conflicting claims.

Settlement of special case.

45. Where the special case is to be submitted by the parties it may be agreed to by them, or, if they differ, may be settled by the Comptroller on payment of the prescribed fees.

Order of Court.

46. Where an order has been made by the Court in either of the following cases: viz.—

(*a*) Allowing an appeal under Section 62 of the said Acts;

(*b*) Disallowing an opposition to registration under Section 69; or

(*c*) Under the provisions of Sections 72, 90, or 92 of the said Acts,

the person in whose favour such order has been made, or such one of them, if more than one, as the Comptroller may direct, shall forthwith leave at the Patent Office, Trade Marks Branch, an office copy of such order. The register shall thereupon be rectified or altered, or the purport of such order shall otherwise be duly entered in the register, as the case may be.

Removal of mark from register.

47. Where a trade mark has been removed from the register for nonpayment of the prescribed fee or otherwise, under the provisions of Section 79 of the said Acts, the Comptroller shall cause to be entered in the register a record of such removal and the cause thereof.

Alteration of address in register.

48. If the registered proprietor of a trade mark send to the Comptroller, together with the prescribed fee, notice of an alteration in his address, the Comptroller shall alter the register accordingly.

Notice to Comptroller of applications to rectify register.

49. Four clear days' notice of every application to the Court under Section 90 of the said Acts, for rectification of the register, shall be given to the Comptroller.

Publication of rectification or variation of register.

50. Whenever an order is made by the Court for making, expunging, or varying an entry from or in the register, the Comptroller shall, if he thinks that such rectification or variation should be made public, and at the expense of the person applying for the same, publish, by advertisement or otherwise, and in such manner as he thinks just, the

circumstances attending the rectification or variation in the register.

51. Whenever the registered proprietor of any trade mark intends to apply for the leave of the Court to add to or to alter such trade mark, under Section 92 of the said Acts, the notice to be given to the Comptroller shall be given fourteen days at least before such application. If leave be granted on such application, the applicant shall forthwith supply to the Comptroller such a number of representations of the trade mark, as altered, as he may deem sufficient. **Notice to Comptroller of Order of Court for alteration of trade mark under Section 92 of Acts.**

Inspection of Register.

52. The Register of Trade Marks shall be open to the inspection of the public, on payment of the prescribed fee, on every weekday, between the hours of ten and four, except on the days and at the times following:— **Hours of inspection.**

(*a*) Christmas Day, Good Friday, the day observed as Her Majesty's birthday, days observed as days of public fast or thanksgiving, and days observed as holidays at the Bank of England; or

(*b*) Days which may from time to time be notified by a placard posted in a conspicuous place at the Patent Office;

(*c*) Times when the register is required for any purpose of official use.

Power to Dispense with Evidence.

53. Where under these Rules any person is required to do any act or thing, or to sign any document, or to make any declaration on behalf of himself or of any body corporate, or any document or evidence is required to be produced to or left with the Comptroller, or at the Patent Office, and it is shown to the satisfaction of the Comptroller that from any reasonable cause such person is unable to do such act or thing, or to sign such document, or make such declaration, or that such document or evidence cannot **Dispensing with evidence.**

be produced or left as aforesaid, it shall be lawful for the Comptroller, with the sanction of the Board of Trade, and upon the production of such other evidence, and subject to such terms as they may think fit, to dispense with any such act or thing, document, declaration, or evidence.

AMENDMENTS.

Amendment of documents.

54. Any document or drawing or other representation of a trade mark for the amending of which no special provision is made by the said Acts may be amended, and any irregularity in procedure which in the opinion of the Comptroller may be obviated without detriment to the interests of any person may be corrected, if the Comptroller think fit, and on such terms as he may direct.

ENLARGEMENT OF TIME.

Comptroller may enlarge time.

55. The time prescribed by these Rules for doing any act, or taking any proceeding thereunder, may be enlarged by the Comptroller, if he think fit, and upon such notice to other parties, and proceedings thereon, and upon such terms, as he may direct.

CUTLERS' COMPANY.

Sheffield applications in duplicate.

56. All applications to the Cutlers' Company for registration of a trade mark, under Section 81 of the said Acts, shall be in duplicate, accompanied by the prescribed fees and representations.

Notice to Comptroller.

57. The Cutlers' Company shall, within seven days of the receipt by them of an application to register a trade mark, send the Comptroller one copy of such application, by way of notice thereof, together with two representations of the mark for each class for which the applicant seeks registration.

Time within which Comptroller may object to application made at Sheffield.

58. (1) The time within which the Comptroller shall give notice to the Cutlers' Company of any objection he may have to the acceptance of an application for registration made to the said Company shall be one month from the date of the receipt by the Comptroller of the notice from the said Company of the making of the application.

(2) If no such objection is made by the Comptroller, the Cutlers' Company shall require the applicant to send the Comptroller a wood block or electrotype as the Comptroller may direct, and the Comptroller shall, if satisfied with such wood block or electrotype, advertise the application in the same manner as an application made to him at the Patent Office. Advertisement of application made at Sheffield

(3) The manner in which the Comptroller shall notify to the Cutlers' Company an application and proceedings thereon made as mentioned in Sub-section 8 of Section 81 of the said Acts shall be by sending to the Cutlers' Company a copy of the official paper containing the application of which notice is required to be given, with a note distinguishing such application. Manner of notifying to Cutlers' Company application received by Comptroller.

59. The provisions of these Rules as to forms, representations, the proceedings on opposition to registration, registration, and all subsequent proceedings shall, as far as the circumstances allow, apply to all applications to register made to the Cutlers' Company, and to all proceedings consequent thereon. Similarity of proceedings at London and at Sheffield.

CERTIFICATES.

60. The Comptroller, when required to give a certificate as to any entry, matter, or thing which he is authorised by the said Acts or any of these Rules to make or do, may, on receipt of a request in writing, and on payment of the prescribed fee, give such certificate, but every certificate of registration shall have specified on the face thereof whether the same is to be used in legal proceedings, or for the purpose of obtaining registration in a foreign country, or for purposes other than use in legal proceedings or obtaining registration in a foreign country. Certificate by Comptroller.

DECLARATIONS.

61. The statutory declarations required by the said Acts and these Rules, or used in any proceedings thereunder, shall be made and subscribed as follows:— Manner in which, and persons before whom, declaration is to be taken.

(*a*) In the United Kingdom, before any justice of the peace, or any commissioner or other officer authorised by law in any part of the United Kingdom to administer an oath for the purpose of any legal proceeding;

(b) In any other part of Her Majesty's dominions, before any court, judge, justice of the peace, or any officer authorised by law to administer an oath there for the purpose of a legal proceeding; and

(c) If made out of Her Majesty's dominions, before a British Minister, or person exercising the functions of a British Minister, or a Consul, Vice-Consul, or other person exercising the functions of a British Consul, or a notary public, or before a judge or magistrate.

Notice of seal of officer taking declaration to prove itself.

62. Any document purporting to have affixed, impressed, or subscribed thereto or thereon the seal or signature of any person hereby authorised to take such declaration in testimony of such declaration having been made and subscribed before him, may be admitted by the Comptroller without proof of the genuineness of any such seal or signature, or of the official character of such person or his authority to take such declaration.

Repeal.

Previous Rules repealed.

63. All general Rules as to the registration of trade marks heretofore made by the Board of Trade under the Patents, Designs, and Trade Marks Acts, 1883 to 1888, and in force on the 31st day of December, 1889, shall be, and they are hereby repealed, as from that date, without prejudice, nevertheless, to anything done under such Rules, or to any application pending at the said date.

M. E. HICKS-BEACH,

President of the Board of Trade.

FIRST SCHEDULE.

FEES.

	£	s.	d.
1. On application to register a trade mark for one or more articles included in one class	0	5	0
2. For registration of a trade mark for one or more articles included in one class	1	0	0
3. For registering a series of trade marks, for every additional representation after the first in each class	0	5	0
4. On appeal from Comptroller to Board of Trade—by appellant	1	0	0
5. On notice of opposition for each application opposed—by opponent	1	0	0
6. On hearing by Comptroller—by applicant and by opponent respectively...	1	0	0
7. On application to register a subsequent proprietor in cases of assignment or transmission, the first mark	1	0	0
8. For every additional mark assigned or transmitted at the same time	0	2	0
9. For continuance of mark at expiration of 14 years ...	1	0	0
10. Additional fee where fee is paid within three months after expiration of 14 years	0	10	0
11. Additional fee for restoration of trade mark where removed for non-payment of fee	1	0	0
12. For altering address on the register, for every mark ...	0	5	0
13. For every entry in the register of a rectification thereof or an alteration therein, not otherwise charged	0	10	0
14. For cancelling the entry or part of the entry of a trade mark upon the register, on the application of the owner of such trade mark	0	5	0
15. On request to Comptroller to correct a clerical error, or permit amendment of application under Section 91	0	5	0
16. For certificate of refusal to register a trade mark under Section 77	1	0	0

	£	s.	d.
17. For certificate of refusal at the same time for more than one trade mark, for each additional trade mark after the first	0	10	0
18. For certificate of registration to be used in legal proceedings	1	0	0
19. For certificate of registration to be used for the purpose of obtaining registration in foreign countries	0	5	0
20. For certificate of Comptroller under Section 96, other than certificate of registration to be used in legal proceedings, or for the purpose of obtaining registration in a foreign country	0	5	0
21. For copy of notification of registration	0	2	0
22. Settling a special case by Comptroller	2	0	0
23. For inspecting register, for every quarter of an hour...	0	1	0
24. For making a search amongst the classified representations of trade marks, for every quarter of an hour	0	1	0
25. For office copy of documents, for every 100 words (But never less than one shilling.)	0	0	4
26. For certifying office copies, MS. or printed	0	1	0
27. In cases where the wood block or electrotype of the trade mark exceeds two inches in breadth or depth, or in breadth and depth—For every inch or part of an inch over two inches in breadth ...	0	2	0
For every inch or part of an inch over two inches in depth	0	2	0
28. Manchester Trade Marks Office	Same as above		
29. Sheffield Marks	Same as above		
30. On appeal from Cutlers' Company, Sheffield, to Comptroller	1	0	0

M. E. HICKS-BEACH,
President of the Board of Trade.

Approved :—FRANK MOWATT,
Assistant Secretary for the Lords Commissioners of Her Majesty's Treasury.

SECOND SCHEDULE.

FORMS.

Form of Application for Hearing by Comptroller.
,, Application for Registration.
,, Additional Representation of Trade Mark.
,, Appeal to Board of Trade.
,, Transmission of Registration Fee.
,, Notice of Opposition.
,, Request to Enter Name of Subsequent Proprietor of Trade Mark.
,, Request for Certificate of Refusal.
,, Notice of Application for Alteration of Address.
,, Notice of Order of Court for Rectification of Register.
,, Application to Cancel Entry on Register.
,, Declaration in Support of Application to Cancel Entry.
,, Request to Comptroller for Correction of Clerical Error, or for Permission to Amend Application under Section 91.
,, Request for Certificate of Registration for Use in Obtaining Registration Abroad.
,, Request for Certificate of Registration for Use in Legal Proceedings.
,, Application for Settlement of a Special Case.
,, Request for General Certificate of Comptroller.
,, General Certificate of Comptroller.
,, Request for Copy of Notification of Registration.
,, Appeal from Cutlers' Company.
,, Application for Continuance on Register.
,, Transmission of Additional Fee.
,, Application for Restoration to Register.
,, Application for Registration of Old Corporate Trade Mark.

PATENTS, DESIGNS, AND TRADE MARKS ACTS, 1883 TO 1888.

(N.B.—THIS HEADING SHOULD APPEAR AT THE TOP OF EACH OF THE FOLLOWING FORMS.)

FORM E.

FORM OF APPLICATION FOR HEARING BY THE COMPTROLLER.

(In Cases of Opposition &c.)

SIR,—I [here insert name], of [here insert address], hereby apply to be heard in reference to____________, and request that I may receive due notice of the day fixed for the hearing.

I am, Sir,

Your obedient Servant,

Dated the________day of__________18____

To the Comptroller,
Patent Office, Trade Marks Branch,
25 Southampton Buildings, London.

FORM F.

APPLICATION FOR REGISTRATION OF TRADE MARK.

One representation to be fixed within this square, and two others to be sent on separate half-sheets of foolscap.

Representations of a larger size may be folded, but must be mounted upon linen and affixed hereto.

You are hereby requested to register the accompanying Trade Mark in Class______in respect of [only goods contained in one and the same class should be set out here; a separate application form is required for each separate class] in the name of [here insert legibly the full name, address, and description of the individual, firm, or company; add trading style, if any], who claims to be the proprietor thereof. [Alter to "who claim to be the proprietors thereof" in the case of a firm or company.]

The essential particulars of the Trade Mark are the following:—[see Sub-sections 2 and 3 of Section 64 of the Acts], and I (*or* we) disclaim any right to the exclusive use of the added matter.

(Signed)____________________

[To be signed by the applicant or by an agent duly authorised.]

Dated the____________day of____________18____

To the Comptroller,
Patent Office, Trade Marks Branch,
25 Southampton Buildings, London.

Or, where the application is for a Mark in Classes 23, 24, or 25,

To the Comptroller,
Manchester Trade Marks Branch,
48 Royal Exchange, Manchester.

NOTE.—If the Trade Mark has been in use in respect of the goods since before August 13th, 1875, state length of such user.

FORM G.

ADDITIONAL REPRESENTATION OF TRADE MARK, TO ACCOMPANY APPLICATION FOR REGISTRATION.

One representation of the trade mark to be affixed within this square.

It must correspond *exactly*, in all respects, with the representation affixed to the Application Form.

Any representation of a larger size than foolscap may be folded, but must then be mounted upon linen and affixed hereto.

Two of these additional representations of the Trade Mark must accompany *each* Form of Application.

In the case of a Trade Mark claimed in one of the Classes 23 to 35, four of these additional representations of the Mark must accompany the Form of Application.

FORM H.

FORM OF APPEAL FROM THE COMPTROLLER TO THE BOARD OF TRADE.

I [here insert full name and address of appellant] hereby give notice of my intention to appeal to the Board of Trade from [here insert "the decision" or that part of the decision as the case may be] of the Comptroller of the_______day of_________________18_____, whereby he [here insert the decision complained of].

Accompanying this notice is a statement of my case for the decision of the Board of Trade.

(Signed)____________________________

Dated the_______day of________________ 18____

To the Comptroller &c.

And to [Name of Respondent to Appeal].

FORM I.

FEE FOR REGISTRATION OF A TRADE MARK.

SIR,—In reply to your request, I hereby transmit the prescribed fee for the registration of the Trade Mark No. in Class____.

I am, Sir.
Your obedient Servant,

To the Comptroller &c.

FORM J.

NOTICE OF OPPOSITION TO APPLICATION FOR REGISTRATION.

(To be accompanied by an unstamped duplicate.)

In the matter of an Application
No._____by_______of_______.

I [here state full name and full address] hereby give notice of my intention to oppose the registration of the Trade Mark advertised under the above number for Class________in the Trade Marks Journal of the_____day of_______, 18__, No.______, page __.

The grounds of opposition are as follows:—[Here insert particulars.]

(Signed)________________

Dated the_______day of________________18

Address for Service :—

To the Comptroller &c.

FORM K.

REQUEST TO ENTER NAME OF SUBSEQUENT PROPRIETOR OF TRADE MARK UPON THE REGISTER, WITH DECLARATION IN SUPPORT THEREOF.

I [here insert name, full address, and description] hereby request that you will enter my name in the Register of Trade Marks as proprietor of the Trade Mark No._______in Class_______.

I am entitled to the said Trade Mark and to the goodwill of the business concerned in the goods with respect to which the said Trade Mark is registered.

[Here state whether Trade Mark transmitted by death, marriage, bankruptcy, or other operation of law, and if entitled by assignment state the particulars thereof, as *e.g.* "by deed dated the_______day of____________, 18____, made between so-and-so of the one part &c.]

And I do solemnly and sincerely declare that the above several statements are true, and the particulars above set out comprise every material fact and document affecting the proprietorship of the said Trade Mark as above claimed.

And I make this solemn declaration conscientiously believing the same to be true, and by virtue of the provisions of the Statutory Declarations Act, 1835. [This paragraph is not required when the declaration is made out of the United Kingdom.]

[To be signed here by the person making the declaration.]

Declared at____________this_______ }
day of__________, 18____ }

Before me [signature and title of the authority before whom the declaration is made].

To the Comptroller &c.

FORM L.

REQUEST FOR CERTIFICATE OF REFUSAL TO REGISTER A TRADE MARK IN USE BEFORE 13TH AUGUST, 1875.

In the Matter of an Application for Registration of an Old Trade Mark No. in Class

SIR,—I ________, of ________, the applicant in the above matter, hereby request you to furnish me with your Certificate of Refusal to Register the said Trade Mark.

[Signature of applicant.]

Dated the ______ day of ________ 18___

To the Comptroller &c.

FORM M.

NOTICE OF APPLICATION FOR ALTERATION OF ADDRESS ON REGISTER OF TRADE MARKS.

In the Matter of the Trade Mark No. , registered in Class

SIR,—Notice is hereby given that I ________, of ________, the registered proprietor of the Trade Mark numbered as above, desire that my address on the Register of Trade Marks be altered to ____________

[Signature of proprietor.]

Dated the ______ day of ________ 18___

To the Comptroller &c.

FORM N.

NOTICE OF ORDER OF COURT FOR ALTERATION OR RECTIFICATION OF REGISTER OF TRADE MARKS.

In the Matter of the Trade Mark No. ,
registered in Class in the name of .

SIR,—Notice is hereby given that by an Order of the Court made on the______day of____________18____, it was directed that the entry on the Register of Trade Marks in respect of the Trade Mark numbered as above should be rectified in the manner therein specified.

An office copy of the Order of the Court is enclosed herewith.

[To be signed by the person interested, or his agent.]

Dated the______day of ________18 .

To the Comptroller &c.

FORM O.

FORM OF APPLICATION BY PROPRIETOR OF REGISTERED TRADE MARK TO CANCEL ENTRY ON REGISTER.

Trade Mark No._____Class_____, advertised in Trade Marks Journal No._____, page_____.

Name of Registered Proprietor or Firm____________________

Place of Business______________________________

I the undersigned_________, of_________ [*or* I the undersigned_______ a member of the firm of_________, of_________, on behalf of my said firm], apply that the entry upon the Register of Trade Marks in Class___ of the Trade Mark No._______ may be cancelled.

(Signed)____________________

Dated the ______day of____________18____.

This is the statement marked "O" referred to in the Declaration of__________made before me the______day of_________18____.

A Commissioner &c.

FORM P.

FORM OF DECLARATION IN SUPPORT OF APPLICATION FOR CANCELLATION OF TRADE MARK BY OWNER.

I____________, of____________ [*or* I____________, a member of the firm of____________, of____________], do hereby solemnly and sincerely declare, to the best of my knowledge and belief, as follows :—

(1) The Application signed by me, and dated the__________ day of__________ 18____, and marked with the letter "O." and shown to me at the time of making this declaration, is true.

(2) I am the person whose name appears on the Register of Trade Marks as the Proprietor of the Trade Mark referred to in the said Application marked with the letter "O."

[*Or* My said Firm is the Firm whose name appears on the Register of Trade Marks as the Proprietor of the Trade Mark referred to in the said Application marked with the letter "O."]

And I make this solemn declaration conscientiously believing the same to be true, and by virtue of the provisions of the Statutory Declarations Act, 1835.

(Signed)____________ ____________

Declared at____________
this____day of___________18__
Before me____________

If the declaration be made before a Commissioner to Administer Oaths, it will require to be stamped with a 2*s.* 6*d.* impressed Inland Revenue stamp.

FORM Q.

FORM OF REQUEST FOR CORRECTION OF CLERICAL ERROR OR FOR PERMISSION TO AMEND APPLICATION UNDER SECTION 91.

SIR,—I hereby request that [insert particulars of error].

(Signed) ____________

Dated the____________day of ______ 18____

To the Comptroller &c.

FORM R.

REQUEST FOR CERTIFICATE OF REGISTRATION OF TRADE MARK FOR USE IN OBTAINING REGISTRATION ABROAD.

In the Matter of the Trade Mark No. ,
registered in Class in the name of .

SIR,—I____________, of____________, the registered proprietor of the above Trade Mark, hereby request you to furnish me with your Certificate of Registration for use in obtaining registration of the same in [here state name of country in which registration is to be sought].

I am, Sir,
Your obedient Servant,

Dated the______ day of________ 18____

To the Comptroller &c.

FORM S.

REQUEST FOR CERTIFICATE OF REGISTRATION OF TRADE MARK TO BE USED IN LEGAL PROCEEDINGS.

In the Matter of the Trade Mark No. ,
registered in Class in the name of .

SIR,—I____________, of____________, the registered proprietor of the above Trade Mark, hereby request you to furnish me with your Certificate of Registration to be used in legal proceedings.

(Signed) ____________

Dated the______ day of________ 18 .

To the Comptroller &c.

FORM T.

APPLICATION FOR SETTLEMENT OF A SPECIAL CASE ON APPLICATION TO REGISTER A TRADE MARK.

In the Matter of the Application of ________
and of the Application of________

SIR,—Notice is hereby given that I________, of________, and I________, of________, are unable to agree upon the facts on which the opinion of the Court is to be taken, and that we request you to fix a day on which we may attend before you and obtain your finding on the matters of fact to be submitted to the Court as settled.

[To be signed by both parties.]

Dated the________day of________18___

To the Comptroller &c.

FORM T1.

REQUEST FOR GENERAL CERTIFICATE OF COMPTROLLER (OTHER THAN CERTIFICATE FOR USE IN LEGAL PROCEEDINGS OR FOR USE IN OBTAINING REGISTRATION ABROAD).

In the Matter of the Trade Mark No. ,
in Class

SIR,—I________, of________, hereby request you to furnish me with your certificate that [here set out the particulars which the Comptroller is requested to certify].

(Signature)________

Dated the day of________ 18___

To the Comptroller &c.

FORM U.

GENERAL CERTIFICATE OF COMPTROLLER (OTHER THAN CERTIFICATE FOR USE IN LEGAL PROCEEDINGS OR FOR USE IN OBTAINING REGISTRATION ABROAD).

Patent Office, Trade Marks Branch,
London,______________18___.

I__________________, Comptroller-General of Patents, Designs, and Trade Marks, hereby certify [particulars to be inserted].

FORM V.

REQUEST FOR COPY OF OFFICIAL NOTIFICATION OF REGISTRATION OF TRADE MARK.

In the Matter of the Trade Mark No. ,
registered in Class .

SIR,—I_____________, of_____________, the registered proprietor of the Trade Mark above named, hereby request that you will furnish me with a copy of the official notification of the registration of the same.

[Signature.]

Dated the_______day of______________18___

To the Comptroller &c.

FORM W.

FORM OF APPEAL FROM CUTLERS' COMPANY AT SHEFFIELD TO COMPTROLLER.

(To be accompanied by an unstamped duplicate.)

SIR,—I hereby give notice of appeal against the decision of the Cutlers' Company of Sheffield in regard to my application for registration of a Trade Mark No.______in Class______for_____________ and I beg to submit my case for your decision accordingly. [The statement of the case to be written upon foolscap paper, on one side only, with a margin of two inches on the left-hand side thereof.]

[Signature.]

Dated the________day of____________18___

To the Comptroller &c.

FORM X.

CONTINUANCE OF MARK AT EXPIRATION OF FOURTEEN YEARS FROM THE DATE OF REGISTRATION.

SIR,—In pursuance of the notice received from you, I hereby transmit the prescribed fee of £1 for continuance on the Trade Marks Register of the Trade Mark No.________ in Class________.

[Signature of Proprietor.]

Dated the____________day of______________18

To the Comptroller &c.

FORM Y.

(Additional Fee of Ten Shillings to accompany "Continuance Fee," Form X, within Three Months after expiration of Fourteen Years.)

SIR,—In pursuance of the notices issued by you, and of the provisions of Section 79 (3) of the above Acts, I hereby transmit the additional fee of Ten Shillings (along with Form X) for the continuance on the Trade Marks Register of the Trade Mark No.__________ in Class________.

[Signature of Proprietor.]

Dated the__________day of________________18_____

To the Comptroller &c.

FORM Z.

RESTORATION OF TRADE MARK WHERE REMOVED FOR NON-PAYMENT OF FEE.

(To accompany Form X.)

SIR,—In pursuance of the notices issued by you, and of the provisions of Section 79 (4) of the above Acts, I hereby transmit the additional fee of One Pound (along with Form X) for restoration to the Trade Marks Register of the Trade Mark No.________ in Class________.

[Signature of Proprietor.]

Dated the__________day of________________18_____

To the Comptroller &c.

FORM AA.

APPLICATION FOR REGISTRATION OF OLD CORPORATE TRADE MARK.

You are hereby requested to register the accompanying old Corporate Trade Mark in Class______, in respect of______________, in the name of______________, who claims to be the proprietor thereof.

(Signed)__________________________

Dated the____________day of______________18____

To the Cutlers' Company,
Cutlers' Hall, Sheffield.

M. E. HICKS-BEACH,
President of the Board of Trade.

THIRD SCHEDULE.

GENERAL NOTE.—Any wares made of mixed materials (for example, of both cotton and silk) shall be included in such one of the classes appropriated to those materials as the Comptroller may desire.

CLASSIFICATION OF GOODS.

NOTE.—The goods referred to in the following classes are mentioned by way of illustration, and not as an exhaustive list of the contents of the class.

CLASS 1.—Chemical substances used in manufactures, photography, or philosophical research, and anti-corrosives. Such as Acids. including vegetable acids; Alkalies; Artists' Colours; Pigments; Mineral Dyes.

CLASS 2.—Chemical substances used for agricultural, horticultural, veterinary, and sanitary purposes. Such as Artificial Manure; Cattle Medicines; Deodorisers; Vermin Destroyers.

CLASS 3.—Chemical substances prepared for use in medicine and pharmacy. Such as Cod Liver Oil; Medicated Articles; Patent Medicines; Plasters; Rhubarb.

CLASS 4.—Raw or partly prepared vegetable, animal, and mineral substances used in manufactures, not included in other classes. Such as Resins; Oils used in manufactures and not included in other classes; Dyes, other than mineral; Tanning Substances; Fibrous Substances (*e.g.* Cotton, Hemp, Flax, Jute); Wool, Silk; Bristles; Hair; Feathers; Cork; Seeds; Coal; Coke; Bone; Sponge.

CLASS 5.—Unwrought and partly wrought metals used in manufacture. Such as Iron and Steel, pig or cast. Iron—Rough; Bar and Rail, including rails for railways; Bolt and Rod; Sheet, and Boiler and Armour Plates; Hoop. Lead—Pig; Rolled; Sheet. Wire; Copper; Zinc; Gold, in ingots.

CLASS 6.—Machinery of all kinds, and parts of machinery, except agricultural and horticultural machines included in Class 7. Such as Steam Engines; Boilers; Pneumatic Machines; Hydraulic Machines; Locomotives; Sewing Machines; Weighing Machines; Machine Tools; Mining Machinery; Fire Engines.

CLASS 7.—Agricultural and horticultural machinery, and parts of such machinery. Such as Ploughs; Drilling Machines; Reaping Machines; Thrashing Machines; Churns; Cyder Presses; Chaff Cutters.

CLASS 8.—Philosophical instruments, scientific instruments, and apparatus for useful purposes; and Instruments and apparatus for teaching. Such as Mathematical Instruments; Gauges; Logs; Spectacles; Educational Appliances.

CLASS 9.—Musical Instruments.

CLASS 10.—Horological Instruments.

CLASS 11.—Instruments, apparatus, and contrivances, not medicated, for surgical or curative purposes, or in relation to the health of men or animals. Such as Bandages; Friction Gloves; Lancets; Fleams; Enemas.

CLASS 12.—Cutlery and Edge Tools. Such as Knives; Forks; Scissors; Shears; Files; Saws.

CLASS 13.—Metal goods not included in other classes. Such as Anvils; Keys; Basins (metal); Needles; Hoes; Shovels; Corkscrews.

CLASS 14.—Goods of precious metals (including aluminium, nickel, Britannia metal, &c.) and jewellery, and imitations of such goods and jewellery. Such as Plate; Clock Cases and Pencil Cases of such metals; Sheffield and other Plated Goods; Gilt and Ormolu Work.

CLASS 15.—Glass. Such as Window and Plate Glass; Painted Glass; Glass Mosaic; Glass Beads.

CLASS 16.—Porcelain and Earthenware. Such as China; Stoneware; Terra Cotta; Statuary Porcelain; Tiles; Bricks.

CLASS 17.—Manufactures from mineral and other substances for building or decoration. Such as Cement; Plaster; Imitation Marble; Asphalt.

CLASS 18.—Engineering, architectural, and building contrivances. Such as Diving Apparatus; Warming Apparatus; Ventilating Apparatus; Filtering Apparatus; Lighting Contrivances; Drainage Contrivances; Electric and Pneumatic Bells.

CLASS 19.—Arms, ammunition, and stores not included in Class 20. Such as Cannon; Small-arms; Fowling-pieces; Swords; Shot and other Projectiles; Camp Equipage; Equipments.

CLASS 20.—Explosive substances. Such as Gunpowder; Guncotton; Dynamite; Fog Signals; Percussion Caps; Fireworks; Cartridges.

CLASS 21.—Naval architectural contrivances and naval equipments not included in Classes 19 and 20. Such as Boats; Anchors; Chain Cables; Rigging.

CLASS 22.—Carriages. Such as Railway Carriages; Waggons; Railway Trucks; Bicycles; Bath Chairs.

CLASS 23.—(*a*) Cotton yarn, and sewing cotton not on spools or reels. (*b*) Sewing cotton on spools or reels.

CLASS 24.—Cotton piece goods of all kinds. Such as Cotton Shirtings; Long Cloth.

CLASS 25.—Cotton goods not included in Classes 23, 24, or 38. Such as Cotton Lace; Cotton Braids; Cotton Tapes.

CLASS 26.—Linen and hemp yarn and thread.

CLASS 27.—Linen and hemp piece goods.

CLASS 28.—Linen and hemp goods not included in Classes 26, 27, and 50.

CLASS 29.—Jute yarns and tissues, and other articles made of jute not included in Class 50.

CLASS 30.—Silk, spun, thrown, or sewing.

CLASS 31.—Silk piece goods.

CLASS 32.—Other silk goods not included in Classes 30 and 31.

CLASS 33.—Yarns of wool, worsted, or hair.

CLASS 34.—Cloths and stuffs of wool, worsted, or hair.

CLASS 35.—Woollen and worsted and hair goods not included in Classes 33 and 34

CLASS 36.—Carpets, floorcloth, and oilcloth. Such as Drugget; Mats and Matting; Rugs.

CLASS 37.—Leather, skins unwrought and wrought, and articles made of leather not included in other classes. Such as Saddlery; Harness; Whips; Portmanteaus; Furs.

CLASS 38.—Articles of Clothing. Such as Hats of all kinds; Caps and Bonnets; Hosiery; Gloves; Boots and Shoes; other Ready-made Clothing.

CLASS 39.—Paper (except paper-hangings), stationery, and book-binding. Such as Envelopes, Sealing Wax, Pens (except gold pens), Ink, Playing Cards, Blotting Cases, Copying Presses.

CLASS 40.—Goods manufactured from india-rubber and gutta-percha not included in other classes.

CLASS 41.—Furniture and Upholstery. Such as Paper-hangings Papier-mâché; Mirrors; Mattresses.

CLASS 42.—Substances used as food, or as ingredients in food. Such as Cereals, Pulses, Olive Oil, Hops, Malt, Dried Fruits, Tea, Sago; Salt, Sugar, Preserved Meats, Confectionery, Oil Cakes, Pickles, Vinegar, Beer Clarifiers.

CLASS 43.—Fermented Liquors and Spirits. Such as Beer; Cyder; Wine; Whisky; Liqueurs.

CLASS 44.—Mineral and Aerated Waters, natural and artificial, including ginger-beer.

CLASS 45.—Tobacco, whether manufactured or unmanufactured.

CLASS 46.—Seeds for agricultural and horticultural purposes.

CLASS 47.—Candles, common soap, detergents; illuminating, heating, or lubricating oils; matches, and starch, blue, and other preparations for laundry purposes. Such as Washing Powders; Benzine Collas.

CLASS 48.—Perfumery (including toilet articles, preparations for the teeth and hair, and perfumed soap).

CLASS 49.—Games of all kinds and sporting articles not included in other classes. Such as Billiard Tables; Roller Skates; Fishing Nets and Lines; Toys.

CLASS 50.—Miscellaneous.—(1) Goods manufactured from ivory, bone, or wood, not included in other classes. (2) Goods manufactured from straw or grass, not included in other classes. (3) Goods manufactured from animal and vegetable substances, not included in other classes. (4) Tobacco pipes. (5) Umbrellas, walking-sticks, brushes, and combs. (6) Furniture cream, plate powder. (7) Tarpaulins, tents, rickcloths, rope, twine. (8) Buttons of all kinds, other than of precious metal or imitations thereof. (9) Packing and hose of all kinds. (10) Goods not included in the foregoing classes. Such as Coopers' Wares.

(Signed) M. E. HICKS-BEACH,
President of the Board of Trade.

INTERNATIONAL CONVENTION

FOR THE

PROTECTION OF INDUSTRIAL PROPERTY.

(Signed at Paris 20th March, 1883.)

ACCEDED TO BY HER MAJESTY'S GOVERNMENT 17TH MARCH, 1884.

THE International Convention was initiated and concluded by the several assenting Powers for the purpose of affording their respective subjects and citizens mutual protection in sustaining their rights, chiefly to the abstract species of industrial property constituted by Patents for Inventions, Copyright in Designs, Trade Marks and Trade Names. The original text of the Convention is in the French language, and the following excerpt is from the authorised translation.

The opening paragraphs rehearse the names and titles of the subscribing potentates and plenipotentiaries, and are of but slight interest to the general reader. Since the signature, several changes have taken place, and it will serve a more useful purpose to give the complete list of the Governments which are now either parties to the Convention or have by separate treaty given corresponding advantages to British subjects. These are as follows:—America (U.S.A.), Belgium, Brazil, East Indian Colonies of the Netherlands, France, Great Britain, Guatemala, Italy, Mexico, Netherlands, New Zealand, Norway, Paraguay, Portugal, Queensland, Salvador, Servia, Spain, Sweden, Switzerland, Tunis, Turkey, Uruguay. Germany is not a member of the Union, nor is Austria.

The text of the Convention consists of nineteen Articles, and is followed by a Final Protocol explaining and qualifying the terms of these Articles.

ARTICLE I. contains a list of the original subscribing Powers, which may now be replaced by the list given in the foregoing introduction.

Article II.—The subjects or citizens of each of the Contracting States shall, in all the other States of the Union, as regards patents, industrial designs or models, trade marks and trade names, enjoy the advantages that their respective laws now grant, or shall hereafter grant, to their own subjects or citizens. Consequently, they shall have the same protection as the latter, and the same legal remedy against any infringement of their rights, provided they observe the formalities and conditions imposed on subjects or citizens by the internal legislation of each State.

Article III.—Subjects or citizens of States not forming part of the Union, who are domiciled or have industrial or commercial establishments in the territory of any of the States of the Union, shall be assimilated to the subjects or citizens of the Contracting States.

Article IV.—Any person who has duly applied for a patent, industrial design or model, or trade mark in one of the Contracting States, shall enjoy, as regards registration in the other States, and reserving the rights of third parties, a right of priority during the periods hereinafter stated. Consequently, subsequent registration in any of the other States of the Union before expiry of these periods shall not be invalidated through any acts accomplished in the interval, either, for instance, by another registration, by publication of the invention, or by the working of it by a third party, by the sale of copies of the design or model, or by use of the trade mark. The above-mentioned terms of priority shall be six months for patents, and three months for industrial designs and models and trade marks. A month longer is allowed for countries beyond sea.

Article V.—The introduction by the patentee into the country where the patent has been granted of objects manufactured in any of the States of the Union shall not entail forfeiture. Nevertheless, the patentee shall remain bound to work his patent in conformity with the laws of the country into which he introduces the patented objects.

Article VI.—Every trade mark duly registered in the country of origin shall be admitted for registration, and protected in the form originally registered in all the other countries of the Union. That country shall be deemed the country of origin where the applicant has his chief seat of business. If this chief seat of business is not situated in one of the countries of the Union, the country to which the applicant belongs shall be deemed the country of origin. Registration may be refused if the object for which it is solicited is considered contrary to morality or public order.

Article VII.—The nature of the goods on which the trade mark is to be used can in no case be an obstacle to the registration of the trade mark.

Article VIII.—A trade name shall be protected in all the countries of the Union, without necessity of registration, whether it form part or not of a trade mark.

Article IX.—All goods illegally bearing a trade mark or trade name may be seized on importation into those States of the Union where this mark or name has a right to legal protection. The seizure shall be effected at the request of either the proper public department or of the interested party, pursuant to the internal legislation of each country.

Article X.—The provisions of the preceding Article shall apply to all goods falsely bearing the name of any locality as indication of the place of origin, when such indication is associated with a trade name of a fictitious character or assumed with a fraudulent intention. Any manufacturer of, or trader in, such goods, established in the locality falsely designated as the place of origin, shall be deemed an interested party.

Article XI.—The High Contracting Parties agree to grant temporary protection to patentable inventions, to industrial designs or models, and trade marks, for articles exhibited at official or officially recognised International Exhibitions.

Article XII.—Each of the High Contracting Parties agrees to establish a special Government department for industrial property, and a central office for communication to the public of patents, industrial designs or models, and trade marks.

Article XIII.—An international office shall be organised under the name of "Bureau International de l'Union pour la Protection de la Propriété Industrielle" (International Office of the Union for the Protection of Industrial Property). This office, the expense of which shall be defrayed by the Governments of all the Contracting States, shall be placed under the high authority of the Central Administration of the Swiss Confederation, and shall work under its supervision. Its functions shall be determined by agreement between the States of the Union.

Article XIV.—The present Convention shall be submitted to periodical revisions, with a view to introducing improvements calculated to perfect the system of the Union. To this end conferences shall be successively held in one of the Contracting States by Delegates of the said States. The next meeting shall take place in 1885 at Rome.

Article XV.—It is agreed that the High Contracting Parties respectively reserve to themselves the right to make separately, as between themselves, special arrangements for the protection of industrial property, in so far as such arrangements do not contravene the provisions of the present Convention.

Article XVI.—States which have not taken part in the present Convention shall be permitted to adhere to it at their request. Such adhesion shall be notified officially through the diplomatic channel to the Government of the Swiss Confederation, and by the latter to all the others. It shall imply complete accession to all the clauses and admission to all the advantages stipulated by the present Convention.

Article XVII.—The execution of the reciprocal engagements contained in the present Convention is subordinated, in so far as necessary, to the observance of the formalities and rules established by the constitutional laws of those of the High Contracting Parties, who are bound to procure the application of the same, which they engage to do with as little delay as possible.

Article XVIII.—The present Convention shall come into operation one month after the exchange of ratifications, and shall remain in force for an unlimited time, till the expiry of one year from the date of its denunciation. This denunciation shall be addressed to the Government commissioned to receive adhesions. It shall only affect the denouncing State, the Convention remaining in operation as regards the other Contracting Parties.

Article XIX.—The present Convention shall be ratified, and the ratifications exchanged in Paris, within one year at the latest.

In witness whereof the respective plenipotentiaries have signed the same, and have affixed thereto their seals.

Done at Paris the 20th March, 1883.

[Here follow the signatures of the respective plenipotentiaries.]

FINAL PROTOCOL.

TRANSLATION.

ON PROCEEDING to the signature of the Convention concluded this day between the Governments of Belgium, Brazil, Spain, France, Guatemala, Italy, the Netherlands, Portugal, Salvador, Servia, and Switzerland, for the protection of Industrial Property, the undersigned plenipotentiaries have agreed as follows:—

1. The words "Industrial Property" are to be understood in their broadest sense; they are not to apply simply to industrial products properly so called, but also to agricultural products (wines, corn, fruits, cattle, &c.), and to mineral products employed in commerce (mineral waters, &c.).

2. Under the word "Patents" are comprised the various kinds of industrial patents recognised by the legislation of each of the Contracting States, such as importation patents, improvement patents, &c.

3. The last paragraph of Article II. does not affect the legislation of each of the Contracting States as regards the procedure to be followed before the tribunals, and the competence of those tribunals.

4. Paragraph 1 of Article VI. is to be understood as meaning that no trade mark shall be excluded from protection in any State of the Union from the fact alone that it does not satisfy, in regard to the signs composing it, the conditions of the legislation of that State; provided that on this point it comply with the legislation of the country of origin, and that it had been properly registered in said country of origin. With this exception, which relates only to the form of the mark, and under reserve of the provisions of the other Articles of the Convention, the internal legislation of each State remains in force.

To avoid misconstruction, it is agreed that the use of public armorial bearings and decorations may be considered as being contrary to public order in the sense of the last paragraph of Article VI.

5. The organisation of the special Department for Industrial Property mentioned in Article XII. shall comprise, so far as possible, the publication in each State of a periodical official paper.

6. The common expenses of the International Office instituted by virtue of Article XIII. are in no case to exceed for a single year a total sum representing an average of 2,000 fr. for each Contracting State.

To determine the part which each State should contribute to this total of expenses, the Contracting States, and those which may afterwards join the Union, shall be divided into six classes, each contributing in the proportion of a certain number of units, namely:—

1st class	25 units.
2nd class	20 "
3rd class	15 "
4th class	10 "
5th class	5 "
6th class	3 "

These co-efficients will be multiplied by the number of States in each class, and the sum of the result thus obtained will supply the number of units by which the total expense has to be divided. The quotient will give the amount of the unit of expense.

The Contracting States are classed as follows, with regard to the division of expense:—

1st class ...	France, Italy.
2nd class ...	Spain.
3rd class ...	Belgium, Brazil, Portugal, Switzerland.
4th class ...	Holland.
5th class ...	Servia.
6th class ...	Guatemala, Salvador.*

The Swiss Government will superintend the expenses of the International Office, advance the necessary funds, and render an annual account, which will be communicated to all the other Administrations.

* This classification is now modified by the presence of the additional Powers which have since become adherents to the Convention, for which see list in introductory remarks.

The International Office will centralise information of every kind relating to the protection of industrial property, and will bring it together in the form of a general statistical statement, which will be distributed to all the Administrations. It will interest itself in all matters of common utility to the Union, and will edit, with the help of the documents supplied to it by the various Administrations, a periodical paper in the French language dealing with questions regarding the object of the Union.

The numbers of this paper, as well as all the documents published by the International Office, will be circulated among the Administrations of the States of the Union in the proportion of the number of contributing units as mentioned above. Such further copies as may be desired either by the said Administrations, or by societies or private persons, will be paid for separately.

The International Office shall at all times hold itself at the service of members of the Union, in order to supply them with any special information they may need on questions relating to the international system of industrial property.

The Administration of the country in which the next conference is to be held will make preparations for the transactions of that conference, with the assistance of the International Office.

The Director of the International Office will be present at the meetings of the conferences, and will take part in the discussions, but without the privilege of voting.

He will furnish an annual report upon his administration of the office, which shall be communicated to all the members of the Union.

The official language of the International Office will be French.

7. The present Final Protocol, which shall be ratified together with the Convention concluded this day, shall be considered as forming an integral part of, and shall have the same force, validity, and duration as, the said Convention.

In witness whereof the undersigned plenipotentiaries have drawn up the present Protocol.

[Here follow the signatures of the respective plenipotentiaries.]

TWELVE SHORT PRECEDENTS

OF

Agreements, Assignments, Licences, Mortgages &c.

RELATING TO THE WORKING AND DISPOSAL OF LETTERS PATENTS FOR INVENTION.

The following short examples of Agreements, Assignments, Licences, and Mortgages may usefully serve as a guide to those engaged in preparing such documents.

Modern practice is all in favour of abridging and simplifying the intolerable prolixity which many draftsmen still affect. The Author has therefore in drawing these Precedents endeavoured to make them as concise as possible. Deference to the expressed opinion of one or two authorities entitled to respect has caused him in several of the examples to include a covenant for the validity of the patent, in addition to the use of the words "as beneficial owner"; but this is against his own conclusions, and might in his opinion be omitted.

One notably new feature will be apparent in the examples of Agreements made prior to application: viz., the inclusion of a short description and sketch of the invention spoken of in the Agreement, so that the subject-matter of the Agreement may be identified with the subject-matter of the after application. This course is in all such cases advisable, lest it should be necessary afterwards to seek registration of the document, as such registration would inevitably be refused by the Comptroller if he should be unable to identify the invention referred to in the Agreement with the invention afterwards patented (*re* Parnell's Patent, page 80 *supra*).

With reference to the implied covenants for title &c., and to the position of those who grant loans or make advances under certain agreements of this nature, it may be of use to the lay reader to glance at the extracts from the Conveyancing and Partnership Acts which appear immediately after the last of the precedents.

I.—AGREEMENT between an Inventor who has been unable from want of means to develop or protect his invention, and a second party who proposes to furnish the necessary funds in consideration of receiving a share in the patent to be applied for.

AN AGREEMENT made the______day of________18___, between Andrew Bell, of 15 Leaf Street, Birmingham, in the County of Warwick, Metal Worker, of the one part, and Charles Dendy, of 56 Horne Square, Birmingham aforesaid, Stock Broker, of the other part. WHEREAS the said Andrew Bell claims to be the true and first inventor of certain "Improvements in Apparatus for directly recording and transcribing speech and sounds," which invention he has not been able, from want of means and opportunity, properly to develop and patent: AND WHEREAS the said Charles Dendy has agreed with the said Andrew Bell to provide and pay a sum of money not exceeding Five Hundred Pounds for the further development and patenting of the said invention, but subject to the conditions and for the consideration hereinafter expressed: NOW THESE PRESENTS WITNESS and it is hereby agreed between the parties as follows:—

1. The said Charles Dendy shall upon the signing of this Agreement advance the sum of £100 for the purpose of purchasing materials, tools, and all necessary adjuncts to enable the said Andrew Bell to proceed with his experiments and trials for the further development of the said invention, and if necessary additional sums will be advanced by the said Charles Dendy from time to time to continue the said experiments and trials, it being hereby agreed that the total sum so advanced shall not exceed £250.

2. If when the said sum of £250 shall have been expended the invention is still not sufficiently developed or advanced to warrant

an application for Letters Patent, the said Charles Dendy shall be at liberty to give notice to the said Andrew Bell of his intention to withdraw from this Agreement, and thereupon, within one week after such notice has been given, and when all liabilities incurred in connection with the development of the invention since the signing of this Agreement, and with the knowledge and consent of the said Charles Dendy, have been discharged by the said Charles Dendy, this Agreement shall cease and determine, and the invention will remain the sole property of the said Andrew Bell, who shall not be liable in respect of any sums expended by the said Charles Dendy in pursuance of this Agreement.

3. If the aforesaid experiments and trials should result in the proper and successful development of the invention, the said Andrew Bell shall forthwith make application for Letters Patent, and shall thereafter and in due course file the Complete Specification and take all necessary steps to obtain the Letters Patent, but all at the expense of the said Charles Dendy.

4. As soon as the Letters Patent shall have been issued and obtained, the said Andrew Bell shall execute a proper assignment conveying one half share in the said Letters Patent and invention, and in all further improvements upon the same devised by him, to the said Charles Dendy, as consideration for the moneys expended and to be paid by him; and if after provision for all outstanding amounts and charges the full sum of £500 shall not have been already expended, then the undisbursed balance shall be paid on the execution of the said assignment by the said Charles Dendy to the said Andrew Bell.

5. The said assignment shall contain conditions limiting the mutual rights and liabilities of the co-owners of the Letters Patent, and shall provide that the inventions and patents, however worked or disposed of, shall operate for the mutual benefit of the co-owners, and neither of the co-owners shall be at liberty to work or license the inventions and patent rights for his own benefit alone, but shall account for his share of the profits to his co-owner, the patent or patents being held equally between them as tenants in common, and in like manner the annual taxes which fall due at or before the expiry of the fourth year of the patent or patents shall be paid by the parties hereto in equal shares.

6. In order to identify the invention forming the subject-matter of this Agreement with the invention forming the subject-matter

of the patent or patents to be hereafter applied for under the conditions of this Agreement, and so to provide for the entry of this Agreement upon the Register at the Patent Office, if such entry should hereafter prove to be necessary or desirable in the interests of either of the parties, the following is a short description and sketch of the invention in its present condition.

[Here insert a brief description and sketch of the invention.]

7. It is to be understood that this Agreement shall have no effect as regards the obtaining ownership or working of any foreign patents for the invention, and that these may be obtained and dealt with by the said Andrew Bell at his own expense, and without reference to the said Charles Dendy.

8. The duties, liabilities, and benefits undertaken by and accruing to the parties to this Agreement shall extend and apply as far as possible to the executors, administrators, and assigns of either party.

IN WITNESS WHEREOF the within-named parties have hereunto set their hands the day and year first above written.

ANDREW BELL.
CHARLES DENDY.

(This document would not be capable of registration until after the patent had been applied for and issued, and then only if the invention indicated in the Agreement was, in the opinion of the Comptroller, the same as that covered by the patent. Registration would, however, only require to be sought in the event of the inventor refusing or failing to execute the assignment provided for in Paragraph 4.)

II.—AGREEMENT between an Inventor whose invention has not yet been protected, and a second party, not a co-inventor, who is to join with him in applying for a patent and acquire one half share in consideration of his defraying the costs of applying for the patent and paying the inventor an additional sum of money upon the issue of the patent.

AN AGREEMENT made the ______ day of ______, 18 , BETWEEN Edward Fisher, of 13 Thacker's Row, Preston, in the County of Lancaster, Hairdresser's Assistant, of the one part, and George Hardy, of 35 Thacker's Row aforesaid, Grocer of the other part. WHEREAS the said Edward Fisher claims to be the inventor of "An Improved Apparatus for Heating Curling Tongs by Electricity," of which the following is a brief description and sketch, inserted for the purpose of identifying the subject-matter of this Agreement with the subject-matter of the patent to be hereafter applied for, that is to say [here insert short description and sketch of the invention]: AND WHEREAS the said George Hardy is desirous of acquiring one half interest in the said invention and in the patent to be hereafter obtained for the same, and the said Edward Fisher has agreed to sell one half share and interest as aforesaid for the sum and upon the conditions hereinafter set forth:

NOW IT IS HEREBY AGREED BETWEEN THE PARTIES AS FOLLOWS:—

1. Immediately upon the signing of this Agreement the said George Hardy will instruct a Patent Agent to make a search to ascertain the novelty of the said invention, and if no anticipatory publication is found, then the parties hereto will make application for a patent in their joint names, and will thereafter and in due course file the Complete Specification, and obtain issue of the Letters Patent. The costs of the search and all of the charges incurred in applying for and obtaining the patent will be borne and paid by the said George Hardy as part consideration in respect of this Agreement, and no demand in respect thereof is to be made upon the said Edward Fisher, except that if the search discloses that the invention is not novel, and the matter proceeds no further, then the said Edward Fisher agrees to pay one half of the agent's charges incurred for making the search.

2. Immediately upon the issue of the Letters Patent, and not later than one week thereafter, the said George Hardy will pay to the said Edward Fisher the sum of £100, which, together with the aforesaid search and patent fees, shall constitute the consideration paid by him for the half share in the patent, and the agent who obtains the patent will be instructed to keep the Letters Patent in his hands until payment of this latter sum of £100 has been made.

3. The patent and every extension thereof shall be held and enjoyed by the parties hereto in equal shares as tenants in common, and all renewal fees and expenses connected with the maintenance of the patent when granted shall be borne equally by the parties. Neither of the parties shall be entitled to work the invention for his

exclusive benefit nor to grant licences without accounting to his co-patentee or his representative or assigns for one half share of all net profits derived from such working or licensing. Either of the parties shall be at liberty to sell his share of the patent, and his assignee shall be subject to and be bound by the conditions and restrictions herein set forth.

4. Any further improvements in the invention which may be devised by either of the parties shall be disclosed to the other, and if considered advisable the same shall be patented in their joint names and at their joint expense.

5. Except where the context requires a different interpretation, or where from other causes such interpretation is not reasonable, any expression referring to either or both of the said parties to this Agreement shall extend and be construed to apply also as far as possible to the assigns of the person or persons so designated.

IN WITNESS &c.

(This Agreement would not require registration unless difficulties were to arise in respect of the partition clause in Paragraph 3.)

III.—AGREEMENT between Joint Inventors and intending co-applicants for the purpose of defining their respective interests, rights, and powers into and under the patent to be applied for.

MEMORANDUM OF AGREEMENT made this__________ day of____________, 18____, BETWEEN Isaac Jenkins, of 17 Tuer Street, Manchester, in the County of Lancaster, Cotton Spinner, of the one part, and Kenneth Latham, of The Hawthorns, Palatine Road, Didsbury, near Manchester aforesaid, Engineer, of the other part. WHEREAS the said parties have jointly invented certain "Improvements in Carding Engines," a sketch and description of which is contained in the Schedule attached hereto, and in respect of which it is intended by the parties to make joint application for a patent: AND WHEREAS the said Isaac Jenkins has invented the chief portion of the said improvements, while the parts of the invention attributable to the said Kenneth Latham refer to less important details, it has been thought desirable before applying for a patent to define the respective shares and the terms and conditions in and under which the said invention and any Letters Patent obtainable for the same shall be possessed and worked by the parties:

NOW THESE PRESENTS WITNESS AND IT IS HEREBY AGREED AS FOLLOWS:—

1. The property constituted by the invention and Letters Patent to be hereafter applied for shall be considered as divided into three equal parts, of which two parts or thirds shall be the share of the said Isaac Jenkins, and the remaining one third the share of the said Kenneth Latham.

2. All expenses connected with ascertaining the novelty of the invention and obtaining Letters Patent therefor, and all renewal fees and charges connected with maintaining the patent in force when granted, shall be borne and paid by the parties hereto in the proportion of their respective interests: namely, two thirds by the said Isaac Jenkins, and one third by the said Kenneth Latham.

3. In the same manner, all net profits obtained as royalties or otherwise from the manufacture, sale, use, or licensing of the said invention and Letters Patent shall be shared by the parties hereto in the same proportions: that is to say, two thirds to the said Isaac Jenkins, and one third to the said Kenneth Latham.

4. If either of the parties hereto should manufacture carding engines made in accordance with the said invention, a fixed royalty, to be mutually agreed upon, shall be chargeable upon each machine, and this royalty shall be shared between the parties in the indicated proportions.

5. Neither of the parties shall be entitled to grant licences without the consent in writing of the other, but either of the parties may sell his share of the invention and future Letters Patent without the concurrence of the other, and the purchaser of the share so assigned shall be subject to the same conditions and restrictions and entitled to the same benefits as are imposed upon and secured to the original co-patentees under this Agreement.

6. The conditions of this Agreement shall apply, not only to the parties hereto, but also, as far as possible, to their assigns.

IN WITNESS &c.

SCHEDULE.

[To contain description and sketch of invention.]

(It would be advisable to follow up this Agreement, after the patent is issued, by a proper deed of partition.)

IV.—AGREEMENT for Sale of Patent, between Inventor who has obtained Provisional Protection, and Purchaser who arranges to pay the purchase-money in the following instalments: viz.—One-third on signing Agreement; one-third on acceptance of Complete Specification; and the remainder on the issue of the Letters Patent.

AN AGREEMENT made the______day of________, 18___, BETWEEN Matthew Nash, of 12 Prior's Court, in the City of London, Clerk, of the one part, and Oliver Paley, of Gracechurch Street, London aforesaid, Advertising Agent, of the other part. WHEREAS the said Matthew Nash claims to be the inventor of, and has obtained provisional protection for, an invention entitled "Improvements in Means for Displaying Advertisements," No. 3698, dated 15th March, 1894, which invention and the patent to be obtained therefor he has agreed to sell to the said Oliver Paley: NOW THESE PRESENTS WITNESS that in consideration of the sum of £150 paid by the said Oliver Paley to the said Matthew Nash as hereinafter set forth, he the said Matthew Nash DOTH HEREBY AGREE to sell and assign the said invention and Letters Patent to the said Oliver Paley, the purchase-money to be paid in the following instalments: that is to say—£50 upon the signing of these presents; £50 upon the acceptance of the Complete Specification (which the said Matthew Nash agrees forthwith, and at his own cost, to prepare and file); and £50 upon the sealing and issue of the Letters Patent.

PROVIDED that if the said Matthew Nash shall fail to file the Complete Specification in due course, the said sum of £50 paid upon the signing of this Agreement shall be returned by him to the said Oliver Paley, or if the said Complete Specification after acceptance should be successfully opposed, then the said sum of £50 paid at the signing of this Agreement, and also the sum of £50 paid on the acceptance of the Complete Specification, shall be repaid by the said Matthew Nash to the said Oliver Paley, and these sums shall be recoverable as a simple contract debt. PROVIDED FURTHER that upon the sealing and issue of the Letters Patent the said Matthew Nash shall forthwith execute a proper deed of assignment conveying the said invention and Letters Patent to the said Oliver Paley, or otherwise shall execute such further deeds or instruments as may be considered necessary to more fully vest and secure the said invention and Letters Patent in and to the said Oliver Paley, but at the cost of the said Oliver Paley. Any improvements upon the said invention which the said Matthew Nash may devise during the five years following the signing of this Agreement shall be disclosed and submitted to the said Oliver Paley or his assigns, and shall become his property, with the option of protecting the same by a patent if he or they should think fit, but at the cost of the said Oliver Paley or his assigns.

IN WITNESS &c.

(No registration. The Agreement should be replaced by the deed of assignment provided for, and this deed could be registered.)

V.—AGREEMENT for Sale of Patent to Company, made between patentee and trustee for syndicate about to form a company; agreed consideration, partly cash, partly shares in company; patentee to be a director in company; Agreement to become void in the event of capital not being subscribed.

MEMORANDUM OF AGREEMENT made this_________ day of_________, 18___, BETWEEN William Scott, of Brierfield Hall, Northwich, in the County of Chester (hereinafter called the Vendor), of the one part, and George Scattergood, of 3 Capstan Street, Liverpool, in the County of Lancaster, Solicitor (hereinafter called the Trustee), of the other part. WHEREAS the said Vendor claims to be the true and first inventor of certain "Improvements in Pneumatic Wheel Tyres," for which he has obtained Her Majesty's Letters Patent, No. 14,036, under date the 12th December, 1892, and also certain foreign and colonial patents as set forth in the Schedule A hereto: AND WHEREAS the parties whose names appear in the Schedule B hereto, together with the amounts of their respective holdings or interests, and who are hereinafter referred to as the Syndicate, have duly empowered and appointed the said Trustee to agree to purchase the said invention and Letters Patent, home, foreign, and colonial, from the Vendor, in trust for and on their behalf, for the consideration of £10,000 in cash, together with certain fully paid-up shares, but subject to the conditions hereinafter expressed: NOW THESE PRESENTS WITNESS that, in pursuance of the said agreement and authorisation, and for the considerations and subject to the conditions herein expressed. IT IS HEREBY AGREED between the said Vendor and the said Trustee as follows :—

1. The Trustee shall upon the signing of these presents pay to the Vendor the sum of £250, being part payment of the aforesaid sum of £10,000, receipt of which sum of £250 is hereby acknowledged by the Vendor, and the Trustee shall thereupon inform the Syndicate of the execution of this Agreement.

2. The Syndicate or their agents shall then take the necessary steps to promote and form a limited company, to be entitled "The Scott Patent Tyre Company, Limited," and shall register the said company in terms of the Companies Acts, 1862 to 1893, the registered office to be in Liverpool as aforesaid.

3. The capital of the said company shall be £50,000, divided into 5,000 shares of £10 each, and out of the said 5,000 shares 1,000 fully paid-up shares shall be allotted to the Vendor, in addition to the sum of £10,000 already referred to, and the Vendor shall be placed upon the board of directors.

4. Immediately upon the registration of the company prospectuses and advertisements will be issued and the subscription of capital invited. If the required amount of capital is subscribed the Vendor shall thereupon execute a proper assignment or assignments duly conveying and transferring the said invention and patents, both in this country and elsewhere, and also the benefits of any future improvements devised by him upon or in addition to the said inventions and Letters Patents, as beneficial owner, to the said company or their duly appointed trustees, and the Vendor shall upon the execution of the assignment receive the sum of £9,750, being the amount of purchase money hereinbefore set forth, less the sum of £250 paid at the signing of this agreement, and shall in addition have delivered to him the certificates representing 1,000 fully paid-up shares of £10 each.

5. If sufficient capital should not be subscribed to pay the said purchase money and justify proceeding to allotment, then within three months after the date of the first issued prospectuses or advertisements inviting subscriptions of capital to the company this

Agreement shall become null and void, and the Trustee shall forfeit and the Vendor shall retain the sum of £250 paid at the signing of this Agreement.

IN WITNESS &c.

SCHEDULE A.

(Numbers, dates, and titles of home and foreign patents.)

SCHEDULE B.

(Names of members of syndicate, with amounts of holdings or interest.)

NOTE.—This Agreement, together with any subsequent instrument, should be referred to in any prospectus issued, and should also be filed with the Registrar of Joint Stock Companies, pursuant to Section 25 of the Companies Act, 1867.

VI.—ASSIGNMENT (Absolute) of Invention and Letters Patent by the Patentee to a Purchaser.

AN INDENTURE made the______day of________, 18___, BETWEEN Robert Sheddon, of 29 New Smithhills, Paisley, in the County of Renfrew, North Britain, Iron Turner (hereinafter called the Assignor), of the one part, and Theodore Underwood, of the Clydebank Shipbuilding Yard, Stobcross, Glasgow, in the County of Lanark, N.B., Marine Engineer (hereinafter called the Assigneee), of the other part. WHEREAS the Assignor claims to be the inventor of certain "Improvements in Feathering Paddle-wheel Floats," for which he has obtained Letters Patent, No. 12,342, dated 23rd July, 1893: AND WHEREAS the Assignor has agreed with the Assignee for the sale to him, the Assignee, of the said invention and Letters Patent for the sum hereinafter expressed: NOW THIS INDENTURE WITNESSETH that, in pursuance of the said agreement and in consideration of the sum of £1,000 paid by the Assignee to the Assignor upon the signing of these presents (the receipt of which sum is hereby acknowledged), he the Assignor, as beneficial owner, doth hereby assign unto the Assignee and his assigns absolutely all those the said invention and Letters Patent and the sole and exclusive benefit thereof, and all rights, powers, emoluments, and advantages whatsoever under or in respect of the said Letters Patent, the Assignor hereby covenanting with the Assignee and his assigns that, notwithstanding anything by him the Assignor done, omitted, or knowingly suffered, the said Letters Patent are now valid and subsisting.

IN WITNESS &c.

(This assignment should be under seal, and should be registered.)

VII.—ASSIGNMENT of Half Share of Patent; co-owners to work the invention under the patent independently of each other, but all licences to be granted under the hands and seals of both.

AN INDENTURE made the_______day of , 18___, BETWEEN Richard Mason, of The Phœnix Boiler Works, Pendleton, Manchester, in the County of Lancaster, Boiler Maker (hereinafter called the Assignee), of the one part, and Thomas Johnson, of 40 MacDonald Street, Belfast, County Antrim, Ireland, Engineer (hereinafter called the Assignee), of the other part. WHEREAS the Assignor has obtained Letters Patent, No. 7326, dated the 12th of July, 1892, for "Improvements in the Construction of Steam Generators," of which he claims to be the true and first inventor: AND WHEREAS the Assignor has agreed to sell one half share of the said invention and Letters Patent to the Assignee for the sum of £600, but subject to the conditions hereinafter set forth: NOW THIS INDENTURE WITNESSETH that, in consideration of the said sum of £600 paid by the Assignee to the Assignor at the signing of these presents, and the receipt of which is hereby acknowledged, he the Assignor, as beneficial owner, doth hereby assign and convey one half share of the said invention and Letters Patent absolutely to the Assignee and his assigns, the said assignment being coupled with the following conditions:—

1. Either of the parties may, in carrying out his own business, manufacture and sell boilers made in accordance with the said invention, and under the said Letters Patent, without accounting to the other for profits and royalties derived therefrom.

2. Neither of the parties alone shall be at liberty to grant any licences to third parties to manufacture and sell under the said

Letters Patent, but any such licence shall be granted only with the full consent of both parties, and under their respective hands and seals, and all royalties and profits whatsoever accruing under such licence or licences shall be divided equally between the parties hereto, share and share alike.

3. All renewal fees for maintaining the patent in force and the agency or other charges connected with the payment of such renewal fees shall be borne and paid by the parties hereto in equal proportions, and if either of the parties or his assigns should omit or refuse to pay his or their share of such renewal fees and expenses, the same shall remain a charge upon his or their share of the patent, or otherwise shall be recoverable from the party or his assigns by the other party by action at law as a simple contract debt.

4. Either of the parties shall be at liberty at any time to sell his share of the said invention and Letters Patent to a third party, but only after the other party has had the first refusal of the said share at the price for which the said half share is actually and ultimately sold.

5. The terms "Assignor" and "Assignee," and any other terms herein used to describe the parties to this Agreement, shall be understood to include, as far as possible, their assigns, except where such an interpretation is specifically barred.

IN WITNESS &c.

(To be under seal and registered.)

VIII.—ASSIGNMENT of a Patent to Trustees in Trust for Purchasers having unequal shares, the trustees to exploit the patent, sell the goods, grant licences, draw royalties, distribute profits, call for contributions, and otherwise act generally for the beneficial owners.

AN INDENTURE made the _______ day of _________, 18__, BETWEEN Hiram Potter, of Newark, New Jersey, United States of America, Engineer (hereinafter called the Vendor), of the first part; James Steel, of 12 Victoria Street, in the City of London, Civil Engineer, Alfred Mottershead, of the "Black Bull" Hotel, Chester, in the County of Chester, Wine Merchant, and Philip Stapleton, of Burnley, in the County of Lancaster, Cotton Spinner (hereinafter called the Purchasers), of the second part; and George Kinghorn and Frederick Wilson, both of 133 King William Street, in the City of London, Chartered Accountants (hereinafter called the Trustees), of the third part. WHEREAS the Vendor has obtained Her Majesty's Letters Patent in the United Kingdom for "An Improved Telephonic Transmitter," No. 328, dated 14th January, 1894: AND WHEREAS he has agreed to sell and the Purchasers have agreed to purchase the said invention and Letters Patent for the sum of £5,000 in the following shares and proportions: namely— As to the said James Steel, one half share, for which his contribution to the purchase money is £2,500, and as to the said Alfred Mottershead and Philip Stapleton, one fourth share each, for which their contributions to the purchase money are respectively £1,250 each: AND WHEREAS the Purchasers have requested the Vendor to assign the said invention and Letters Patent to the aforesaid Trustees, in trust for the purchasers, subject to the payment of the purchase money and to the conditions herein expressed: NOW THIS INDENTURE WITNESSETH that, in pursuance of the said agreement and request, and in consideration of the said sum of £5,000 paid at the signing of these presents, and the receipt of which the Vendor hereby acknowledges, he the Vendor, as beneficial owner, doth hereby assign and convey to the Trustees the aforesaid invention and Letters Patent, upon trust for the Purchasers as tenants in common in the shares already set forth: namely, one half share to the said James Steel, and one fourth share each to the said Alfred Mottershead and Philip Stapleton. AND THE VENDOR doth hereby covenant with the said Trustees jointly, and also with each of the Purchasers separately, that, notwithstanding anything by the Vendor done, omitted, or knowingly suffered, the said Letters Patent are now valid and subsisting and not void or voidable. PROVIDED FURTHER and it is hereby agreed and declared as follows:—

1. Except under licence granted by the Trustees, none of the Purchasers or their assigns shall be entitled to make, use, exercise, or vend the said invention and Letters Patent within the United Kingdom.

2. The Trustees shall work and exploit the patent and premises to the best advantage of the Purchasers, and shall, subject to the

direction and advice of the Purchasers, or a majority of the Purchasers representing three fourths of the value, manufacture the patented apparatus and grant licences for the manufacture, use, and sale of the invention at royalties to be fixed by the Purchasers or a majority as aforesaid, and all net profits, royalties, and emoluments accruing to the Trustees from and by such manufacture, licensing, and exploiting of the invention and Letters Patent shall form part of the trust estate, and, subject to the payment of all costs and expenses, shall be held by the Trustees in trust for the Purchasers and paid to them in accordance with their respective shares as hereinbefore set forth.

3. The Trustees may, and shall at any time during the continuance hereof, at the request in writing of the Purchasers or their assigns, or such of them as hold a majority in value of not less than three-fourths of the entire value of the patent and premises, sell the said Letters Patent, and the purchase-money so obtained, after deducting all necessary costs and expenses, shall be divided among the Purchasers or their assigns in accordance with the amounts of their respective holdings.

4. The Trustees shall, out of the trust estate, pay the renewal fees necessary to maintain the said patent in force, or to obtain and maintain any further patents which may be applied for or bought by or under the direction of the Purchasers, or for any extension or extensions of the said patent or patents, and, generally, the Trustees shall pay out of the trust moneys all costs, expenses, and liabilities strictly chargeable against the estate.

5. Any proceedings at law or otherwise necessary for the protection and maintenance of any Letters Patent aforesaid, or for the protection and maintenance of the rights of the owners therein, and for the prosecution of infringers pirating the invention or inventions, or slandering the title or titles of such Letters Patent or Patents, shall be taken and prosecuted by the Trustees when required so to do by the Purchasers or by a three-fourths value majority of the Purchasers, the costs of such proceedings to be borne by the trust estate, and any moneys recovered in the form of damages or otherwise, or sums paid to compromise actions, shall be paid and accrue to the said trust estate, less costs and charges paid in recovering or obtaining the same or judgments to that effect.

6. The Trustees shall present accounts as between themselves and the respective Purchasers half-yearly, such accounts to be made out as extending from the 1st day of January in each year to the 30th day of June in each year, and from that day to the 31st day of December in each year, such accounts to be presented and a proper balance struck, audited by independent auditors appointed by the Purchasers and settled not less than fourteen days after the termination of the respective periods over which the accounts extend. If on the presentation of accounts it should be found that there is an adverse balance against the trust estate or the respective Purchasers, then the Trustees shall apportion the sum to be paid by each Purchaser, having regard to his (the Purchaser's) share, and shall require him in writing to pay such sum within fourteen days, and if default in payment is made the said sum due shall bear interest at five per cent. per annum, and shall until paid remain a charge upon the defaulting owner's share in the estate.

7. For each half-year or portion thereof, each Trustee shall during the continuance of his trusteeship receive the sum of £100, such payment to come out of the moneys of the trust estate generally and not to be chargeable as a debt against any of the Purchasers particularly.

8. The Trustees or either of them may be removed by the Purchasers, but such power of removal shall be exercised only by a majority representing two-thirds in value of the entire ownership.

9. If any difference shall arise between the parties—that is to say, between the Vendor and the Trustees, or between the Trustees, or between the Purchasers, or between the Trustees and the Purchasers—in respect of the construction of this instrument, or of the respective rights, duties, or liabilities of the parties, the same shall, if competent and desirable, be referred to two arbitrators, one to be appointed by each of the parties, and such arbitrators, or their umpire, may accordingly make an award in respect of the said difference, and the costs of or incidental to such reference and award respectively, and the person or persons by whom and in what manner the same shall be paid; and the submission may be made an order of the High Court of Justice upon the application of either party, who may consent or instruct counsel to consent thereto for the other of them, the death of any party not to operate as a

revocation of the submission or otherwise be a bar to proceedings in respect thereof.

IN WITNESS &c.

(NOTE.—Although dealing with a trust, this deed can and should be registered as an assignment. Registration will not, however, refer to the trusts therein set forth. See Section 85 of the Patent Acts.)

IX.—LICENCE (Non-Exclusive) in Consideration of Royalties to be paid half-yearly.

AN INDENTURE made the_______day of__________, 18 , BETWEEN Henry Dickenson, of 4 Saxby Street, Salford, in the County of Lancaster, Mill Mechanic (hereinafter called the Licensor) of the one part, and John Booth, trading as Jacob Booth and Co., of the Penelope Works, Burnley, in the same county, Manufacturer (hereinafter called the Licensee), of the other part. WHEREAS the Licensor has obtained Letters Patent, No. 393, of the 8th day of January, 1893, for a certain invention entitled "Improvements in Shuttle Tongues": AND WHEREAS the Licensee has applied to obtain and the Licensor has agreed to grant the Licensee a licence to use the said invention in consideration of the royalties and upon the terms hereinafter set forth: NOW THIS INDENTURE WITNESSETH that, in pursuance of the said agreement, and in consideration of the royalties hereinafter reserved and the covenants on the part of the Licensee hereinafter contained, the Licensor doth hereby grant unto the Licensee full liberty, licence, power, and authority to make, use, exercise, and vend the said invention within the United Kingdom and the Isle of Man: TO HAVE, HOLD, exercise, and enjoy the said licence and premises unto and by the Licensee and his successors in business for and during all the residue now to come and unexpired of the term of fourteen years for which the said Letters Patent were granted: YIELDING AND PAYING unto the Licensor half-yearly, on the 30th day of June and the 31st day of December in each year, for every gross of shuttle tongues manufactured and sold by the Licensee in accordance with the said invention and Letters Patent, the sum of ten shillings as royalty: PROVIDED ALSO that the Licensee shall keep at his usual place of business all proper books of account, and will enter therein all particulars relating to the manufacture and sale by him of the said patent shuttle tongues, and will produce the said books to the Licensor or his authorised agent at all reasonable times for inspection and the taking of copies or extracts therefrom, and will at the end of each half-year aforesaid deliver or send to the Licensor a statement in writing of all essential particulars of the manufacture and sale during such half-year of the said patent shuttle tongues, together with a statement showing the amount of royalties payable to the Licensor, and shall, if required so to do, verify the said statement and particulars by statutory declaration.

AND IT IS FURTHER PROVIDED that if the amount of royalties payable under this licence should for any continuous two years fall beneath the aggregate sum of £100, then the Licensor may terminate and withdraw this licence by giving three months' notice to that effect. FURTHER, if, as the result of proceedings at law or otherwise, the aforesaid Letters Patent should in the High Court or in any Court of Appeal be declared null and void, either wholly or in respect of their essential features, this licence shall therefrom cease and determine, and the Licensee shall be at liberty to manufacture the said shuttle tongues without the payment of royalty to the Licensor, notwithstanding that this licence is expressed to be for the full term of patent right. In the event of the Licensee wishing to terminate and withdraw from this licence, he may do so by giving the Licensor three months' notice to that effect, and nothing in the licence mentioned shall operate as estoppel to prevent the Licensee, after his licence has determined, from challenging the validity of the patent, either as plaintiff or defendant, in any action at law commenced and prosecuted after the termination of this licence.

THE LICENSEE shall stamp all shuttle tongues manufactured by him in accordance with the said invention and Letters Patent or otherwise. The shuttles to which the tongues are applied shall be stamped with the words "Dickenson's Patent," and also with the number of the patent.

LASTLY, the Licensor shall, during the continuance of this licence, pay the renewal fees necessary to keep the patent in force, and shall, if required, produce the certificate of payment fourteen days before the last day for such payment, or otherwise shall allow the Licensee to pay the said renewal fees, the amount thereof to be deducted from the royalties then or thereafter due to the Licensor.

IF THE LICENSEE should at any time fail to pay the royalties due to the Licensor within three weeks from the end of the half-year in respect of which such royalties are payable, the Licensor may thereupon by notice in writing revoke this licence without prejudice to his right of recovery of any moneys then due to him or to any right of action in respect of breaches of this licence.

IN WITNESS &c.

X.—LICENCE (Exclusive, save in respect of Licensor) for a Single County at Rent and Royalties.

AN INDENTURE made the_____day of________, 18__, BETWEEN George Champion, of the Tubal Brass Works, Tubal Lane, Manchester, in the County of Lancaster, Brass and Tin Worker (hereinafter called the Licensor), of the first part, and Frederick Perkins, of 12 Grove Street, Bury, in the same county, Tinsmith (hereinafter called the Licensee), of the second part. WHEREAS the Licensor claims to be the true and first inventor of and has obtained Her Majesty's Letters Patent, No. 12,333, of 12th October, 1890, for an invention of "Improvements in Humidifying and Ventilating Apparatus": AND WHEREAS the Licensee has agreed to take, and the Licensor has agreed to grant an exclusive but (except as hereinafter limited) non-assignable licence to the Licensee to make, use, exercise, and vend the said invention in accordance with the said patent at the rent and royalties and under the conditions hereinafter specified: NOW THIS INDENTURE WITNESSETH that, in pursuance of the said agreement and conditions, and in consideration of the said rent and royalties reserved, the Licensor, as beneficial owner, hereby grants, and the Licensee agrees to accept, an exclusive licence upon the following terms:

1. The licence hereby granted shall continue for the full term now to come and unexpired of the aforesaid patent rights, subject to the hereinafter contained conditions as to terminating the licence.

2. For each year during which the licence shall continue, dating from the date of this indenture, the Licensee shall pay to the Licensor an annual rent of £50, payable in advance, the first payment of £50 being made at the signing of these presents and acknowledged by the Licensor to be so paid.

3. In addition to the said annual payment of £50, the Licensee shall pay to the Licensor, for each humidifier manufactured by him during the continuance of this licence, the sum of £1 as royalty, such payments to be made half-yearly. The first payment of royalties, if any should be due, shall be made fourteen days after the expiry of six months from the date of this indenture, and thereafter half-yearly as provided.

4. The Licensee shall keep proper books of account at his usual place of business, and shall enter therein all particulars of humidifying and ventilating apparatus manufactured by him in accordance with the invention and patent, and shall allow the same to be inspected, and copies and extracts made thereof and therefrom, by the Licensor or his authorised agent, at all reasonable times, and shall allow the Licensor or his authorised agent, at all reasonable times, to inspect his works if the Licensor should desire so to do. The Licensee shall at the end of each half-year furnish true statements showing the number of humidifiers manufactured by him during the half-year then expired, and shall accompany the said statement by an account showing the amount of royalties due to be paid to the Licensor, and shall verify the said statements and accounts by statutory declaration if required so to do by the Licensor. All sums due as royalties from the Licensee to the Licensor shall be paid to the Licensor not less than fourteen days after the expiry of each half-year.

5. Although this indenture is set forth as an exclusive licence, the Licensor reserves to himself the right to manufacture and sell humidifying apparatus in Lancashire, under his patent as aforesaid, but at prices which shall not be lower than those quoted by the Licensee, and all humidifiers sold by the Licensor shall be strictly those of his own manufacture, made at his works in Tubal Lane as aforesaid, or in any other workshop to which he may hereafter remove, or in which he may carry on his business.

6. The Licensee will not during the continuance of this licence manufacture any humidifying apparatus except in accordance with the said invention, and will not, while the licence is in force, dispute the validity of the said Letters Patent, and will do all in his power to detect infringers and assist the Licensor in any proceedings at law or otherwise which the Licensor may institute to protect his patent rights and interests.

7. Each humidifier and ventilating apparatus manufactured and sold by the Licensee shall bear upon the casing, or upon some prominent part of the apparatus, a stamped brass plate, of not less than two inches in length by an inch and a quarter in breadth, bearing the words "Champion's Patent" and the numerals "No. $12{,}333^{90}$"; but to this the Licensee may add his name and address as maker. These brass plates will be consecutively numbered, and will be supplied at cost price by the Licensor to the Licensee, the latter binding himself to use only such brass plates as are supplied to him by the Licensor, and no others, and all humidifiers in accordance with the patent identified as having issued from the hands of the Licensee and not bearing a brass plate so supplied shall be chargeable with triple royalty, hereby agreed to represent liquidated damages suffered by the Licensor, unless a reasonable explanation is forthcoming.

8. The Licensor binds himself to maintain the patent in force during the continuance of this licence by the payment of the annual renewal fees, the certificate of each payment of the said renewal fees to be shown by the Licensor to the Licensee not less than fourteen days before the payment shall have become due; and if from any cause the Licensor shall omit or fail to pay any such renewal fee, the Licensee shall be at liberty to pay the same, together with any fine, if such should have been incurred, and shall charge the same against the Licensor, and deduct it from any moneys due to the Licensor at that time or thereafter in the hands of the Licensee.

9. If any rent, royalties, or other sums due from the Licensee to the Licensor should remain unpaid for one month after the time when they shall have become due, or if a breach of any of the conditions herein contained should be committed by the Licensee, the Licensor shall be at liberty to terminate this licence by giving two months' notice, and at the expiry of that time this licence shall cease and determine.

10. If the Letters Patent in respect of which this licence is granted shall, as the result of proceedings at law between the Licensor and third parties, or by revocation or otherwise, be finally declared void, either wholly or as to a material part thereof, then this licence shall forthwith cease and determine, and the Licensee shall be at liberty to manufacture and sell the invention without accounting to the Licensor for rent and royalties; and in any case, if at any time after the expiry of three years from the date hereof the Licensee should wish to terminate this licence, he may do so by giving six months' notice to that effect, whereupon this licence shall cease and determine.

11. The Licensee shall not be at liberty to sell or assign this licence, during its continuance, to another or to others; but in the event of the death or withdrawal from business of the Licensee, this licence shall continue to his representatives and successors in business upon the terms and under the conditions hereinbefore set forth as enjoyed by and binding upon the Licensee himself.

IN WITNESS &c.

(NOTE.—This Licence should be entered in the Register of Patents.)

XI.—NOTICE BY LICENSOR TO TERMINATE LICENCE.

(Address and date.)

IN ACCORDANCE with the power given me under Clause ________ of the Licence dated the day of ___________ 18 granted by me to you in respect of Letters Patent No. 15,342 of 18th December, 1892, for "Improvements in Skates," I hereby give you notice that the said Licence shall as and from the ________ day of ___________ next absolutely cease and determine.

(Signature) ________________________

To A.B., of

(NOTE.—An intimation of this withdrawal should be sent to the Comptroller-General of Patents.)

XII.—MORTGAGE OF A PATENT.

AN INDENTURE made the ______ day of ______, 18 , BETWEEN Sidney Smith, of The Hollies, Cleworth Street, Barnstaple, in the County of Devon, Hat Manufacturer (hereinafter called "the Mortgagor"), of the one part, and Walter Pym, of Newport, Barnstaple aforesaid, Gentleman (hereinafter called "the Mortgagee"), of the other part. WHEREAS the Mortgagor has obtained Her Majesty's Letters Patent, No. 1,236, dated 24th February, 1887, for an invention entitled "An Improved Filter": AND WHEREAS the Mortgagor has applied to the Mortgagee for a loan of £500, to be secured, together with interest thereon, by a mortgage of the said invention and Letters Patent as hereinafter expressed: NOW THIS INDENTURE WITNESSETH that, in consideration of the said sum of £500 this day paid by the Mortgagee to the Mortgagor (the receipt whereof is hereby acknowledged), the Mortgagor doth hereby covenant with the Mortgagee that he (the Mortgagor) will pay to the Mortgagee, on the ______ day of next, the sum of £500, together with interest thereon at the rate of six per cent. per annum. AND THIS INDENTURE ALSO WITNESSETH that, for the consideration aforesaid, the Mortgagor, as beneficial owner, doth hereby assign unto the Mortgagee all those the said invention and Letters Patent and the sole and exclusive benefit thereof, to hold the said invention, Letters Patent, and premises unto the Mortgagee and his assigns, subject to the proviso for redemption hereinafter contained. PROVIDED ALWAYS that if the Mortgagor shall pay to the Mortgagee the sum of £500, with interest for the same in the meantime at the rate of six per cent. per annum, on the said ______ day of next, then the Mortgagee will at any time thereafter, at the request and cost of the Mortgagor, re-assign to him the said Letters Patent and premises; but otherwise if the said sum of £500 or any part thereof shall remain unpaid after the said ______ day of ______ next, he the Mortgagor shall pay to the Mortgagee, so long as the said sum or any part thereof shall remain unpaid, interest on the said sum or unpaid part thereof at the rate of six per cent. per annum by equal half-yearly payments on the ______ day of ______ and the ______ day of ______. PROVIDED ALSO that if the said Mortgagor shall at the said periods or within fourteen days thereafter make payment to the Mortgagee of the said interest and shall perform and observe all the covenants and conditions herein contained, and on his part to be performed and observed, then the Mortgagee will not call in the said sum of £500 or any unpaid portion thereof until the_______day of__________18 . PROVIDED ALSO that in such case provided the Mortgagor shall not before the said day of 18 compel the Mortgagee to receive the said sum of £500 or the unpaid portion thereof.

AND THE MORTGAGOR doth hereby covenant with the Mortgagee that the said Letters Patent are now valid and subsisting and not void or voidable, and that the Mortgagor will during the continuance of this security pay all fees necessary for the renewal and maintenance of the said Letters Patent at least one month before the day when such renewal fees shall become due, and shall forthwith send or deliver to the Mortgagee the receipt for every such payment; and if the Mortgagor should fail to pay such renewal fee, then the Mortgagee may, if he think fit, himself make payment of the fee, and the amount, together with the expenses, fine, or other charges, will remain on the security hereof as further moneys advanced. PROVIDED ALSO that until the Mortgagee shall become entitled to exercise the power of sale to be implied herein, the Mortgagor shall be at liberty to use and work the said invention without interference from the Mortgagee, and may also, in the joint names of himself and the Mortgagee, grant licences to make, use, exercise, and vend the same.

LASTLY, it is hereby declared that, except when the context requires a different interpretation, each of the expressions "Mortgagor" and "Mortgagee" shall, wherever used herein, be also applicable, as far as possible, to the assigns of the parties hereby designated.

IN WITNESS &c.

(NOTE.—This Mortgage should be registered.)

EXTRACT

FROM THE

PARTNERSHIP LAW AMENDMENT ACT, 1865.

(28 & 29 VICTORIA, CHAPTER 86.)

The advance of money on contract to receive a share of profit not to constitute the lender a partner.

1. The advance of money by way of loan to a person engaged or about to engage in any trade or undertaking upon a contract in writing with such person that the lender shall receive a rate of interest varying with the profits, or shall receive a share of the profits arising from carrying on such trade or undertaking, shall not, of itself, constitute the lender a partner with the person or the persons carrying on such trade or undertaking, or render him responsible as such.

* * * * * *

In case of bankruptcy &c., lender not to rank with other creditors.

5. In the event of any such trader as aforesaid being adjudged a bankrupt, or taking the benefit of any Act for the relief of insolvent debtors, or entering into an arrangement to pay his creditors less than twenty shillings in the pound, or dying in insolvent circumstances, the lender of any such loan as aforesaid shall not be entitled to recover any portion of his principal, or of the profits or interest payable in respect of such loan.

EXTRACT

FROM THE

CONVEYANCING AND LAW OF PROPERTY ACT, 1881.

(44 & 45 VICTORIA, CHAPTER 41.)

(THIS ACT DOES NOT EXTEND TO SCOTLAND.)

Covenants for Title.

7. (1) In a conveyance there shall, in the several cases in this section mentioned, be deemed to be included, and there shall in those several cases, by virtue of this Act, be implied, a covenant to the effect in this section stated, by the person or by each person who conveys, as far as regards the subject-matter or share of subject-matter expressed to be conveyed by him, with the person, if one, to whom the conveyance is made, or with the persons jointly, if more than one, to whom the conveyance is made as joint tenants, or with each of the persons, if more than one, to whom the conveyance is made as tenants in common, that is to say: Covenants for title to be implied.

(*a*) In a conveyance for valuable consideration, other than a mortgage, the following covenant by a person who conveys and is expressed to convey **as beneficial owner** (namely): On conveyance for value by beneficial owner.

That, notwithstanding anything by the person who so conveys, or any one through whom he derives title, otherwise than by purchase for value, made, done, executed, or omitted, or knowingly suffered, the person who so conveys, has, with Right to convey.

the concurrence of every other person, if any, conveying by his direction, **full power to convey the subject-matter expressed to be conveyed,** subject as, if so expressed, and in the manner in which, it is expressed to be conveyed, and that, notwithstanding anything as aforesaid, that subject-matter shall remain to and be quietly entered upon, received, and held, occupied, enjoyed, and taken, by the person to whom the conveyance is expressed to be made, and any person deriving title under him, and the benefit thereof shall be received and taken accordingly, without any lawful interruption or disturbance by the person who so conveys or any person conveying by his direction, or rightfully claiming, or to claim by, through, under, or in trust for the person who so conveys, or any person conveying by his direction, or by, through, or under any one not being a person claiming in respect of an estate or interest subject whereto the conveyance is expressly made, through whom the person who so conveys derives title, otherwise than by purchase for value; and that, freed and discharged from, or otherwise by the person who so conveys sufficiently indemnified against, all such estates, incumbrances, claims, and demands other than those subject to which the conveyance is expressly made, as either before or after the date of the conveyance have been or shall be made, occasioned, or suffered by that person or by any person conveying by his direction, or by any person rightfully claiming by, through, under, or in trust for the person who so conveys, or by, through, or under any person conveying by his direction, or by, through, or under any one through whom the person who so conveys derives title, otherwise than by purchase for value; and further, that the person who so conveys, and any person conveying by his direction,

Quiet enjoyment.

Freedom from incumbrance.

Further assurance.

and every other person having or rightfully claiming any estate or interest in the subject-matter of conveyance, other than an estate or interest subject whereto the conveyance is expressly made, by, through, under, or in trust for the person who so conveys, or by, through, or under any person conveying by his direction, or by, through, or under any one through whom the person who so conveys derives title, otherwise than by purchase for value, will, from time to time and at all times after the date of the conveyance, on the request and at the cost of any person to whom the conveyance is expressed to be made, or of any person deriving title under him, execute and do all such lawful assurances and things for further or more perfectly assuring the subject-matter of the conveyance to the person to whom the conveyance is made, and to those deriving title under him, subject as, if so expressed, and in the manner in which the conveyance is expressed to be made, as by him or them or any of them shall be reasonably required:

(c) In a conveyance by way of mortgage, the following covenant by a person who conveys and is expressed to convey as beneficial owner (namely): On mortgage, by beneficial owner.

That the person who so conveys has, with the concurrence of every other person, if any, conveying by his direction, full power to convey the subject-matter expressed to be conveyed by him, subject as, if so expressed, and in the manner in which it is expressed to be conveyed; and also that, if default is made in payment of the money intended to be secured by the conveyance, or any interest thereon, or any part of that money or interest, contrary to any provision in the conveyance, it shall be lawful for the person to whom the conveyance is expressed to be made, and the persons deriving title under him, to enter into and upon, or receive, and thence- Right to convey. Quiet enjoyment.

forth quietly hold, occupy, and enjoy or take and have, the subject-matter expressed to be conveyed, or any part thereof, without any lawful interruption or disturbance by the person who so conveys, or any person conveying by his direction, or any other person not being a person claiming in respect of an estate or interest subject whereto the conveyance is expressly made; and that, freed and discharged from, or otherwise by the person who so conveys sufficiently indemnified against, all estates, incumbrances, claims, and demands whatever, other than those subject whereto the conveyance is expressly made; and further, that the person who so conveys and every person conveying by his direction, and every person deriving title under any of them, and every other person having or rightfully claiming any estate or interest in the subject-matter of conveyance, or any part thereof, other than an estate or interest subject whereto the conveyance is expressly made, will from time to time and at all times, on the request of any person to whom the conveyance is expressed to be made, or of any person deriving title under him, but, as long as any right of redemption exists under the conveyance, at the cost of the person so conveying, or of those deriving title under him, and afterwards at the cost of the person making the request, execute and do all such lawful assurances and things for further or more perfectly assuring the subject-matter of conveyance and every part thereof to the person to whom the conveyance is made, and to those deriving title under him, subject as, if so expressed, and in the manner in which the conveyance is expressed to be made, as by him or them or any of them shall be reasonably required:

Freedom from incumbrance.

Further assurance.

On conveyance by trustee or mortgagee.

(*f*) In any conveyance, the following covenant by every person who conveys and is expressed to convey as trustee or mortgagee, or as personal representative of a deceased person, or as committee of a lunatic so found by inquisition, or under an order of the Court, which covenant shall be deemed to extend to every such person's own acts only (namely):

That the person so conveying has not executed or done, or knowingly suffered, or been party or privy to, any deed or thing whereby or by means whereof the subject-matter of the conveyance, or any part thereof, is or may be impeached, charged, affected, or incumbered in title, estate, or otherwise, or whereby or by means whereof the person who so conveys is in anywise hindered from conveying the subject-matter of the conveyance, or any part thereof, in the manner in which it is expressed to be conveyed. Against incumbrances.

(2) Where in a conveyance it is expressed that by direction of a person expressed to direct as beneficial owner another person conveys, then, within this section, the person giving the direction, whether he conveys and is expressed to convey as beneficial owner or not, shall be deemed to convey and to be expressed to convey as beneficial owner the subject-matter so conveyed by his direction; and a covenant on his part shall be implied accordingly.

(4) Where in a conveyance a person conveying is **not expressed to convey as beneficial owner,** or as settlor, or as trustee, or as mortgagee, or as personal representative of a deceased person, or as committee of a lunatic so found by inquisition, or under an order of the Court, or by direction of a person as beneficial owner, **no covenant on the part of the person conveying shall be, by virtue of this section, implied in the conveyance.**

(6) The benefit of a covenant implied as aforesaid shall be annexed and incident to, and shall go with, the estate or interest of the implied covenantee, and shall be capable of being enforced by every person in whom that estate or interest is, for the whole or any part thereof, from time to time vested.

Covenants for title.

(7) A covenant implied as aforesaid may be varied or extended by deed, and, as so varied or extended, shall, as far as may be, operate in the like manner, and with all the like incidents, effects, and consequences, as if such variations or extensions were directed in this section to be implied.

Covenants to extend to heirs &c.

59. (1) A covenant and a contract under seal and a bond or obligation under seal, though not expressed to bind the heirs, shall operate in law to bind the heirs and real estate, as well as the executors and administrators, and personal estate of the person making the same as if heirs were expressed.

(2) This section extends to a covenant implied by virtue of this Act.

* * * * * *

Effect of covenant with two or more jointly.

60. (1) A covenant and a contract under seal and a bond or obligation under seal, made with two or more, jointly to pay money or to make a conveyance, or to do any other act to them, or for their benefit, shall be deemed to include, and shall by virtue of this Act imply, an obligation to do the act to or for the benefit of the survivor or survivors of them, and to or for the benefit of any other person to whom the right to sue on the covenant, contract, bond, or obligation devolves.

THE STAMP MEDICINES ACT, 1812.

According to this Act, where any person prepares and sells medicaments for inward or outward use, alleged to be compounded from some secret recipe, or claims to have an exclusive right or title to the making or preparing of the same, **or where such medicaments are exposed for sale under the authority of any Letters Patent,** the packet, box, or bottle must bear a Government stamp applied in such a way that the contents cannot be reached without tearing the stamped label or cover. Penalty for non-observance, £10 for each offence. (See remarks on "Patent Medicines," page 89, *supra*.)

INDICES.

NOTE.—The following Indices are arranged according to subject-matter—viz., Patents, Trade Marks, and Designs. An alphabetical list of the Foreign Countries and Colonies whose Patent Laws are dealt with will be found in the Table of Contents, pages x and xi.

PART I.—PATENTS.

PART II.—TRADE MARKS.

PART III.—DESIGNS.

KK

Printed in Dunstable, United Kingdom

91220858R00298